Welcome to the
Jungle Inn

The Story of the Mafia's
Most Infamous Gambling Den

Allan R. May

ConAllan Press

Published by ConAllan Press, LLC
Cleveland, Ohio, USA

May, Allan R.
Welcome to the Jungle Inn : the story of the Mafia's
most infamous gambling den / by Allan R. May. -- 1st ed.
p. cm.
Includes bibliographical references and index.
LCCN 2011910213

1. Mafia--Ohio--Trumbull County--History.
2. Criminals--Ohio--Trumbull County--Biography.
3. Gangsters--Ohio--Trumbull County--Biography.
I. Title.

HV6452.O3M39 2011   364.106'09771'38
                                            QBI11-600144

Design by Lynn Duchez Bycko, Commoner Company

First published 2011

This book is dedicated to

Jan Vaughn

Thank you for your encouragement and
support, but most of all your friendship

Welcome to the Jungle Inn

"Conceived in infamy!"

That's how famed Youngstown Police Chief Edward J. "Eddie" Allen described the tiny village of Halls Corners, Ohio, located in the southeast corner of Trumbull County, just over the northern border of Mahoning County. The hamlet was fourteen miles away from the city of Warren, but only four miles from downtown Youngstown.

For years this rural gambling den served the gambling populace of not only neighboring Warren and Youngstown, but also gamblers from Akron, Canton, Cleveland and Pittsburgh.

That is until the night of August 12, 1949, when Governor Frank Lausche sent agents of the Ohio Department of Liquor Control to close the Jungle Inn forever. Welcome to the Jungle Inn is the story of this infamous gambling den and its near tragic demise on that hot summer night.

Welcome to the Jungle Inn is also a concise history of organized crime in the city of Warren, Ohio and surrounding Trumbull County. It contains stories about five of its most famous underworld personalities. Jimmy Munsene, whose famous nightclub, the Hollyhock Gardens, launched the career of singer Perry Como. Munsene's five trials for bribery brought local hometown celebrity Clarence Darrow to town to represent him.

Twin brothers John and Mike Farah were Cleveland bootleggers until relocating to Warren to oversee the Cleveland Mafia's gambling interests. Detroit Mafia transplant Frank Cammarata was deported and illegally returned to the United States and settled into a nice Trumbull County neighborhood. Finally Anthony "Tony Dope" Delsanter, who rose to the position of under boss of the Cleveland Mafia family.

◆　◆　◆

"Extra, extra, read all about it! The Jungle Inn is closed forever."

The story the Jungle Inn and all the colorful figures associated with it could not have been told without the wonderful reporting of the two premier newspapers of the Mahoning Valley: the Warren Tribune Chronicle and the Youngstown Vindicator. The Tribune Chronicle is Ohio's oldest newspaper, with its roots dating back to 1812. The Vindicator was founded in 1869. Both newspapers continue to serve their communities successfully to this day.

Allan R. May is an organized crime historian from Cleveland, Ohio. May began his writing career with a brief stint working for the Dean of organized crime writers, Jerry Capeci at his popular "Gangland News" website. May moved on to write for Rick Porrello's AmericanMafia.com, Court TV's "CrimeLibrary" and CrimeMagazine.com.

This is May's third book. The first was Mob Stories, a compilation of his columns that appeared at AmericanMafia.com. The second was Gangland Gotham: New York's Notorious Mob Bosses. May has taught classes on the history of organized crime at Cuyahoga Community College's Senior Adult Education Program and gives lectures throughout northeastern Ohio. May is the historian at Lake View Cemetery and is on its Speaker's Bureau.

In Memoriam

During the course of writing this book and working to get it published, two important contributors passed away within weeks of each other. Carol Willsey Bell died on October 2, 2010. Carol oversaw the local history and genealogical departments at the Warren-Trumbull County Public Library. She was a certified genealogical librarian and founded the Mahoning and Columbiana County chapters of the Ohio Genealogical Society.

Carol loved history, as could be seen by the many societies that she held membership in: Ohio Historical Society Library, Daughters of the American Revolution, the Huguenot Society of Ohio, Daughters of 1812, Colonial Dames of the 17th Century and First Families of Ohio.

The knowledge she held of the area helped lead to the writing of this book. Please read more about her contributions in the Acknowledgments section.

◆　　◆　　◆

On October 27, 2010 organized crime writers and those fans of what was known as The Mid-West Crime Wave 1933-34 lost one of the greatest writer/researchers of our time – Rick Mattix.

I knew of Rick and his reputation before I even decided to be a writer. In late 1998 I started working for Jerry Capeci's Gangland News, before moving over to write for Rick Porrello's AmericanMafia.com the following year. While I received a few modest commendatory notes on my work, my greatest compliment arrived in my inbox on August 29, 2003:

Hi Allan,

Just thought I'd drop you a line and let you know I'm a big fan of your work. Have read many of your articles on the Internet about organized crime and they are among the most factual and well researched I've seen. Being an Iowan, I especially enjoyed your recent piece on Luigi Fratto, aka Lou Farrell, a guy I've always been fascinated with.

Later,
Rick Mattix

In getting a note like that from someone who was as admired and respected as Rick Mattix, remains one of the greatest compliments I have received as a writer.

Known as Rick, Riktor, and the Mad Dog, Rick was a sort of icon when it came to knowledge of the Mid-West Crime Wave and other Chicago and Mid-West criminals. Rick was quite a character, but what was so great about him was that he always had time to help someone out. Anyone who ever had any dealings with him walked away calling him a friend. A dominant figure in the group Partners In Crime, Rick always shared his insight with members of the group and gave freely of his thoughts and opinions.

I spoke with Rick in the hospital a couple weeks before he died. I didn't know how ill Rick was at the time, I'm not sure he knew. He told me all he wanted to do was go home.He did go home, and he will be sorely missed by all who were blessed with the opportunity to know him.

Table of Contents

Acknowledgements   x

Prologue   xiii

Introduction   ixx

Chapter 1   The Place of Salt Licks   1

Chapter 2   James "Jimmy" Munsene   16

Chapter 3   The Jungle Inn   63

Chapter 4   The War Lords of Trumbull County:
             John & Mike Farah   118

Chapter 5   The Saga of Frank Cammarata   198

Chapter 6   The Story of "Tony Dope"   231

Chapter 7   A Few Selected Biographies   237

Chapter End Notes   259

Appendix   274

Bibliography   284

Index   286

Acknowledgments

I did not set out to write a book about the Jungle Inn, or Trumbull County gangsters, or organized crime in Warren, Ohio. This book was an offspring of a collaboration effort with popular crime writer Rick Porrello to co-author a book on the history of organized crime in Pittsburgh and Youngstown. As I dug deeper into the research and began writing, the subject matter expanded to the point that the Youngstown piece alone will become two or even three volumes, while Rick continues to produce the Pittsburgh book on his own.

Even after the decision to split Youngstown and Pittsburgh, the Warren / Trumbull County piece was still scheduled to be part of the Youngstown book. That was until I stepped into the Warren-Trumbull County Public Library, where I met Jan Vaughn and Carol Bell. Jan, who at that time was program director of the library, immediately began booking me for lectures on the chapters of the Youngstown book that I had already completed. She became a good friend and a constant source of support for my writing. The talks I gave drew audiences of 100 or more local residents, who had a keen interest in the Mahoning Valley's rich organized crime history.

On my first visit with Carol Bell I told her what I was working on and that I needed information on the Jungle Inn. It was during this initial conversation that she introduced me to the county's most famous gangster – Jimmy Munsene, whom I had not come across in my research at the Youngstown Public Library. She provided me with lots of information on Munsene, as one can clearly see by his prominence in this book.

When Jan Vaughn suggested that I put together a program on the Jungle Inn and Trumbull County gangsters, I did so and we packed the place that night. The start of the program was delayed as library personnel ran around getting chairs for the overflow crowd of patrons.

It wasn't long after this that I took an inventory of all the material I had on Warren and Trumbull County and made a decision to do a separate book. I decided to focus on the Jungle Inn for the title since the notorious gambling den got mention during the Kefauver Crime Committee hearings during the early 1950s.

I owe a lot to these two women, Carol and Jan, for all the support they gave me throughout this project.

I want to thank Rick Porrello for initiating the idea that turned into Welcome to the Jungle Inn. I would be happy to enjoy a fraction of the success Rick has achieved during his writing career, which includes having one of his books, To Kill the Irishman turned into successful film. Rick also played a key role in helping me make the decision to self-publish this book. It kind of came across as an order, something Rick is good at giving, since he's the Chief of Police in a local Cleveland suburb.

I also owe a great deal of thanks to Krista Goering, who was my agent and worked tirelessly in trying to find a fit with a publisher for my book. The brick wall we continuously ran into was that it was too "regional" to be a big money maker for the publishers. After nearly two years we finally were offered a contract by a local publisher only to have the rug pulled out from under us at the last moment when they wanted the Jungle Inn book to be combined with the book I was completing on Youngstown.

At the moment the deal fell through I realized the only way this book was ever going to make it to a book shelf was if I self-published it. I wasn't sure that I had the moxie to do this myself so the first person I went to was Lynn Duchez Bycko from the Special Collections Department at Cleveland State University. Over the past decade Lynn has served as an advisor, counselor and therapist to me, not to mention a best friend. I asked her out to dinner and then sprang my idea on her. She assured me that "we" could get it done. Lynn has been a major influence in helping me get this book published and establishing my website and moving this project, not to mention my career, in a positive direction. She has been invaluable.

In addition to having Rick order me to self-publish and Lynn helping me to self-publish, I want to thank Ellen Poulsen. Ellen has self-published her two classics, Don't Call Us Molls: Women of the John Dillinger Gang and The Case Against Lucky Luciano. Ellen was a wealth of knowledge and support in providing information and tips in making the decision for me to self-publish. I also want to thank Robert I. Gross for helping me to navigate the financial end of this decision.

A very special thank you to the following gentlemen of Warren, who spent time with me and helped me understand the people and the times: Bruce Birrell, Lynn B. Griffith, Jr., Nick DeJacimo, David McLain and Joseph L. Wyndham. Mr. Birrell also provided most of the photographs for this book.

I would like to thank the following library personnel around Northeastern Ohio for their help in this project that has stretched out over so many miles and years – Pete Ewell, Ryan Jaenke and Melinda Schafer (Cleveland Public Library), Carol Bell, Carol Genova and Jan Vaughn (Warren-Trumbull County Public Library) Theresa Cousins and Carole Anderson (Youngstown Public Library), Audrey John (Niles Historical Society); John Anderson (Ashtabula County Library) and finally from outside Northeastern, Ohio, Leslie Broughton, (Arizona Historical Society – Tucson).

Charlotte M. Versagi has provided me with encouragement and support for this project for the past decade. She and her father Frank Versagi have provided technical support, advice, counsel and guidance since the day I began writing.

As always, I owe a special thanks to Charles R. Molino, the most knowledgeable guy I know on the history of organized crime in America. "Charlie Moose" has tirelessly reviewed every chapter in Welcome to the Jungle Inn, sat through all my lectures at the Warren-Trumbull County Public Library (and stayed awake), and has been a constant source of information, but more importantly a good friend for the past dozen years.

A special thank you and a good luck to John Chechitelli, who is pursuing a film adaptation of this work in Tinseltown.

I want to thank my friends who have provided me with encouragement over the past decade with my writing. My apologies for leaving anyone out: Jay Ambler, Patrick Downey, Abby Goldberg, Jerry Kovar, Tom Leahy, Fred Merrick, Jimmy Monastra, John Murray, David Pastor, James Trueman, and Fred Wolking. And a special thanks to family members: Tammy Cabot, Gary May, and the Vaciks – Nelda, Bob, Melanie and Robbie.

I want to offer a final thanks to the late great Riktor "Mad Dog" Mattix. In my acknowledgments section in *Gangland Gotham*, I wrote of Rick "There simply isn't a more knowledgeable person when it comes to the Midwest crime wave and different facets of organized crime history in Chicago; he is the best." He was a key contributor to the Midwest crime wave section of this book, as well as to that section of my Youngstown book. It's sad to think I will not be working with him again.

As always, I have left the most important person until last, my wife Connie. Over the past two years she has battled back from a serious illness. It could not have come at a worse time. During that period I was unemployed for all but five months. Despite her illness Connie missed very little work and has amazed everyone with the battle she has waged in her incredible comeback. She has been an inspiration to me and those that have witnessed what she has gone through. For all her hard work I have rewarded her with helping me to promote this book. God knows I couldn't do it without her.

Prologue

"Conceived in infamy!"

That's how Youngstown Police Chief Edward J. "Eddie" Allen described the tiny Village of Halls Corners, located in the southeast corner of Trumbull County, just over the northern border of the Mahoning County line. The hamlet was fourteen miles away from the city of Warren, but only four miles from downtown Youngstown.

In 1936, when Liberty Township voters cast their ballots abolishing the serving of alcoholic beverages in public places, nine registered voters pulled the wool over the eyes of Ohio state officials by creating their own private illicit haven. The incorporation of Halls Corners was done for the sole purpose of allowing liquor by the glass to be sold in a less than swanky gambling palace on Applegate Road. For the next thirteen years this casino operated with little law enforcement interference as The Jungle Inn.

While its birth may have been in infamy, Jungle Inn's demise nearly ended in tragedy when the casino's operating boss ordered a guard to open fire on unarmed state liquor agents who had the temerity to raid the illegal gambling den. Though the order was not carried out, the raid and the closing of the Jungle Inn, on a warm summer night in August 1949 made it one of the most infamous gambling casino tales in the history of organized crime in the United States.

The Hollywood version of the illegal casino reveals a glittery, highly affluent bunch. Dressed to the nines, these sophisticated people sip cocktails and enjoy the romantic sense of being out on the town for an evening in an illegal setting. Compare this movie version to a reporter's unflattering description of women enjoying a night at the Jungle Inn:

> "Women as drab as the barn-like setting are crowded at the north side of the gaming room, listening attentively for the numbers. They are women of all ages and all types, from farms and apartments, but all with a single aim.
>
> "The Jungle Inn doesn't draw smart, sophisticated women with money to throw away and the few reasonably well-dressed ones stand out among the

cheap prints and loose hanging sports coats like the proverbial sore thumb

"Hats are a novelty, and straggly hair, frizzled with low-cost permanents, do a good job of matching shabby pocketbooks worn thin at the locks from constant opening."

The Jungle Inn reached its peak of popularity after World War II, when a combination of returning servicemen and factory workers, their pockets fresh full of cash from the furnaces of the Mahoning Valley steel mills, went in search of illegal entertainment. Gambling had always been a source of recreation for the thousands of foreigners who came to Ohio's Steel Valley looking for work and a place to raise their families.

Surprisingly, in this post-war atmosphere, the average patron of the Jungle Inn was the middle-aged housewife, who came to seek a fortune, or at least a new kitchen appliance, during the daily bingo games that were the trademark of the Trumbull County casino.

Perhaps the operating concept of the Jungle Inn came from Al Capone. During Prohibition Capone ran a brothel that was located on the Illinois/Indiana state line. When raiders from Illinois appeared on the scene, the patrons and employees would move to the Indiana side of the establishment; when the Indiana raiders came, vice versa. The trick was making sure that both groups never showed up at the same time. The Jungle Inn operated with a similar philosophy, one which dictated that to stay in business they had to out-think the local authorities. During the late 1940s most important gambling house raids in Ohio were carried out by the State Liquor Board, since it seemed like most of the local authorities were in one way or another under the influence of the gamblers to look the other way.

Bars, restaurants, taverns and inns with state liquor licenses were not permitted to have any form of gambling on the premises. If they were found to be in violation, they could have their license suspended or revoked. Jungle Inn got around this by not allowing their patrons to drink alcoholic beverages in the gambling hall. Patrons had to walk to a separate building, the Jungle Inn nightclub, located just five feet away. This facility contained a barroom and restaurant, but was not technically connected to the casino.

The other trick to keep the Jungle Inn free of raids was practiced by county officials. The Trumbull County prosecutor's position was that he would not act as a law enforcement official; it was up to the county sheriff to conduct the raids. The Trumbull County sheriff's position was that the policing of Halls Corners and the Jungle Inn was up to village law enforcement. The catch-22 was that with only nine registered voters in Halls Corners, the village had no law enforcement officers.

While this ridiculous policy allowed county officials to wash their hands of the casino, it generated disdain from law enforcement officials to the south in Youngstown and Mahoning County. The *Vindicator*, Youngstown's premier newspaper, was the Jungle Inn's greatest adversary until Chief Eddie Allen assumed office in 1948.

The Jungle Inn was averaging crowds of 400 to 800 a night during the pre-war years of 1936 to 1942. With America's entry into World War II, and the advent of gasoline and tire rationing, Jungle Inn was about to get hit in its own pocketbook. The casino's operators tried to take the patriotic approach and tell patrons they were closing for the duration of the war to help in the war effort. In reality, Ohio Governor John W. Bricker had just ordered the closing of the Arrow Club in Geauga County, which catered to the gambling society of Cleveland. With the *Vindicator*'s help the Jungle Inn was about to come under the same scrutiny, but opted to close on its own terms.

The post-war years became a financial boom for the operators of the Jungle Inn. When it reopened in the spring of 1947 the crowds suddenly increased to 2,000 and 3,000 per night. On one occasion a *Pittsburgh Post-Gazette* columnist wrote that the Jungle Inn "was jammed with about 2,000 chance-takers, the local [Pittsburgh] folk report, and they couldn't get near the tables." The disappointed Pittsburgh gamblers "came home with their money." One night in the fall of 1947 a crowd of 5,000 patrons was reported on the premises.

When gambling returned to the Applegate Road casino in 1947 it was described as "running wide open." New owners had sunk a reported $75,000 into the gambling den to spruce it up. Patrons jammed the reopened gambling Mecca sinking coins into its 80-plus slot machines, rolling dice at the crap tables, placing bets at the roulette wheel, playing poker or trying the chuck-a-luck games. Still the main feature was the always-present bingo tables, which seemed only to wet the appetite of the fortune seekers. During the afternoons horseracing took center stage at the Jungle Inn, a lucrative business that was said to bring in $50,000 a day.

There was no age-discrimination at this place. In addition to the blue-hair special crowd, the doormen allowed in children of high school age – all seeking their own fortune. People came as they were, as one story noted, "Evening dress isn't necessary to get into the 'Jungle.' Patrons were clad in work clothes. They may have just ended a turn in one of the shops. There were old army uniforms and a smattering of 'Zoot suits.'" There was no problem for patrons who didn't own automobiles; the Jungle Inn operators paid for taxicab service to and from Youngstown and other places to bring in the "suckers."

Still, the mainstay of this gambling den was always the housewife. The *Vindicator's* continued bashing of the gambling den reached a point where some people thought the criticism was serving as free advertising for the Jungle Inn. In a "Letter to the Editor" a *Vindicator* subscriber suggested that if the newspaper truly wanted to discourage patrons they should "bring out" the following points about the women who gamble there:

> "Few women want to admit they are getting along in years – would it make the [Jungle Inn] less popular if you pointed out that by far the greatest number of patrons are elderly women? It's true. Why not tell about the unbreathable air, blue with smoke from hundreds of cigarettes held by the same women? Couldn't you describe the look on the scared faces as trembling hands feed the last nickel, dime or quarter into the hungry slot machines?
>
> "How many patrons would come back night after night if they realized the men behind the tables – with their beautiful, well manicured, useless hands – make more money in a week than most of the widows they are so charmingly and politely robbing, receive in a month or more.
>
> "Why don't you deglamorize the joint?
>
> "The middle-aged women get their thrills at the Jungle Inn…The churches are competing with the gambling houses. In the meantime too many of our young people are turning into juvenile delinquents. Who is responsible?"

The housewife seemed unaffected even when the church was affected. The Jungle Inn once challenged local parishes for the dollars of the Sunday afternoon church sponsored bingo players. The ill-fated attempt aroused the ire of Dr. Roland A. Luhman, pastor of the First Reformed Church. After preaching a fiery sermon he was inspired to rewrite the following biblical verses, making them applicable to the Valley's gambling addicts:

> "Come unto me, ye gullible, and I will give you grief.
>
> "Foolish are the gullible for they shall inherit life in the Poor House. (At the expense of the tax-payer.)
>
> "Foolish are the duped: for theirs is the kingdom of regret.
>
> "Foolish are they which hunger after bingo and slot machines: for they shall go empty away.
>
> "Foolish are they which trust in one armed bandits: they shall see worse days.
>
> "Foolish are they which are taken in for gamblings' sake: theirs is the kingdom of folly.
>
> "Foolish are they which lose all kinds of money with which to buy Cadillacs and sea-shore mansions for the proprietor: your own house shall fall to pieces and you will drive around in a pile of junk.

"Foolish are the gamblers: for they shall be called the children of stupidity."

The Jungle Inn survived despite the efforts of the *Vindicator*, the church and Chief Allen – not too mention World War II – to close it. A noted fire-trap with its makeshift electrical connections, it was by the grace of God a fire didn't occur as there were never adequate exits. Just when business at the casino seemed to be at its peak, a governor was elected whose record of being a staunch adversary of commercialized gambling and the under-world would be put to task. Making use of the state liquor enforcement department Governor Frank J. Lausche sent agents to close the Jungle Inn forever on the night of August 12, 1949, but its legacy lives on.

This book, in addition to telling the complete story of the rise and fall of the Jungle Inn, discusses the underworld bosses who dominated orga-nized crime in this region from the Prohibition years to the 1970s.

James Mancini ran the underworld bootlegging and gambling in the county beginning in the mid-1920s. Known to all as "Jimmy Munsene," he was one of the most popular figures in the Warren area. His bribery trial for trying to "buy" the county sheriff was one of the most notable ever to be held in this area of the state. The case went to trial on five separate occasions before Munsene finally cut a deal that kept him from serving any prison time. His lawyer for the last three trials was Clarence Darrow, America's most noted criminal defense attorney. Darrow was trying to have a last hurrah in the area where he was born, grew up and began his long and prestigious legal career.

During the mid-1930s, Munsene ran the immensely popular Holly-hock Gardens Night Club, which became famous as the most renowned nightspot between Cleveland and Pittsburgh. The nightclub became thespringboard for the successful singing career of Perry Como. When the club began to cater to the gambling crowd it came under fire from local crime crusaders and went out of business.

Munsene was looking to move in on the Jungle Inn in 1941. The gam-bling den run by the Farah twins, John and Mike, from Cleveland, which drew underworld attention from Detroit, Cleveland and Buffalo, was not about to kowtow to the local underworld element. In March 1941 Munsene and his nephew were shot down in cold blood by Detroit hitmen in his new establishment, the Prime Steak House.

Several years later the FBI captured Munsene's killer, Thomas "Tommy" Viola in Tucson, Arizona at a mob operated hotel. His trial was one of the most colorful ever held in Warren. It also marked one of the few times in the history of the underworld in this country where the family of a murdered mobster helped track down and testify against the hitman accused of the murder.

The lives of the Farah brothers, John and Mike are chronicled from their bootlegging days in Cleveland and the murder of a rival there, to their running of the Jungle Inn as front men for the Cleveland Mafia. The closing of the Jungle Inn brought the brothers a decade of tax problems with the Internal Revenue Service.

During the post-Jungle Inn years Mike Farah became involved in Trumbull County politics. When an Election Board worker was fired, a near deadly confrontation took place outside the Farah home when Trumbull County Democratic Chairman Jean Blair failed to see things Mike's way. The subsequent arrest and booking of Farah caused a community outrage due to the preferential treatment shown the hoodlum. The handling resulted in a civil service review board looking into the actions of the Warren Police Chief.

The end of the Farah regime came on a pleasant summer morning when Mike was the recipient of a shotgun blast while practicing golf strokes on his lawn.

Frank Cammarata was a Detroit hood related by marriage to the Licavoli clan. Sent to prison after a bank robbery conviction, Cammarata found himself deported to Italy only to return to the country illegally three years later. When the government found him living with his family outside of Cleveland, his arrest triggered a twelve-year saga that would test our legal system's will to deport an undesirable member of the Mafia. Cammarata's escapades involved Michael J. Kirwan, one of the Mahoning Valley's most respected Congressmen, who would be pitted against the law enforcement wits of the legendary Chief Eddie Allen.

In the end, Cammarata would leave on his own volition, but not before a final showdown before the McClellan Crime Committee and its lead counsel Robert F. Kennedy.

Anthony "Tony Dope" Delsanter is the final entry. The book looks at his life from his upbringing in Cleveland, to his relationship with legendary mob-turncoat Aladena "Jimmy the Weasel" Fratianno, his role in the Jungle Inn management and his position with the Cleveland Mafia family.

Introduction

I was a late-comer to the mob scene in the Mahoning Valley, but not so late that I missed some of the events Allan R. May relates here.

In fact, in my dozen years as police reporter for the *Warren Tribune Chronicle*, I wrote some of the newspaper reports he quotes here.

As a newspaperman, I still regret that I arrived on the scene just after the closings of the Jungle Inn and the Hollyhock Gardens you will read about.

Mr. May's accounts fill in these events and make me all the more sorry that I missed them.

I was, however, on hand for the trial of Mike Farah for his alleged pistol-whipping of Jean Blair that he describes.

And I was in the emergency area of Trumbull Memorial Hospital after Farah was brought there, having been shot-gunned in the side yard of his home.

I do remember one of Farah's sons, at the hospital, yelling, "Where's Tony, where's Tony," referring to Tony "The Dope" Delsanter.

The sons refused to be interviewed, and I don't recall we ever knew if the son was blaming Delsanter for the slaying.

May had a few surprises here for me.

For instance, I never heard that in a mob trial here, one defense lawyer had been famed Trumbull County native Clarence Darrow.

The author has a historian's obvious patience for the deep research that underlies this fascinating book.

Long time Mahoning Valley residents who lived through these mob years, and younger people who have only heard bits and pieces about those years, will find the May's picture well-drawn and fascinating.

Welcome to the Jungle Inn belongs in every area historian's reference collection.

By Richard G. Ellers
Police Reporter, *Warren Tribune-Chronicle*, 1956-1965

1

The Place of Salt Licks

A Brief History of Trumbull County

The region that came to be known as Trumbull County, located in Ohio's Mahoning Valley, was occupied long before white settlers moved in by tribes of Indians. Initially, Trumbull County lay along the path the warriors and hunters followed between what would become the cities of Pittsburgh and Detroit. Soon Indians began to settle in the area due in part to the salt licks located near the Mahoning River. The valley was said to have taken its name from the Indian word Mahoning, which means "the place of salt licks."

Members of the Erie tribe were first to fully inhabit the area. Around 1655 these Indians lost in battle to warriors of the Iroquois tribe and were forced to abandon the valley. The Iroquois then took control of the entire region.

The events of the Revolutionary War (1775-1783) had little effect on Trumbull County, except for one incident. The American commander of Fort Pitt ordered an expedition westward in the direction of the Cuyahoga River. The purpose was reportedly to head off any collusion between the Indians and British in that area. The only Indians the force came across were a group of squaws in the Trumbull County area, who were gathering salt from the salt licks. In an action called "ridiculous and cowardly," the men attacked the women, killing or capturing all of them. The expedition became known as the "Squaw Campaign" and an angry General George Washington personally ordered the removal of the fort's commander.

After the cessation of hostilities following the Revolutionary War, Americans looked forward to continuing the westward expansion. The states of Connecticut, Massachusetts, Pennsylvania, New York and Virginia claimed ownership of land west of the Allegheny Mountains – how far west could not be determined.

After some squabble, all the states ceded their claims to the Federal government, "in the interest of national unity," with the exception of Connecticut. The "Constitution State," said to be "Yankee bred and stubborn," wanted their just deserve. With other states pressuring her to back off, Connecticut yielded its claim in 1786, but reserved a single strip in Northern Ohio. This area, which became known as the Connecticut Western Reserve, ran westward for 120 miles from the Pennsylvania line and was bounded by Lake Erie on the north and the 41st parallel to the south (roughly where US Route 224 runs today).

The Connecticut legislature now had to determine how to distribute the land. During the Revolutionary War, loyalists to the British crown ransacked and put the torch to a number of towns along the Atlantic Coast of Connecticut, displacing 1,870 residents. Some ten years after the war ended, Connecticut set aside 500,000 acres of land in the Western Reserve for these victims. The land, located on the western edge of the Reserve became known as "The Fire Lands." Considering that the new residents would be forced to settle with local Indians, this didn't seem like such a great deal. Permanent settlement by white pioneers did not begin until after General "Mad Anthony" Wayne defeated the Indians at the Battle of Fallen Timbers in 1794 leading to the signing of the Treaty of Greenville a year later.

At that time the Connecticut legislature approved for sale the remaining land of the Western Reserve. It was purchased for $1.2 million by the Connecticut Land Company, a syndicate of 35 land speculators. Involved in the negotiations were members of the Iroquois tribe who still lived in the area. Members of the Connecticut Land Company's surveying party met with Iroquois Chief Joseph Brandt. Purchase of the lands from the tribe was negotiated for $500, two beef cattle and 100 gallons of whiskey. Most likely, portions of the whiskey were sampled prior to the consummation of the deal.

The general agent of the Connecticut Land Company was Moses Cleaveland, who led the first expedition of settlers and surveyors into the territory. The city of Cleveland would later be named in his honor. By 1798 fifteen families inhabited the entire Western Reserve. Incredibly, within two years the population would climb to 13,000.

The new settlers brought their New England ways of life with them to the territory, even naming some of the towns – New London and Norwalk – for Connecticut towns. Farms and homes were built in the New England tradition, matching the same architectural style. Making it easy on the new arriving settlers was the fact that the Indians who had once occupied the territory had completed much of the clearing that was needed for the planting of crops.

As the territory grew, with new families arriving daily, the question of title and government arose. Connecticut officials put forth a petition for a New Connecticut territory, but were turned down by Congress. Likewise, a request to make the Western Reserve a county of Connecticut was declined. In April 1800, under an act written by future US Supreme Court Chief Justice John Marshall, Connecticut renounced all claims to the area. The Western Reserve was no longer attached in any capacity to the state of Connecticut.

The Western Reserve region became Trumbull County, named in honor of former Connecticut Governor John Trumbull, who guided that state from 1769 to 1784. At one time Western Reserve / Trumbull County consisted of the entire areas of Ashtabula, Cuyahoga, Erie, Geauga, Huron, Lake, Lorain, Medina and Portage Counties, as well as portions of Ashland, Mahoning and Summit Counties.

Founding of Warren

During the fall of 1798 Ephraim Quinby and Richard Storer ventured into Trumbull County from Washington County, Pennsylvania looking for new lands to settle. After examining the area and checking the soil they headed home. Over the winter Quinby purchased some 440 acres of land from the Connecticut Land Company. In the spring of 1799 he returned accompanied by family and friends.

It took a year for Quinby to begin laying out the town. When he did he named it in honor of Moses Warren, a surveyor who accompanied Moses Cleaveland on his initial expedition into the new territory. One of Quinby's first civic minded moves was to donate four acres in the center of town to be used as a village square – this area remains the same to this day, highlighted by a domed courthouse.

Although the cities of Cleveland and Youngstown were older and more established, Northwest Territorial Governor Arthur St. Clair designated Warren the county seat and the "capital of the Western Reserve." The decision was politically based. St. Clair felt there were more Federalists in the area from which he could count on for support for his political agenda. Due to the fact that Youngstown was overlooked, when Mahoning County was later formed an intense rivalry existed between the two counties for years.

Once established as the county seat, one of the first orders of business was to divide the county into townships. During the first meeting on August 25, 1800, "held between Ephraim Quinby's corn cribs in Warren," eight townships were determined – Cleveland, Warren, Youngstown, Hudson, Vernon, Richfield, Middlefield and Painesville. The action was approved by St. Clair and "the organization of Trumbull County was completed and civil government was established in the Western Reserve," according to the book *Cleveland and Its Environs*.

Next on the agenda was to select a jail. Apparently more consideration was given to this than the construction of a church and schoolhouse, which were to follow. The group decided on a room inside Quinby's log cabin to serve as the jail and Warren's first citizen was now the city's first jailer.

With the growing population it didn't take long for the first criminal act to take place. It occurred in 1800 and was perpetrated against local Indians who were still in the district. White settlers and several Indians got together to discuss the layout of the City of Warren. The drinking of whiskey accompanied the session. When the Indians finished their supply they were angered when the white settlers refused to share theirs. Arguing began and the city planning exercise came to an end. On their way home after the preempted meeting some of the Indians stopped and harassed the family of James McMahon, scaring his wife and children.

McMahon was one of the first white settlers to arrive in the area, building his cabin in an area that the Indians had cleared for crops. He wasn't the most popular settler in the valley. One account claimed he had "none too good a reputation for stability in the community and was looked upon as a squatter."

Incensed by this offense to his family, McMahon and several others, including Ephraim Quinby and Richard Storer, headed to the Indian settlement to "talk things over." The following account was a result of the "talk":

> "There they met Captain George, a Delaware, and Spotted John, a half-breed, and during the argument over the behavior of the Indians toward McMahon's family, McMahon shot and killed Captain George. In the excitement, Storer, believing that Spotted John was aiming at him, shot and killed the half-breed. Somehow the bullet that killed Spotted John also injured his squaw and son and daughter. McMahon was taken into custody, but Richard Storer escaped and never returned to the Ohio country."

To head off any retaliatory efforts by the Indians, Governor St. Clair immediately called a conference of the Indians in the area to let them know justice would be served. McMahon was taken to Fort Pitt to be incarcerated until his trial. Unfortunately, the decision makers hearing the case "did not regard the killing of a red man as a grave offense." McMahon was acquitted and released.

Many of the Indians who remained in the region took the side of the British during the War of 1812. After their defeat the Indian population vanished and did not return.

Economic Growth in the Region

During the early decades of Warren's development the town's growth, like that of Trumbull County, was fueled by agriculture. The area became known for its dairy farming and milk production. The region also produced a large volume of cheese. This continued until the development of the railroad and the introduction of the refrigerator car. Next to dairy goods, poultry was an important product. Because of Trumbull County's central location to the cities of Cleveland, Akron and Canton to the west and Youngstown and Pittsburgh to the east, it was a ready supplier of corn, potatoes, vegetables, fruit, chicken, milk, cheese and butter to these expanding metropolitan areas.

Trumbull County's desire to capitalize on its agricultural products by supplying them to an outside market was achieved during the "Canal Era" with the opening of the Ohio and Erie Canals. Initially the plans didn't call for the canal to pass through Trumbull County, but that all changed on May 23, 1839 when Warren celebrated the arrival of the first canal boat via the new Ohio-Pennsylvania Canal. In addition to providing an outlet for the region's farm produce, it opened the door for the county's iron and coal products.

The "Canal Era," like the "Pony Express" was a short-lived era. By 1856 the "Iron Horse" was coming to prominence in the Mahoning Valley. Soon the region would be crisscrossed by the New York Central, Baltimore & Ohio, the Erie and the Pennsylvania railroads.

Oil was a commodity few settlers in the county had much use for. By the time the Civil War began, however, uses for kerosene and lubricating oil were on the rise. The first shallow well was sunk in 1860 in Mecca Township, which "became the scene of an almost unpredictable oil boom." An additional 2,500 wells were soon sunk in Trumbull County. Vast quantitiesof oil, selling as high as $20 per barrel were being siphoned out of the earth in this small township. By the end of the 1870s the reservoir of "black gold" had all but run dry.

Another form of industry prior to the Civil War were the mills – saw mills, grist mills and carding mills – all fed by water power provided by the Mahoning River.

Warren also had a piece of the automobile industry at one time. The Packard brothers – J. Ward and William – sons of a local industrial leader had their first taste of success in the electrical business, founding Packard Electric Company. J. Ward owned several patents in the electrical industry. By the early 1890s, however, he had a new interest – the automobile.

In 1898 Packard purchased a Cleveland-made Winton automobile and deconstructed it. Assisted by two former Winton Company employees, J. Ward rebuilt the car into a much improved model. The next year Packard automobiles began appearing on the streets of Warren. Seeking financing for their manufacturing, the brothers bypassed local financers and secured funding from Detroit. They soon transferred their base of operations there, thus helping it to earn the title of The Motor City.

The product that was to give Trumbull County and the Mahoning Valley its greatest source of wealth and notoriety was steel. Beginning with a foundry and blast furnace in Brookfield Township in 1836 the industry would expand to the point where the Mahoning Valley would be dubbed the "Steel Valley."

In 1912 the Trumbull Steel Company was offered a free factory site in an area of Warren known as the "Flats." In return, the steel company promised to construct six mills and hire 600 workers. The steel industry in Warren was on its way.

Two years later the war in Europe created an unprecedented demand for steel. In addition to the war, this country had developed a huge demand for steel for the railroads, the automobile and the building industry. From the book *Warren and Trumbull County* comes a brief narrative of the industry and its affect on the local populace:

> "The Flats were transformed into a gigantic workshop, covered with acres upon acres of buildings. Mills, converters, rollers, these were the evidence of the new steel empire.
> "And here on the Flats rose a new city. It was peopled with strangers speaking a foreign tongue, living in the very shadow of the mills where they labored. They were burley men, Serbs, Croatians, Slovaks, and other middle-Europeans; they were prolific women. Not only was the foreign element increased, but hardy American stock came, attracted by the promise of steady work and high wages.
> "At the end of the first decade of the twentieth century, as more and more new homes rose on the Flats, the older families retreated to the north and west where they also built new homes, leaving the valley to the new-comers.
> "As a result the city is divided conspicuously into two elements. In the north section of town live the old families who are proud of their New England heritage handed on by their grandfathers. Here the Kinsman,

Packard, and Perkins homes preserve something of the past, the time when Warren was a smaller city in an agricultural community. It is said that some of these people who lived on Mahoning and Park Avenues vigorously opposed the coming of the steel mills into this quiet town.

"In the southern sections of Warren, across the railroad tracks in the Flats, the big Republic Steel mills stretch in one long line of stacks and factory buildings. They furnish a vivid background for the rows of shabby, unpainted, frame houses where live the mill workers who came in from the Monongahela district to the east or directly from abroad.

Dominated though it is by steel, Warren is still a marketing and social center for outlying districts. When the farmers come in on Saturday and throng the public square, they give the town a rural character; but through the week, when the mill workers walk the streets, Warren is again the city of industry."

The dichotomy of the city, brought to bear by the division of the foreign born steel workers living in the Flats and the descendents of the early white settlers sitting in the higher-up sections of Warren, enforced the adage of "being from the other side of the tracks."

During this time the city's population grew by 130 percent. Like Youngstown, Warren would thrive on the steel industry until the mid-1970s when the bottom fell out of the steel market.

Crime in Trumbull County

The influx of foreign-born workers into the valley created a market to help them blow off steam after a grueling six or seven day work-week of ten or more hours per day. Saloons were plentiful around the mills up and down the Mahoning Valley. Gambling dens and houses of prostitution soon sprang up. With the end of World War I came Prohibition. The foreign workers who enjoyed their alcohol were not about to let a new morality law known as the Volsted Act prevent them from quenching their thirst after a long hot day at the mill.

The combination of thirsty overworked foreign factory men and the law prohibiting the manufacture, sale and transportation of intoxicating beverages initiated a long period of lawlessness in both Mahoning and Trumbull Counties. While Youngstown would earn the nickname "Crime-town, USA," for its continued underworld activities, Warren would have its own legacy of organized crime and political corruption.

The "Roaring '20s" were all of two days old when a public corruption scandal splashed across the front pages of the local newspapers. Charles

D. Kistler was a married father of three, who had a sterling reputation as a bank teller and as city treasurer of Warren. One day after leaving office, voted out after six years as treasurer, Kistler was arrested and charged with embezzling $50,000. Once behind bars the 56 year-old made a startling confession about the theft of the money blaming a Cleveland woman for his fall from grace. Kistler, a grandfather, became infatuated with the woman and purchased a home for her, spending freely of the city's funds to decorate the house in lavish fashion.

Kistler's paramour, Lillian Jane Wilson, a married mother of two daughters, denied she had ever received any money from the former city official and was prepared to fight the charges of receiving stolen property. Authorities filed an injunction to keep Wilson from disposing of any property or possessions. While at first admitting that she knew Kistler, in a later interview with police she claimed, "I do not know Mr. Kistler and I do not know why anyone should seek an injunction against me. Further than that, I do not care to discuss the case."

Kistler was able to keep his embezzling from being discovered because he served as teller at the Western Reserve National Bank for 20 years, maintaining the position while holding the office of city treasurer. After Kistler's initial confession, he refused to say anything more about his crime. The newspapers hinted that another man in the Cleveland area was being sought. Whether Kistler was being blackmailed for his illicit love affair with Mrs. Wilson was never revealed.

On January 30, Kistler pleaded guilty and received a term of from one to twenty years in the Ohio Penitentiary. He was fined $100,640, exactly twice the amount of the sum he stole from the city. No family members were present in the courtroom during the sentencing. Mrs. Wilson was reported by the newspapers to be "absent."

Kistler was released from the penitentiary on October 14, 1922. Good behavior was cited for his early freedom. As for Mrs. Wilson, she was reported to have married a Cleveland real-estate man. The property that Kistler purchased for her was awarded to the city of Warren by the courts.

During the early years of Prohibition the bootleg liquor of choice in Youngstown as well as Cleveland was a product called "raisin jack." This concoction was produced prior to corn sugar being utilized in the distilling process. The Mahoning Valley's first arrests under the new law were of a man and woman caught selling "raisin jack" in Warren. This case involved a woman whose husband had lost his job at Youngstown Sheet and Tube, and had gone to Detroit to look for work. The boom times, which the nation enjoyed during the 1920s, had not yet arrived. It was not uncommon for defendants to come before a judge and claim they produced and sold liquor as a means to support their families.

Prior to the Italian underworld's entry into bootlegging, the crime of choice was Black Hand extortion. This heinous crime was vicious in nature and usually perpetrated on fellow Italians. One of these gruesome crimes occurred on July 2, 1920 involving an Italian from Calabria. The body of Dominick Scallechia was discovered along Howland Road near Niles. The 33 year-old Girard resident, like several other recent victims, had his head nearly severed from a blow from a meat cleaver or an axe. In the dead man's back, the numeral "7" had been carved. The newspapers called the murder "one of the most atrocious in the criminal records of Trumbull County."

Police went immediately to the Girard boarding house where Scallechia was living, which was owned by Joseph Perillo. In Scallechia's room police discovered a set of clean sheets on the bed and that the floor had recently been scrubbed. A closer inspection of the bed revealed a heavily bloodstained mattress. Police at first theorized that Scallechia had been murdered while in bed and his body taken out to Howland Road. They could not, however, explain why the body was clothed in a "natty Palm Beach suit." Scallechia was known to wear the latest fashions despite the fact he had no visible means of support. A roommate of the murdered man packed all his possessions into a trunk and left stating a cousin would come by to pick up his belongings. The cousin, as well as Perillo and his wife were arrested for the murder when police found out Scallechia had recently received a Black Hand extortion threat.

Just days after the Scallechia murder, Bruno Pugalise, described as the leader of a group of Black Handers in the Niles – Warren area, was murdered while he slept. A gunman entered Pugalise's Third Avenue home in Warren and shot him three times in the head and body killing him instantly. Bruno Pugalise had been busy with his Black Hand practice trying to raise a $10,000 bail to get his brother Pasquale "Patsy" out of jail. Patsy had been carrying on a love affair with the wife of Dr. George Ormeroid, a well-known Warren dentist. Mrs. Ormeroid was the daughter of the former superintendent of the Warren school system. Ormeroid became aware Patsy was on "intimate terms" with his wife and bravely told the Black Hand gang member to keep away from his home. On Sunday afternoon June 2, Ormeroid returned home to find the two in bed together. A fight ensued and Pugalise pulled a gun and fired. The bullet grazed the dentist's vest. Later, Pugalise claimed he fired only after Ormeroid hit him over the head with a gun. In November, Patsy Pugalise was convicted of shooting with intent to kill and was sentenced to 15 years in the Ohio Penitentiary. Pugalise was asked if he had anything to say before he was sentenced, to which he stated he still believed in and had love for the Lord. The judge responded that Pugalise would now have plenty of time "to develop this love further."

In addition to Black Hand extortion, bootlegging, gambling and political corruption during this lawless period in America, prostitution was also on the rise in Warren and Trumbull County. The practice was known as "white slavery" at the time. In July 1921 an investigation by agents from the Justice Department uncovered a white slavery ring operating in Warren. Authorities initially arrested two young women from Erie, Pennsylvania at a Warren "resort." The women told investigators that they were "lured" to Pittsburgh from their homes in Erie. They described their treatment by the brothel keepers as "inhuman."

Justice Department officials arrested Viola Belledaire, the proprietor of the brothel, and two Greek men, Thomas Gust and James Mallo. The ring operated by "importing" young women to Warren for immoral purposes and then transferring them to other cities for prostitution in order to keep a fresh supply of new faces. The three were charged with violating the Mann Act, which banned the interstate transportation of females for "immoral purposes," and sent to prison.

A few random murders took place in the Mahoning Valley during the Prohibition years; while in Cleveland the era was dominated by the Lonardo-Porrello Corn Sugar War. During this bloody fray three Lonardo brothers and four Porrello brothers were slaughtered, as well as a dozen other gang members. The Corn Sugar War spilled over into Warren on August 5, 1930 when the body of Salvatore Randazzo was found with 34 wounds on a stretch of road in Vienna. According to Trumbull County Coroner J.C. Henshaw, the killers took regular shotgun shells, emptied the buckshot from them and filled them with heavy lead slugs. With one exception, all the wounds suffered by Randazzo were to the upper chest, face, head and neck. A coup de grace was fired from close range into the side of the bootlegger's head as he lay on the road. Witnesses spotted four men running from the scene and getting into a waiting automobile.

Another bootleg murder, based on local competition, occurred around the same time. "First there were four or five shots fired and then there was a rat-tat-tat which lasted for nearly a minute. There must have been 50 shots fired. Then there were four or five more distinct reports." These were the words of a witness prior to discovering the body Pietro Fedele near Woodford's Corners in Vienna. The slaughter was brutal. Revolvers, sawed-off shotguns and a Thompson sub-machinegun were employed. Fedele's body had 34 wounds including a shotgun blast that nearly obliterated his face making it nearly impossible for friends to identify him. His automobile had been hit with 48 slugs.

Fedele had arrived in America around 1923. He settled in New York City for a while with relatives, but for some reason never completed the plans to bring his wife here from Italy. In the late 1920s he moved to Ashtabula

County and became involved in bootlegging. Fedele moved into a rooming house on Springfield Avenue in Youngstown a year before he was gunned down. He told the boarders there he was a macaroni and olive oil salesman. Residents at the home considered Fedele a "mystery man." He spoke little English and had made no apparent attempt to learn the language other than what he needed to get by. He was described as having few close friends.

When he was murdered the newspapers wrote that Fedele "had been 'put on the spot' in Chicago gangster style." Investigators believed Fedele was a liquor runner who began undercutting the competition in an area of Trumbull County called "Little Canada," a notorious "wet strip" in Brookfield Township along the Pennsylvania State line near Sharon.

While searching the room where Fedele lived, detectives found a form letter from the United Natural Gas Company of Sharon informing their customers of a pending two-hour gas shut off to make repairs. Authorities believed Fedele had a location in Trumbull County where he was manufacturing liquor, while living in Youngstown in an attempt to throw off his enemies. A bill found in Fedele's pocket revealed that he had recently purchased $800 worth of corn sugar in "truck load lots" from a Youngstown supplier. Police immediately tried to link his killing to three recent murders in Cleveland – James and Joe Porrello and Salvatore "Sam" Tilocco – in that city's ongoing Corn Sugar War.

The investigation concluded that Fedele was taken at gunpoint and forced to drive his car to Vienna. There he was ordered to stop in the middle of the road at 11:45 at night. Told to get out of the vehicle, Fedele stood next to the car while at least four gunmen blasted away, the shooting continuing even after he fell. Local residents say they saw four or five men running from the murder scene to a car that headed off in the direction of Belmont Avenue.

"What's going on here?" a farmer called out as the group passed by.

"Get the hell out of the way or we'll show you," replied one of the shooters, nearly out of breath.

Neighbors rushed to the scene of the carnage to find Fedele with his face and chest "horribly torn" and his automobile still running. The *Vindicator* reported, in what was a custom of the day, that several hundred people viewed the "bullet-riddled" body at the undertakers.

The police announced they discovered the shotguns used in the slaying were purchased from a gun dealer in Farrell, Pennsylvania. Several people questioned by police said the "method employed by the killers indicate there was a woman (involved) in the case." The hunt for clues uncovered a rumor that Fedele had recently been seen with a woman in Meadville, Pennsylvania and was threatened by the lady's boyfriend. The police investigation concluded that Fedele was murdered while attempting to undersell his rivals in the liquor business.

During the investigation Trumbull County authorities claimed their work led them to speakeasies, illicit distilleries and corn sugar plants they "never knew existed." Trumbull County Sheriff Jack Risher claimed Fedele's "slayers are sure making it tough for others in the racket." When told of Risher's comment and asked if that was the case in Youngstown, Vice Squad Chief J.C. Huffman stated, "No! That's because we have been making it as tough as possible for them right along and you can't make it any tougher than as tough as possible."

On August 8, a private service was held at Hall's Funeral Home in Warren. There were only three mourners – Fedele's brother, brother-in-law, and a cousin. His body was cremated at Oakwood Cemetery later that day. Fedele's killers were never identified.

Even bombings and union violence had an early entry into Warren's crime history. On the morning of January 18, 1933 Gus Macris froze in his tracks when he arrived at his East Market Street place of business, the Victory Barber Shop. Leaning against the front door of his establishment was a small pasteboard box containing a can filled with powder and other material. From the top a half-burned fuse protruded.

Macris was under pressure since December from men who told him to make his barber shop an organized shop. To emphasize their point, a stink bomb was released into the shop one night. Local barber establishments were in the middle of a price war. Macris was charging only 25 cents for a haircut. He was receiving anonymous calls at his shop daily from people telling him to raise his prices or else. Barbers Union officials claimed they had nothing to do with the phone threats or the attempted bombing.

Mid-West Crime Wave 1933-34

If the Prohibition years gave birth to organized crime in America, then the criminal era that succeeded it should be acknowledged for establishing this country's greatest law enforcement agency – the Federal Bureau of Investigation. The Mid-West Crime Wave of 1933-1934 spawned a group of bank robbing criminals, sensationalized by the media and Hollywood, who still remain household names 70 years after their demise. John Dillinger, Charles Arthur "Pretty Boy" Floyd, "Baby Face" Nelson, Ma Barker and her sons, George "Machine Gun" Kelly, Alvin "Creepy" Karpis and Bonnie and Clyde were the marquis names during this colorful, yet short-lived era. Their criminal activities helped establish the FBI as the premier-law enforcement agency in the United States and catapulted its director, the self-promoting J. Edgar Hoover, into the limelight as America's Number One crime fighter.

Trumbull County played a role in the activities of one of this era's bank robbing *extraordinaires*, while a fictionalized account of another's presence is still part of local folklore. On August 11, 1934 the Warren *Tribune Chronicle* ran a story about the "racket friends" of John Dillinger in the area. The famed bank robber had been killed in Chicago three weeks earlier The article began, "John Dillinger is dead but the fear he inspired still lives. The reporter discovered this when trying to talk about him to the Trumbull racketeers and gamblers who knew him during the short time he was in Masury and the vicinity."

The article claimed that Dillinger worked in several gambling houses during a two-month period the previous summer. The gist of the piece was that although the infamous outlaw was dead, people were still afraid to talk about him. One of the interviewees declared, "That guy is still hot. See me in ten years and I'll tell you all I know."

Fast-forward almost 60 years and now it's the *Vindicator* reporting on the "friends" of the legendary bank robber. Two old-timers claiming to have known Dillinger in Masury were quoted. One stated, "To me, he was always a real gentleman. And when it came to the kids, you couldn't beat him. As far as we were concerned, he'd get us anything we wanted – moonshine, you name it."

The other man recalled nostalgically that one of Dillinger's "favorite tricks" was to stand on the roof of the gambling club every Friday night and toss a hat full of pennies to the children waiting below. "We'd scramble for these pennies, and then head up to the Gable movie theater on Saturday and put two cents down on a Tom Mix or Buck Jones western."

Although colorful, there are a couple of major flaws in the story that these two gentlemen told. The article, which appeared on January 9, 1994, stated:

> "Dillinger worked for a brief time in the Brookfield-Masury area in the early 1930s.
> "'If he had five dollars, he'd give it to you...John Dillinger was just a regular fella dealing cards for chuck-a-luck, until 'Legs' Diamond was killed by the mob that was backing him.'
> "Well known racketeer Jack "Legs" Diamond, gunned down in Albany, N.Y., in 1931, was Dillinger's boss at a gambling club in the "49" district of Masury."

The problem with the story is that Diamond was murdered on December 18, 1931. Dillinger was serving time in prison for a botched robbery from the fall of 1924 until May 22, 1933. He never met Diamond, let alone worked for him.

After Dillinger's release from Michigan City Prison, he returned home to Mooresville, Indiana where he vowed to change his life. Within two weeks he was robbing stores, food markets and drugstores and embarking on his famous bank-robbing career. Incredibly, Dillinger's legendary career lasted a mere 14 months. Activities early on in that career brought him to western Ohio. On June 10, 1933 he robbed the New Carlisle Bank in New Carlisle, Ohio of $10,600, and on August 14 at the Citizens National Bank of Bluffton he got $2,100. Between June 4 and September 23, when he was arrested in Dayton, Ohio, Dillinger was identified in eleven robberies. An accomplice who was captured by police put the number of robberies Dillinger was a participant in at 24.

It is difficult to believe that with all this criminal activity Dillinger could have found two months to spend working gambling houses in Masury, which is located on the eastern edge of Ohio near the Pennsylvania border in Trumbull County. The furthest east Dillinger is known to have traveled into Ohio was Bluffton, which is approximately 50 miles inside the Indiana-Ohio border. None of the many biographies written about the prolific bank robber place him anywhere near the Mahoning Valley.

One of the Mid-West Crime Wave notables who did "pull a job" in the Valley was Alvin "Creepy" Karpis. Born Albin Karpowicz to Lithuanian parents living in Montreal, Canada, Karpis was a killer, kidnapper and bank robber. As a member of the feared Barker-Karpis Gang he participated in two highly publicized kidnappings – St. Paul brewer William A. Hamm, Jr. on June 15, 1933 and St. Paul banker Edward G. Bremer on January 17, 1934. The first kidnapping earned the gang $100,000; the second twice that amount.

After the Bremer kidnapping Karpis needed a place to lie low until the marked ransom money could be laundered. For a brief time he worked at the Harvard Inn in Cleveland. The gambling house was closed during a spectacular raid in January 1936 in which legendary law enforcement official Eliot Ness, Cleveland's newly appointed Director of Public Safety, participated. Years after the raid a false story emerged that Karpis was present when the club was raided. Karpis, in two books he later authored, never discussed being at the club the night of the raid.

Karpis, the last of the infamous criminals of this period to be captured, robbed the payroll of the Youngstown Sheet & Tube Company from a mail delivery truck on April 24, 1935 making off with $72,000. Karpis was working without Barker brothers Freddie (killed by FBI agents in Florida along with Ma) and Doc (captured by Melvin Purvis in Chicago). His new accomplices were Harry Campbell and Joe Rich.

In 1971, after spending a quarter century on Alcatraz, second longest of any inmate, he penned his autobiography *The Alvin Karpis Story*. Karpis recalled the Warren robbery in the book, admitting that it almost didn't make it off the ground. He explained that after tracking the payroll delivery process he discovered that once the money arrived by train it was picked up by the post office and delivered to two different banks. Karpis wrote, "The idea was to intercept it while it was being switched from train to truck or, failing that, to stop the truck later and hold up the driver."

At the train station several railroad employees were gathered, as well as a number of bystanders. Harry Campbell began to lose his nerve. Karpis related:

> "By that time, Harry was beginning to come unhinged. He and Joe walked back to the car.
>
> "'Do you realize,' he said to me, 'that we're going to have to kill a lot of people to take this payroll?'
>
> "I told them to climb in the car, and I pulled out of the station parking lot. Harry was clearly upset. I drove a couple of blocks hoping to calm him down. A black cat crossed in front of the car.
>
> "'That was a black cat,' said Harry.
>
> "'Forget it,' I said. 'That cat had white marks all over its chest.'
>
> "'That cat was black as coal,' he said.
>
> "'Harry, for chrissake,' I said, 'a cat isn't going to make a damn bit of difference. The question is, are we going to get this job done or aren't we?'
>
> "What a ridiculous situation, arguing over a goddamn cat!"

Karpis concluded, "Harry got a grip on himself," they found the mail truck, forced it to a stop, and pulled off the robbery without a hitch.

On May 1, 1936 the FBI arrested Karpis in New Orleans. Hoover, who had been criticized up to this point for never having personally made an arrest, flew to Louisiana while Karpis was under surveillance so that he could "throw the cuffs" on the outlaw. According to Karpis, Hoover was kept in an alley while agents surrounded him after he got into his car. When it was safe, the director stepped forward. Karpis claimed that not one of the army of FBI agents had remembered to bring a set of hand cuffs so his hands were tied together using the necktie of one of the agents.

"If Munsene had visited the sheriff and made him two hours late for his Sunday dinner, neither his wife nor the cook would ever have allowed the sheriff to forget the incident. That is not the way with woman and cold dinners." –Clarence S. Darrow, May 10, 1928, during final arguments of the third James Munsene vs. State of Ohio trial for trying to bribe Trumbull County Sheriff John H. Smith.

2

James "Jimmy" Munsene

James Mancini, known locally as "Big Jimmy" Munsene, was Trumbull County's most well known gangster during the first half of the 20th Century. Munsene's rise during Prohibition, his heyday during the days of the old Hollyhock Gardens Night Club, to his sensational murder at the hands of hired Detroit hitmen left him a legendary figure in the Steel Valley. Part of Munsene's mystique was his personal aversion to weapons. He never carried a firearm for his personal protection.

Munsene was born in 1890 in Collelongo, on the southern tip of Italy. He arrived in America around 1903, eventually settling in the city of Steubenville, along the Ohio River. As a teenager he found work as a water-boy on a railroad construction site outside Morgantown, West Virginia. He next found employment in a local tin mill, where he was trained as a "doubler's helper." After completing his apprenticeship, he went on to be a doubler in mills in Farrell, Pennsylvania and Steubenville. In 1914, one year after he was naturalized, he married Lucy Durandetti and their first child, Nofry, was born later that year. A second son, Tullio, was born in 1916, and later the couple had a third son, Warren, and a daughter, Marian, to round out their family. During the World War Mancini moved to Warren where he found work at the Trumbull Steel Company plant (later purchased by Republic Steel).

Then came Prohibition. Munsene left Republic Steel in 1921 (some sources say 1919) to work with his brother-in-law, Bernard Monfrino, at a grocery concern in Pittsburgh. By 1924 the two became aware of the tremendous profits that were being made from bootlegging and operating a new business venture called the speakeasy. As a bootlegger Munsene developed an air of arrogance due to his success. He once told Trumbull County Sheriff John H. "Jack" Smith about the confiscation of a carload of beer by police on the city's south side. While this was taking place, he claimed he was unloading another carload of beer on the north side. Munsene boasted, "I made enough money on that second car load to pay [for] the loss of the other and make a nice profit." It was during this time that Mancini became a public figure and took on the persona of "Jimmy Munsene," the last name adapted simply because of the way most people pronounced it.

In 1924 Munsene and Monfrino went to Atlantic City, New Jersey where they operated the Follies Bergere, a restaurant and cabaret. The next year, running the operation on a seasonal basis, Munsene was there from April until mid-October.

Mancini's next illegal venture was one that would separate the steel factory workers from their weekly earnings – the operation of gambling dens. Deputy sheriffs raided one of these operations, a gambling club on South Street, on March 29, 1925. Munsene and 53 others were arrested. Sheriff Smith, who claimed he did not order the raid, arrived soon after and personally slapped the handcuffs on Munsene.

This was not the first time a Munsene operation was raided. In fact, Munsene felt the sheriff was singling out his gambling houses and he began to have discussions with the county's chief law enforcement officer to work out a solution. In his first visit with the sheriff, Munsene demanded to know how much longer Smith would continue "ramming" his operation. To which Smith replied, "As long as you keep violating the law."

Munsene passed the summer months of 1925 attending to his Atlantic City operation, returning to the Warren area in October. In late November Munsene paid another visit to the sheriff. Arriving at the front door of the Smith home, which was attached to the jail, he was let in by Deputy Charles Clemens, the sheriff's father-in-law. This time during their discussions, Munsene offered the sheriff $500 to look the other way. Smith declined the offer, but the next evening, Friday, November 27, Munsene showed up at the jail with a pink envelope full of cash and handed it to the sheriff's wife. On the envelope was a handwritten note:

"Mr. Smith; I will see you every first of the month. I expect to do better later."

The sheriff's cook, Helen Wilkins, witnessed the transaction from the hallway. Mrs. Smith took the envelope to her husband's private office and handed it to him. Smith opened it in the presence of Jay Buchwalter and the chief jailer. Buchwalter, an attorney, counted the contents, which totaled $500, and told Smith to note the date and time, 9:10 p.m. Smith swore out an affidavit the next day and Munsene was arrested late Saturday night and taken before a justice of the peace who released him on a $5,000 bond.

Bribery Trials

On January 18, 1926 Munsene was charged with bribery in a secret indictment. The language in the indictment stated Munsene "gave Sheriff Smith the sum of $500 with intent to influence him with regard to his official duty." This would become one of several points of contention as the Sheriff never did see the money delivered, nor was it ever specified as to what the money was for. Munsene pleaded not guilty at arraignment and was released on a $5,000 bond. If convicted he was looking at a term of one to ten years in the Ohio Penitentiary. Realistically, he was facing as much as three years behind bars.

There was a media frenzy as the trial opened on Monday, February 22 in the courtroom of Common Pleas Judge William C. Duncan. Handling the prosecution was Wick W. Pierson. Despite the publicity, a jury of six men and six women was seated in just over an hour. During the impaneling process, each juror said "no" when asked if they would vote guilty if it were proved Munsene operated gambling joints and speakeasies and not proved that he offered a bribe. The defense team, consisting of former Trumbull County Prosecutor Harvey A. Burgess and R.I. Gillmer, made it clear that Munsene was being tried solely for bribery, not for running a gambling house or selling liquor.

On the first day of trial the courthouse was filled to capacity. The Warren *Tribune Chronicle* reported, "In the crowd were some trial fans, a score of women, friends of Munsene and the sheriff, some court house attaches, two ministers and many lawyers." The first witness for the state that morning was Sheriff Smith, who discussed the private conversations he had with Munsene. Smith recalled a conversation, which took place the night before the money was delivered at the county jail, where Munsene asked him, "Suppose you would receive a letter with $500 in it?"

"I said, 'Whoa, stop right there, I would prosecute.' Then he said, 'Suppose you would receive $500 and did not know where it came from? 'I told him, 'I would turn it over to the prosecutor.'"

Smith then described the events that took place the next night, November 27. The sheriff then endured a vigorous cross-examination by Gillmer. At the heart of the questioning was whether the sheriff knew at the time the money was handed over if Munsene was in fact operating a speakeasy or gambling house. Smith answered that he didn't know.

Ten witnesses were called that afternoon including Mrs. Smith, whose testimony was essential to proving that Munsene was the man who delivered the envelope. On the night the envelope was delivered there was a knock on the door and the Smith's young son answered. A man asked to see Mrs. Smith and when she came he handed her the envelope. She claimed the man was Munsene and that she knew this because she had seen him at the jail after the South Street raid in March 1925. On cross-examination, defense counsel tried to discredit her claiming that because of the lighting and layout of the home it would have been impossible to see the man clearly. Despite the effort to shake her testimony, Mrs. Smith remained adamant that the man who handed her the envelope was the man sitting at the defense table.

Additional witnesses included Buchwalter and the chief jailer, who were both present when Smith's wife delivered the envelope to the sheriff.

The prosecution rested its case at 4:30 Monday afternoon. The defense asked the judge to declare the charge "not sustained" by the evidence. Duncan denied the request. Since the jury had already filed out of the courtroom, many thought that the proceedings were over for the day and left. Those who stayed got to see the trial's best arguments.

Smith's admission that he didn't know if Munsene was operating a speakeasy or a gambling joint at the time of the alleged bribe was behind a motion by the defense. Attorneys contended that the money could not have been offered for protection because the sheriff was not aware of any operation that needed "protection." Simply stated, there was no official act to perform on acceptance of the money. Gillmer declared there was no law in the state covering "attempted bribery," and that "a proffer of money is not bribery unless given for a specific reason."

A legal argument began as Pierson stated that "the crime was complete on Munsene's part by delivering the money and that the sheriff did not have to commit a crime to make the deed complete." After several minutes of heated exchanges, Judge Duncan overruled defense counsel's motion.

The *Tribune Chronicle* thought the mix of spectators was an interesting one and wrote:

> "The crowd was again a strangely mixed one. Ministers, lawyers, insurance men, doctors, police off duty, court house attaches, W.C.T.U.

members, friends and foes of the accused and accuser, a few who had been convicted of booze connections, some who never drank and at least one who had drunk plenty today."

On Tuesday morning Munsene took the stand. He testified that in his conversation with the sheriff he discussed having a club where the members "might have social poker games." Munsene said Smith responded, "I'll tell you, Jim, myself personally I'm not against those things, but what am I going to do when a man loses money and his wife comes to me?"

Munsene said he replied, "But nobody can play poker, only club members, and I'll guarantee there won't be any niggers and no roughnecks."

Munsene related that Smith told him that if he opened such a club he would send his deputies over and arrest him. With that, Munsene said he left saying, "Goodnight, sheriff, we're not going to start this club."

During cross-examination Pierson asked, "If the sheriff told you he would not bother you, you would have opened up this gambling club?" To which Munsene replied, "Yes."

He denied that he had offered the sheriff money or that he had handed over $500 to Mrs. Smith. He claimed he was on South Pine Street the entire evening before heading home to bed. As evidence of this, he said he witnessed a raid being carried out by police on South Pine Street shortly before 10:00 p.m. According to the sheriff and other prosecution witnesses, the money was delivered at approximately 9:20 that night.

During the long cross-examination Munsene blurted out comments like, "This is a frame-up, Mr. Pierson!" On another occasion he said, "This is a frame-up and you know it!" At one point, when being reminded of Smith's testimony, he responded to the prosecutor that the sheriff had "made up" things. Pierson replied, "Do you mean the sheriff was lying?"

"Absolutely," Munsene shot back, "and he knows he's lying."

To a claim by Mrs. Smith and Helen Wilkins that Munsene had walked past the jail building during the summer of 1925, the defendant declared he was in Atlantic City from April to October, except for two days when he returned to visit his family.

Defense counsel then called several alibi witnesses to support Munsene's testimony that he was on South Pine Street. Mrs. Smith claimed the defendant was wearing a light brown hat when he arrived at the door. Two police officers testified they saw Munsene twice that evening and both times he was wearing a green hat. P. J. Durkin, an Irish officer, said he "kidded" Munsene about the color of the hat, "I said, where do you dagoes get that stuff, wearing green hats?" The other officer, Thomas Fagadore, claimed he kept his eye on Munsene from a police call box as he sat with friends at Murphy's restaurant on South Pine Street. Two other witnesses, Michael Gillett and Andrew Sargent, businessmen from Farrell, Pennsylvania, claimed they ate spaghetti while talking with Munsene at Murphy's the night of the alleged bribe.

The defense rested its case at 11:20 Tuesday morning and the state began its closing argument shortly afterward. During defense counsel's closing Burgess stated, "Jim is not saint and doesn't pretend to be. They say he is a big bootlegger and a big gambler, but Jim has lived in this county ten years and is accused of having been busy here for several years but he has never been convicted of a booze selling or gambling house keeping charge by either city or county.

"If Jim Munsene had done half the things he is reputed to have done wouldn't anyone know that he was too smart to go to the sheriff's residence and hand $500 to the sheriff's wife after the sheriff had told him he would arrest him and throw him in jail if he opened a card club?"

At 3:20 that afternoon the jury began their deliberations. The comments of attorney Burgess had scored well with many members of the panel. In addition, the testimony about Mrs. Smith's ability to identify Munsene in less than ideal lighting raised some doubts. Yet, when the jury broke for dinner at 5:15 it had taken eight ballots and a unanimous decision was just one juror away. After dinner the jury returned and came to a decision on the ninth ballot.

At 7:30, after a brief wait for Munsene and defense counsel to make their way to the courtroom, the jury returned. As 100 hundred spectators looked on, the *Tribune Chronicle* reported, "Vigorously chewing gum as the court preliminaries were run through [Munsene] stopped for just a moment when the words, 'find the defendant guilty of bribery as charged,' were read."

Burgess and Gillmer immediately filed a motion for a new trial. Judge Duncan said he would rule upon it before passing sentence. Munsene and his counsel quickly left the courtroom. The next day Munsene let his feelings be known. Claiming the charges were a "political frame-up," he accused Sheriff Smith of lying under oath. Munsene told reporters, "What else could the sheriff do? He got $500 in an envelope and opened it in front of Jay Buchwalter and others. He had to look for someone to be a scapegoat, he picked me out. I was unjustly convicted and another trial will prove it."

On Saturday, February 27, Munsene was back in court before Judge Duncan, where the defense team presented their motions for a new trial. One of the claims made during the hearing was that "political enemies" of the sheriff sent the $500 to him in hopes he would not report it. Gillmer complained, "It was unfortunate that newspapers printed so much about it."

A disgusted Pierson responded to the accusations that there was never any evidence produced to indicate that the handing over of the money was political in nature. He also stated that if there was any doubt about Munsene receiving a fair and impartial trial in Trumbull County that defense counsel had every opportunity to ask for a change of venue.

After hearing arguments, Duncan denied the motion. The judge listened to each point the defense made and gave his opinion. In discussing the jail house situation, Duncan responded that he personally went to the jail and examined the hallway area in question, that was said to be too dark to identify Munsene. He concluded by stating, "I believe this man was guilty and that the trial was fair and partial." Munsene had no comment as the judge sentenced him to three years.

The attorneys announced immediately that they would file an appeal. Munsene was allowed to remain free on a $5,000 bond. The Appellate Court would not get around to hearing the case until September 1926. In March 1927 the Appellate Court ruled that Duncan had erred in his charge to the jury and the verdict was set aside and a new trial ordered.

On May 17, 1927 the second trial got underway with several new faces. Lynn B. Griffith was the new Trumbull County Prosecutor; hearing the case was Judge William M. Carter; and joining Burgess on the defense team was G. C. Locke and Luther S. Day, the latter one of Cleveland's best trial lawyers and the son of William L. Day, the late Chief Justice of the United States Supreme Court.

Jury selection took two and a half hours and when completed consisted of eight men and four women. One of the questions asked to potential jury members was if they were members of the Ku Klux Klan. One woman who claimed to have been a member and a man who said he was affiliated were both removed with peremptory challenges.

In the defense counsel's opening statement for round two, attorney Day claimed they would prove three points:

> ‣ That Munsene did not go to the residence of the sheriff on the night of November 27, 1925, that he was elsewhere and that the defense would show where he was at the time
> ‣ That he did not offer $500 to Sheriff Smith for protection
> ‣ That if he did do what the sheriff claims he did, "he is the most stupid man, the dumbest man in the wide, wide world."

This time, with fewer motions filed by the defense, the trial moved along rapidly. When opening statements were completed the second trial began, like the first one, with the testimony of Sheriff Smith. While attorney Day uncovered some discrepancies from his previous testimony, there was nothing major.

Meanwhile, Helen Wilkins Walker, the sheriff's former cook now married, had her testimony torn apart by Luther Day. She testified that on one of Munsene's visits to the sheriff, an afternoon affair, he was in there so long that dinner was held up until 3:00 or 3:30. Day questioned her, "Mrs. Walker, do you know that the sheriff has testified in the first trial and this one that the only time he talked to Munsene was at night; [and that] Sheriff Smith has testified he never saw Jim Munsene in the daytime?" Mrs. Smith was caught in the same predicament. She testified that Munsene had come to the house one day about noon. Sheriff Smith said he didn't recall the afternoon meeting and stated further that he couldn't remember ever meeting with Munsene during the day.

Defense witnesses included Munsene, the two police officers who saw him on South Pine Street, and the two Farrell men who dined on spaghetti with him at Murphy's restaurant.

The closing arguments were described as "dramatic pleas to the jurymen." Prosecutor Griffith's closing statement was brief. He told the jury that the crime of bribery was a serious one and that the state had a right to know who tempted the sheriff to "wink at a law violation." He explained that the state's witnesses "were endeavoring to tell the truth and if they erred in the minute details it was not their intention to do so."

In Luther Day's closing he paid "high tribute" to Griffith stating, "It has been a pleasure to appear here and try the first criminal case I have ever tried in this county. It has been a pleasure to be associated with your young prosecuting attorney who is square as a die, honest and fair." He then approached the jury with the doctrine that they must be convinced of guilt beyond a reasonable doubt or find the defendant not guilty. He then pointed out all the discrepancies and near discrepancies he could find in the testimony of the state's witnesses.

Day also went back to his opening statement and now followed up on his point of Munsene being the "world's dumbest man." Reiterating the testimony, that the $500 had come the night after Sheriff Smith's comment that he would raid Munsene's club if he ever opened it, Day asked the jurors, "do you think Munsene or anyone would be a big enough fool to send money to him the very next night, much less take it there personally?"

In his closing rebuttal, which was described by the *Tribune Chronicle* as being "forceful, dynamic and impressive," Griffith scored a direct hit on Day's "world's dumbest man" defense. "Why, the penitentiary is full of fools," the young prosecutor pointed out.

His statement, which stirred the jury's soul, contained a mixture of humility and Bible verses. The *Tribune Chronicle* reported:

"Modestly the attorney declared that he was not an expert trial lawyer. 'I cannot embellish or adorn or dramatize testimony' he declared – I can simply offer it to you as plain evidence, just as near the truth as I can get from witnesses. I do not come before you clad in the armor of a giant – I come clad only in the garments of a righteous cause to meet these Goliaths of the bar.'

"He praised the jury system and said jurors have a high duty to perform that requires courage and steadfastness. He said perfect juries are not easy to obtain. 'The Savior of Men set out to find a jury of twelve to witness evidence of His Divinity' he declared and the Savior found a Peter to deny him and a Judas to betray him.'

"He declared the Munsene case 'means more to the community than any case since 1900.' He hit an alibi as 'easily manufactured' and in closing quoted the Scripture taking the words of Elijah – 'Choose ye this day whom ye will serve.'"

After deliberating just 50 minutes, the panel returned with a guilty verdict. For the second time a jury derailed Munsene's high-priced legal team. Unlike the first trial where the first ballot was 7 to 5 for conviction, this time it was 10 to 2 and required just four votes to come to a unanimous decision. Judge Carter sentenced Munsene this time to not less than three years or more than six, but refused to grant a stay while he appealed.

The newspaper claimed, "The verdict is another great victory for Lynn B. Griffith … who in a few short months of service has scored notably over older and much more experienced trial lawyers." Unimpressed with the homage being paid to the new prosecutor by both the newspaper and his own counsel was an infuriated Jimmy Munsene. Through his attorneys he declared he would appeal the case all the way to the United States Supreme Court if necessary. On June 10 the Appellate Court authorized Munsene to file a petition in error and granted a stay of his prison sentence until the case was heard.

As in the first case, the Appellate Court ruled that Carter had erred in his instructions to the jury in reference to Munsene's alibi. Again the higher court cast aside the verdict and ordered a new trial. Despite havingone of the area's most well known attorneys representing him at his second trial – Luther Day – Munsene now sought the best. At his third trial Clarence Seward Darrow would represent him.

Because of Darrow's local roots he was excited to try what he felt would be the last case of his legendary career near his hometown in Trumbull County. Darrow was born in Farmdale on April 18, 1857 and as a child moved to Kinsman, which many consider his hometown.[1] After earning his law degree from the University of Michigan and passing the Ohio bar Darrow served as solicitor (law director) of Ashtabula, beginning in 1885 when it was still classified as a village. Hoping to establish a home there, Darrow went to a local bank to borrow money to purchase a house. He was rejected by the financial institution. The experience caused him to pack up his belongings and move out of the area and he soon found a new home for himself in Chicago, where his legal career began in earnest. Early on Darrow built his reputation on championing causes, especially his opposition to the death penalty, fighting to keep clients off death row, many times taking cases on a pro bono basis.

His most famous cases didn't occur until Darrow was in his late 60s. The two trials he was most noted for were the Leopold-Loeb case, in which he defended two teenaged boys from wealthy families who murdered 14 year-old Robert Franks for the "thrill" of it in Chicago in 1924. Darrow succeeded in saving both young men from the electric chair. The second case, a year later, was known as the "Scopes' Monkey Trial," in which he defended John T. Scopes, a high school biology teacher from Tennessee, for teaching Darwin's theory of evolution in his classroom. Darrow, a staunch agnostic, battled William Jennings Bryan, a three-time Democratic candidate for president, in a classic court case.

According to stories, Darrow wanted to win a case in his hometown before he retired. Some fifty years earlier Darrow tried his first case in Ashtabula, defending a man accused of stealing a set of harness. He lost the case. Munsene heard of his desire and after finding out that Darrow was coming to visit Kinsman, he waited at the village limits for the old attorney to appear. Munsene flagged down Darrow's automobile and discussed the case with him. The old attorney was excited by the prospect and agreed to defend Munsene. Darrow reportedly said, "It won't cost you a cent, win or lose."

Later, Darrow addressed the matter himself when being interviewed by the *Ashtabula Star-Beacon*:

> "You know, I have tried to retire several times, and when I had an opportunity to become associated with other attorneys in the defense of Mr. Munsene, I decided that Trumbull County, where I was born, would be a good place to do it. No, I did not offer to sit in on the case, just as a friend. I was retained the same way as any other lawyer would be retained.
>
> "However, I am not interested in taking cases of this kind for the fees that are in them. That was not my motive in this case. There are some cases in which I am employed, though, where the fees are interesting."

Darrow received a welcome home treatment reserved for conquering heroes. Crowds jammed the courthouse corridors and courtroom, where it was standing room only. Friends and former colleagues dating back to his days as law director were anxious to renew acquaintances. Despite not having seen many of the well-wishers for half a century, Darrow amazed most of them by remembering their names and intimate details of events which occurred long ago. The old attorney had two scheduled addresses for later in the week, for which tickets were being sold. Darrow's wife, who was described as looking more like a daughter, attended the hearing on the first day and spoke openly with reporters at the press table where she sat.

Despite the lawyer's 70-plus years of age, many were waiting to watch the old lion roar one more time. His bouts with witnesses in which they were brow beaten, yelled at and scoffed at were part of his legendary reputation, as well as his impassioned pleas to the jury. In this case, the makeup of the jury would mark a first for Darrow; it was the first one he faced on which there were women.

Along with the improved defense team, attorney Burgess sought greener pastures in which to have his client tried. Claiming that the case received too much publicity and that there was too much local prejudice in Trumbull County for Munsene to get a fair trial, Burgess asked for, and was granted, a change of venue.

On Monday morning, May 7, 1928 a pool of 28 potential jurors was on hand in the century old Ashtabula County Court House in Jefferson, Ohio, the county seat. The newspapers crowed about the "greatest array of legal talent" ever brought together in Northeast Ohio for a trial. On the defense side was Burgess, Darrow, H.J. Redmond of Ashtabula and Francis Poulson of Cleveland. Opposing them were Lynn Griffith and his assistant, 24 year-old William M. McLain.

With the talent laden pool of defense attorneys there was bound to be some ego problems. Redmond was described as being one of the "leading attorneys" in Ashtabula County, who over the past 25 years had participated in nearly all the major trials. On the first day Redmond "assumed leadership practically ignoring the other attorneys for the defense." The next day, to no one's surprise, Darrow took charge.

The judge allowed Darrow to have a soft cushioned, armchair brought in for his 71 year-old body. He told the judge, "I have one bad ear, I will turn the other one to the court." Darrow then moved the chair to face the potential jurors. Throughout the trial he sat in a sideways position.

As in Munsene's earlier trials in Trumbull County, there was a large delegation of Women's Christian Temperance Union (WCTU) delegates from Warren in attendance. The women mingled with newspaper reporters covering the trial from cities as far away as Chicago.

The new trial had an auspicious beginning. The first twelve potential jurors were brought in and seated, while the others found seats in the court-room's gallery. Griffith began his questioning and to the first person, a married woman from Ashtabula, he asked, "Would the fact that this defendant has been twice convicted...?" Before Griffith could complete the question, attorney Redmond was on his feet barking, "I object, your honor. This is misconduct on the part of the attorney, and the question is prejudicial. I demand that the case be continued."

Common Pleas Judge Charles F. Sargent, who was overseeing the trial, sent the potential jurors to the jury room and called counsel for both sides into chambers. After a thirty-minute meeting all parties returned and Redmond again renewed his motion that the entire panel of prospective jurors be dismissed. Sargent ruled that despite the fact that Munsene was convicted twice in Trumbull County, this could not under any circumstances be introduced. Since other members of the jury pool had been present in the courtroom the judge decided that no admonition from the court to disregard the question could remove the revelation from their minds. Sargent dismissed all 28 members and ordered the trial to begin again, with a fresh jury pool, the next morning at 9:30.

As it turned out, had Redmond allowed Griffith to complete his question without jumping to object, it would have been allowed. Curious about this when the trial ended, Griffith wrote the complete question out and handed it to Darrow for his opinion. The complete question asked, "Would the fact that this defendant has twice been convicted and each conviction set aside by the court of appeals, influence you in any manner in your judgement of the case?" Darrow deemed the question to be a proper one and, when asked, other lawyers agreed with him.

Prosecutor Griffith began his second day of questioning by asking only the normal questions about residence and occupation. Darrow, on the other hand, questioned each person about lodges and organizations they belonged to, and their religious affiliation. Of each potential juror, Darrow asked, "If you are selected to sit on this jury would you let any man be convicted by the jury if you were not convinced beyond the existence of a reasonable doubt, that he was guilty?"

The jury selection process for the third trial took longer than the first two trials. Darrow assumed a leading role, questioning all the prospective jurors. By Tuesday afternoon the panel, consisting of 10 men and 2 women, was completed. After the jurors were sworn in, Griffith made a motion that they be taken to Warren to visit the scene of the crime, the sheriff's residence where Munsene allegedly appeared and handed the envelope containing the alleged bribe money to Mrs. Smith. Members of the defense team declined to go along.

While Munsene may have been the celebrity in the Warren courtroom, in Ashtabula it was clearly Darrow that people lined up to see. A *Tribune Chronicle* article proclaimed:

> "Eliminate Clarence Darrow from the Munsene trial and the case would not attract any more attention from Jefferson and Ashtabula county people than the passing of a last year's Ford car. The only real interest in the outcome of the hearing is shown by people from down Warren way, and even they give one glance at the prisoner at the bar and then crane their necks to get a view of the great Chicago criminal lawyer who has figured in the Leopold and Loeb defense and many other notable cases."

On Wednesday morning the jury heard the trial's first testimony. Sheriff Smith and his wife took the stand and proceeded to answer the same questions they had during the first two trials. If spectators expected to see the state's witnesses attacked by the famed defense attorney they were disappointed. Darrow's cross-examinations were described as "unexciting."

None of the state's witnesses were questioned at length with the exception of Jay Buchwalter.[2] He was asked by Darrow if he was a member of a "certain organization" of which Smith was also a member, to which he replied, "No." Then the attorney asked him if he "represented any order of which the sheriff was a member?" Buchwalter answered that he had. The *Jefferson Gazette* reported that Buchwalter was the "alleged" counsel for the Ku Klux Klan in Trumbull County.

When Smith was questioned about being a member of the unnamed organization the exchange went as follows:

> Smith: I couldn't say as to that.
> Darrow: Don't you know whether you were or not?
> Smith: I can't say.
> Darrow: But if you were, you would remember it, would you not?
> Smith: I don't remember.
> Darrow: Have you ever seen Buchwalter at meetings of an organization to which you belong?
> Smith: I may have, but I can't recall any particular one.

During the defense's case several new witnesses appeared. Thomas Thomas, a former turnkey at the jail, testified Helen Wilkins Walker told him that she couldn't believe that Munsene would be fool enough to bring the money to the jail himself. Recalled to the stand, Walker denied she had ever made such a statement to Thomas.

While being cross-examined by Griffith the one-time turnkey was asked, "Isn't it true Mr. Thomas, that Sheriff Smith fired you because you got drunk?"

"Yes," replied the witness. "I took one drink too many."

The defense then put on a surprise witness, James Bane, who served as a special deputy during Smith's first term as sheriff and was now operating a hotel in Niles. Bane made the following statement, "About two months after Smith became sheriff, I went to the jail to talk to Sheriff Smith and asked him how he and Jim Munsene were getting along. The sheriff said to me, 'Munsene does not like you very well,' and told me to look out for him. Smith then said to me he was going to frame Munsene on a bribery charge and I replied, 'I would not do that.'"

Smith was recalled to the stand and asked if he had ever made such a statement. "Positively not!" was his emphatic reply. During cross-examination it came out that Smith had recently "replevined" (repossessed) an automobile from Bane, and that the sheriff had once defeated him in a Republican primary for sheriff.

Griffith was not without his own surprise. Officer Fagadore was again called to the stand to testify how he watched Munsene in Murphy's restaurant from a police call box. The prosecutor called a city engineer to the stand who told the court the call box closest to Murphy's was over 100 feet away from the restaurant and on the same side of the street. It would have been impossible for him to see into the restaurant from that vantagepoint.

When Munsene took the stand it was reported that Darrow "became vexed" with his client's spit-fire answers. The attorney wanted short, concise responses and on a few occasions Judge Sargent stopped Darrow from moving to his next question, telling him to allow the witness to finish his answer.

On Thursday afternoon closing arguments began. Assistant Prosecutor McLain went first. He noted that the state was outnumbered 100 years to 20 in legal experience, declaring, "No such array of legal talent has ever been arrayed in defense of a criminal." McLain pointed out that both Munsene and Smith agreed that the two met the night prior to the alleged bribe being offered, and that they both agreed on the conversation that took place, with the exception of the offer of the $500. McLain asked the jury, "If Munsene was intending to open a place why did he have to go to the sheriff about it, if not to seek protection."

In his final comments it was clear McLain was concerned that jury members would be focused on the fact that it was the great Clarence Darrow who would be closing for the defense. He stated, "What Darrow says will be remembered by you. What I say will soon be forgotten, but what you do will remain with you. Mr. Darrow will go into another state and not be affected by the result of this trial, but to us here it is of vital importance." He then offered that the panel would have better "peace of mind" if they made their decision based on the evidence as opposed to the "eloquent appeal" they were about to hear.

Darrow's closing was not the articulate piece of oratory the jurors had been prepped to hear. The *Tribune Chronicle* reported, "It was not eloquent but it carefully analyzed the testimony and made an instinct impression." He began by saying, "If you are satisfied of my client's guilt, find him guilty. If not, set him free." Darrow focused on creating reasonable doubt in their minds based on discrepancies in the testimony of the state's witnesses.

The attorney started by recounting the testimony of the sheriff's wife and Mrs. Walker, the cook, about the Sunday dinner which was two hours late. Since the sheriff said he didn't recall the incident and further stated that he had never met Munsene during day light hours, Darrow said the women were mistaken in their identity. "If they were mistaken in the identity of Munsene then, why would they not be mistaken as to his identity on the night of November 27," he queried. He cleverly pointed out, "If Munsene had visited the sheriff and made him two hours late for his Sunday dinner, neither his wife nor the cook would ever have allowed the sheriff to forget the incident. That is not the way with women and cold dinners."

Darrow then hit upon Mrs. Walker's identification of Munsene on the night the envelope arrived. "How much of a view would Mrs. Walker have of a man standing in a 23-inch door when Mrs. Smith was standing between her and the visitor at the door?" asked Darrow. During the trial Darrow had gotten Mrs. Smith to admit she weighed 250 pounds. "Are you going to take away the liberty of my client on this sort of testimony?" he inquired.

Darrow then discussed former deputy Thomas Thomas. He declared, "This man Thomas was good enough to be hired by the sheriff. Are you going to condemn the man as a liar because he took a drink? I've seen people that took a drink and still tell the truth, and I've seen men that took too much and still retain their honesty. If people are all to be condemned, who take a drink, then we will have to throw into the discard the greater number of our statesmen orators, any amount of lawyers, and a goodly number of the preachers."

Next he reviewed the note that accompanied the bribe money. Darrow questioned, "About that envelope and that letter. Why was no effort made by the state to find out who wrote the letter and the address on the envelope? There has been nothing shown to connect my client with the writing of that letter or with having sent the money." Prosecutors could have perhaps brought up the same point. The defense had every opportunity to prove the writing wasn't Munsene's.

The old attorney's closing was not without humor. In describing Jay

Buchwalter's testimony he quipped, "Mr. Buchwalter is honest, I know because he is an attorney."

Darrow wound up his closing by stating, "Members of the jury, all that is needed to establish an alibi is to produce enough evidence to raise in the minds of the jury a reasonable doubt as to whether or not our client was there. If there was ever a case that had not been made it is here.

"Talk of justice as between man and man. I know there is prejudice because my client is a foreigner, yet none of us can trace our pedigree very far before it takes up beyond the ocean. The only real Americans are the Indians, and we have killed them nearly all off. Where he was born and where he came from is none of our concern.

"They say that my client wanted to start a gambling place. I don't like hypocrisy. Is that such a heinous offense? There is a great deal in life that is a gamble and we take chances on many things.

"I want to say to you that if Munsene took that letter up to the jail and handed it in that night, he ought to be in a crazy house instead of being sent to a penal institution. Every person is entitled to the same protection in law in this country. I want to make you realize what it is to convict a man unfairly. I ask you to forget what he is, where he was born. Not only have they failed to convict him, but the weight of the evidence is against his guilt.

"Render a verdict that appeals to your sense of justice and we will be satisfied with your verdict."

Griffith's closing rebuttal was brief, just 15 minutes before court adjourned for the afternoon. He pointed out to the jury that "the defense had to go beyond the state to get men to establish an alibi for the accused." The next morning Griffith finished his rebuttal in ten minutes, touching again on the key evidence. Judge Sargent then gave the jury their instructions, closing with, "Perform your duty without fear or favor, without vengeance or pity. Your duty is an intellectual one and not an emotional one."

The jury began deliberations at 10:05 that morning. On the first ballot the panel was deadlocked 6 to 6. A total of ten ballots were taken and the balance never grew greater than 8 to 4 for conviction. At one point the jury was brought back to the courtroom to ask the judge a question. Sargent admitted, quite frankly, he didn't understand what they wanted to know and sent them back to the jury room to reframe the question. Instead, the jury came back at 8:55 p.m. stating that after nearly eleven hours of deliberation they were deadlocked. Judge Sargent had no choice but to dismiss the panel.

No one was more disappointed than Darrow who was hoping to win one in his hometown. He told a reporter, "Doesn't it beat all that I could not come back to my old home town and a win a law suit. It was my ambition to do so. But I am coming back. I never quit a case when I once start on it. They do not need to worry about the money. I have all I need and will come back without pay."

By the time the fourth annual State of Ohio vs. Munsene bribery trial came to pass on Thursday, May 23, 1929, there were significant changes in the lead players. Munsene and Darrow were still the defendant and lead defense attorney, but Griffith had been replaced as prosecuting attorney by George H. Birrell and the state's star witness, John Smith, was now the ex-sheriff.

This time around ex-sheriff Smith now recalled that Munsene was in his office on a Sunday afternoon, right around dinner time; a fact that he had denied during previous trials. His statement was supported from a new witness introduced by the state. Charles Clemens was Smith's father-in-law and the custodian of the jail. He testified that he was sent to the sheriff's office by his daughter to let Smith know dinner was ready. When he arrived he saw Smith and Munsene "closeted in conference."

Also offered into evidence in this trial was that Munsene had once employed Evelyn Nesbit[3] as a hostess at his Follies Bergere in Atlantic City. While being cross-examined by Birrell, the prosecutor brought out that Nesbit had been a hostess at the club. When asked how long she had been employed there, Munsene answered, "Eight months, and I think she is a nice woman." Judge Sargent ordered the comment stricken from the record.

What this trial did feature was a move by the defense to catch the prosecutors off guard. With testimony concluded, the prosecution began its closing statement. Birrell used 20 minutes of 80 allotted to him, saving the last 60 minutes for his rebuttal. When the defense was notified that it was their turn to begin, however, Darrow shocked the courtroom by announcing, "You may instruct the jury, your honor." He told the court that the defense did not wish to argue the case.

At 1:30 the case went to the jury. Although deliberations went on until almost midnight, by 5:30 that Friday afternoon it was clear that the jury was in an unbreakable deadlock. At 11:00 Judge Sargent brought the panel back to the courtroom to question them on their progress. Three members all expressed different opinions as to the possibility of a united verdict. The judge sent them back to deliberate a while longer, but an hour later he declared a mistrial. It was reported the jurors stood at 10 to 2 for conviction for the last seven hours of deliberations.

At the time of the dismissal only Munsene and Burgess were there from the defense. Darrow had left at 7:30 with his wife, taking a train back to Chicago. The old attorney was getting ready to set sail for England where the couple planned to tour Europe for several months.

After the disappointment of a second hung jury, the *Ashtabula Star-*

Beacon stated, "There is no probability of a fifth trial. Sentiment is against the retrial of Munsene, owing to the impossibility of securing conviction. Jury disagreement in the trial completed, and of a year ago, combined with public sentiment, will probably cause the case to be dropped."

Disregarding the newspaper's prognostication, Prosecutor Birrell immediately announced his intentions to try the case for a fifth time.

On Monday, June 2, jury selection for the fifth trial began after a two-hour delay to find more potential jurors. In contrast to the opening day of the first trial in Jefferson two years earlier, where acquaintances and curiosity seekers jammed the courtroom and corridors, only a half-dozen spectators where now on hand. Darrow was again active during the questioning of jurors. Soon twelve tentative panelists had been selected, but it was all for naught.

On Tuesday morning, after a lengthy meeting in Judge Sargent's chambers, Munsene agreed to plead guilty for a one-year paroled sentence. Attorney Redmond made the suggestion and Prosecutor Birrell agreed and recommended it to the judge, who accepted it. The provisions of the sentence called for Munsene to report once a month to his appointed parole officer, Warren attorney Louis L. Guarnieri, who would report to Judge William Carter. In addition, Munsene was ordered to reimburse all taxable costs associated with the five trials. Because of this last provision, the Trumbull underworld figure was not fined.

At 11:00 a.m. the parties returned to the courtroom where Redmond made the official plea. There was no report of Darrow's[4] role in the plea agreement, if any. Redmond in making the plea told the court the five-year odyssey had taken a toll on Munsene and his family and that the defendant had "suffered great mental agony."

Munsene was then called before Judge Sargent. The judge addressed the defendant, "It has been rumored that you have repeatedly violated the laws against gambling and liquor. Let me warn you that any such charge made against you may be the cause of you going to the penitentiary. It will not be necessary to obtain a conviction if the evidence is clear enough to convince me that you are guilty of such infraction. I will immediately send you to prison."

The five-year ordeal was over except for the disposition of the $500 bribe. The judge declared the money belonged to Munsene, who was approached by a *Tribune Chronicle* reporter and questioned about it.

"What's going to happen to the $500? The judge says it's yours," the reporter asked.

"I don't want the money," claimed Munsene.

"Then let me tell you what to do with it," said the reporter, "just give it to the Warren Community Fund."

"That's a good idea," replied Munsene.

The Hollyhock Night Club

Munsene's prolonged court battle on the bribery charge didn't occupy all his time during the latter half of the 1920s. Munsene expanded his activities into other rackets with success. A *Vindicator* story said of the gangster, "Munsene was king of rackets in Warren and his word was virtually 'law' in Niles, but in Niles [located between Warren and Youngstown] he remained friendly with the men who operated the 'numbers' racket, handled race bets or had gambling rooms. Through friendship, rather than gangster-like authority, his power was respected."

As the numbers rackets became more prominent in this country, Munsene took over the activities in Warren and Trumbull County. He insulated himself from the writers, but whenever any of them were arrested his "lieutenants" were quick to appear and provide bond. Court fines were paid with the writers rarely having to appear for the formalities.

One of the rackets Munsene steered clear of was white slavery. He abhorred prostitution and in twenty years as an underworld leader in Trumbull County was never known to be involved in any activities that involved women, including the use of "shills," beautiful women used as decoys to attract men to the gambling tables, in his gambling dens.

A *Vindicator* story about Munsene declared he "was a power in Warren politics and often spent thousands in a campaign." If this statement was true, Munsene carried this out in low key fashion. Neither the Warren nor Youngstown newspapers ever reported any politicians as beholden to him.

With his profits Munsene built a beautiful home on Tod SW Ext. just outside of Warren, where he led the life of a "gentleman farmer" raising dogs and pheasants. It was said to be his "pride and joy." A large fence was later built for the protection of his family, to whom Munsene was extremely devoted. One newspaper report stated Munsene, "was a generous donor to charitable institutions and was known as one 'who would take off his shirt' to help one in need, especially children and aged persons and those whom he considered his friends."

Those closest to Munsene, however, knew he possessed a dark side, that he had an "insatiable appetite for power." In the late 1920s Munsene had a controlling interest in a speakeasy / nightclub located at the corner of Pine Street and Clinton Avenue in the "Flats" section of Warren. The establishment became famous – and at one time nationally known – as the Hollyhock Gardens Night Club. Before the days of television, noted entertainment personalities from the stage and radio, as well as sports' celebrities, appeared at the club. Sophie Tucker, "Pinky" Hunter, Estelle Taylor, Irene Bordoni, FiFi D'Orsay[5] and former heavyweight boxing champ Max Baer were some of the marquis names who were seen at the Hollyhock. The club's most notable personality was crooner Perry Como, who came to the attention of bandleader Ted Weems,[6] during a performance at the nightclub. Signed by the popular bandleader, Como's career took off while he was a singer for Weem's orchestra.

Under the guidance of Munsene the Hollyhock became one of the chic establishments in the area. In addition to top name entertainment the club was noted for its large kitchen, which prepared "some of the best dishes served in Warren." The entry doors to the club were affixed with "peep holes" so Munsene's underlings could keep an eye on what was happening outside. No one was allowed to enter without the approval of club lookouts.

As the "Roaring '20s" were coming to an end, Munsene found his adversary was a familiar face, George Birrell the Trumbull County prosecutor. During the final years of Prohibition Birrell carved out a reputation by leading a number of raids on the Hollyhock in which furniture, booze and slot machines were destroyed with axes. Birrell earned the nickname the "Ax-buster," which helped him in later years when he became a well-respected common pleas judge in the county.

In late 1930 the second floor of the Hollyhock was operating as a gambling joint known as the Chase Athletic Club. Police were no strangers to the club. They had raided it a number of times – smashing gambling equipment and furniture, one time even tearing the linoleum off the floor. The police, like most people in town, knew that Munsene had a hand in the club. In what capacity they weren't sure.

On the night of December 20 there were approximately 35 gamblers in the club. Around 10:00 an automobile containing six men arrived. One waited behind the wheel, a second stood in the downstairs hallway, while the other four ascended the stairs to the gambling room. Described as "sheik-looking," the four surveyed the room before one told the door-keeper, "We want some action on craps – where's the layout?"

After searching the four-some for weapons, the doorman directed them to a table in the back. Shortly after the men began rolling dice, they disappeared – two at a time – into the bathroom. After emerging around 10:40, the group's leader shouted, "Everyone get 'em up – don't move out of your tracks and get ready for a searching party." The four men who had passed muster with the armed doorkeeper now had revolvers aimed at the patrons in the club. One of the victims later reported that inside the men's room was a window facing the roof of the building next door. The guns were probably passed to the men by an accomplice.

The first order of business was to disarm the doorman. "Over your head with them mitts, boy – and let me have that rod on your hip," one of the gunmen called out. As the patrons moved to a wall and prepared to be searched, a few of them already knew what was in store. One threw his money "roll" into a "cuspidor" (spittoon), and recovered it later. Another tossed an expensive diamond ring into a wastebasket. After the patrons had taken their place along the wall, the gang leader turned to one of his men and stated, "You, Charlie, frisk 'em – every damn one of them and let's see what kind of collection we can get out of 'em."

Two gang members searched the patrons, while the other two covered them with a gun in each hand. The bandits took cash, except in the case of one man who was carrying only $1.45. "You're a little short on the collections, buddy – guess I'll take this ticker to make up for it," the robber declared. He then removed the man's watch.

With the gamblers fleeced of an estimated $3,500 to $5,000, the bandit leader announced, "We're shoving off now fellows – sorry to have bothered you all, but you know its all for the benefit of the unemployed." As the quartet made their way down the stairs and toward the door, a man entered from the outside. "Don't go up there, the place is being raided," he was told.

Shortly afterward the nightclub closed. For nearly two months it remained dark until State Prohibition agents received a tip that liquor was being stored on the premises. On the evening of March 11, 1931, state agents, backed by Warren police led by Captain George Salen, went to the Pine Street address. Finding the premises locked, the officers battered down a door to obtain entry. The Warren *Tribune Chronicle* reported:

> "The officers located an electric button which controlled a special panel leading to an especially constructed room built inside the place. Huge quantities of corn whiskey, bonded goods, gin and wine were found behind the panel
>
> "The state men report they found several barrels of alleged corn whiskey, about four cases of alleged bonded whiskey, several cases of gin, cognac, bourbon whiskey, dry gin, creme de menthe, rum, burgundy and champagne. They also confiscated 1,000 bottles of beer."

In addition, officers found a keg containing 19 gallons of wine, four barrels of beer, a complete brewing outfit, sixteen 30-gallon stone crocks, 24 cases of malt extract and quantities of yeast and other brewing ingredients. They proceeded to smash open barrels and watched as 400 gallons of corn whiskey made its way into the city's sewer system. Police questioned 25 customers inside the place before releasing them. A 20 year-old man found in the closed club was arrested and charged with violation of the

Crabbe Act, the Ohio state liquor law.

During the early part of the 1930s the Hollyhock operated as a restaurant. Around January 1934 the nightclub opened with a wine license. In May the license was changed to a nightclub permit, which allowed it to stay open and sell all types of alcoholic beverages until 2:30am. The license was obtained in the name of Agostino Sansone, Munsene's brother-in-law. Munsene made sure that he always insulated himself. Whether it was the numbers rackets, the dog track, the Hollyhock or later the Prime Steak House, Munsene kept the activities in the names of relatives or lieutenants to shield himself.

After the repeal of Prohibition the club improved its entertainment and the second floor was turned over to gambling. The Hollyhock garnered national attention as the night club's reputation made it one of the top hot spots in the country, and the upstairs gambling den became noted as one of the finest between Cleveland and Pittsburgh. During the 1930s it was the premier place for Trumbull County citizens to be seen. During this pre-Las Vegas era, it was reported that some of the most well known gamblers in the country gathered to try their luck on the club's second floor. To cover themselves during a raid or robbery, a special steel-plated "Money Room" was constructed, which served as a counting room.

During 1934 authorities raided the club nine times and made 40 gambling arrests; 23 of which came after the Hollyhock received its nightclub permit. In early January 1935 State Liquor Control officers made three visits on consecutive nights to the club where they gambled and ordered drinks after the 2:30 a.m. closing time. By questioning several people at the club they were able to determine that Munsene was the true owner. Most people knew it was Munsene's operation, but a *Tribune Chronicle* article around this time stated, "Munsene is not a citizen and is therefore not eligible to obtain a liquor license."

After a hearing held in Columbus on January 23, 1935 the Ohio State Liquor Board revoked the Hollyhock's license to sell liquor. A week later Munsene went to Columbus to argue the revocation. Munsene maintained that he was not the owner of the Hollyhock that Sansone was. He declared that he was the nightclub's booking agent and sometimes served as master of ceremonies. Munsene claimed he had recently booked Max Baer for a one-night appearance at the club for $5,000.

In their battle, state liquor inspectors argued that ownership of the Hollyhock had been misrepresented, a gambling den was operating on the second floor, and liquor was being sold after hours. Official records showed the club's permit had been issued to Augustino Sansone. Inspectors claimed Sansone was the owner in name only. Sansone argued he was the rightful owner of the club and that Munsene was his employee. Sansone brought out the big guns to represent him. One of his attorneys was a member of the Democratic State Central Committee; the other was chairman of the Mahoning County Democratic Committee.

The battle over the revoked liquor license continued through the fall and winter of 1935. The Hollyhock Gardens operated for a few months during this period without serving alcohol, but after being open on New Years' Day 1936 the club shut down. By late 1935 Munsene had already moved his base of operations from the Hollyhock to the Prime Steak House[7] at 602 South Park Avenue, on the next street over from his old nightclub.

Despite the restaurant being closed gambling was still carried on there. On the night of February 17, 1936 Warren police made two numbers raids. The first was at 443 South Street, a reputed numbers headquarters, where 18 people were arrested. The second was at a backroom at the closed Hollyhock, where police didn't find any numbers activity, but they arrested two men for loitering. While officers searched the closed Hollyhock, Munsene followed them around uttering "smart remarks." Sergeant John O. Heinlein got irritated with Munsene and arrested him for "provoking a quarrel." The Trumbull County underworld boss spent the next two hours in solitary confinement in the women's detention area of the jail before being released.

During the summer of 1936 plans were being made to reopen the restaurant section of the club. A new license was obtained by Donato Scarpitti and redecorating was already in progress. A new grand opening was planned and then delayed pending the anticipated reopening of the club's cabaret.

That all changed on September 27, 1936. Around 11:15 that Sunday night three witnesses saw "men" race from the Clinton Avenue entrance of the club to awaiting cars parked on the street. One of the men was seen carrying "an object." The witness claimed "the man stumbled, almost dropped the object, and fell to one knee in an effort to retain a good hold on the package." The cars then raced north on Pine Street.

Minutes after the cars disappeared an explosion occurred inside the nightclub. The blast blew out plate glass windows, showering glass down upon the automobile of a local mill worker, who was driving past on his way home. The man stopped and called the fire department.

When firemen arrived at 11:30, the entire downstairs of the restaurantwas ablaze. It took fire fighters nearly three hours to bring it under control. Flames had swept through the dining area and bar. In addition, the cabaret and stairway leading to the gambling rooms on the second floor were damaged. Kitchen equipment and an expensive bar were ruined while the dining room furniture was destroyed.

Fire inspectors were in for a surprise when they entered. They found rags, soaked in oil, burned newspapers and six five-gallon cans, that had contained kerosene, scattered about the premises on the kitchen floor, in the bar room and in the doorway leading to the cabaret. The doors leading into the various rooms had been tied open with the oil-soaked rags. In addition to the fire damage, on the second floor investigators discovered gambling tables and a bookie room where a tickertape was located. A large blackboard for horserace results was about to be installed.

Investigating officials made several trips into the damaged club. Assistant Warren Fire Chief George Mock estimated that the damage exceeded $25,000. That would change, however, the next day. Fire Chief Edwin Oldacres downgraded the loss to $10,000, claiming that while the damage looked bad, it was not as bad as first believed. He said little actual loss resulted due to the quick response and actions of the firemen. Insurance on the building, owned by an Amsterdam, Ohio company was only $5,000.

Munsene had gone to Columbus that Sunday for a scheduled meeting the next day with state liquor officials in anticipation of reopening the club. When he returned Monday night he was questioned by Police Chief Barney J. Gillen, Captain George Salen, Deputy State Fire Marshall Walter Paull and Fire Chief Oldacres. The fire chief believed the fire was set by men responsible for two other area arsons – the Gray Wolf Tavern and the Fowler Dog Track. Oldacres told reporters, "Although no definite clues are available it is reasonable to believe that 'racketeers' wishing to bring their rackets into the county are responsible for the three fires."

Munsene told officials he had no idea who would want to set the fire, but the incident seemed to be the first blow to his undisputed underworld leadership in the county. Was it possible that the out-of-county racketeers Oldacres was referring to were members of the Licavoli clan, who were recently pushed out of Detroit and Toledo and were setting up shop in other parts of Ohio? Could it have been mobsters from Cleveland's notorious Mayfield Road Mob using the Farah brothers – John and Mike – who were making inroads into a gambling den of their own that fall that would be known as the Jungle Inn? They certainly would not have wanted local competition cutting into their profits.

Whatever the case, whomever the muscle, wherever the threat was coming from, Munsene declared that he was uncertain that he would pursue the reopening of the Hollyhock Garden Night Club, which he had planned to do in the coming weeks.

Instead, Munsene focused his attention on the Prime Steak House. He soon found city officials were doing the same. Over a two-year period more than a dozen arrests were made. Mayor Daniel Gutelius "waged a campaign" against the club to stop the gambling. At one time a police officer was assigned inside the club to make sure no gambling occurred. The restaurant owners filed a lawsuit to rid the place of the officer. The case was heard by now Judge Lynn Griffith, who upheld the right of city officials to keep the officer on duty.

In July 1939, Warren Solicitor George Buchwalter, the only son of attorney Jay Buchwalter, filed for an injunction against the restaurant asking for it to be padlocked as a public nuisance. Stating that the establishment "constitutes a threat to the moral welfare of the community," Buchwalter claimed in his petition:

> "By reason of its continued and never ending source of demoralization to the lawful institutions and law abiding citizens of the community and by reason of its continued and purposeful disturbance in spite of and in the face of every law enforcement agency, the establishment constitutes a public nuisance and ought to be abated for the best interests of the public at large."

The petition also called for a permanent order restraining Felix Monfrino, Munsene's nephew, from conducting the operation. In September 1939 Monfrino was arrested for possession of liquor without a license at the club. During the 1930s Felix Monfrino, the son of Bernard Monfrino became one of Munsene's closest associates. His name appeared on the police blotter after many of the gambling raids at the Prime Steak House.

The Prime Steak House, like the Hollyhock, was noted for its fine food, but the new owner of record had trouble obtaining a liquor license. At onetime a liquor permit, issued to George Mustakes, was revoked by state liquor authorities. In March 1941, after Ohio Lieutenant Governor Paul Herbert appeared at a hearing on behalf of Angeline Sferra, on paper the owner of record, a liquor permit was finally granted.

In the late 1930s Munsene became involved with dog racing. He was a member of a partnership that operated the Fowler Dog Track. In 1938 the partners had a disagreement which ended in the track being closed for the remainder of the season. The next year Munsene was involved in a new dog track venture at Milton Lake. The track was built on the Mahoning County side of Milton Lake. Operations at the new track, which employed 40 workers, did not get off to a smooth start. Construction of the track began on May 29, 1939. The workers received paychecks for the first three weeks. Payments were then stopped and checks that were issued bounced. Employees were told they would be paid when the track opened on July 1 and began to generate money. When it did it was initially reported that attendance was good, but the betting at the mutual windows was "extremely poor." On July 13 a bomb exploded in the parking lot destroying one car and damaging two others. Speculation was that it was due to, "ill feeling among dog track operators in the Eastern Ohio district." Track officials downplayed the incident, claiming the explosion was caused by lightning from an approaching storm.

Newspaper advertisements stated the track held eleven events every night except Sunday. Ladies were admitted free on Tuesdays and Fridays. The highlight of the season was a race featuring 1936 Olympian Gold Medallist Jesse Owens, the "World's Fastest Human," who attended Ohio State University. Owen's opponent was a greyhound named Didder. Owens was given a 90-yard head start.

The next year several legal battles ensued and closings by the sheriff followed. The track was then relocated across the lake on the Portage County side of Milton Lake and operated until the fall of 1940. The track became a popular betting place with gamblers from the Pittsburgh area. On several occasions special trains were chartered between Pittsburgh and Youngstown, a 1940's version of the gambling junket, and the betting crowd was delivered to the track by bus. In this group from the Steel City were a number of underworld figures and lottery men. In June 1946, after five years of inactivity, the Munsene family sold the track to two speculators.

Around 2:30 on the afternoon of January 30, 1941 Munsene was at the wheel of a "big expensive sedan," said to be a 1941 model, driving two miles west of North Jackson on Route 18 (Mahoning Avenue). With Munsene were four other men. Freezing drizzle was falling on the road making travelling hazardous. Suddenly the car began to skid. As Munsene tried to bring the vehicle under control, the backend fishtailed, crossed the center of the road and was struck by a tractor-trailer laden with steel traveling in the opposite direction. The force of the impact caused the truck to plunge into a ditch, its driver leaping from the cab to avoid injury. The Munsene automobile spun around and flew off the road, crashing into a telephone pole. The injury toll from the Munsene sedan was much greater.

Frank Rock, a tailor, and Ambrose DiPaola, a retired grocer, were killed instantly after being ejected from the back seat of the car. Dominic "Muggsy" Rossi was in critical condition with head injuries and a fractured jaw, while Guy Lombardi suffered a broken arm and a concussion. Munsene, who suffered the least of the group, incurred chest injuries. The survivors were transported to South Side Hospital, the two dead men directly to funeral parlors.

Munsene was charged by the state highway patrol with failure to present a driver's license and operating a motor vehicle with tags issued for another car. Although Munsene did not have a license, he obtained one within five hours after a local registrar accepted a notarized application from a man who claimed it was for a "sick friend." On February 21 Munsene appeared in a Canfield court with his attorney, George Buchwalter, and pled guilty to both charges. Munsene left the courthouse after paying a reduced fine of $20 and court costs.

Murder in the Prime Steak House

On Monday night, March 24, 1941, Warren witnessed its first double murder and its most infamous one. On that evening Jimmy Munsene was in his usual haunt, the Prime Steak House. With him were his brother Tony, son Nofry, nephew Felix Monfrino and brother-in-law Bernard Monfrino. Munsene had plans to meet with Earl B. Huffman, manager of the Co-operative Adjusting Co. and Physicians & Hospital Credit Bureau. The purpose of the meeting was to discuss the unpaid hospital bill from Munsene's recent accident.

Shortly before 9:30 p.m. two well-dressed men entered the barroom area of the Prime Steak House using the Clinton Avenue entrance. There were approximately eight people in the bar at the time, while another twenty were in the main dining room being served dinner. Anthony Shero and Jack Harris were tending to customers at the bar. Shero, known as "Tony the Hawk" and "Tony the Killer," doubled as a bodyguard and driver for Munsene. The strangers ordered Scotch and Harris poured two glasses of Haig & Haig and brought two glasses of water to them. Huffman and Munsene were standing in the bar area waiting for a third man to join them. Huffman explained what happened next:

> "As I was talking I noticed two men walk up and stand at the bar to Jim's left. Jim was between me and the two men. They ordered Haig and Haig (Scotch whisky). I turned around wondering who was ordering Haig and Haig. I noticed the men were exceptionally well-dressed. They were both in their early 30's.
> "I turned back to Jim and he said, 'I'm going up on Pine St. and look for my friend.' Just then I heard sounds like fireworks going off. I whirled around and saw the man nearest Jim motion to me with his gun.
> "'Keep away. Keep out of this,' he said.
> "The other man forced most of the men in the barroom to line up against the wall. Then he walked to the open side door. I presume he was to act as guard or something.
> "Just then Monfrino rushed into the bar from the restaurant. He saw Jim beginning to slump down with his back to the bar. He yelled something and leaped toward the gunman next to Jim. As he did, the

man at the door opened fire and shot Monfrino. He then shouted to the man beside Jim, 'Come on, let's go.'

"Instead of leaving, the gunman said, 'I'll make sure he's done,' and fired a couple more shots into Jim. Then the two ran out the side door on to Clinton St. Someone yelled, 'Get their license number.' We ran out but we couldn't see anyone. Later someone said they saw a coupe speeding north on S. Park toward the business district."

Huffman was standing so close to the gunfire that two of the bullets grazed him; one on the right forearm, the second hit his left knee. Felix Monfrino had come on the run from the dining room to his uncle's aid when the shots rang out. The first shot at Monfrino may have been fired as a warning, as it ripped through his right shoe entering his foot. Once hit, Monfrino staggered a few steps, nearly reaching the gunmen. The second bullet entered Monfrino on the left side of his chest, passed above his heart and exited out his right armpit and into his right arm. He fell to the floor face up, his body twitching. Monfrino died minutes later.

Another version of the shooting, which appeared in the Warren *Tribune Chronicle* stated, "As Munsene slumped to the floor, his left shoulder and head lying over the bar rail, his assailant started for the door. A groan escaped Munsene's lips and the man who had done the shooting turned and said to the other, 'Finish him off.' The second killer fired two shots at the prostrate victim."

When the shooting ceased, customers panicked and ran – except for one. A Youngstown woman, who had once trained as a nurse, knelt next to Munsene and felt his wrist for a pulse. There was none. Moving over to Monfrino, she discovered a "fleeting" heartbeat.

Both gunmen fled through the Clinton Avenue door. There were conflicting reports from the parking lot on how they escaped. One witness claimed the two jumped into a waiting coupe that headed north on South Park, another stated the pair disappeared on foot into the darkness.

Police officers and sheriff's deputies rushed to the restaurant. One of the first deputies to arrive was Jean P. Blair, who would later become Chairman of the Trumbull County Republican Party. Authorities grilled customers and employees who had not already fled the restaurant. It was reported that "important witnesses" were transported to Cleveland and Pittsburgh to review a collection of mug shots in hopes of identifying the shooters.

The bodies of Munsene and Monfrino were removed from the restaurant and taken directly to the Peter Rossi Funeral Home, where autopsies were performed by Trumbull County Coroner Dr. J.C. Henshaw.[8] Monfrino's wife, Genevieve collapsed after viewing the bloodstained corpse of her husband and was carried from the room.

As word of the double-murder spread, a frenzy to obtain more details erupted throughout the county. The *Tribune Chronicle* reported:

> "It took two officers at police headquarters to answer calls regarding the murders. From 10 p.m. until the wee hours of the morning the phones continued ringing with curious citizens on the line, wishing to know about the slayings.
>
> "The lobby of the station was crowded with inquisitive persons and officers were forced for a time to lock the door from the lobby to the desk room.
>
> "Telephone company officials reported that operators who were ready to go off duty were asked to remain in order to alleviate the heavy increase in calls between 10 p.m. and midnight."

Detectives determined that since Munsene stood so close to his killers without recognizing or acknowledging them that they were unknown to him. Police had a decent description of the gunmen and the killers had provided a vital clue – they left their fingerprints behind on the glasses at the bar from which they drank their scotch and water. Anthony Shero, the son of a Niles police officer, had placed a towel over the glasses to preserve the prints. The glasses were taken to the police station where Sergeant William E. Johnson of the Identification Bureau examined them, dusting them for fingerprints. He was able to obtain one solid print, the left index finger of one of the killers. A few days later Captain George Salen took the glasses to the FBI lab in Washington D.C. Unfortunately the bureau was unable to match the print to any in their "single print division."

Soon, another important clue proved fruitless. A new waiter at the club, who left before the shooting, had worked his first shift that night. He told investigators that two men seated in the dining room inquired "if the heavy-set fellow strolling around the room was Jim Munsene?" The wait staff had been schooled never to point out Munsene to anyone. Instead, the waiter told the customers that Angeline Sferra operated the restaurant and that Munsene was no longer involved. At first police believed the two customers, whose descriptions did not match those of the shooters, had gone to the restaurant ahead of time to spot Munsene and "finger" him for the gunmen. The next day, however, after reading the waiter's account in the newspaper, the two customers in question went to police headquarters and explained they had inquired about Munsene simply to satisfy their own curiosity.

Another clue that fell to the wayside was that the gunmen escaped in a coupe. Police Chief Barney J. Gillen soon declared that this story was a figment of someone's imagination. The chief declared, "No one can tell how the two men escaped!"

Investigators tried to determine a motive for the murders. Chief among them was that someone wanted to move in on Munsene's dog track business. Another possible motive was the numbers racket, a rumor claimed Munsene had tried to cut in on someone else's territory, possibly in Steubenville. Others claimed it was a disgruntled numbers' player. Police received word that on Saturday, March 15 there was a dispute over the winning number. The payoff was made on 652, while two reporting centers listed the winning number as 650. Complaints were said to have been lodged from Cleveland and Pittsburgh and "every city in between." It's unlikely this latter incident could have been responsible for the mobster's death. Munsene was said to have had a record, two decades long, of never failing to pay on a winning number. Whenever confusion over a winning number occurred his banks willingly paid off on both numbers in order to keep the customers satisfied.

The city of Pittsburgh seemed to garner a lot of attention in the search for the killers, as it was reported Munsene had many business interests there. The first arrest in the investigation was of a Pittsburgh man who was questioned about Munsene's "connections in that city."

The murder theory involving the Milton Dog Track soon went by the wayside. While this seemed to run high in speculation within days the police, without divulging any details, declared the killings had no connection with the facility.

On Thursday afternoon the funeral service for Felix Monfrino was held in his home at 801 Woodbine. The Reverend W.L. Burner, pastor of the Second Christian Church of Warren conducted the services at both the home and Pineview Memorial Park. Among the pallbearers were Munsene's sons, Nofry, Tullio and Warren.

The next day Munsene's funeral was conducted from his Tod SW Ext. home. Hundreds of friends, family and onlookers lined the road outside the fenced-in home of the Warren underworld kingpin. A private service was held at 10:00 a.m. in the home's small front room, where Munsene's open casket was surrounded by flowers. Reverend Burner delivered the sermon, based on the verse "Jesus wept," before fewer than a dozen mourners.

After the service Munsene's casket was carried to Peter Rossi's funeral coach for transporting to Oakwood Cemetery for burial. A procession, a mile and a half in length followed the coach containing 110 automobiles, including 12 flower cars. At the cemetery hundreds of mourners and on-lookers surrounded the open-sided funeral tent, while others lined Niles Avenue. Jimmy Munsene's funeral was described by some as the largest ever held in Warren.

The murder investigation was soon at a standstill. Police Chief Gillen,[9] 71 years of age, had taken ill by the end of the week and was trying to run the investigation from his sick bed. On the Monday after the shooting witnesses were taken to Pittsburgh to view a suspect, but none recognized him. A coroner's inquiry was held, but testimony was not released. The murder investigation ground to a halt.

Arrest and Trial of Tommy Viola

Nearly three years passed after the double slaying. Then, in December 1943, a confidential informant from Youngstown provided Warren Sergeant William Johnson with pictures and the names of the two assassins – Thomas "Tommy" Viola and Charles "Black Charlie" Monazym, both of Detroit.

Viola was born in Baltimore, but his entire criminal career took place outside of that city. On Viola's rap sheet were convictions for counterfeiting, and arrests for armed robbery, grand larceny and assault with intent to kill. While Viola was reputed to be "a trigger man" for gangs in Michigan, Ohio and New York, most of his arrests occurred in Detroit between 1931 and 1934. The most notorious was a counterfeiting arrest in June 1933 when he was picked up, along with 140 others, by the United States Secret Service. Viola was indicted with hitman Elmer Macklin, future Detroit Mafia heavyweight Mike Rubino and three others. While all six were convicted, Viola received the lightest sentence of the group – two years and a $500 fine. During the early 1940s Viola was reputed to be a top gunman for the underworld. In addition to the Munsene / Monfrino double murder, he was considered a suspect in the highly publicized murder of State Senator Warren G. Hooper, from Michigan's 9th District, which took place on January 11, 1945. Hooper, who was to be questioned by a grand jury about a payoff scheme, was found shot and set afire in his automobile. Viola was also a suspect in the murder of Eddie Sarkesian, a one-time collector for the Detroit mob who began holding up numbers banks and paid for it with his life on August 16, 1944.

Charles Monazym, a career criminal since the age of 16, was born in Pottsville, Pennsylvania into a family of Syrian origin. The family moved to

Missouri when Charlie was a teenager. There he stole an automobile, was arrested and served 14 months in the Missouri State Penitentiary. Upon release he rejoined his family in Detroit, where he developed a reputation as a burglar, bootlegger and hijacker. Monazym became acquainted with James Tamer and the two developed a long friendship. In August 1932, after stealing a ring from a cabaret operator, he was sentenced to a term in the State Prison of Southern Michigan[10] in Jackson. Monazym became a trusty at the prison and lived at the home of the prison chaplain. Far from a model prisoner, Monazym was involved in a narcotics smuggling ring until Christmas Day 1934 when he walked out of the prison, never to return. He was unaware at the time of his escape that he was due to be paroled in two weeks.

On May 1, 1936 Monazym was involved in one of the richest bank robberies in Detroit history – the Oakland-Woodland branch of the Detroit Bank. Monazym, wielding a Thompson sub-machinegun, held bank employees and customers at bay as his accomplices grabbed $64,740. Within a short time all the participants were captured with the exception of "Black Charlie." Included in the roundup were three women who were convicted of hiding $12,000 of the loot in a Cleveland safe deposit box. One of the women, Margaret Allen, was a 35 year-old, married mother of four young children. Allen escaped and in November 1938 J. Edgar Hoover named her and Monazym as two of the "Nation's 10 Most Desperate Criminals."

On January 21, 1942, nearly ten months after the Munsene and Monfrino double slaying, Monazym was arrested in Buffalo, New York where he was hiding with his wife, under the alias of John Vincent. An anonymous caller tipped off Buffalo police to his whereabouts. Arrested with them was Buffalo mobster, Sam Pieri, who was suspected, but never charged, of being the getaway driver on the night of the Warren murders. At the time of his arrest Monazym was not a suspect in the murders. Returned to Detroit, "Black Charlie" was tried in Federal Court and convicted on April 29 on two counts. Federal Judge Arthur F. Lederle sentenced him to 25 years on the first count and two years on the second count, to run consecutively; he was also fined $20,000. Monazym was sent to Leavenworth Federal Penitentiary in Kansas to serve his sentence.[11]

◆　　◆　　◆

Police Sergeant William Johnson, who would later serve as police chief of Warren,[12] was credited with affecting the capture of Thomas Viola. A

June 29, 1948 *Tribune Chronicle* article stated, "Equipped with a smudged partial print of one of the killers…and an eyewitness description, Johnson, as a member of the Bureau of Identification, tracked the killer thru 37 states [another report claims 24], until the capture." While the story seems a bit incredible, another article stated Viola's "arrest ended better than a four year search that covered many cities and states during which Viola was almost within the grasp of pursuing officers several times but managed to make his getaway." This story was supported by a *Tribune Chronicle* article from August 1945, which stated Johnson's search took him to:

> "Los Angeles, Miami, New York, St. Louis, Kansas City, Washington, Baltimore, Louisville, Cleveland, Toledo, Steubenville, Conneaut, Geneva-on-the-Lake, Wheeling, Columbus and many other cities. Approximately $2,000 has been spent from the Reward Fund in the hunt for the killers. The Reward Fund derives its revenues from the annual police dance held in November.
>
> "The sergeant revealed that on several occasions he was less than a half-hour behind Viola in some of these cities. The closest Viola came to Warren since the crime was when he was at Geneva-on-the Lake and Youngstown…"

With Viola's identity established, Johnson again approached the FBI. When they initially received the print from the Warren Police back in April 1941 they couldn't match the left index fingerprint because they were looking only at their single fingerprint files. After they were provided with the suspect's name they found a card on Viola in their main index. On St. Valentine's Day 1944 four grand jury murder indictments were returned, two for Viola and two for Monazym for the killings of Munsene and Monfrino. Since there was credible information that the pair fled to New York after the murders, the FBI was brought into the case due to a federal law making it illegal for flight to avoid prosecution for a felony.

Viola remained on the run. On July 2, 1945 he arrived at the Frontier Motel at 227 West Drachman Street in Tucson, Arizona where he checked into cabin #3, registering as Frank N. Salerno of New York, one of 15 aliases he was known to have used. There was little mystery as to why Viola had chosen Tucson to lie low. Earlier that year Detroit Mafia boss Peter Licavoli purchased a ranch in Wrightstown,[13] which he renamed the Grace Ranch, after his wife. In addition, former associates of the Cleveland Syndicate had relocated there and set up a handbook and wire service. Sam "Gameboy" Miller[14] was overseeing these and other operations from the Santa Rita Hotel.

By early August Viola's presence in Tucson was brought to the attention of the FBI through the Assessor's office when Viola applied for a license for a 1941 Pontiac station wagon, listing his address as Pete Licavoli's Grace Ranch. Around 8:00 p.m. on Tuesday, August 7, FBI agents, under the command of Tucson Special FBI Agent Herman E. Tickel, followed Viola to the Santa Rita Hotel. The hotel had a popular bar, where a crowd swung the night away on the dance floor. The FBI had no way of knowing if Viola was armed, so to avoid a potentially dangerous encounter the agents, reinforced by Tucson city detectives,[15] surrounded the Santa Rita's exits and waited for Viola to come out. It would be a long wait. Viola, using another alias Sam Lavigne, was with four friends – Ralph Barrasso, William Dillas, Jimmy Aaran and Jacob Lerner – enjoying the company of several women. Lerner, from Pittsburgh, had been associated with the Cleveland Syndicate in a dog track operation in Steubenville and was now fronting for "Game Boy" Miller at the Santa Rita Hotel.

Around 1:00 Wednesday morning, as the dance crowd was thinning out, Viola became aware of the officers who appeared to have the place surrounded. As Viola attempted to leave three men armed with a machinegun, a shotgun and a revolver confronted him. Viola retreated and headed toward another door on the run. Agents and detectives moved quickly and he was apprehended without a struggle. Viola was searched and found to be unarmed. Agents recovered $340 in cash and two checks totaling $650 drawn on a Detroit bank.

There were several unanswered questions in the wake of Viola's arrest, mostly brought about by the newspaper reporting. The *Tucson Daily Citizen* reported that his capture "climaxed several days of vigil and investigation on the part of the officers." If the FBI knew where he was living, why wasn't he apprehended at the cabin where there would have been less risk of others being harmed? The same newspaper, however, claimed his identity was not ascertained until that Tuesday evening, which doesn't quite fit in with the "several days of vigil and investigation." The story states, "A strong clue… was the fact that he is known as a drinker of only Scotch whisky, with which he had been imbibing with friends while officers waited outside to apprehend him." Then there was confusion in the reporting of the weapons that were recovered. The *Arizona Daily Star*[16] reported, "agents found a .25 caliber Spanish-type automatic and a .32 caliber Colt automatic in his cabin at a tourist court." Meanwhile, the *Tucson Daily Citizen* stated that two of Viola's friends [Ralph and Buddy Barrasso, brothers who owned the Frontier Motel] went to the cabin after the arrest, "ransacked his room… and took the two pistols and gave them to Lt. Syracuse. It was from Syracuse that the guns were later recovered." The newspaper claimed Viola was sharing the cabin with a Lieutenant Samuel Syracuse, which raises the question was this man related to Detroit Mafia killer Russell Syracuse.[17] Lieutenant

Syracuse was working at Davis-Monthan Air Force Base,[18] where he was suspected of running a handbook. Army records showed his home address as Falconer, New York, located near Jamestown, some 50 miles south of Buffalo.

Once in custody Viola gave his occupation as a "bookmaker," readily admitted who he was, and that he knew he was a wanted man. He denied, however, having any knowledge of the crimes for which he was being sought. Two of Viola's companions – Aaran and Lerner – offered to put up $2,500 for his release, but agents said he would be held until arraigned by a federal commissioner, at which time bond would be officially set. On Wednesday Viola was brought before United States Commissioner C. Wayne Clampitt. He was dressed in expensive clothing, a silk shirt and "snappy" trousers from which officers had removed the belt. Viola stated he wanted lawyer, John L. Van Buskirk to represent him. Counsel James Silver, who appeared with the prisoner, asked for a continuance as Van Buskirk was currently in Nogales, Arizona. The continuance was granted, and Clampitt ordered the prisoner held under a $50,000 bond. Viola's belt was replaced and he was led back to jail by U.S. deputy marshals with his hands cuffed behind his back.

The next day Viola was back in court represented by Van Buskirk. This time it was Assistant U.S. Attorney K. Berry Peterson who requested a continuance, stating he was awaiting the arrival of documents "from the east." Clampitt approved the motion, setting a hearing date of August 16. Van Buskirk then objected to the $50,000 bond that had been set for his client. The attorney claimed that under federal law the maximum that could be imposed was $5,000. Clampitt stated that the bond was set on the recommendation of Don C. Miller, the U.S. Attorney for Northern Ohio.

On August 17 a hearing to determine if Viola's removal to Ohio should be granted was held. Van Buskirk first objected to the affidavit of removal, claiming the FBI agent who signed the document was not authorized to do so. Peterson quickly remedied this by amending the affidavit and signing it himself. Van Buskirk stated that since the hearing was solely on the violation of the federal flight law, and since the statute of limitations had run out, Viola should be set free. Clampitt called the attorney's contention an "interesting theory," but claimed allowing it would give fugitives a precedent to circumvent the law. After the motion was heard, Bernard Monfrino, who had traveled to Tucson with Sergeant Johnson, identified Viola as the gunman who shot his son and brother-in-law. At the end of the brief hearing Clampitt ordered Viola held for removal to Ohio.

The legal battle to return Viola to Ohio[19] dragged on until December. On December 12 Viola arrived at the Cuyahoga County jail. The Cleveland jail was selected over the Trumbull County facility as it was felt "a jailbreak attempt would be less likely."

On December 19 a three-car caravan of well-armed law enforcement officers made its way from Cleveland to Warren at 5:30 in the morning. Viola sat in the back seat of the middle vehicle handcuffed to Warren deputies, Earl J. Bash and Henry Rose, while Sheriff Ralph R. Millikin drove. Later that morning at arraignment, Viola stood with counsel Wick W. Pierson and Charles Margiotti and pleaded not guilty to two counts of first-degree murder. One reporter commented that Viola was composed and denied participation in the murders, "as calmly as he were ordering a cup of coffee."

Wick Pierson was a former Trumbull County prosecutor who, ironically, successfully prosecuted Munsene in the first of his five bribery trials in the mid-1920s. Margiotti was a nationally known criminal defense attorney from Pennsylvania. He had once served as attorney general of that state and was a long-time political leader. His most famous case was the murder of Pennsylvania State Trooper Brady Paul, in which he won conviction of two defendants, a man and a woman, sending both to the electric chair. During the arraignment of Viola, Pierson asked for, and was denied bond for his client.

In addition, Donald J. DelBene was asked by Margiotti to join the defense team, but declined. At the time DelBene was the city solicitor (law director) of Warren. He would later serve as legal counsel to the Farah brothers. With a high priced legal team, and the fact that Viola had no visible means of support, many were left wondering who was paying the defendant's legal fees.

A week before the trial was scheduled to begin defense counsel filed notification with the court that they were going to present an alibi defense. Viola claimed he was in Youngstown at the time of the murder, but precisely where was not stated. The prosecution filed a motion requesting that Viola be required to be more specific.

On Monday, March 25, 1946 the trial of Thomas Viola got underway in the Trumbull County Courthouse before Judge George Birrell. The trial was for the murder of James Mancini only. It's possible that the prosecutor might have decided to try the cases separately in case the first one failed, but oddly, there was no mention in the newspapers to this affect. Handling the state's case were Trumbull County Prosecutor Paul J. Reagen and his assistant William M. McLain. The Tribune Chronicle reported, "The defendant, well and nattily dressed, took but little interest in the proceedings in which his life was at stake." Relatives in the courtroom included Munsene's sons, Warren and Nofry and three sisters of Viola.

The jury of seven men and five women were seated and sworn in by Wednesday and the trial began with opening statements. During defense counsel's statement, Pierson told the panel, "Viola was never in the city of

Warren, he didn't know Munsene, had no reason or motive for killing him and doesn't even know where the Steak House is."

The state began its case by calling Bernard Monfrino, who testified he saw Viola and Charles Monazym shoot his son and brother-in-law in the bar of the Prime Steak House. After identifying Viola as the shooter, Monfrino was subjected to a grueling four-hour cross-examination by Margiotti over a two-day period. On Wednesday afternoon, in the middle of the cross-examination, the judge granted a request for the jury to be taken to the scene of the double-murder. When testimony resumed, Monfrino said that he and Anthony Shero made many trips with Sergeant Johnson in an effort to identify the killers. These trips took the men to many cities around the country. During the trial it became a point of contention by defense counsel that the Monfrino and Munsene families bankrolled the investigation, an accusation which Bernard Monfrino adamantly denied.

Margiotti questioned Monfrino about his identification of Viola in Tucson after the defendant's arrest there in August. The attorney asked if it wasn't true that Johnson was "nudging" Monfrino to get him to identify Viola. Monfrino declared, "Sergeant Johnson wasn't anywhere near me. I didn't need anyone to tell me who Viola was."

The defense attorney tried time and again to shake Monfrino from his identification of the defendant. Margiotti read from the testimony Monfrino gave during the coroner's inquest where Bernard stated, "I couldn't recognize the shorter man. I might recognize his face – it might come to me." Monfrino responded that at the time of the inquest he was still upset over the deaths of his son and brother-in-law. "I stayed upset for a couple of years, "he added. The attorney pointed out that on several occasions Monfrino had viewed suspects and made tentative identifications. Monfrino countered that on closer viewing he had cleared those suspects. The witness also stated that Monazym and Viola had been in the Prime Steak House the Saturday night prior to the Monday evening murders. When the attorney pointed out that Monfrino had taken a great interest in hunting down the murderers, the witness responded, "Sure I was interested in getting the men who killed my boy. If I live a thousand years I'll never forget the face of the man who killed my son."

During the trial Judge Birrell kept a tight rein on the courtroom. Standing room only was banned by the jurist and after warning the gallery that he expected them to conduct themselves properly, he had four men removed for laughing during Monfrino's testimony.

On Thursday afternoon Anthony Shero took the stand. He told the court of his trips around the country with Johnson and Monfrino, stating again that the police sergeant picked up the expenses. In describing the shooting Shero stated, "Viola shot Jim in the back. As he was on the ground, Monazym fired at him too, just before the men left the place." Shero then identified a picture of Monazym as the man he had seen at Leavenworth prison. Like Monfrino before him, Shero was put though a long cross-examination by Margiotti. Shero seemed to revel in telling the court how he told bartender Jack Harris to hand him a bar towel, which he placed over the four glasses left on the bar by the killers, stating that he had read about the procedure in *True Detective* magazine.

On Friday morning Nofry Munsene told the court that he had paid close attention to Monazym and Viola when they entered the restaurant because he thought the two looked like "hoodlums." Nofry's account of the night of the shooting was being heard publicly for the first time, as he had not testified at the corner's inquest. Munsene's oldest son was the only witness to testify as to what happened outside the restaurant. He recounted that Monazym, armed with a revolver, ran past him heading south on South Park. When Viola came out he started to run north.

"This way, Tom, let's get out of here," Nofry testified Monazym called out to his partner. As Viola changed directions, Munsene got a good look at him.

During cross-examination, Munsene told Margiotti he had no diffi-culty picking Viola out of a lineup at the Cuyahoga County jail. "His face has been in my mind since that night."

The Friday morning session featured a bickering contest between Reagen and Margiotti as Special FBI Agent Herman Tickel of Tucson testi-fied about Viola's arrest. Margiotti objected to nearly every question asked of Tickel by the prosecutor on the grounds that it was "immaterial and irrelevant."

The *Tribune Chronicle* reported:

> "Considerable time was spent by counsel in conferences with the judge regarding Tickel's testimony. Margiotti objected to Reagen's questions as to whether Viola had been tipped off that the police were waiting for him to come out of a hotel dining room; as to Viola's conduct when he did come out of the room; as to any conversation Tickel had with Viola after the arrest and as to investigation of Viola's personal belongings."

When the trial began Judge Birrell let the jury and both sides know that he was going to extend the days of testimony by a half-hour and hold a Saturday session. A good portion of this time was taken up with a motion filed by the defense to have the fingerprint information withheld from the jury. Margiotta argued that the police couldn't prove the chain of custody of the glasses to show that they were indeed the ones handled in the Prime Steak House the night of the murders. Birrell overruled counsel's motion and the FBI's fingerprint expert would be on the stand when trial resumed.

On Monday, April Fools Day jurors heard some of the most compelling evidence in the case. Sebastian F. Latona, an FBI fingerprint expert from Washington D.C., took the stand. As with Special Agent Tickel, attorney Margiotti raised numerous objections. The first was to question the agent's qualifications. Latona responded with a sterling tale of his reputation, informing the court that in his 14 years with the bureau he conducted classes in fingerprinting for all new FBI agents as well as refresher courses for field agents. In addition, he was an instructor in police academies around the country. Judge Birrell had no problem ruling Latona competent to testify.

"No two fingers on any person are alike," Latona told the jury. "It would be impossible for one person to have the same fingerprints as another. The same finger made the impression on the two glasses and on the cards furnished the FBI. No other finger made it or could have made it." Latona's use of a blowup of the left index fingerprint from the glass, comparing it to an enlarged print from the FBI card, proved conclusive. He then outlined the 12 points by which the identification was made. Also called as witnesses were several law enforcement officers who testified to the chain of custody of the glasses since the night of the shooting.

One of the last witnesses called Saturday afternoon was Sergeant William Johnson. He testified that a confidential informant disclosed to him the identity of the killers in December 1943. Provided with photographs of the pair he was able to get positive identification from witnesses, which led to the grand jury indictment of Monazym and Viola in February 1944.

On cross-examination Margiotti tried to get Johnson to reveal the informant's name. Johnson replied, "I'll never reveal the source of information to anybody."

Judge Birrell ruled, "A police officer should have the right to protect his source of information."

During another line of questioning, Johnson declared that the funding for his trips, and that of witnesses, was paid for by the public and not by the Monfrino or Munsene families.

As the trial moved into its second week FBI fingerprint expert Sebastian Latona was still on the stand. Margiotti, as was his pattern, put the agent through an exhausting four-hour cross-examination. Numerous objections and sidebar discussions highlighted the testimony. The bickering between Margiotti and Reagen had by now become a regular part of the trial. On several occasions the judge warned the jury that comments from the two should not be considered evidence and only the testimony as it came from the witnesses was relevant.

Latona said the fingerprints from the glasses had been received by the Bureau after the double murder. But it wasn't until Johnson secured the suspect's identity that he was able to match it to a card with Viola's name and prints, which had been obtained during Viola's prison term for counterfeiting in 1934. Prints taken in Warren, upon Viola's return there in December 1945, matched both sets. The FBI agent testified that no fingerprints from Monazym could be found on either of the glasses. The only other fingerprint Latona could identify belonged to bartender Jack Harris. "It took me about 10 minutes to make sure that the prints on the glasses were the same as those on Viola's card in our files," Latona confirmed.

Margiotti continued to hammer away at Latona trying to shake his identification of the print. Irritated by the long hours of questioning, Latona shot back at one point, "I have never made a mistake when I said fingerprints were identical where there are as many points present for comparison as there are in this case. No other fingerprint expert could possibly make any other finding!"

On Tuesday, April 2 the defense began its case with Ellmonte Saylor, a Tucson police sergeant who participated in the arrest. He was called to refute testimony given by FBI Agent Tickel about Viola's actions at the time of his arrest, stating that the defendant had not run away as the agent had described. He testified he saw Sergeant Johnson "nudge" Bernard Monfrino at the time that latter identified Viola in Tucson. Under cross-examination Saylor said his brother ran a local dry cleaners and the defense had paid his way to Warren and was reimbursing him for time lost from his job in Tucson. Reagen asked Saylor when he was being questioned by Assistant County Prosecutor McLain before the trial why he didn't mention the "nudging" incident. Saylor replied he didn't mention it because McLain didn't ask.

The next two witnesses called for the defense were Anthony DiCenso and Thomas Cage. Both had been conversing with one another at the Prime Steak House on the night of the murders. Each claimed that when the killers entered they thought they were black men until they got a closer look at the pair.

DiCenso testified, "I'm not interested in the outcome of this case. I was a good friend of Munsene and Felix Monfrino and I'm on good terms with the Munsene and Monfrino families now." Under cross-examination he said he wasn't sure who else was in the barroom that night and denied he was impaired due to liquor consumption. Cage admitted under cross that at the coroner's inquest he admitted he hadn't paid much attention to the two men that walked in and that he couldn't identify them unless they were dressed the same way they were when they entered the bar that night.

Bartender Jack Harris told the court that Viola "is positively not one of the two men who engaged in the shooting that night." He claimed that he didn't see Nofry Munsene in the restaurant that night and that he could not recollect giving Anthony Shero a towel to cover the glasses on the bar. He claimed that in Cleveland, where he had gone to view Viola upon his return from Tucson, that Bernard Monfrino grabbed him by the coat and demanded, "That's him, don't you recognize him."

Under cross-examination Harris denied that he had made up his mind not to identify Viola; that he told Sergeant Johnson he wanted no part in this case; and that he had ever stated he was scared to testify. At an inquest in April 1944 he told investigators, "I don't believe I could identify them."

Another witness called by the defense confirmed he heard Bernard Monfrino say to Harris during the lineup in Cleveland, "that's the man, he hasn't changed a bit." He denied, however, that Monfrino had grabbed Harris.

The defense called a nurse from Detroit who testified that a Samuel Levigne came to the Alexander Blaine Hospital in that city for treatment of gonorrheal rheumatism[20] in December 1944. The treatment involved a recommendation by the doctor that the patient go to Arizona for his health. Her testimony was to show that Viola had gone to Tucson for his health, not because he was on the run.

Margiotti was pulling out all the stops. He then tried to question two local optometrists who treated Bernard Monfrino to show that he had poor eyesight. The judge denied testimony about his examination claiming Monfrino was protected by doctor-patient privilege.

The defense then put on its own fingerprint expert who, after a long and arduous examination, claimed that there were too many indistinct identifying marks left on the glasses to prove that the print belonged to Viola. During cross-examination McLain got the man to admit that the FBI was recognized throughout the world as the authority on fingerprinting. "I don't know of a single case where the FBI made a mistake in comparing and identifying a latent finger print," he stated.

On Thursday, April 4 Louis and Lee Tiberio, operators of the Tropics Night Club in Youngstown, were called to the stand. They testified that Viola was a regular at the club from late 1940 to late 1941. They said Viola didn't work while in town, but took bets on sporting events. Cyril Barbarus, a student at Ohio University, related how he had been arrested with Viola during a raid at the Savoy Club in Youngstown. During the booking process he said he used a fictitious name and didn't know what name Viola gave because the defendant was already using the alias Tommy DeNota. Barbarus stated that at the time of the booking Viola "had shown no fear of the police."

On Saturday the defense rested and the state called a couple of rebuttal witnesses. One was Special FBI Agent Tickel who, over the objections of Margiotti, was permitted to testify that Sergeant Johnson stood twelve feet away from Bernard Monfrino at the commissioner's hearing in Tucson, making it impossible to "nudge" him during his identification of Viola.

It is interesting to note that Earl B. Huffman, the man standing closest to Munsene and the killers, was never called to testify. No reason was given in the newspapers for his absence.

With testimony completed Margiotti asked Birrell to carry the case over until Monday, because he would need three hours for his closing statement. "I don't like to be limited in the matter of time for an argument," declared the attorney, who had already proved he didn't like to be limited "in the matter of time" for a cross-examination either. Reagen had no objection, telling Birrell he would need a mere hour and fifteen minutes. Claiming he didn't want to confine the jury over Sunday, the judge agreed to hear closing arguments Monday morning.

On Monday, April 8 closing arguments were heard. Prosecutor Reagen told the jury, "The murder of Munsene was the coldest, most brutal ever committed in Trumbull County. It was a planned, paid killing and there isn't a single circumstance to warrant the granting of mercy. The only way to stop such killings is to tell Thomas Viola by your verdict that it can't be done in this county."

Reagen hit on Viola's failure to testify stating, "The only man who could tell us if he was in the Prime Steak House on the murder night didn't take the stand." He then attacked Viola's alibi defense declaring that even though witnesses had him living in Youngstown from 1940 to 1941, there wasn't a shred of evidence to his whereabouts on the night of the slaying. "The alibi doesn't mean a thing," Reagen bellowed. "He wasn't even known as Viola when he lived in Youngstown but as Tommy DeNota."

In covering the fingerprint evidence Reagen pointed out that the defense "expert" never said the prints didn't belong to Viola, but only that he was unable to identify them because they were not distinct. "The FBI doesn't let that kind of evidence be offered unless it is positive," Reagen declared. "The FBI doesn't make mistakes in comparisons of fingerprints and even the defense expert agreed with that. Are you going to accept the evidence of an FBI agent, paid by the government, or are you going to believe the story of a man who for a fee, will testify to anything."

The prosecutor finished by saying, "I am satisfied that the state has proven its case beyond a reasonable doubt and I have all the confidence in the world that you will exercise your most careful judgment and bring in a proper verdict."

Margiotti seemed clearly on the defensive as he began his closing argument. "The defendant has come into this court presumed to be innocent until the state proves beyond a reasonable doubt that he is guilty," Margiotti began. "The defendant is not required to show that he is not guilty."

Margiotti thanked the jury for the consideration they had shown and reminded them of their promise to cast aside their prejudice and feelings about the defendant when they were sworn in. He then correctly pointed out that the prosecution had failed to establish a motive for the slaying or that Viola had any connection to Munsene and his activities. He then attacked Munsene's character stating, with "the kind of life that Munsene was living he could expect to die in the manner that he did."

The attorney also pointed out that no evidence had been offered to show that Viola and Monazym had ever known each other. He reminded jurors that no murder weapon had ever been produced. He then downplayed the eyewitness identification calling it the "least reliable information that can be offered in court." Next he attacked Bernard Monfrino, Anthony Shero and Nofry Munsene for being "very much interested" in the outcome of the case. But when it came to the fingerprint evidence, Margiotti must have felt licked. He simply offered up that in the chain of evidence trail the officer who accompanied the glasses to Washington D.C. could not say for certain that they were taken from the Prime Steak House. Recalling Latona's comment that it had taken him only ten minutes to make positive identification, Margiotti asked the jury, "Are you going to send Viola to the chair on a 10 minute investigation? If you do no man is safe if his life or liberty can be taken away on testimony of that kind."

Margiotti closed with, "Your verdict must assure every citizen in Trumbull County that he has a right to live a full life and work out with his God the salvation of his soul."

Throughout the trial Viola had sat stoic, if not disinterested. During Margiotti's closing the defendant was seen to wipe his eyes with a handkerchief, while his sisters wept silently.

In his rebuttal argument Assistant County Prosecutor McLain stated, "I am willing to stake the result of this case on the findings of Latona – a trusted employee of the FBI for more than 14 years. If we don't believe the FBI on fingerprints, whom are we going to believe?"

McLain closed with, "You face an unpleasant task but you must emblazon a message to the world that we here in Trumbull County live in peace and security. Your verdict must not only punish a person guilty of crime but it must deter others from coming to this community and committing like and similar crimes."

After Birrell gave his instructions to the jury the panel began its deliberations late Monday afternoon. The makeup of the jury had changed during the trial. One woman was released, due to an illness in her family, and was replaced by a male alternate; the jury was now eight men and four women. After a dinner break the jury resumed deliberations at 6:45. At 7:55 the jury room buzzer sounded and panel members reported that someone had been seen outside the door. A deputy was stationed to prevent anyone else from getting near. At 8:48 the buzzer was sounded again as panel members had two questions they wanted resolved. They inquired if the finger print card blowup was in evidence and if they should consider evidence from the coroner's inquest. Birrell answered yes to the first and no to the latter question. Birrell then had Sheriff Millikin bring Viola to the courtroom so he could explain what had transpired, thus avoiding a trial error.

At 11:18 p.m. the jury buzzer sounded for the final time. They had reached a verdict. The 13-day trial tied a record in Trumbull County set back in 1931.[21] The courtroom was silent as Birrell asked the jury foreman if they had arrived at a verdict.

"Yes, your honor," came the reply.

The clerk of courts handed the verdict to Birrell, who then handed it back to the clerk to read, "Guilty, with a recommendation of mercy." Viola turned white and his sisters sobbed openly. As the jurors were polled, Viola sat looking at the panel incredulously.

It was later learned that six ballots had been taken and that most of the time was spent – in vain – trying to convince a single holdout juror to put Viola in the death chair. The holdout juror, later revealed to be the alternate, was described as "an active politician in and around Warren." It was also reported that the conviction was swayed by the fingerprint testimony of agent Latona.

Defense counsel announced immediately that it would file a motion for a new trial. Judge Birrell said he would consider the motion before passing sentence. The motion was filed and in Birrell's hands the next day.

On Friday, April 12, Judge Birrell called all the parties back to his courtroom. Margiotti was not present as the judge overruled the defense motion for a new trial. He then asked Viola if he had anything to say before sentence was passed.

Viola answered, "Just that I'm not guilty of this crime, your Honor."

The sentence was pre-determined by the jury's verdict. Viola was sentenced to prison for the rest of his natural life, but new Ohio laws would allow the prisoner to be considered for parole after serving 20 years.

Viola was returned to the county jail. Sheriff Millikin was determined not to keep him there any longer than necessary. Two of Viola's sisters and a brother-in-law visited him for the last time. Before leaving he gave them all his extra clothing.

Within an hour of his sentencing Viola was on his way the Ohio Penitentiary in Columbus. Like his trip from Cleveland to Warren, Viola was in a three-car caravan handcuffed in the back seat of the middle car next to Deputy Sheriff Earl Bash, while Sheriff Millikin and Deputy Cliff Wilson were in the front seat.

Attorney Margiotti promised to appeal the case all the way to the U.S. Supreme Court. His first step was on September 6, 1946 when he appeared before the 7th District Court of Appeals. Margiotti challenged the weight of the evidence for his client, while Reagen claimed guilt was proved beyond a reasonable doubt. There was a long delay because the Ohio Supreme Court had to rule on whether the Appellate Court had jurisdiction.

On May 29, 1947 the Appellate Court ruled that while some errors had been committed during the trial, they were not of such prejudicial magnitude as to warrant a new trial. Appellate Judge William M. Carter, who was on the bench during Munsene's first two bribery trials in the 1920s, noted, "We found that substantial justice has been done by the jury in this case and that the verdict was justified under the evidence offered at the trial."

On September 17, 1947 Margiotti made his appeal to the Ohio Supreme Court for a new trial claiming there were "numerous errors of law" during the trial. On November 13 Margiotti and McLain argued before the high court. Margiotti had a novel argument. FBI Director J. Edgar Hoover had signed the letter giving the bureau's finding that the fingerprint on the glass was Viola's. Margiotti stated that the fingerprint match had not been made by Hoover but by Sebastian Latona and the director signed the letter as a matter of routine. "That letter did the damage," Margiotti argued. He claimed Hoover's name would be harmful to his client's case and insisted he had objected to it during the trial. McLain simply argued that there was no record of Margiotti ever objecting to the offering of the letter into evidence.

Margiotti also challenged the fact that Judge Birrell had answered questions from the jury, giving them instruction without Viola present. This occurred, but Birrell realized his mistake, and its possible consequences, and had the sheriff bring Viola to the courtroom and in front of the jury explained what had transpired. Six days later the Ohio Supreme Court refused to review the decision of the 7th District Court of Appeals.

As promised, Margiotti filed a motion to take the case to the U.S. Supreme Court. On May 10, 1948 in Washington D.C., the highest court in the land refused a writ of certiorari.[22] Viola was staying put in the Ohio Penitentiary – or so people thought.

By 1960 Viola had spent nearly 15 years behind bars and had earned a position as a trusty in the Ohio Penitentiary. On the afternoon of September 22, Viola finished his workday as a clerk in the prison's business office, but instead of returning to his cell he casually walked out of the penitentiary, still attired in prison garb, and escaped. Some speculated he might return to Warren and seek revenge against William E. Johnson, now the retired chief of police, who had pursued him relentlessly. New Warren Police Chief Manley English[23] doubted that, stating, "I should think he'd stay as far away as possible."

Viola's escape had been well planned. A safe-house had been rented for him in Detroit the day he walked out of prison. By mid-January 1961 Viola was still at large. On January 17 he was placed on the FBI's "Ten Most Wanted" list. Around that same time he moved to an apartment at 250 Merton Road, which had been rented for him by Gertrude M. Sloan, a manicurist from Windsor, Ontario. Viola used the name Jim Sloan and told anyone who asked that he was a salesman. On February 12 Viola's picture appeared in the Sunday edition of the *Detroit News' This Week Magazine,* in an article written by FBI Director J. Edgar Hoover.[24] A Detroit resident recognized Viola as the Jim Sloan on Merton Road and contacted the local FBI office. The FBI began a three-week surveillance using the "anonymous tipster's" information. Around noon on Monday, March 27 FBI agents moved in to make the arrest. They telephoned Viola and informed him that he was surrounded and to come out. The escapee answered that he would be "out in 15 minutes." Viola, after looking out the windows and realizing that he was indeed trapped, called from the window and said he would be "right out." Agents arrested him without incident when he stepped into the hallway.

While in hiding, Viola had dyed his graying hair black and grew a mustache, which he also dyed. During a search of his apartment, agents found two handguns wrapped in a towel and $4,016 in cash. When questioned, Viola said he had won the money gambling. Viola admitted to the arresting agents, "I knew my free time was up the minute the FBI put me on the top 10. I knew you would get me." Viola was taken to the Wayne County Jail. At his arraignment the next day, Viola waived extradition and bail was set at $75,000. On April 19, after the completion of extradition proceedings, Ohio Penitentiary Warden Beryle C. Sacks and three prison officials escorted Viola from Detroit back to the Columbus prison facility.

In November 1962 Viola was named in a federal indictment along with two other men – James "Biffo" Maccagnone, described as a "Mafia crime syndicate section leader in Detroit in testimony before the McClellan Senate Committee," and Louis LaHood Sarkis – for conspiracy in the harboring of a murder fugitive and failure to report a felony. Maccagnone helped arrange for the apartment to be rented on the day of Viola's escape.

On January 23, 1963 U.S. Marshals from the Motor City took Viola from the Ohio Penitentiary to the U.S. District Court in Detroit, where a plea of not guilty to a charge of harboring a fugitive – himself – was entered. Viola was back in Columbus three days later. Referring to Gertrude Sloan as "the one-time girlfriend" of Viola, the Associated Press reported that two FBI agents recognized her walking on a residential street in Detroit and arrested her on May 15, 1963. Reports stated Mrs. Sloan shared the apartment with Viola. Eventually the list of indicted grew to include Joseph F. "Eddie" Kory and Sargon John Ballo. Viola was refused release from the Ohio Penitentiary by Governor James A. Rhodes when the trial began on April 14, 1965. The defendants were represented by Joseph W. Louisell. After several days of testimony Maccagnone and Sloan were convicted while the other three went free due to lack of evidence. The two were facing a maximum sentence of 18 years in prison and $20,500 in fines for their actions.

In the mid-1960s health officials at the Ohio Penitentiary diagnosed Viola with advanced lung cancer. In December 1965 x-ray therapy was initiated, but his condition grew worse and doctors claimed surgery would be futile. In early March the chief surgeon of the Ohio Penitentiary gave Viola from 60 to 90 days to live. Both the chief surgeon and the warden recommended the prisoner be released under an Ohio law which provides "imminent danger of death" releases. On March 15, 1966, Viola was released to relatives in Detroit, where the U.S. Attorney was still considering conspiracy charges against him. Viola outlived the surgeon's prediction by over 100 days. Then on October 26 Viola succumbed to cancer in Grace Hospital at the age of 54.

A news article proclaimed, "Police and FBI agents are expecting Mafia mobsters from all over the country" to attend the funeral and burial at Mount Olivet Cemetery. If they were waiting, they were disappointed.

"We were against naming this village Halls Corners because of that gambling house. It's a disgrace to the family name. And when you tell someone you are from Halls Corners, they always smile." – Mrs. Charlotte Halls, *Cleveland News* August 16, 1949.

3

The Jungle Inn

Welcome to Halls Corners

According to famed Youngstown Police Chief Edward J. Allen, "The Village of Halls Corners, Ohio was conceived in infamy as a 'front' for a brothel operated by a Trumbull County criminal syndicate. The brothel, which later became the Jungle Inn and eventually "Ohio's most notorious gambling den," was constructed without a building permit. Located on Applegate Road near Ohio Route 62, on the northern boundary of Mahoning County, many residents of the two counties referred to the area as "Jungle Inn Village."

The village took its name from the family of Calvin Halls, whose great-grandfather, Calvin Applegate, was one of the earliest settlers in the area when it was commonly referred to as the Western Reserve. The name was chosen by Charles E. Sedore, Jr. who became the first and only mayor of the village. The Halls family operated a trailer camp site within the village and due to the notoriety of Jungle Inn were less than excited that the little hamlet bore their family name.

Charles Sedore had a colorful reputation in the area. "Charley" started out as a cab driver in the 1920s until he realized, like thousands of others during that era, the profits that could be realized from bootlegging. He soon opened a speakeasy behind the Landsdowne Airport, which catered to the city's "leading citizens." Perhaps being around the airfield got him interested in flying. He soon became one of the first licensed pilots in the area. In 1932 he crash-landed a plane which resulted in the death of his 13 year-old nephew. When Prohibition ended he took the profits he earned and opened one of the first night clubs in the area. It stood where the Jungle Inn would later operate. The club competed with Jimmy Munsene's Hollyhock Gardens Night Club and the Gray Wolf Tavern in Masury. Sedore ran the club until the mid-1930s when Edward A. "Sheriff" Flannigan, a Niles gambler, moved in and brought a "gambling crowd" with him. Sedore, reduced to overseeing the restaurant and bar operation, was soon forced out completely. He wisely didn't put up a fight and later benefited greatly from that decision. Friends said of him, "He always flirts with trouble but never gets involved seriously."

William M. McLain, assistant Trumbull County prosecutor, gave the following characteristics of Halls Corners:

> "The incorporation was made solely for the purpose of securing a liquor license and to defeat the purpose of the Liberty Township electors who in November, 1936, voted against permitting the sale of liquor by the glass.
> "The fact that the incorporation is a fraud is further indicated by the failure of the electors in Halls Corners to hold municipal elections… though the ballots for this purpose were sent to the community by the Board of Elections."

Officially, Halls Corners Village came into existence in 1936 after Liberty Township residents decided to go dry. At the time the village was incorporated it had only one business – the Jungle Inn, which Edward Flannigan is credited with establishing. Situated in the southeast corner of Trumbull County, municipal records show the boundaries of Halls Corners to be: Applegate Road, to the north; Hubbard Township, to the east; the Mahoning County line, on the south; and the Erie Railroad tracks on the west. The entire area consisted of just a little over 200 acres. The village consisted of just nine voters when it was incorporated, "All of whom," Chief Allen claimed, "became city officials and were connected with the Jungle Inn either personally or through some relative." Board of Election officials remarked that never in the history of Halls Corners did a candidate file a nominating petition. All office holders were "write-in" candidates for their positions. By 1949 Halls Corners had expanded to include nearly 400 acres and 100 citizens.[1]

The Jungle Inn itself consisted of two frame buildings, one 57' x 125', the other 53' x 88'. The larger building was used as a bingo hall, horserace book and game room; the smaller one contained a restaurant, bar and living quarters. At different times over the years the restaurant operated under separate management from the gambling hall.

When stories about the casino appeared in the newspapers, or were broadcast on local radio news reports, it was referred to in one of two ways; "the Jungle Inn" or simply "Jungle Inn." Also, when being discussed, it was seldom clear as to whether the casino or the restaurant was being talked about. In many people's minds there was no difference between the two and both were referred to as the Jungle Inn. At different times the names Jungle Nite Club, Jungle Restaurant and Jungle Casino were used, but most of the locals and nearly all of the regulars knew it simply as the Jungle Inn, no matter who was running it.

In his book *Merchants of Menace* Allen gave this brief early history of the Jungle Inn:

> "The wide-open character of the joint attests to the immunity with which they were able to operate in Trumbull County with no apparent fear of law enforcement interference. Over the fourteen years of its existence it became the focal point for a number of gangland murders and "disappearances." The Farah brothers, Mike and John, have been identified with it from the beginning. Their reign remained uncontested until the late thirties when Jim Munsene, or Mancini, moved in from Cleveland. A deal was consummated with the Farah brothers and henceforward Munsene also became an underworld bigshot in the area."

The chief's facts about Munsene were a bit off. Munsene was the underworld leader in Warren since the mid-1920s and was not from Cleveland; there is no indication he was associated with anybody from that city.

Munsene's role as a "bigshot" ended in March 1941 when he was cut-down by two Detroit hitmen in his Prime Steak House restaurant. After his murder the Farah brothers were again recognized as the "gambling king-pins" of Trumbull County. Despite the Farahs outward status as underworld leaders in Warren, other Cleveland and Detroit gangsters appeared on the scene in the 1930s and 1940s. Where the Farahs stood in the pecking order is uncertain. Were they "in charge" or were they just front men for a larger syndicate, whose members included James Licavoli, Frank Cammarata, Frank Brancato and Anthony "Tony Dope" Delsanter?

◆　　◆　　◆

The Jungle Inn first made news after the April 23, 1937 disappearance of James "Jimmy" Muche, a popular ex-boxer and gambler. That night Muche had been fired from his job at the gambling spot by management after he "failed to report receipt of certain money at the inn." It was rumored that outside the club that night Muche argued with mobsters from Cleveland. When her husband didn't return home, Margaret Muche and the missing man's brother, Louis, went to Cleveland where they visited several gambling joints in search of Jimmy. Mrs. Muche believed her husband had been "taken for a ride" because he knew too much about local gambling operations.

Days after the disappearance it was reported that two men, "connected with a Cleveland gang," visited the home of Jimmy's parents and advised family members that "no harm would come to him." Margaret Muche didn't believe their claim and told reporters, "If anyone knows my husband is lying low, why don't they tell where he is? How does anyone know he is hiding out without knowing where he is? My husband is not a hunted criminal and has no reason to leave town for a few days to hide."

With the publicity the Jungle Inn was receiving it suddenly went dark. Patrons were told by an employee, "They closed us down," never explaining who "they" were. Another employee remarked that the Jungle Inn would be closed until Muche was found. The search for Muche led to Detroit and Gary, Indiana without success. Years later, in 1946, a skeleton was unearthed in a shallow grave near New Kensington, Pennsylvania. An autopsy revealed a bullet hole in the skull and it was rumored that Muche's body had finally been recovered. Further medical examination, however, ruled out that it was Muche's skeletal remains. Muche was never found alive...or otherwise. For years whenever a body was discovered anywhere near the Mahoning Valley speculation was always ripe that Jimmy Muche had finally been found.

Few doubted that the Cleveland mobster's had carried out the underworld's ultimate sentence on Muche only to have it backfire on their own pocket books. The boxer's disappearance and the notoriety it brought caused the Jungle Inn to close until the publicity subsided; when it did it was business as usual.

Nearly two years later, on Sunday night, January 8, 1939, patrons arriving at the casino were turned away by a sign announcing that the Jungle Inn was closed for "alterations." Sunday nights were always a busy night at the casino and scores of automobiles that pulled into the parking lot left with disappointed gamblers. The real reason for the closing was unknown. While management claimed a new plumbing system was being installed, another source claimed a new heating system was the cause. While heat may have been the reason for the closure, many believed it was the heat coming from Trumbull County Sheriff Roy S. Hardman, who had recently warned gamblers that they were not welcome. It was quite possible, however, that following the holidays this year; regular patrons were simply strapped for cash.

On April 29 the Jungle Inn was open again for business featuring bingo and keno games, with prizes of up to $600 being offered. A "bank night" extravaganza was planned for mid-week. Nearly 500 patrons attended the opening night. Hardman described the activity as the same types of games being played in many churches. This, despite reports that visible inside were two dice tables, two blackjack tables, a table for chuck-a-luck, a horserace board and a pinball machine. On the wall was a schedule announcing that the Jungle Inn would be open for business seven nights a week.

Despite the hype, the bingo and keno games were not a large draw and the other tables remained idle. On Tuesday evening, May 2, a sparse crowd of less than 150 were in attendance. Staff members began turning away patrons before 11:00 p.m. and by 11:10 the gambling den and the parking lot were nearly deserted.

The Jungle Inn struggled for the next three weeks, then on May 20 horserace betting opened and 32 slot machines were suddenly placed into service. As patrons were enjoying "real gambling entertainment," management announced the Jungle Inn would be in "operation seven afternoons and evenings each week," with free transportation provided from the Paddock Bar on West Federal Street in Youngstown four times daily. The bar was operated by Dominic "Moosey" Caputo and his brother Frank. While it seemed as if Sheriff Hardman was on top of the gambling den's operations, making comments in each article about the inn, once the illegal activities began the sheriff appeared to have nothing to say.

The Jungle Inn remained in operation, but out of the news, for nearly a year. Then on April 12 a theft occurred at one of the dice tables. A man was loitering near one of the craps games until the crowd, "intent on the last game of keno," suddenly drifted away. At that moment the man grabbed a pile of bills, estimated to contain $500, and raced out the door. He ran to an automobile, where two accomplices waited, which sped out the driveway. Employees of the inn jumped into a waiting taxicab, which gave chase. The cab, outfitted with a device to prevent the driver from speeding, was quickly left in the dust. It was four days later before the theft was reported in the newspapers, the story having been leaked by patrons. When Jungle Inn management was questioned about the theft they denied it took place. There would be another daring robbery in August 1947. This time the thief, described as a youth, grabbed a bag of money from an employee who was delivering it to the dice tables. Instead of escaping by automobile, the young man simply ran into the woods.

In November 1940 the operators of the Jungle Inn were named publicly for the first time when Helene Ingle filed a lawsuit against the gambling den to recover nearly $1,200 she claimed to have lost while playing bingo. According to the suit the operators were Dominic B. "Moosey" Caputo, Emanuel H. Dupuy, Mike Farah and Edward A. Flannigan. The woman, a Youngstown resident, was represented by Clyde W. Osborne, a noted local attorney.

According to Ohio law, any lawsuit filed to recover losses from a game of chance had to include the dates and amounts of the loses. Ingle kept a complete log of her losses from October 1938 through August 1940. Some of the losses were as little as $2 and as much as $70 in a single night. The petition showed that Ingle had frequented the club on more than 100 occasions. In addition to the gambling losses, Ingle also sought $500 for "exemplary damages and court costs."

While Ingle's petition may have seemed a bit outlandish, it was no match for a second petition she filed on December 3. In that lawsuit, filed for $25,000 in damages, she claimed "unlawful and forcible arrest and detention." In September, according to the petition, Ingle had won some $750 playing keno. Afterwards she said she was told to stay away from the inn "because other patrons were beginning to think that the games were 'fixed' as a result of her winnings."

Ingle failed to heed the order and on September 21 she arrived at the inn with three friends. After purchasing $8 worth of keno cards, she was notified by an inn employee that she was wanted on the telephone. After finding the telephone receiver in place she went back to the keno area where "Moosey" Caputo headed her off. Ingle claims she was ordered "in a stern and peremptory tone and manner" to follow Sam Sanfillipo, who led her to the barroom in the restaurant next door.

Here, according to Ingle's suit, she was told she would have to remain until the keno games were concluded. When she objected, Emanuel Dupuy shoved her into a chair and stated, "You stay where we have put you and obey orders." Ingle claimed that despite her friends inquiring about her she was not allowed to leave the barroom. She was held that night from 9:30 until 11:30, "filled with fear and terror and caused to become in a highly nervous condition" which later caused "nervous illness." The suit also claimed that the "incident materially injured and damaged her reputation and impaired her ability to secure employment."

The response to the latest charges were addressed on January 31, 1941 when Caputo filed a joint reply that declared Ingle had been "treated with the utmost respect and at no time was she denied freedom by any of the defendants, agents or representatives during said times, to go and come as she pleased." The first case was scheduled to be heard in late January 1942. Just days before the trial, Helene Ingle went to Clyde Osborne's office and ordered him to drop both law suits. The stunned attorney stated Ingle "gave no reason for doing so." On January 22 charges were "officially" dismissed against the four defendants in front of Mahoning County Common Pleas Judge David G. Jenkins.

During the early hours of January 5, 1941 Trumbull County Sheriff-elect Russ Stein stopped at the club and told the operators they would have to close voluntarily or face being raided, once he took office. The Jungle Inn had operated for nearly a year and a half without any interference from the law. The action by Stein drew the praise of the *Vindicator* in an editorial.

Two days after Sheriff Stein's decree, Jungle Nite Club manager, Charles Sedore announced that only the Jungle Novelty Club, the building where the gambling took place, was closed. The nightclub would continue to operate, offering food and entertainment. A newspaper advertisement showed the club offering "Dining 9:30 till 2:30 every night" and continuous entertainment featuring "SHOWS – 11:30 and 1:30." The January headliner was the "Gay Boy Revue" with additional entertainment provided by "The Three Sophisticates." Admission to the club was 25 cents on weeknights and 40 cents on Saturday nights.

By mid-March 1941 rumors were circulating that "as soon as things were straightened out," the Jungle Inn would be open again for gambling. Before that happened Jimmy Munsene was gunned down in his restaurant. Whether his murder had anything to do with the Jungle Inn has never been determined. The motive for his killing remains a mystery. The *Vindicator* reported that, "The Munsene murder had a quieting effect" on the efforts to reopen the inn.

By mid-June the inn was back in business. There was no official word of its reopening; instead notification was strictly by word of mouth. At first it had been rumored that the inn would only be offering bingo, "adding other games gradually, and consequently with less fanfare." In reporting the reopening, however, the *Vindicator* stated:

> "More than 450 people, most of them women, crowded into the large game room Saturday night to play various games of chance.
> "Besides the crap table and other gambling paraphernalia, the club… boasted two long rows of slot machines arranged in much the same manner as they were in the old days."

On May 10, 1942 the newspaper published a descriptive article by an unnamed reporter who spent an evening at the Jungle Inn. The article was introduced with an editor's note stating: *Jungle Inn, notorious gambling resort on Applegate Road, has been a stumbling block in law enforcement in the Mahoning Valley for several years. Almost every effort to clean up the city or Mahoning County has been characterized by some groups as a move to throw business to 'the Jungle Inn crowd.' With an extensive investigation of crime and rackets impending here,² it seemed appropriate to send a reporter to find what Jungle Inn was doing.*

The anonymous *Vindicator* reporter wrote:

When I arrived at the Jungle Inn about 9:45 p. m. Friday, I found more than 1,000 persons from 16 to 75 years of age in the place, and all but a few were either playing bingo, chuck-a-luck, craps, five-card stud poker, or the slot machines.

At least 650 were seated at the bingo tables with from one to five bingo cards in front of them. At the time I went into the gambling hall, the 12th game of the 16-game bingo party was in progress. When the 15th game was completed, the announcer on the loud-speaker system declared a recess.

As he made this announcement, the bingo players dashed en masse to the chuck-a-luck tables and the slot machines. Within a few minutes every machine was being played and at some of the machines (the five-cent and dime variety) the patrons were lined up three and five deep awaiting their turn to play.

The same was true at the chuck-a-luck tables, with many of the patrons failing to get a chance to play before the final bingo game was called. The prize in the last bingo game was $150.

After the bingo was over, about 700 of the 1,000 patrons left the place, while the others went to the other methods of gambling.

In the crowd of bingo players were a number of teen-age boys and girls who looked like seniors in high school. Others in the crowd were aged people who probably came to blow their pension checks.

Off hand I would say that 60 per cent of the patrons were women or girls, many of them accompanied by male escorts.

I noticed, too, that most of the players of the chuck-a-luck games and the slot machines were women, while the majority of the poker and crap players were men. At one of the crap tables, I noticed a woman with a wad of money that was big enough to choke a horse and each time she bet $5. At one time I saw her win about $80.

The least amount that could be bet at the crap tables was $1 while the minimum in the chuck-a-luck games was 10 cents. The sky was the limit at the poker tables, apparently, although I never saw anybody bet more than a dollar at a time. Most of the opening bets were five cents.

The price of the bingo was a dollar for 16 games and then 10 cents for each extra card in the final game.

During the final bingo game, the man running the affair made an announcement that bank night was held every Tuesday, Thursday and Saturday nights. He also announced that the three persons whose names were drawn out Thursday night were not present and failed to win the money. The first prize award Thursday, he said, was $1,200.

Saturday night's bingo prizes, he announced, would be two $500 awards and a third of $300.

In inspecting the gambling hall, which is a huge building at the rear of the night club, I found there was only one entrance, at the back. All the bingo players had to pass the long rows of slot machines when they entered the building. There was no separate entrance to that part of the building where the bingo tables were located.

On the walls in back of the chuck-a-luck tables were huge boards on which the results of the Friday races at the country's major horse racing tracks were posted. The boards were complete in information on the names of the horses, jockeys, scratches, time of race and the mutuals (sic).

By actual count, there were 60 slot machines, two of which were of the 50-cent type, seventeen 25-centers, eighteen 10-centers and 23 five-centers. There were two huge crap tables, four chuck-a-luck tables and two poker tables with a seating capacity of eight players and the dealer.

In the parking lot at the rear of the gambling hall, I counted over 400 automobiles and in addition there were about 200 more scattered around the place. Most of the cars had license numbers issued in Mahoning and Trumbull counties, with the majority of them from Mahoning. Others had plates from Columbiana and Ashtabula counties. About one-third of the cars were from Pennsylvania.

In the crowd I saw several people from Salem, East Liverpool, and Alliance, indicating that the inn has a wide drawing power.

During the summer of 1942 the *Vindicator* reported a cheating incident involving the Jungle Inn's horserace betting. A "trusted" employee of the inn, who was responsible for calling the horse races, decided to do a little side business with an accomplice. The race caller, who received his information over the wire and in turn relayed it to the Jungle Inn bettors, would delay his call for a few seconds. This would give him time to provide secret hand signals to his partner, thus allowing him to place a bet after the race had been completed, but before the winner was announced.

The newspaper pointed out, "a lucky streak is one thing, but winning too regularly is another." While it was not reported how the Jungle Inn operators broke up the betting scheme, it was stated that the two cheaters were spared a death sentence – once the $3,000 they won was repaid.

◆　　◆　　◆

During the early 1940s the Arrow Club, located on Pettibone Road in Geauga County just across the Cuyahoga County line, was the most notorious gambling club in the Cleveland area since the highly publicized closing of the Harvard Club by famed "Untouchable" lawman Eliot Ness back in 1936. Reputedly corrupt Geauga County officials, Sheriff Stuart Harland and Prosecutor Harold K. Bostwick, were the reason for the Arrow Club's continued existence. The gambling club was an operation of the Cleveland Syndicate – Moe Dalitz, Morris Kleinman, Lou Rothkopf and Sammy Tucker. In addition, Cleveland Irish mobster Thomas "Tommy" McGinty had a role in both the Arrow Club and the soon-to-be-popular Mounds Club in Lake County.

Ohio Governor John W. Bricker received numerous complaints about the Arrow Club, just as he had about the Jungle Inn. The governor was a firm believer in leaving local law enforcement in the hands of local law officials and was reluctant to take action. With America's involvement in World War II and the advent of tire rationing, however, trips to the Geauga County gambling palace were being called wasteful to the nation's resources. The Cleveland Press shamed the patrons of the Arrow Club by recording the license numbers and then printing the owner's names and addresses in the newspaper.

Joining the fight were the Office of Price Administration (OPA) and the Office of Defense Transportation (ODT). The two departments issued a joint statement declaring, "A man may have the title to his tires, but they are no longer his for unrestricted use. He is holding them in trust for the national welfare, and it is his duty to make them last as long as possible." The OPA and the ODT asked local police departments to report cases of "rubber-wasting" to the office in order that the future benefits from tire rationing could be withheld from these offenders.

The governor used the "rubber wasting" to his benefit. He claimed, "Tires are being consumed that ought to be used in the war effort and money is being gambled away that ought to be used to purchase Defense Bonds." Bricker took action against the Arrow Club on October 5, 1942 sending letters to Sheriff Harland and Prosecutor Bostwick with the following message:

> "If you do not take steps to see that the Arrow Club and any similar operation in your county are closed immediately, I shall on [October 10] instruct the attorney general to proceed in this matter and to take such steps as may be necessary to enforce the law in your county."

Gamblers, worried that they were jeopardizing their opportunity to purchase tires in the future, stayed away from the Arrow Club in droves. This made it an easy decision for the Cleveland Syndicate to close the club on the date ordered by Bricker, without the sheriff having to worry about enforcing the governor's decree. The club would remain closed for the duration of the war, before reopening in 1946 as the Pettibone Club.

On October 6 a *Vindicator* editorial pointed out that Cleveland / Cuyahoga County officials couldn't close the Arrow Club because it was over the county line, "but the governor could." The editorial stated that the Jungle Inn was just across the Mahoning County line in Trumbull County, making it impossible for local officials to close it and allowing Youngstown residents to continue to be fleeced nightly. The newspaper seemed to relay only concern for Youngstown, blaming Trumbull County for the problem. The editorial urged Bricker to now address the Jungle Inn stating:

> "With the Arrow Club closing, Jungle Inn is going to attract some of the gamblers and racketeers who frequented the Geauga County casino. There is no other gambling spot to match the Inn between Cleveland and Pittsburgh. If conditions have been bad in the past, they will get worse as the gambling crowd migrates to a casino just north of Youngstown.
>
> "The wide-open Arrow Club showed the breakdown of local law enforcement. Governor Bricker's action showed the remedy. But it will solve nothing if the racketeers simply move down here. Youngstown will be the sufferer. If Mr. Bricker is given the sorry facts on the flow of war workers' checks into gamblers' pockets at Jungle Inn, he cannot overlook Trumbull County's plague spot."

Ironically, the first person to come to the defense of the Jungle Inn was Sheriff Russell Stein, the man who once ordered the club to close before he was even sheriff. He stated it was wrong for the *Vindicator* to compare the Jungle Inn with the Arrow Club. Stein claimed that the Geauga casino drew crowds of nearly 2,000 nightly, while the Jungle Inn "usually entertains between 400 and 500 on week nights and between 600 and 800 persons on Saturday nights." The sheriff added that there were a multitude of complaints from residents about the Arrow Club, but he claimed he had "received no complaints" about the Applegate Road casino. Stein failed to address the *Vindicator's* concerns that the now 2,000 casino-less patrons would soon be invading the Mahoning Valley to suppress their gambling appetite.

On October 9, 1942 the *Vindicator* responded to Sheriff Stein's comments with a stinging rebuke:

> "The weakest statement of public policy heard here in many a day is Sheriff Stein's explanation that the Jungle Club's gambling joint north of Youngstown is not in the same class with the Arrow Club near Cleveland, because it entertains 400 to 800 persons while the Arrow outfit attracts 2,000, and because the Jungle Club runs a nice, quiet place with no disorders.

"Sheriff Stein might as well say that if a man steals $2,000 he should be jailed, but if he steals only $400 to $800 it's all right. He might as well say that if you commit a nice, quiet, efficient murder with no outcry or disturbance, it's different from a noisy, messy kind of murder.

"The law is the law, whether it is violated 2,000 times a night or only 400, whether it is broken in genteel or rowdy fashion. Ohio law is the same in Trumbull County as in Geauga. There is now the added consideration that America is at war and can afford no use of rubber which does not help to sustain either the war effort or the civilian structure which must be kept up behind the war effort.

"Courtney Riley Cooper, in his expose of government-racket combinations after his experience in the FBI, wrote that wherever there were open, organized, commercial rackets, there were crooked connections with government, involving a pay-off. Sheriff Stein lays his office open to suspicion by his lame defense of the Jungle joint."

The war of words subsided on Sunday, October 19, 1942 when Jungle Inn patrons arrived at the club to find a sign hanging on the door stating, "Closed for the Duration." The previous night an official at the club told patrons shortly before the last game of bingo that the closing "was our contribution towards winning the war. We hope it will help" It was reported that business at the casino had been down for the past few months and now with the advent of gasoline and tire rationing more patrons were expected to stay away. The club's operators made the closing of the casino sound patriotic, but few doubted that Bricker's recent order to close the Arrow Club, and the *Vindicator*'s urging of the governor to do the same with the Jungle Inn, were the driving influences behind the casino's sudden gambling hiatus.

After the war there was evidence the Jungle Inn served as a sort of headquarters for Valley mobsters and that members of Detroit's infamous Licavoli Gang had arrived to organize and take charge of local gambling operations. The early months of 1945 had seen the murder of Cleveland's slot machine czar, Nate Weisenberg on February 24, followed by the disappearance of Youngstown's Jerry Pascarella, another slot machine operator, two months later. Even though the gambling den didn't reopen for business for another two years, some believe the plot to murder Pascarella was concocted behind the Jungle Inn's doors. James Licavoli was a prime suspect in both incidents.

The Post-War Boom

The Jungle Inn remained in hibernation for over four and a half years. Nothing was heard about the casino from the night it closed, October 18, 1942, until June 23, 1947, when the *Vindicator* suddenly announced the Jungle Inn was running "wild." The return of the gambling den caused a flurry of newspaper articles. The next day the *Vindicator* reported, "Gambling of all types now is flourishing at the 'hot spot' on a scale seldom approached before the war."

The newspaper ran into a brick wall when it tried to question Trumbull County officials regarding the wide-open activities on Applegate Road. County Prosecutor Paul J. Reagen was reportedly "out of town to reporters," while acting sheriff Earl J. Bash declared, "We have no reports on Jungle Inn and no action is contemplated at the present time." Bash was filling in for Trumbull County Sheriff Ralph R. Millikin, who was recovering from a heart attack. The sheriff took ill in the early spring, spent seven weeks in Phoenix, Arizona convalescing, and had returned home just a week before the new hoopla began.

In the rash of new stories it was reported that "a new gang of operators" had taken over and spent $75,000 to remodel the inn. The new additions included:

> - A light brown veneer paneling covering the walls, ceilings and pillars
> - Fluorescent lights in the latest style illuminating the spacious 30,000-square-foot gambling section
> - Handsome leather chairs and poker tables
> - New bingo accommodations, and an arrangement of comfortable benches and long, shelf-like desks with troughs to hold the cards and markers
> - Large red and black blocks of linoleum covering the floor

In the confines of this modernized pleasure palace, the slot machines were pulling in coins at a record rate, the afternoon action of horseracing was bustling, bingo catered to the early evening "family" crowd, and when the late gamblers "flooded" in from Youngstown, chuck-a-luck, craps and high-stakes poker games awaited them. The inn promoted their free taxicab service to and from Youngstown and other places; the new management was hoping that by the time the patron was ready to head home it would be without enough money to pay the fare. Mayor Charles Sedore operated the bar concession at the Jungle nightclub. When the casino closed in October 1942, Sedore began operating the Hickory Grill on South Phelps Street in Youngstown. When the inn reopened in 1947, Sedore offered free taxi service to Halls Corners from the Hickory Grill.

The *Vindicator* was quick to attack in an editorial comment. On June 24 the newspaper placed the blame on the sheriff and county prosecutor with the following caustic comment: "Such places can't operate long without a two-way fix – county and state. The local fix has seldom been hard to arrange in Trumbull County. Is there now a state fix with someone in the liquor department, or are the promoters making a test to see what they can get away with under the new administration?" This latter comment was seen as a shot at Governor Thomas J. Herbert's recent statement that local law enforcement was up to the counties. The latest stories also confirmed rumors that John and Mike Farah had "resumed" their positions as operators of the casino.

When reporters were finally able to get a comment out of Sheriff Millikin he stated, "I know nothing about gambling at Jungle Inn. It is a job for local enforcement officers." He said there would be no investigation by his office, unless requested to do so by Halls Corners' officials. To this, a new *Vindicator* editorial replied:

> "So now the circle of buck-passing is complete. Governor Herbert says law enforcement is up to counties. Sheriff Millikin says it's up to local officials of Halls Corners. The local officials of Halls Corners are Jungle Inners, and Halls Corners is really Jungle Inn."

Having heard from the sheriff, reporters were still trying to chase down a comment from Paul Reagen. By mid-July, four weeks after the reported re-opening, the prosecutor had still not been heard from. On July 24 Reagen was recuperating at his Girard home after being released from University Hospital in Cleveland, where he was being treated for a "hay fever-asthma ailment" he had suffered while on vacation. He issued the following statement:

> "Arrests in this county are the job of peace officers. I have always diligently prosecuted cases brought to me and will do so in the future. The cases include a lot of Youngstown thugs who have received sentences to long prison terms but the Vindicator has not given me credit for diligent prosecution."

What made the positions of both the sheriff and the prosecutor so laughable was that Halls Corners had no peace officers, no police, and no constables!

Curious as to whom the prosecutor was referring to when he mentioned the "peace officers," reporters called Reagen at home. The angry prosecutor responded, "You have my statement, I don't want to say any more about it. I'm ill at home and I don't want to be bothered any more about this."

Responding to the prosecutor's comments, the *Vindicator* unleashed its most scathing editorial to date on the matter:

> "Trumbull County Prosecutor Paul J. Reagen puts off The Vindicator's query about what he intends to do about gambling at Jungle Inn with the remark that he is sick at home and doesn't 'want to be bothered about Jungle Inn.'
>
> "Jungle Inn is one of the most notorious gambling dens in Ohio, ... owned by vicious Cleveland racketeers. Evidently they have political pull in Trumbull County or they would not be allowed to run. What their connection with Mr. Reagen is, only he can say. He is responsible for their being in his county. His excuse that law enforcement in Halls Corners, where Jungle Inn is located, is up to local officials won't stand up. He knows that Halls Corners is a fake village and that every voter who lives there is a Jungle Inn employee.
>
> "If 'Mayor' Charles Sedore and his officers don't close up Jungle Inn, then it is up to county officials. Sheriff Ralph Millikin, who has been away for an extended period because of illness, has now returned. Mr. Reagen has used his absence as an excuse for inaction. If Mr. Millikin does not act, all that Mr. Reagen needs to do is to send in his detective – which he should have done long ago.
>
> "Since Mr. Reagen has failed to do this, Trumbull County voters have a right to ask why he violates his oath of office, and what interest he has in Jungle Inn that he allows it to keep open."

On September 7, the *Vindicator* changed its tactics. Switching to propaganda type methods, the newspaper called the Jungle Inn a "fire trap." The newspaper attacked the gambling joint for not having adequate fire safety in mind. Describing the inn as a "dried out, wooden structure," the article noted, "No smoking signs are posted about the inn, but no one enforces the rule and smoking continues. Fire extinguishers required for this type of establishment could not be found." The newspaper also pointed out that screen doors on two of the three exits swung inward to open.

One week later the *Vindicator* printed a letter from an anonymous reader who profiled three women and how they fell prey to the gambling bug at the Jungle Inn. One woman had collected several thousand dollars from an accident and then lost it all at the poker table. Another, a mother of young children, neglected her family while losing hundreds of dollars at the casino.

The next week another anonymous reader, in a letter to the *Vindicator* titled, "Tells of 'Odd Circumstances' In Jungle's Bingo Operation," hinted that cheating was going on regularly at the inn during bingo games, which featured large pots.

During the early morning hours of September 29 armed gunmen pulled a daring robbery at the Mounds Club in Lake County. The infamous robbery of Tommy McGinty's gambling palace was rumored to have netted the participants between $250,000 and $500,000. Just days after the robbery the *Vindicator* spit out another editorial defending their attacks on the Jungle Inn. In the editorial the newspaper declared, "Trumbull County is conspicuously lacking in public spirited citizens." The editorial went on to suggest who was behind the gambling operations at the inn:

> "Jungle Inn is reputed to be controlled by Buffalo gangsters who upon threat of an underworld war, have lately cut in some of Youngstown's undesirables. Who are these men, and what is going on here beneath the surface while Youngstown also sleeps? Are there public officials among them? What bargain has been made to buy off the Youngstown gangsters who lately were complaining that Jungle Inn was taking away their business but now are strangely silent?"

By now it was no secret that the "Big Three" – Joe "the Wolf" DiCarlo, Jasper Joseph "Fats" Aiello and "Moosey" Caputo – were collecting tribute from the bookmaking fraternity in the Mahoning Valley. While both Aiello and Caputo had earlier ties to the Jungle Inn, there was no clear-cut connection between Buffalo mobster DiCarlo and the casino.

Two days later, citing the corruption that allowed the Mounds Club to operate unmolested, along with Governor Herbert's lack of interest in the matter, a new editorial asked:

> "Who gets the protection money in Trumbull County? Why is law enforcement in Trumbull County in a perpetual state of breakdown? And what is the alliance between rackets and public officials in Trumbull, Mahoning and Cuyahoga Counties?"

In August 1947 Steve Paparodis, a 23 year-old veteran, who served 19 months in the Pacific Theatre during World War II with the US Navy, purchased the Jungle Inn Nite Club, the restaurant section, for $20,000 from John Yavorsky and Walter Petrosky. Handling the legal work for the young man was attorney, and future judge, James A. Ravella. The money to purchase the nightclub, and install a new dining room that could seat up to 250 customers, was borrowed from family members.

During the fall of the 1947 agents of the Ohio State Liquor Control Board began an investigation of the Jungle Inn, focusing on the building where Paparodis operated his bar / restaurant where liquor was served, the only area where the board had jurisdiction. One of the agents, who visited the bar on Sunday, September 28, filed a report stating that gambling was being conducted "in a building only a few feet away" from the bar area. Paparodis was cited for operating a liquor establishment where gambling was conducted "in, or about" the premises.

A hearing was scheduled in Cleveland on November 7 before members of the State Liquor Board to determine if the liquor permit issued to Paparodis should be revoked. The hearing got underway with Attorney Fred Garmone, representing Paparodis, and Assistant Attorney General Charles G. Schnur representing the State of Ohio. Both sides quickly realized that due to the number of witnesses and testimony to be heard that the allotted time for the hearing would not be sufficient. The case was rescheduled for December 2 in Columbus. When the hearing reconvened a state liquor agent testified how the entrance to both the casino and the bar were reached through a common driveway. One of the key factors board members would consider in making their decision was that this common driveway and the parking lot served the gambling den and the tavern. The agent described the scene at the Jungle Inn from his September 28 visit, testifying he saw between 400 and 500 automobiles in the rear parking lot of the establishment. Once inside people were "lined four deep in front of a battery of 82 slot machines and that bingo games, black jack tables and chuck-a-luck devices, as well as other games of chance were underway." The agent estimated that 1,500 patrons were in the large, one story frame building that housed the games.

The State's contention was that Paparodis profited by having the casino located "six to eight feet" behind his tavern. Garmone's argument was that after Paparodis officially took over the bar / restaurant on August 7, the State issued him an additional permit in September authorizing a 2:30 a.m. closing time. Therefore, the liquor department had in effect approved of the conditions under which the bar operated.

Subpoenaed to appear was Halls Corners' Mayor Charles Sedore. While it was reported he was in the hearing room earlier, when his name was called to testify he had disappeared.

In closing statements Schnur declared, "It is high time that we serve notice upon the people of northern Ohio that this board will not tolerate this type of operation. If the authorities of that county and that village fail to accept responsibility for suppressing gambling, the board should act to ban sales of liquor in proximity to gambling joints."

Garmone urged the board "to protect this boy in a business that was given to him by the state of Ohio" He pleaded that even if there were "violations in proximity to his place, don't make a guinea pig of him."

The hearing was completed that afternoon. On the morning of December 4 the State Liquor Board announced its decision to revoke the beer, wine and liquor permits granted to Paparodis.

Despite the loss of the liquor license, the Jungle Inn's operators established a "lushly" decorated private bar on the second floor of the building housing the restaurant for the "inner circle" of the casino's elite gamblers. The carpeted area had a small bar with wicker stools, comfortable lounge chairs, a television and a radio. In the corner was a horserace ticker.

On January 19, 1948 the Jungle Inn received more negative publicity after a patron claimed four casino employees "gave me the beating of my life," after he had a lucky streak at the dice table. John Hurley of Sharon, Pennsylvania stated, "Within a few minutes after I arrived at the place I had won between $50 and $60 and then decided to plunge with a $20 bet on aces turning up. The woman chucked the dice and up came the aces and out I went because I protested their refusal to pay off. They told me they didn't accept bets as high as $20 on aces.

"Only one of those big fellows would have been enough to handle me, but four, oh, I can still feel their blows. Hadn't I been in good physical shape as the result of service in the navy during the recent war I know I couldn't have stood it."

After the beating, Hurley claimed he crawled from the spot where he was left, managing his way to the Youngstown-Hubbard Road, where he got on a bus headed for Sharon. A week after the incident was reported in the newspapers, the 25 year-old Hurley was thrown in a Sharon jail after his wife filed charges against him for desertion and non-support.

In late January 1948 Judge George Birrell launched a grand jury investigation into law enforcement in the county. On Monday morning, January 26 sheriff's deputies issued subpoenas to 23 people to appear that same afternoon. Called to appear were all the mayors, police chiefs and marshals of cities and villages throughout Trumbull County, including County Sheriff Ralph Millikin, Warren Mayor Henry C. Wagner and Halls Corners' Mayor Charles Sedore. The grand jury was under the supervision of County Prosecutor Paul Reagen.

In anticipation of the probe, Jungle Inn management had all the slot machines and gambling equipment removed from the Applegate Road casino, leaving only the bingo tables behind.

The first person questioned by the grand jury was James Maxwell who published "The Lowdown on Warren," a pamphlet highly critical of Mayor Wagner, just prior to the November 1947 election. In his attack he called Warren, "Little Chicago," because of the crime and corruption.

After just an afternoon of questioning, some say a little as two to three hours, the grand jury announced it had completed its investigation. A few of the men called were questioned for thirty minutes; the majority were before the grand jury for less than ten minutes. Mayor Sedore was reported to be vacationing in Florida. In the grand jury's report to Judge Birrell, they stated:

> "In the course of our investigation, we subpoenaed the mayors and chiefs of police of every incorporated city and village, and the county sheriff.
>
> "We, the members of this jury, find that the primary obligation of the suppression and elimination of these evils rests with the peace officers of the county and the municipalities therein. Progress will be made in combating these social problems only through the vigorous and combined efforts of arresting officers. We have impressed the sheriffs, mayors and the heads of the police departments with their important duties and have received positive assurances that places in which gambling and vice exist will be closed forthwith."

The grand jury also commented about the *Vindicator's* attacks on County Prosecutor Paul Reagen, calling the statements "unwarranted and absolutely false."

A week before the grand jury heard testimony, the *Vindicator* thanked Judge Birrell in an editorial, praising his actions and pledging Youngstown's "hearty cooperation." Once the grand jury's report was released the *Vindicator* called it "The Trumbull Whitewash" and attacked Reagen for its failure:

> "Mr. Reagen arranged a parade of mayors and law-enforcement officers; after hearing them for two or three hours the jury made a report concerned with clearing the prosecutor's skirts rather than attacking the evils to which the judge had directed its attention."

The grand jury investigation caused some concern for gamblers around the county. Warren Police Captain John O. Heinlein, head of the city's newly established vice department, claimed that everything in the city was closed down. This did not include, however, private clubs over which the authorities had no jurisdiction. By Thursday night, January 29, the Jungle Inn's gambling den was dark. Inn run bingo games had been halted and taxi service cancelled. Only the non-alcohol-serving restaurant was operating. Carloads of gamblers arrived to find the inn closed.

Until mid-March 1948 the only activity taking place at the Halls Corners den of infamy was bingo, sponsored by the Blue Star Mothers of Niles,

Ohio. But the operators had other plans for the Jungle Inn. Soon post cards were mailed to former patrons announcing the grand opening of the Army-Navy Union Garrison Post 504, of Halls Corners – a private club.

On Saturday night, March 13, Garrison Post 504 was open for business. The Warren *Tribune Chronicle* reported that "1,500 eager patrons… spent the evening playing bingo. No other gambling was seen in the place." The *Vindicator* reported, "The same old hands were calling off the bingo [numbers], the same old faces were selling the cards and the Farah brothers…were watching the proceedings as usual."

The building housing the restaurant was open, still managed by Steve Paparodis. The only thing missing was the big circular bar. This area of the club had been "paneled off" for exclusive use, in which membership in Garrison Post 504 was required for admittance. The newspaper claimed, "Because of the fact that it was virtually impossible to learn who the officers of the organization are, the requirements for membership are strictly secret."

Two weeks after the opening of Army-Navy Union Post 504, legitimate chapters in Warren and Youngstown began to protest. The commander of Warren Post 283 issued a statement disavowing any connection with the Jungle Inn. He also declared that he had mailed an official protest to the national headquarters of the Army-Navy Union complaining about the lax control in issuing charters. The Jungle Inn was able to obtain their charter by claiming to represent the war veterans of Halls Corners. Members of both posts were concerned about the bad image they would receive for the perception that they were some how associated with the infamous gambling joint. To make matters worse, the Jungle Inn operators had installed bright electric lights, one on the casino and one on a sign at Applegate and Hubbard Roads, reading "Army-Navy Garrison No. 504."

During the ensuing months Garrison Post 504, in name and activities, reverted back to the old Jungle Inn days. Crowds of up to 2,000 patrons appeared nightly to play poker, roulette, chuck-a-luck and other games and to feed the more than 80 slot machines on the premises. A majority of the people still played bingo. An insight into the goings on was provided by a *Vindicator* report:

> "Chief attractions at Jungle Inn still are bingo and the 80 odd slot machines which line the walls. Horse racing is the main afternoon feature at the spot, with the big 'run-down boards' indicating that bets are accepted for all the leading tracks.
>
> "Two poker tables continue to keep 22 card 'sharks' interested, and the chuck-a-luck, crap and dice games retain their specialized patrons. The roulette wheel is drawing more fans than in the past, however, as

district gamblers get used to such fancy devices.

"As usual, the crowd ranged from the very young to the very old, but the chief 'customer' of the Jungle still seems to be the motherly appearing middle-aged woman. The young gamblers were there in spite of signs warning: 'No minors allowed.'

"The bingo crowds come in the free taxis provided by the gambling spot's management, or in thousands of automobiles parked in the spacious lots around the place. Many of the cars bear Pennsylvania licenses."

Through the spring and summer of 1948 Garrison 504, aka the Jungle Inn, continued to flourish, unmolested by law enforcement. The fact that the casino was unable to offer alcoholic beverages to its patrons never seemed to keep the players from coming in droves. The *Vindicator* kept an eye on its nemesis to the north, reporting on everything from thunderstorms that knocked out the electricity to the addition of 20 "shiny new" slot machines. The newspaper never failed to get in a dig when it could. In one article the newspaper referred to the Jungle Inn as "the notorious fire trap north of Youngstown." With much of the club's clientele still made up of middle-aged housewives, management continued to come up with ideas to keep them coming. They started a "Queen for a Day" contest, giving away free refrigerators. The newspaper quipped, "an armed guard concealed over the door in a sort of turret device probably wouldn't hesitate to fire upon these same housewives if there was any attempt to walk off with club funds."

During this time a partnership was formed known as the Jungle Novelty Company. The purpose was to operate a gambling casino called the Jungle Inn. The partners of record were John and Shamis Farah; Ralph and Tessie Coletto; Edward F. and Catherine Tobin; and Anthony Delsanter.

By many accounts the Jungle Inn ran a reputable operation, despite strong commentary to the contrary by the *Vindicator*. This was no clip joint. Following the philosophies of New York City crime bosses Frank Costello and Meyer Lansky, the men operating the Jungle Inn knew the two basic results of running a crooked casino. One, that it would only yield temporary dividends, and two, word of a fixed game spreads like wild fire. Lansky biographer Robert Lacey pointed out the pitfalls of a rigged game in *Little Man: Meyer Lansky and the Gangster Life*, "A crap game or a casino can be dead in a matter of hours, and once dead, it stays dead." The real gamblers knew that the odds were always with the house, there was no need to cheat honest patrons. In the Jungle Inn's case, even though the bingo games lost money for the operators they still gave away a large home appliance, from the Farah's own place of business, each night as a prize. Patrons without transportation were brought to and from the club by taxi, free of charge. Any big winners, especially the women, were offered escorts to their homes at the end of the night. On more than one occasion John Farah paid the wives of degenerate gamblers from his own pocket when informed their husbands had lost their weekly paychecks gambling at the casino.

Enter Eddie Allen

Keeping an eye on the happenings at the Jungle Inn was newly appointed Youngstown Police Chief Edward J. Allen. The former Erie, Pennsylvania police officer was hired to clean up Youngstown after the November 1947 election of Charles P. Henderson as mayor. Allen, who had been recommended for the position by FBI Director J. Edgar Hoover, was the perfect law enforcement official to carry out Henderson's promise to "Smash Racket's Rule."

Allen was sure that the underworld element that ran the Jungle Inn was involved in other criminal activity in Youngstown. He was looking for a way to tie the two together. Two incidents gave Allen his opportunity. The first occurred when the Jungle Inn operators approached a Youngstown police patrolman to work as a security guard at the gambling casino. Allen refused to name the officer and the only information he would release was that the patrolman was asked to work on his time off and one of his duties would be to saw down shotguns.

The second incident involved the robbery of the Green Acres casino in Struthers, Ohio on September 17, 1948. During the early hours of the morning five masked gunmen entered the club, in which Joe DiCarlo was alleged to have been at, and robbed the tables and customers of anywhere from $8,000 to $30,000, depending on which account you read. It was rumored that a ring worth $2,000 was taken from DiCarlo. As the robbers fled someone fired at them, wounding at least one seriously.

Several hours later Julius Petro checked into a Cleveland hospital with a bullet wound. Petro had a long criminal record in Cleveland and was suspected of being one of the holdup men in the Mounds Club robbery. Police from Struthers and Cleveland wanted to see if the bullet in Petro's body matched ones fired at the Green Acres casino; however, Petro would not allow the bullet to be removed. On the day he was released from the hospital one of his associates, Sam Jerry Monachino was shot to death and found in the gutter outside his home. Police recovered two .38 Smith & Wesson revolvers after the murder.

The investigation into Monachino's murder revealed that one of the revolvers was traced from the Smith & Wesson Company factory, to Sandusky and then to Youngstown, where it was purchased by Robert Hildebrand, a former gun shop employee from Lowellville who purchased it in August 1947 from a local gun dealer. Hildebrand then sold the weapon to Raymond S. "Legs" Mashorda, a Youngstown resident who was a card dealer at the Jungle Inn. When Chief Allen questioned Mashorda, he stated that he gave the revolver away, but he refused to say to whom, claiming if he did he "would be signing his own death warrant."

Hildebrand and Mashorda was questioned about the Monachino murder by Cleveland police and released. On October 15 Youngstown police arrested them. Hildebrand admitted to Allen that he had purchased 10 to 12 weapons and sold them to Mashorda, each for a $5 profit. Mashorda said he in turn sold them to his employers without realizing any profit. Mashorda claimed he had no idea why they wanted the weapons. The next day the two men were taken before Youngstown Municipal Judge John J. Buckley. Hildebrand pled guilty to unlawful sale of firearms and Mashorda to unlawful purchase of a firearm. Each was fined $200, with $150 suspended. No jail time was given. A few days later, Howard Trigg, owner of the Gun, Lock & Key Shop on East Boardman Street, which had once employed Hildebrand, was arrested for unlawful sale of a weapon. The charge was for selling a .38 revolver to Hildebrand without a police permit, just three days after he had been fined in court. Trigg told Allen that he sawed down and sold two shotguns to Mashorda.

These incidents led Chief Allen to request a sit-down with Sheriff Millikin. Allen traveled to Warren with his vice squad chief, Sergeant Dan Maggianetti. When they arrived Sheriff Millikin and his sidekick Chief Deputy Earl Bash met them, but refused to allow Maggianetti into the meeting.

In requesting Millikin to close the Jungle Inn, Chief Allen relayed the story of the gun used in the Monachino murder being traced to the Jungle Inn card dealer. "I asked Sheriff Millikin to close down the Jungle Inn as a crime prevention measure because my investigations have led me to believe that the establishment is now hiring dangerous individuals," Allen stated.

The sheriff refused Allen's request without elaborating, stating only that he would not consent to anything without warrants for specific individuals. Allen quoted Deputy Earl Bash as saying, "There is something political about this. You know the sheriff is running for re-election." As he was about to leave, Allen asked Bash to repeat his comments in the presence of Maggianetti. Bash refused and ordered the two men to leave. Allen revealed the details of his meeting with Millikin to the *Vindicator* two days later. The newspaper quickly contacted the Trumbull County sheriff to get his side of the story. Millikin's response was, "No comment." When the reporter pressed the sheriff, he replied, "You can talk all day but I still have no comment." When the reporter brought up the murder of Monachino, Millikin asked, "Why don't the Cleveland police come down here then?" Ironically, in a political advertisement, which appeared in the *Vindicator* on October 28, the sheriff proclaimed he had "closed the Jungle Inn."

Due to the remark about the upcoming elections Allen held off contacting the sheriff again. Allen also waited so his attempts wouldn't be construed locally as a political move, which the chief seemed to be accused of constantly by his detractors no matter what time of year it was. After Election Day the chief sent a letter to Millikin stating his concerns and seeking a joint effort to handle the problems. The sheriff never replied.

Allen promised to take action against the Jungle Inn. "The hoodlums who frequent the gambling dives are a menace to Youngstown," Allen stated. "People over in Warren are too far away to be affected by inn activities, but many of the men who work out there live here in Youngstown." Allen checked with his law department to determine what state statutes, if any, would allow him to seek "recourse" against the Jungle Inn. Allen's efforts were rebuked by Youngstown City Council, with one councilman advising, "Stay on your own dunghill, chief, and give Youngstown the benefit of your great talents."

The *Vindicator* was in full support of Allen's efforts and in their latest editorial put in print what everyone else suspected: "the people who own the Jungle Inn also own the sheriff's office in Trumbull County."

The night after Allen's comments were made public, reporters paid a visit to the Jungle Inn only to find the 80-plus slot machines[3] had been removed; only four remained in the building housing the restaurant. This was due to the fact that when law enforcement officials raid gambling joints and break up the equipment, the slot machines are the most expensive to replace. The Jungle Inn operators obviously took Allen's remarks about raiding the casino seriously. A taxicab driver who made runs from Youngstown to the inn reported that as soon as the *Vindicator*, which reported Allen's comments, reached Halls Corners, the staff began removing the machines. Despite nearly 2,000 people on hand to play bingo, poker and patronize the chuck-a-luck wheels and dice and roulette tables, a report claimed others stayed away in droves, concerned that Chief Allen might decide to conduct a raid. Patrons that night also noticed increased security at the doors.

On October 21 Chief Allen exercised one of his "recourses" and had the Ohio Bell Telephone Company cut off phone service to the Jungle Inn. The telephone, in the name of Halls Corners' Mayor Charles Sedore, was used in connection with gathering horse race results. The lines actually went into the Sedore's Hubbard Road home, from where operators of the casino rigged the wires, extending them to the Jungle Inn horseracing room. "You call the Sedore number and get the odds and instructions on how to place a bet," Allen told reporters. That night there was a different atmosphere in the club with the door drawing more security and guards watching the patrons carefully. It was obvious that both Allen and the *Vindicator* were getting all their information about the operations of the Jungle Inn from reporters and undercover police entering the casino as patrons.

The loss of telephone service prevented phone-in wagers from small-time bookies and bettors, from nearby towns in Ohio and Pennsylvania, as well as the elimination of regular phone service from the two buildings. Allen was still trying to get Western Union to cut the wire service to the Jungle Inn, which provided the actual horserace results from the tracks. The day after the telephones went dead, afternoon attendance at the casino, during peak horseracing hours, swelled as bettors arrived to place their wagers directly at the inn. By Thursday night, convinced that the threat of an Allen raid was over, patrons returned and the parking lot was again full for the evening bingo sessions.

Not long after the phone lines were disconnected a separate line was hooked up using the home of 23 year-old Halls Corners Councilman Louis McLain. Jungle Inn operator John Farah secured the assistance of McLain by giving him a deep freezer and a refrigerator from his Girard appliance store. McLain hauled garbage away from the Jungle Inn's restaurant, using the refuge to feed his pigs. When questioned by Chief Allen, McLain revealed that the telephone connection took place shortly after the other telephone was removed by Ohio Bell.

During his interview with the chief, McLain stated, "It's a lot of hooey at the council meetings, and they don't talk much about anything. I went to the meetings to get the $3 for each attendance, and I haven't got my money yet." McLain also explained that the new treasurer of Halls Corners, the 22 year-old nephew of Mayor Sedore, "gained his financial experience by working at the Jungle Inn as a parking lot attendant."

Allen's scrutiny of state laws uncovered a seldom-used statute that gave local police courts and municipal courts jurisdiction over "any misdemeanor" within four miles of the city or county line. On the surface it looked as if Chief Allen had the right to raid the Jungle Inn. The Youngstown law director, however, cast doubts and, since Allen was not about to get the support of city council, these plans were abandoned. With the threat of Allen crashing through the doors put on hold, the slot machines were soon back in action, at full force, at the inn.

The tenacious chief was not ready to give up the fight. In mid-November he announced, "We have made a couple of hits with our long range artillery and now since slot machines have returned to Jungle Inn, a D-Day operation would be effective." Paramount to the lawman's efforts was the cooperation of Western Union to discontinue wire (telegraph) service. By removing the service Allen figured it would bring an end to the estimated $50,000 a day the Jungle Inn was allegedly reaping from horseracing. At first Western Union wrote back advising Allen that they were taking immediate steps to close down the wire. A second letter then arrived on November 17 stating the action to cut service was going before the company's board of directors. In the end there was no indication that the company ever discontinued the service.

Allen had recently ordered his vice squad to raid Charles Sedore's Bridge Club, the former Hickory Grove, on South Phelps Street in Youngstown. Officers arrested four men in possession of football betting slips. Allen used the opportunity to call the Halls Corner chief executive in for a chat. Sedore agreed, but brought with him attorney Russell Mock. During the meeting, Allen asked the mayor for assistance in his efforts to close the Jungle Inn, reciting all the recent violations, especially the gun trafficking, calling it a hazard to law enforcement. Attorney Mock responded to Allen's efforts by telling Sedore, "Let's go," and the two men walked out of Allen's office.

In talking to reporters afterward Allen "hinted" that a raid was being planned. "It'll come when the gamblers least expect it," he promised.

By the end of November 1948 it appeared that Chief Allen's efforts to close the Jungle Inn had been held in check by the casino operators. But the battle was now being fought on a new front. The gambling joint decided it was going to open its bingo tables to attract the church crowds on Sunday afternoons. This put the Jungle Inn in direct competition with Our Lady of Mount Carmel in Niles, which had been running a Sunday bingo operation for the past five years – most recently from the Tri-Lan Dance Hall in McKinley Heights.

On November 28, the bingo caller for the church, aware of his new competition on Applegate Road, informed the afternoon crowd that the money collected by the church went into a building fund designated for the construction of a new school for the parish. He also mentioned that neither himself nor the 20 people assisting him received any compensation, it was strictly volunteer work.

It didn't take long for the religious community to react. The next Sunday, December 5, Dr. Roland A. Luhman, pastor of the First Reformed Church, delivered a fire and brimstone sermon aimed at the Jungle Inn. Luhman denounced the public's apathy toward gambling and racketeering, pointing out that the "lawlessness fostered by Jungle Inn's operations spreads from gambling to strong-arm attacks on woman and children and general corruption of a city."

The pastor told his congregation, "An evil such as Jungle Inn extends its influence bit by bit until it has a community so corrupted there is nothing we could do about it even if we wanted to.

"As long as vices are general, we think they don't affect us. However, an evil that affects any individual also affects a community as a whole. Unfortunately, we don't pay attention until it hits us personally.

"If any type of gambling becomes so professional that individuals are thrown on a community for support and it hits your pocketbook, then you begin to see evil."

Pastor Luhman chastised people who were "willing to swell the pocketbooks of gambling house proprietors who in turn use the money to build seashore mansions and buy expensive cars while the player takes a short walk over the hill to the poor house." He denounced the wasting of this money in gambling dens when there so many worthwhile causes "begging for funds."

Luhman declared, "We have to break our necks to get $10,000 for a cancer fund or $25,000 for crippled children's work. Yet the total of all the funds raised for worthy causes would not equal the sum taken in at Jungle Inn on a single night."

Aware of the negative publicity, the Jungle Inn announced it was canceling its Sunday matinee bingo games immediately. For the bingo players that showed up, "Hot dogs, complete with all the mustard you wanted, were passed out in huge quantities without charge, and the regular $1.50 dinner was offered for only 50 cents." Meanwhile, the patrons were urged to play the numerous slot machines until 7:00 p.m. when the regular night bingo games began.

Before the end of 1948 two more incidents would draw negative attention to the Jungle Inn. The first involved a doctor who was accused of bribing a Youngstown health department inspector to cover up an abortion case. The doctor apparently used the money he received from the illegal operation for a gambling addiction; he was an inveterate horserace bettor. In late November the doctor was robbed at gunpoint in his office. The suspect the police arrested turned out to be a Jungle Inn bookie. When the doctor refused to identify him, it raised speculation that perhaps it wasn't a robbery, but that the doctor owed the Jungle Inn money. Allen used the incident to reiterate, "All this points again to the fact that Jungle Inn harbors hoodlums responsible for crimes committed in Youngstown. As long as it is allowed to operate this sewer of septicity will continue to permeate Youngstown with its poison."

The second incident involved three young men from Columbiana County, all in their early-to-mid-twenties. The *Vindicator* claimed the names of "the boys" were withheld because one said, "We do not want to wind up as corpses out in the woods somewhere." Three days before Christmas 1948 they went to Sharon, Pennsylvania to visit friends. On the way back they planned on doing some Christmas shopping in Youngstown. While driving down Hubbard Road their attention was drawn to the numerous automobiles parked at the Jungle Inn. The men parked their car and went to see what all the excitement was about.

Impressed with the hustle and activity of the casino the men decided to try their luck at the slot machines. At two successive quarter-machines the men won jackpots. When they looked closer at their winnings, however, they realized they had more lead slugs than quarters. They brought this to the attention of one of the employees at the dice tables, asking for money for the worthless slugs. The men were scoffed at and told only "not to use the slugs in the machines." Feeling that they had been cheated, that's exactly what the men did.

One of the burly "floor walkers," who kept an eye on things, spotted the men using the slugs. He grabbed one of them while the other two fled making their way to the woods alongside Applegate Road. The two soon spotted several armed men searching for them. They took refuge in a nearby home where the owner allowed them to call the sheriff's office.

According to the young men, they poured their story out to a deputy, who laughed at them and said there were no slot machines or any other kind of gambling at the inn, only bingo. He then proceeded to tell them that the sheriff's office had no jurisdiction there, the mayor [Sedore] was in charge.

The two men walked down Hubbard Road and into Youngstown. Worried about their companion, they waited until dark and then went back to the casino to find their automobile. When they did, they discovered the ignition wires disconnected and $250 hidden in the glove compartment gone. The two got the car started and drove out of the parking lot. They soon discovered their friend walking along Hubbard Road.

The third companion told his friends he had been taken into a private bar, "used only for the better-paying customers." There he was "cuffed around" by five Jungle Inn thugs, who relieved him of $25. During the beating he was knocked to the ground and kicked several times in the ribs. He said he was worried more about his companions than himself because he was present when one of the thugs handed out revolvers to the others and gave them orders to find the other two.

Whether the story the three men told was real or fabricated was never proven. It was certainly possible the three entered the casino with the slugs to see how far they would get. Whatever the case, while putting the Jungle Inn in a bad light again, the story faded quickly from the newspaper after just one day.

On January 27, 1949 another dubious story appeared in the *Vindicator*, which seemed baseless, self-serving to the newspaper, and printed only to cast negativity on the casino. Without offering any names, and even less detail than the story of the three young men, the article quoted a "habitue who contributed liberally to support of the mobsters for many years." Described as a one-time regular of the casino, and having been upset over the years with the *Vindicator's* reporting on the Jungle Inn, the man was quoted, "You guys were right when you said the damned place is full of thugs. And when that Chief Allen started calling the boys names I thought he was hitting below the belt, too. But now, I admit you guys were 'on the beam.' There are more thugs, 'rats,' 'vermin,' punks and hoodlums around that joint than you'll find in Alcatraz. I think maybe I'll quit going there."

The Jungle Inn continued to operate unmolested through the early months of 1949. The *Vindicator* continued with its Jungle Inn-bashing articles, which sometimes seemed to prove more like free advertising to the casino as opposed to a detriment. A February article advised that additional slot machines were added and people could now play the one-armed bandits in the building housing the restaurant. The article made sure it mentioned the free taxi service to and from the casino.

On March 9, 1949 a front page *Vindicator* article reported, "About 50 dealers, stickmen, slot machine attendants and bingo operators," learned that there had been a 20 percent salary cut upon receiving their pay the previous Saturday night. There had been no warning of the pending pay reduction. The newspaper reported "five veterans walked out," while others decided they were still doing well even at the reduced pay. There was no indication as to why the pay cuts were made, the article pointing out that "crowds bigger than ever" were patronizing the casino.

◆　　◆　　◆

In November 1948 Ohio voters returned Democrat Frank J. Lausche to the governor's mansion in Columbus. Lausche was born in Cleveland where he began his legal and political career. While serving as a common pleas judge from 1936 to 1941 he was instrumental in helping to close the notorious Harvard Club and Thomas Club gambling houses. He served his first term as governor of Ohio from 1945 to 1946. He was defeated for re-election by Republican Thomas J. Herbert, before being re-elected in the fall of 1948, and would serve as governor through 1956.

It would only be a matter of time before Lausche moved against the lawbreakers. A staunch adversary of commercialized gambling he would soon set his sights on the various gambling houses around the state. In March 1949 Lausche presented two anti-gambling bills to the state legislature. One of the bills would allow the governor to direct the state's attorney any county sheriff who refused to enforce local gambling laws. This latter general to initiate padlock proceedings against casinos if the local prosecutor failed to do so. The second would give the governor authority to remove bill was expected to draw much opposition from the rural counties, and was voted down by the Ohio General Assembly.

During a news conference on March 12 to promote the bills he was sponsoring, Lausche blasted commercialized gambling in the state, labeling it "the multi-million dollar racket," and discussed the four worst violators. He named the Mounds Club, in Lake County; the Pettibone Club (formerly the Arrow Club), in Geauga County; the Continental Club, in Lawrence County (the southernmost county in the state); and the Jungle Inn, in Trumbull County. The Benore Club, in Lucas County near Toledo, was also on the governor's list.

The *Vindicator* sought responses from county officials where each of the named gambling joints were located:

> ➤   The Mounds Club was currently closed. Tommy McGinty felt that the "smart money" headed for Florida during the winter months, so the casino was open on a seasonal basis. The new county prosecutor and sheriff in Lake County were said to be "in complete agreement on gambling conditions and in particular on closing the Mounds Club

> ➤   Longtime sheriff Stuart Harland denounced the governor's intrusion on elected county sheriffs. "I feel that Geauga County is capable of electing its own rather than having Columbus tell who it should have," Harland responded.

> ➤   In Lawrence County, Common Pleas Judge James Collins was already on the move, having ordered a special grand jury. "It is common talk," Collins sated, "that gambling interests are buying protection by paying off officials from constables on up. If you find evidence get the real culprits, the owner of the buildings, and the operators, not some minor employee paid to sweep out the place."

> ➤   In Trumbull County, Sheriff Millikin couldn't be located and new County Prosecutor William M. McLain was vacationing in Florida.

By the summer of 1949 Ohio's notorious gambling dens began to fall like dominoes. The first hit was the Benore Club near Toledo, closed by a court action on June 29. Next came the Mounds Club. The infamous Lake

County casino, which catered to the ritzy Cleveland social set, was raided late on the night of Saturday, July 9. The club was being raided for liquor law violations that had been reported by undercover agents visiting the club, which did not possess a valid liquor license. State Liquor Enforcement Chief Anthony A. Rutkowski and State Liquor Director Oscar L. Fleckner conducted the raid.

Once the raiders crashed the front gate of the Mounds Club on Chardon Road (Route 6), it took them fifteen minutes to gain entry into the club, due to safeguards including a six-inch thick safety door. As agents waited to get inside they could hear employees smashing telltale evidence of liquor violations. At the first sign of the raiders, the patrons were notified by club personnel, "Everybody pick up your chips and put them in your pockets. Go back to your [dinner] tables."

In addition to the bottle smashing, employees grabbed gambling tables and carried them off to storage areas. Once inside, the raiders found a crowd of 500 "glittering" patrons, seated at dinner tables listening to music and sipping soft drinks. In the gaming rooms 50 men were engaged in games of gin rummy, without a cent in sight.

Behind the bar, John Kocevar, a liquor agent who would have a dubious record over the years, found a full bottle of cognac and a partially filled bottle ofrum. In the kitchen, garbage pails filled with smashed whiskey glasses were found.

In his report, Rutkowski called the Mounds Club a firetrap because of its locked exits and windowless walls. He said this evidence would be presented to the state fire marshal. Ironically, the next night, Sunday, the Mounds Club was back in full operation. It was reported that patrons "were laughing and joking" about the previous night's raid.

Rutkowski would have the last laugh. At 1:15 Saturday morning, July 16 the Mounds Club was raided for the second time in a week. Joining Rutkowski this time was Chief State Fire Marshal Harold Callan and a state building inspector, a building division chief and several other state officials. Facing a list of violations – including inadequate exits, barred and locked doors, sealed windows, no building permits for original structure and no buildinpermits for remodeling – the Mounds Club was closed as a fire trap for good.

The Jungle Inn Raid

The raid Chief Allen hinted about back in November 1948 would come, but it would take nine months to materialize and it would not be Allen leading it. On Friday night, August 12, 1949 Anthony Rutkowski and Oscar Fleckner would close the Jungle Inn forever[4] during a raid that would live in infamy in Trumbull County.

In July Fleckner and Rutkowski began to formulate their plans. The two had a "dry run" on July 11 with the Mounds Club raid and subsequent closing of the Mounds Club. Their assault on the Jungle Inn would be well planned too. Prior to the raid undercover agents frequented the Jungle Inn playing the slot machines and gambling, all the while making notes about the layout of the place. The night before the raid Fleckner obtained a search warrant from Trumbull County Common Pleas Judge Lynn B. Griffith at his home. The search warrant, in effect, made Rutkowski an officer of the Trumbull County court. Local law enforcement personnel were not notified of the intended action in order to prevent any information from leaking out.

Rutkowski later described the raid to reporters:

> "My men, approximately 19 in number [and all unarmed], entered the main gambling room about 8:30 pm. Exactly at 9 pm on the dot I entered the room side by side with Fleckner.
>
> "I inquired from a man standing at the door if he could locate the manager. He gave me no answer. I then walked over to the bingo microphone in the center of the room and told the man operating the mike that I had a search warrant for liquor and gambling equipment.
>
> "I asked him to announce to the patrons that they should leave the premises. He answered me 'let me finish the game.' I repeated my request. He then told me he would have to get the orders from his boss. I then asked him where was the boss and he pointed to John Farah standing in the doorway.
>
> "I told him to go to your boss and get your orders. He hesitated for a moment, but then removed the microphone from a holder attached to his shoulders and walked over to Farah.
>
> "I took the microphone and addressed the people in these words, 'Ladies and gentlemen my name is Anthony Rutkowski, state liquor enforcement chief, and I am in the company of Oscar Fleckner, state liquor director, and other inspectors. We have a search warrant issued by the Trumbull County Court of Common Pleas to search this place for intoxicating liquors and gambling devices. We will be unable to perform our duty unless you leave the premises. I request that you leave.

"When I made this announcement there was a howl from the patrons. Some of the people asked 'how about our money?' I answered them by saying I regret exceedingly that I can not answer your question. When I said this there was another howl from the patrons.

"One of the inspectors came to me at this time and said the owner had informed him he would refund the money to the patrons. I made this announcement over the microphone and asked the patrons to go to the cashier's desk and get their money.

"Immediately all the patrons got up in an orderly fashion and approached the cashier's desk and received their money. The refunding was performed by Jungle Inn employees under the supervision of Fleckner who by now was inside the cashier's cage."

Over the years, one of the forgotten people involved in the raid was Mrs. Frances Marts, the wife of the inspector in charge of the State Liquor Department's Cleveland district. Charles Marts and his wife entered the Jungle Inn as a gambling couple that night. When the raiders entered, Mrs. Marts was instrumental in helping to identify the dealers, clerks and other employees for the liquor agents (See Appendix 1). Her "special assignment" was to keep an eye on the money changers at the rear of the casino. "I watched them empty money from their aprons and put it into bags. The bags were later found hidden behind slot machines," she stated. Asked if she was frightened by the ordeal, she responded, "I guess I wasn't any more frightened than a man would be in a bargain basement."

After Rutkowski's request to the crowd to vacate the premises the 1,000 patrons began to cash out and leave. The *Tribune Chronicle* wrote, "Since no liquor was found on the premises the raiding party found itself in the awkward position of being unable to make any arrests and it was then that the call for Sheriff Millikin was made." Assistance from Millikin would be required to make the arrests. Millikin and two deputies were tracked down before 9:30 at the Trumbull County Fair, informed about the raid and told that their assistance was required immediately. Millikin would later claim he "didn't have his watch on and didn't know what time he was notified." Whatever the reason, Millikin and his men did not arrive at the Jungle Inn until 11:30.

The sheriff later claimed "he had had no complaints about liquor sales at the Jungle Inn" since the revocation of the liquor license that had been issued to Garrison Post 504, which previously operated the place. It's for certain that the undercover agents who cased the gambling den prior to the raid would have known if liquor were being sold there. The newspaper seemed to imply that Rutkowski was surprised by the fact that no liquor was being served, raising the question: Did word of the intended raid leak out in spite of the precautions made?

Somewhat lost to history was the whereabouts of Mike Farah on the night of the raid. There was only one mention of him that night. One newspaper reported, "Mike Farah came on the scene and cursed at Rutkowski and the other agents. But just as quickly as he appeared, he disappeared roughly shoving one of the agents out of his way during his departure."

Meanwhile management and employees of the gambling casino were getting testy. One man approached Rutkowski and questioned his authority to search the premises. Rutkowski later retold the story, "I said I had a warrant and he could examine it, if he was able to identify himself as an owner or a manager."

"He was very angry and began to call me vile and indecent names. While hurling these epithets at me he turned and started to walk through the main entrance. I saw him push Inspector Henry Fearon. (Perhaps this was the person the newspaper identified as Mike Farah).

"I issued orders to hold that man. At this time John Farah commenced to question my authority to search, and he became very angry and proceeded to call me vile and indecent names.

"I informed him where the warrant was issued, but he still continued to call me vile and indecent names. However, he did not ask to see the search warrant."

Then in the midst of the "vile and indecent" name calling the night almost turned deadly.

Farah spun around and in a loud voice called out, "Kill him, Jock, kill him." When there was no response, the incensed mobster called out again, "Shoot him, shoot him." Rutkowski recalled, "It was at this time Fleckner and I looked up to the right of the cashier's cage and saw a turret in the wall with two guns pointing out of semi-circular slots. Both of us ran against the wall of the cashier's cage." Farah then ran to the cashier's cage.

John Kocevar, one of the liquor agents, climbed a three-foot ladder leading into the gun turret and wrestled with the hood holding the shotguns. Farah, who had tried to hide in a private office next to the cashier's cage,[5] was then ordered out by agent Kocevar, now in command of the two guns (See biographical entry on Kocevar in Chapter 7). After five minutes, Farah vacated the office and the two-hour wait for Sheriff Millikin dragged on. It was here that one of the mysteries of the night occurred, what happened to the shotguns and why didn't the liquor agents hang on to them for their own protection?

It's inconceivable to think that the Jungle Inn could have operated as long as it did without bribes being paid to public and law enforcement officials. While no one was ever charged with paying or accepting a bribe, three factors seem to bear witness that payoffs were made. First, it was state liquor agents, not police or sheriff's deputies who were called upon in secrecy to carry out the raid. Second, the lack of assistance from the county sheriff's officers and state police after the raid. And third, during an April 2000 interview with John Farah's son, he claimed his father had paid large amounts in cash and services to authorities in order to continue their gambling operations. The elder Farah's outrage in ordering the turret gunman to open fire was because he felt the authorities had welshed "on their part of the bargain." The younger John Farah declared his father had been robbed by the people he had paid to protect him. "Who's the crook there?" he questioned.

Disappointed patrons were aided out of the area by the state highway patrol. These officers then retired leaving the 20-man, unarmed, liquor force on their own. After the parking lots were emptied hoods from the inn placed crates, saw-horses, pieces of wood and anything else they could get their hands on to barricade the entrance to the parking lot, thus keeping cars out and two trucks the liquor agents brought to remove the gambling equipment blocked in. The hoods then took up positions around the buildings and surrounding grounds.

The liquor men remained inside, where the telephones were dead (having been turned off at Chief Allen's request); their only communication was a two-way radio in one of the agent's cars. Using this radio Fleckner broadcast several messages asking for support. One request went to Youngstown Police Chief Allen, but he replied sadly that his police force could not legally make any arrests in Trumbull County. Allen promised to keep a "full shift of men on call in case some means of deputizing the men in Trumbull County could be worked out."

An attempt was made to contact Governor Lausche. He was at Cleveland Municipal Stadium, however, watching the Indians lose to the Chicago White Sox by the score of six to five.

As the night dragged on Farah and other members of the Jungle Inn management continued to taunt the liquor men "telling them they were licked; that they hadn't found any liquor and couldn't make gambling arrests and that they might as well take their big trucks and go back to Columbus."

Meanwhile, outside the Jungle Inn, another battle was going on; this one between hoodlums and three Youngstown *Vindicator* employees. After receiving a tip that state liquor agents had just raided the Jungle Inn, reporter Adrian M. Slifka raced to Halls Corners where he began questioning the agents. Slifka was joined by "acting city editor" Irving L. Mansell and staff photographer Edward Shuba. As the men tried to enter the casino several "scowling" men blocked their path.

"You can't go in there, it's private property," one of the man growled.

"Who's in charge here," demanded Mansell.

"I'm in charge," said one burly hood. "Now, you get out."

The unruly hoodlums, who had grown to about 20 in number, began to shove the newspaper people around. Photographer Shuba was the main target as one of the men tried to take his camera, while others stole his film holders and broke the flash attachment to his camera. Someone suddenly called out, "No rough stuff." It was a voice the hoods recognized and complied with. The newspaper employees returned to their automobiles.

Discouraged, the trio of *Vindicator* employees made one last-ditch effort to retrieve the stolen photography equipment. The state highway patrol was contacted and asked for help in getting back Shuba's property. They were informed that the "law permits them to intervene only in traffic law enforcement."

By now Sheriff Millikin had finally arrived and entered the besieged gambling den. Mansell got word to the sheriff that they wanted to enter only to be rebuked by Millikin whose answer was, "We don't want any *Vindicator* men in here." The sheriff's presence didn't offer the state liquor men much support. Belittling the raider's efforts, the sheriff took a sample from a bottle of liquor that had been confiscated. He later claimed it was a wine vinaigrette used for salads.

The raiders had confiscated 83 slot machines, 2,100 poker chips, dice, roulette wheels, chuck-a-luck and black jack tables, as well as horserace betting equipment. It was unclear whether or not the bingo prizes were actually seized; however, one newspaper report claimed that refrigerators, television sets, radios and toasters were ordered returned to the Jungle Inn's operators. Rutkowski ordered one of the trucks backed up to the door and the gambling equipment was about to be loaded and removed to Columbus to be held for trial. Millikin immediately protested any such move. He dispatched a deputy to the home of County Prosecutor McLain to confer on the legal issue of removing the evidence. Fleckner later revealed, "In the meantime we contacted Judge Griffith at his home and he informed us to keep the equipment under guard and wait for a decision scheduled at a hearing" to be held Saturday morning.

While waiting for a response the sheriff chartered a bus to remove 15 of the employees he had to arrest – clerks, bartenders and a maintenance man – to the county jail. They arrived to be booked just prior to 3:00 a.m. Five other men, including John Farah, were allowed to remain at the casino pending disposition of the gambling equipment, valued at $35,000, and money seized in the raid that was estimated at $30,000.

At 9:00 o'clock Saturday morning all 20 men (See Appendix 2) appeared before Judge Griffith. Attorney George Buchwalter, counsel for the defendants, claimed that no liquor had been retrieved from the Jungle Inn. He told Judge Griffith that he "could not recall an occasion when the liquor department had ever before made a gambling raid." Asserting that this type of law enforcement was strictly up to Trumbull County officials, he moved that the men be set free and the equipment released.

Griffith disagreed with the lawyer's argument and quickly fixed bond at $500 for the men who were local and $1,500 for those who resided outside the district. Even though none of the men arrested had been charged with a crime, Griffith explained that "It was not the purpose of the law to let persons languish in jail over a weekend without charges filed." Because John Farah had ordered the turret guard to kill Rutkowski, the judge set bond for him at $2,000. Prosecutor McLain told the judge that Sheriff Millikin requested that the evidence be held in Trumbull County since the case would have to be prosecuted there. The judge agreed and granted the request.

The last issue to be settled was the $30,000 confiscated from the cashier's room. The judge ruled that the money be returned to its rightful owner. Rutkowski explained that this was impossible, the money could not be traced back to the patrons who lost it. Judge Griffith then decided to have the count verified by local bankers after which it be turned over to Youngstown attorney Russell Mock, one of four members of the Jungle Inn "defense team," who would act as trustee for the defendants. The total the bankers came up with was less than $6,000, which shocked both Fleckner and Rutkowski.

When informed the next morning on details of the raid in Cleveland, a disgusted Governor Lausche issued a statement: "My men have been on their feet for more than 30 hours. The whole thing could have been closed easily if it had not been for the preventive action of Sheriff Ralph R. Millikin who blocked the removal of the slot machines and the $30,000 to Columbus and insisted the 'evidence' remain in the county. I have no personal criticism to express, but I cannot help note an attitude of protraction."[6]

After the Saturday morning hearing, Rutkowski told reporters that he had already asked the Cleveland Police Department to assign a detail to his home as threats had been made against his family because of the raid. The vigil on the Rutkowski home was short lived after the liquor enforcement officer "entered a discussion about children" with John Farah, the father of two, and his brother Mike, who had several of his own. The Farah brothers and their attorney, Russell Mock, assured Rutkowski no harm, and no further threats, would come to his family.

On Saturday the *Vindicator* printed the following front-page article. The author of the biting piece was not identified:

Jungle Inn's Suckers Responsible for Bringing Criminals Here
By a Vindicator Reporter

You simple-minded suckers!

Yes, I mean you if you were at Jungle Inn Friday night – or any other night!

And don't give me that time-worn story: "I was just there to play bingo. That is harmless."

For if you resort to that old one, it's time someone gave you the facts of life. If you honestly believe your own story, you don't have enough intelligence – even to play bingo.

What Dollar Did

For here is what that lowly dollar of yours helped to do in the Trumbull County thieves' den Friday night:

1. Allowed a gang of pug-ugly (sic) toughs to defy, threaten and virtually hold captive Ohio's liquor director and his agents. These are the men who have sworn to uphold the laws of Ohio which your elected representatives have made.

2. Permitted some of this same gang to rough up three newspaper men and damage a photographer's camera. Of course, it wasn't you, but remember, a man was kicked around at Jungle Inn earlier this week. It might have been you.

You still aren't convinced? Well, how do you suppose Jungle Inn was able to operate in defiance of your laws? Sure, that dollar goes back into prizes for some of you "luckier" people.

Bingo Just the Come-On

But even you should know that bingo is just a come-on at the Jungle. It sets the stage for the slots, roulette, craps and other games of "chance."

And if you have been there, you have seen the piles of money that change hands – mostly into the house's hands during an evening. The liquor agents seized $30,000 cash and slots worth $35,000.

And who is "the House?" Well, the operators both have prison records. They are former members of the old Maple Heights gang of thugs in the Cleveland area. Now, instead of doing their own dirty work they can hire it done – thanks again to that dollar of yours.

And your dollar helps to keep them in limousines while you, poor sucker, don't even have a car and are glad to accept free taxi service to lose that dollar, or dollars.

By now some of you are probably trying to justify your presence at Jungle Inn with the phony argument that "This is just "The Vindicator popping off again. Why doesn't it keep quiet and do some good for the people?"

Well, The Vindicator is trying to do some good for the people. It has been trying to do it for some time. It doesn't run banner lines on Jungle Inn just to advertise it so more of you can go out and lose your money.

Have Seen the Poison

The men who have been pressing the campaign to wipe out this den have been able to see the poison such a place can spread in the government and daily life of this community.

But I suppose you will go back to the Jungle if it continues to operate.

And you will be the first to cry about the lack of law enforcement when some thug robs your home, holds you up at gunpoint, or attacks your daughter or wife.

The man the article mentioned that was "kicked around" was an unnamed 55 year-old who didn't obey orders on the night of August 8. In a headline article titled "Jungle Inn Goons Whip Man Crowding to Exit," the newspaper explained that, "After the last bingo cover-all, the players... head for the exit door so they can catch a taxi quickly." To slow down the mad rush that night one of the doorman scolded the crowd, "Do I have to spank you ladies every night?" The older gentleman who had ventured too near the door against orders had been shoved back several times. Angered, he let a fist fly. The doorman, aided by another employee, dragged the man outside and pummeled him, breaking his glasses, in front of his "gray-haired wife," who protested in vain. The man was told to "get out and never come back again."

At 1:30 Saturday afternoon, after the court hearing, Fleckner, Rutkowski and the liquor agents returned to the Jungle Inn to finally remove the gambling paraphernalia. With them were two *Vindicator* employees, reporter Adrian M. Slifka and Lloyd S. Jones (the latter a photographer who was assaulted by Youngstown lottery house operator Frank Budak after his indictment back in June 1943). Both were there to take photographs. By this time John Farah and a host of goons had returned to the casino and were in a foul mood. When Farah was told that the photographers were there to snap pictures for the state's records, the mobster informed Fleckner that no cameras would be permitted in the casino. When the photographers protested Farah warned Fleckner, "If you want rough stuff, we'll give it to you."

One of the *Vindicator* men called out to attorney Russell Mock, who was pacing nervously in front of the casino, "I thought you told the judge this morning there would be no disturbance at the inn this afternoon." Mock turned away from the photographer's glare and did not say a word.

One of Farah's goons, overhearing the comment, shouted, "I'm warning you. You're going to get into trouble over this."

The photographers were physically removed from the area by a group of hoodlums. Both were roughed up and their equipment damaged. Lloyd Jones broke lose from the mob and ran to the automobile of James Leisy, a photographer from the *Tribune Chronicle.* Jones pleaded, "Get me out of here those guys are getting rough." With that Leisy sped away to where Jones had parked his vehicle nearly a mile away.

Slifka, who apparently hadn't suffered enough abuse the night before, took refuge in the arriving automobile of Sheriff Millikin. The sheriff advised him, "Listen, I've got enough trouble on my hands now. I've got a fair to take care of and then this raid, and so I don't want to have any trouble with [newsmen] trying to get pictures taken."

The newspapers claimed the Jungle Inn had been "reinforced Saturday afternoon by more than 100 hired thugs." The "thugs" showed as much respect for the sheriff as they did the photographers. Several tried to break into Millikin's car to pull Slifka out. Millikin's deputy quickly drove off stopping at Jones' automobile to release him. Depositing Slifka with his fellow employee, the deputy gunned the engine and he and the sheriff disappeared in the direction away from the Jungle Inn.

Earlier in the day *Tribune Chronicle* photographer Leisy had problems of his own. He had gone to the warehouse of the J.M. Barbe Company to snap pictures of the exterior. The company had been designated by Judge Griffith to maintain the confiscated gambling equipment. J.M. Barbe took exception to the photograph being taken and grabbed Leisy in an attempt to get the film. The photographer was able to escape. Later that day Chief Allen ordered police to watch the homes of both Lloyd Jones and Adrian Slifka. The latter received several telephone threats.

As Saturday night arrived the once thriving casino was quiet. To pass the time a dozen of the "goons" left to guard the place shot dice with a few "selected customers." The barricades remained in place at the driveway entrances keeping the curious from entering the parking lot. A number of curiosity seekers drove slowly past the Jungle Inn during the night.

◆   ◆   ◆

By Monday, August 15 Governor Lausche had already developed a four-pronged strategy against the notorious gambling den and the people who protected it. The first step was to serve a citation to Halls Corners' Mayor Charles Sedore to show cause as to why he should not be removed from office for allowing gambling to continue unmolested at the Jungle Inn. The mere issuing of the citation, served on Sedore at midnight Monday by the state highway patrol, placed the mayor under suspension. He was given until August 31 to respond. Under Ohio law the governor has the right to remove a mayor from office if charges of misconduct can be proved. Lausche had recently sought the same power over county sheriffs, but the state General Assembly voted the measure down after a strong lobbying effort on the part of the state association of sheriffs. During the past winter a citation for Sedore's removal had been issued, but the mayor ducked the serving of it by going to Florida on an extended vacation. On August 30, the day before the suspended mayor was to respond to charges, Sedore announced, "I am not going to appeal the governor's decision."

The next day Governor Lausche heard testimony for an hour on the misconduct of Mayor Sedore. Testifying were Anthony Rutkowski, Chief Eddie Allen, and state liquor enforcement agents Charles Marts, John Kocevar and Morris Stearns, the latter having visited the Jungle Inn to investigate claims on three separate occasions. Sedore, as he announced, did not attend the hearing nor had anyone arrived to represent him or testify on his behalf. Lausche declared that the charges against him had "obviously been sustained" by the testimony of the witnesses.

Lausche concluded that it "appears to me that these people had set up a government of hoodlums in Halls Corners as a means of having other enforcement officers resort to the proposition of letting local officials handle their own problems. My view is that enforcement of law and order is never just the concern of local officials, but is the concern of all law enforcement agencies of the state and of the people of the state."

The governor also attacked Sedore's right to possess a liquor license and he directed state liquor department officials to investigate Sedore's proprietorship of the Hickory Grill in Youngstown.

In the second step of Lausche's plan he forwarded a telegram to Trumbull County Prosecutor McLain "suggesting" that he officially have the conduct of the management and staff of the Jungle Inn reviewed by the common pleas court. He called attention to the incidents on Friday and Saturday where men were "interfering with the investigation, assaulting citizens and taking charge of the highways."

The governor's next two moves were aimed at code violations. "I am going to order representatives of the industrial relations department into the building to check the entire place to see if it conforms to the code," Lausche promised. "I am also going to order the state fire marshal to check the building for fire hazards." No sooner had he made the promise that Lausche asked Harold Callan, the Ohio State Fire Marshal, to check the

Jungle Inn for fire hazards and to make sure it conformed to code. He wrote Albert Woldman, Director of the State Industrial Relations Department, to have representatives of the building construction and building safety divisions inspect the gambling house. (Woldman had sent three of his men to inspect the Jungle Inn the day prior to the raid. They spent several hours there as casino management showed the inspectors around the club.) These last two tactics were used by the governor to secure the closure of the equally notorious Mounds Club in Lake County during July 1949.

All parties involved responded with urgency to Lausche's plans to put the Jungle Inn out of business for good. McLain immediately began working with Fleckner and Rutkowski on charges to be filed against the 20 defendants arrested as a result of the raid. Part of the process would include filing charges against the property owner. Court records showed that Mike Farah's wife, Grace, was the listed owner.

Trial of Those Arrested

Prosecutor McLain was also busy putting the finishing touches on charges against the men who were taken into custody. The charges were in the form of "informations," described by McLain as being "tantamount to indictments and can be filed only in misdemeanor cases which involve fines and or jail sentences."

The men would be indicted in two groups and face one or more of the following charges; "keeping a room and building for gambling [punishment consisting of a $30 to $50 fine and 10 to 30 days in jail], exhibiting gambling devices for gain [punishable by fine of $50 to $500 and 10 to 90 days in jail], and gambling [punishable with a fine of up to $100 and jail time of 10 days up to 6 months]."

Rutkowski, who had returned home for a few days, was scheduled to return and work with McLain on additional charges against John Farah for his order to "kill" the liquor chief. Arraignment, originally scheduled for August 18, was pushed back two days.

Attorneys Russell Mock, George Buchwalter, John Anderson and Donald DelBene – were busy planning their strategy. They planned to attack the legality of the raid by the state liquor men. Foremost in their minds was the right of Judge Griffith to appoint Anthony Rutkowski to the position of "special bailiff," in order to conduct the raid. Mock declared, "Rutkowski, as a resident of Cleveland, was not eligible for appointment as court bailiff and constable. A bailiff must be a deputy sheriff who must reside in the county in which he is authorized to act as such official." In the meantime, Mock was already hinting at one of his normal delaying tactics – jury trials for each of the men.

On Friday, August 19, a week after the raid, all twenty of the arrested were arraigned before Judge Griffith. The men appeared one at a time and each entered a not guilty plea through attorney George Buchwalter. The judge then set a trial date of September 6 after Mock requested additional time due to another pressing matter – the razing of the Jungle Inn. As early as August 23 at least 100 Trumbull County residents were being called for jury duty in preparation of the pending trials.

The entire arraignment proceeding went smoothly until the subject of the shotguns was addressed. An argument ensued between Mock and Rutkowski when the liquor agent claimed the attorney had given his "professional word" to turn over the weapons to Sheriff Millikin. Mock responded that he had promised to turn them over only if he could find them. "I have never seen the guns and I promise the court that if I find out where they are or if they are brought to me I shall bring them in," Mock told the judge. When Rutkowski suggested that the attorney ask Farah where the guns were, Mock angrily replied, "You go get the guns." With that he wheeled around and walked out. Judge Griffith then revealed that Deputy Sheriff Earl Bash and another deputy searched the Jungle Inn days earlier, but had found no trace of the guns. It was never revealed how they got back into the hands of the mobsters after agent John Kocevar seized them from the guard in the turret the night of the raid.

In a surprise move, on September 2 at 10:00 a.m., all twenty defendants appeared in Judge Griffith's courtroom and pled guilty to the counts they were charged with. Sixteen of the men, categorized by Griffith as "helpers, clerks and flunkeys," were fined $100 and court costs. Three men, described by Rutkowski as "seeming to own" the Jungle Inn were fined more; Claude Hoagland $300; Edward Tobin $500; and Ralph Coletto $700. John Farah was handed the heaviest fine, $1,000. In addition to the higher fines, the four men paid court costs and were ordered to each post a $500 bond "for one year's good behavior."

Before Judge Griffith handed down the sentences and fines, totaling $4,100 –which he ordered to be retrieved from the money collected from the slot machines – he allowed attorneys, prosecutors and the state liquor authority to argue their sides. Mock claimed "that although a lot of technicalities could be raised as to the legality of the raid, the guilty pleas were made to save time." Taking a final shot at Rutkowski, Mock continued, "Time which…the liquor department could well use elsewhere in checking up on liquor permit holders instead of raiding gambling establishments." Mock then stated, "If the liquor department considers the fact that they have work of their own, in the future they'll realize that they can't prohibit gambling."

Prosecutor McLain was quick to question what Mock meant by "not being able to prohibit gambling" and asked if he was, "inferring that the defendants would continue their gambling operations."

Mock smugly told McLain that gambling "was going on before our time and will probably continue after we are gone."

At the end of the proceedings Judge Griffith announced that he was going to destroy the $35,000 inventory of gambling equipment. He stated, "These 100 slot machines have grabbed their last nickels from the gullible public."

With the hearing over Farah, Tobin and Coletto walked over to the clerk's office to post their "good behavior" bond. As they stood there *Tribune Chronicle* photographer James Leisy, who had been chased off the Jungle Inn grounds, snapped a picture of the three. Leisy quickly removed the film and handed it to a fellow employee to sneak out of the courthouse. Mock grabbed Leisy by the arm and led him to Judge Griffith to question the photographer's right to take pictures in the clerk's office. Griffith refused to make a ruling, claiming that the clerk "runs her own office." The other Jungle Inn men were still milling around the corridor as the episode played out and several threats were leveled at Leisy. The slick photographer, satisfied he got the last laugh, left the courthouse smiling…and in the company of a state patrolman.

The courtroom hearing and subsequent sentencing did not include the charges against Farah or Albert Sudetic for their attack on the newspaper people. That would be handled in a separate trial. In late September Rutkowski and Fleckner were called before the Trumbull County grand jury and questioned about the "shoot to kill" order shouted by Farah on the night of the raid. When the grand jury was finished reviewing a record 120 cases, there was no indictment against Farah. One report claimed that by this time Rutkowski had a change of heart and decided not to pursue additional charges against Farah for ordering the guard to kill him.

Trial for Assaulting the Newspaper People

On August 20 two arrest warrants were sworn out for the attack on *Vindicator* employees Lloyd Jones and Adrian Slifka. Police set out to arrest

John Farah and Albert Sudetic, an in-law of "Fats" Aiello. On the issuing of the informations McLain wrote:

> "The gathering and disseminating of news is a public service. Few people realize the difficulties encountered and hazards faced by those engaged in this work. It is imperative that they be fully protected in both person and property."

Sheriff's deputies were dispatched to pick up the 24 year-old Sudetic. But Farah, upon hearing of the warrant, went to the jail accompanied by attorney Donald J. DelBene. After he was booked Farah was released on a $1,000 cash bond. Sudetic showed up at the county jail to be served the warrant the next day and was released on a $500 bond.

John was having trouble staying out of trouble. A couple of weeks after the Jungle Inn raid he was arrested by an Ohio State trooper for driving 65-mph in a 35-mph zone on Route 422. Farah stopped his vehicle after a long chase and "used abusive language" with the trooper, after which the patrolman ordered Farah to follow him to the Girard City Jail. On September 10 Russell Mock accepted a $5 reckless driving fine for his absent client, but pled him not guilty to the charge of being abusive to the officer. On October 8, after hearing testimony from both parties, Girard Mayor Clyde Helman dismissed the charges due to insufficient evidence.

In addition to John's other problems, a former patron was suing Farah and the Jungle Inn for $10,000 after he "suffered internal hurts" from eating food at the gambling club in April 1949. The patron claimed he became ill and had to be hospitalized after eating two pork sandwiches. His lawsuit claimed the food served to him was unfit for human consumption, that it was "putrefied, poisonous and adulterated." The plaintiff claimed that as a result of eating the Jungle Inn food he was placed on a diet of fruit, vegetables and milk.

◆   ◆   ◆

On Tuesday, September 6, 1949 the assault trial of John Farah and Albert Sudetic began in Common Pleas Judge Griffith's courtroom. The charge was assault and battery. Prosecutors claimed Governor Lausche had promised that pictures of the Jungle Inn would be taken and made available to the public. Lausche requested that arrangements be made with the *Vindicator* so that Rutkowski and Fleckner would have the photographs to use as evidence. This arrangement was agreed upon by Prosecutor McLain and Sheriff Millikin and all were supposed to arrive at the closed casino at the same time. Jones drove out and left his car near the area, was picked up by Rutkowski and Fleckner and driven the rest of the way.

Jones' account of the afternoon's harrowing encounter at the Jungle Inn first appeared in the *Vindicator* on August 15:

> "I was picked up by the state car at Applegate Road and Logan Row, and was assured that I would be given protection to obtain the pictures requested by Governor Lausche. They also informed me that they would need some 20 pictures.
>
> "We were driven directly into the grounds of Jungle Inn, going through the barricade of guards and wooden horses, and stopped at the rear entrance to the Inn.
>
> "Rutkowski moved directly to the door to obtain entrance, whereupon it was slammed shut from inside. Shortly, several persons, including John Farah, appeared at the door and inquired what Rutkowski wanted. He informed them he wished to enter, but was immediately informed that he would have to wait until the sheriff arrived. Rutkowski said that he would gladly wait as the sheriff was coming along very soon.
>
> "As I moved to the door with the camera equipment, I noticed numbers of men moving from various entrances and spots surrounding the building, toward our direction. The numbers increased, and I asked one of the state officers how many of the increasing number of men were state agents, and he informed me that just the small group of about 10 men, and the rest were Jungle Inn boys.
>
> "John Farah opened the door and called Fleckner and Rutkowski and told them point blank that there would be no pictures taken, and he didn't want any photographers around. Rutkowski stepped up and said, 'This photographer is here under orders of Governor Lausche to take official pictures for our case.'
>
> "'I don't care who gave the order,' Farah shouted, 'there will be no pictures taken. Do you want us to get rough, and show you just how tough we can get?'
>
> "'No!' Rutkowski shouted.
>
> "'There will be no pictures,' Farah said.
>
> "'All right, no pictures,' Rutkowski said.
>
> "Immediately, additional men from the Inn moved around the entrance in increasing numbers.
>
> "Slifka stepped up to Rutkowski and said we would need protection, now that it was evident that the state men were planning to enter the building and leave us there at the entrance. Rutkowski said that we could go get in the car.
>
> "Slifka said they brought us in, and they should give us protection to leave the grounds.
>
> "Farah opened the door, gave a hand signal to his boys and said, 'OK boys, throw those newspaper bums out of here.'
>
> "We looked at the state men, and they shrugged their shoulder and turned in the direction of the entrance, leaving us there.

"Immediately the Jungle Inn Boys closed in and started shouting angry threats. 'Get going – get out of here – we'll bust your damn neck.'

"With no choice but to go, I started across the lot. The men moved in on me and grabbed the camera from my hand while another held and twisted my arm, making it impossible to do anything but give up the camera.

"They shoved me, and I informed them that I was going, that I had no other choice, and they didn't need to be so tough, after all I came in under orders of the state men, and they knew that I hadn't taken a picture.

"The thug that held me by the left arm then grabbed me by the neck, twisting it, and telling me that I had better not look at him like that or he would break my neck.

"Additional men hurled threats. When I reached the barricade I insisted that they hand over the camera. Slifka also told them not to destroy the camera because no pictures were taken.

"One of the number that had the camera said yes, he was giving me the camera, and started to give it to me. But after it passed through several hands, they removed the holder, and then gave me the camera and holder, minus the slides. I yelled for the slides, showing them that the exposed film was in the open holder that I had. So they gave me the slides at the request of one of the group.

"I turned and noticed a press car from the Warren Tribune, and I got into the car and asked them to take me to my car on Logan Ave. Slifka was getting into the sheriff's car.

"As we started to drive away, some of the gang hurled threats about coming back, and several followed the car down the road for some distance.

"As we reached our car on Logan Road, and left the sheriff there was a station wagon with three women in it that drove up, and stopped their car and waited to see where we were going. As I drove away, with Slifka in my car, these girls took up our trail and followed us to the edge of Youngstown city limits, where we turned off from Logan Ave."

Perhaps it was the *Vindicator*'s zealous reporting about the Jungle Inn that led to the abuse of the two newspaper employees. The lack of effort on the part of the two state officials to see to their personal safety was another story. Upon returning to Cleveland that Saturday night, Rutkowski told a *Plain Dealer* reporter, that he and his inspectors were helpless to intercede under the circumstances. "We had no weapons or arms of any kind," he stated. "There were 30 or 40 musclemen, and we weren't in a position to do anything and it was useless to call on the deputy sheriffs who were there."

At the trial two Warren bankers, who were on hand to "guard the money" at the casino testified that they were concerned for their own safety when they witnessed Jones and Slifka being pushed around. One stated that when the assault started with the grabbing of Jones' camera, attorney Mock shouted, "Give it back to him." At that point both bankers took up positions beside Mock.

The defense's case was Farah had never called out to any one to "get those newspaper bums out of here," and that Sudetic was in Youngstown, nowhere near the Applegate Road casino that afternoon. To support Sudetic's claim, his sister-in-law and wife testified he was at home. On the stand later Farah also claimed Sudetic was not there.

In addition to Farah, other defense witnesses included a number of deputy sheriff's, none of whom said they witnessed "the disturbance."

Rutkowski testified for the state and told the court he had heard Farah's shout to "get the bums off the property." Fleckner claimed, however, he walked into the casino and was not aware of any commotion outside.

After two days of testimony the jury received the case late Wednesday. The panel of eight men and four women deliberated for a few hours before telling the judge they were deadlocked, their final vote tallying 8 to 4 for conviction. It was apparent Griffith was unhappy with the jury after they first announced they couldn't come to a unanimous decision. Brought into the courtroom, the judge stated, "We're in the habit of getting verdicts in this court. You are intelligent, able jurors and should be able to reach a verdict."

Griffith then told them, "Jurors should not be obstinate. A good juror listens to his fellow jurors and considers their views carefully, calmly and dispassionately. He then votes as his conscience directs."

Despite the impassioned plea, after a total of four fruitless hours of deliberations and ten votes the jury remained hopelessly deadlocked. At 6:15 that evening, Griffith dismissed the jury. It was later reported that the jury felt Sudetic was innocent.

When informed that Prosecutor McLain planned to confer with Griffith on a retrial, attorney Mock remarked, "a silly expenditure of public funds – all this for a misdemeanor."

Destruction of the Gambling Equipment

On August 25 a "slot party" began at the J.M. Barbe Inc. warehouse on South Street. Judge Griffith ordered that the slot machines be opened, emptied of their contents, the coinage counted by tellers from separate banks, and the money turned over to the clerk of courts.

For some unexplained reason the proprietor, J.M. Barbe, was hostile toward the newsmen who came to cover the event. He allowed photographers to enter and take only two pictures each. Reporters, who were told the previous day that they could view the proceedings, were banned from entering and could observe only through a wire fence door. One reporter went to Judge Griffith and obtained a letter requesting Barbe allow entry to the media. The proprietor's response was a terse, "If you're not satisfied with watching through this door you can get out!"

Rutkowski, who drove from Columbus to observe the emptying of the slot machines, engaged in a heated argument with attorney DelBene about two "slot machine mechanics" who were present. Rutkowski claimed he needed the names for his report. DelBene claimed the men, who held two large containers of slot machine keys, were not identified in the court papers and were not required to give their names.

"You're looking for publicity," DelBene charged. "Some people aren't."

The machines yielded the following counts:

39 Nickel machines	$ 714.25
24 Dime slot machines	1,67.20
31 Quarter slot machines	1,797.75
5 Half-Dollar slot machines	1,146.50
1 One-Dollar slot machines	407.00
Total	$5,132.70

The process was a tedious one. The two slot machine mechanics had to manipulate the wheels to create pay-off combinations with one hand and then pull the lever with the other to force the coins to drop out. The entire process took six hours to perform. In addition, there was one machine officials couldn't open, which contained an estimated $72. Bank officials also reported "the presence of a small number of washers, war time meat ration plastic tokens and several English and Canadian pennies."

The contents of each machine were placed in separate bags and tagged with a number representing the serial number of the machine from which it was recovered. The coin sacks were then placed in a large canvas bag and taken by a county patrol car to the Warren bank for counting and safe keeping.

◆   ◆   ◆

On September 8 Griffith ordered that the gambling paraphernalia seized at the Jungle Inn – slot machines, tables, roulette wheels, etc. – be destroyed. A bid of $115 was accepted by the county from Warren Scrap Iron & Metal Company to destroy the equipment and keep the remains. The destruction of the equipment would be under the supervision of Sher iff Millikin and Rutkowski, who had been appointed co-custodians of the gambling devices.

A legal battle quickly began to halt the destruction of the Jungle Inn slot machines and other gambling equipment. One day after ordering the equipment destroyed Judge Griffith stayed his own order to allow attorneys for John Farah to appeal to the Seventh District Court of Appeals. Farah's petition to the appeals court, which required a $1,000 bond, declared that the slot machines were not gambling equipment "in and of themselves" and should be returned to the owner as personal property. Farah went on to claim that Griffith "usurped" his authority by issuing a search warrant that made it possible for Rutkowski to confiscate the gambling equipment."

The state did win the battle to destroy the slot machines when the Appellate Court on March 3, 1950 upheld Judge Griffith's order for the one-armed bandits to be demolished. On April 19, amid much fanfare, 83 slot machines, three dice tables, a roulette wheel and a chuck-a-luck board were removed from the J.M. Barbe warehouse and taken to the Warren Scrap Iron & Metal Company to meet their fate. As the gambling equipment was being loaded, Rutkowski, on hand to witness the demolition, took a metal piece from the roulette wheel to keep as a souvenir. Deputies ordered him to put it back.

First the gambling tables and devices were reduced to splintered wood. Then at 11:30 the sledgehammer began to fall on the slot machines. The hammering resulted in the recovery of an additional $434.33, which had been stuck in the mechanisms of the machines. Rutkowski[7] was concerned that pieces of the machines could be salvaged and used to rebuild other machines. The concern became moot after a huge, magnetic iron ball was used to pulverize the remains.

The Battle to Raze the Jungle Inn

State Fire Marshal Harold Callan and Charles R. Scott, chief of the state fire prevention bureau, arrived at the Jungle Inn Monday evening August 15 along with Roy A. Skipton, acting chief inspector of the division of factory and building inspection of the department of industrial relations. Unfortunately, upon arriving at the Halls Corners' casino they found the place locked tight.

Reporters accompanied the inspection team as well as photographers from the *Tribune Chronicle* and the *Vindicator*. The grounds were deserted except for two caretakers who claimed they had been hired the day before. They gave their names as J. B. Brown and John Smith. When asked the whereabouts of John Farah, one replied, "We don't know...guess a lot of people are looking for him."

After making an inspection of the outside of the two frame buildings the group made their way to a telephone to call Judge Griffith to obtain legal access to the building. With a promise to help them the next morning, the inspection team retired to a Youngstown hotel for the night.

The next morning the judge issued an order allowing the inspectors to enter the building. The order stated that the men were to be given immediate access to the buildings "without being hampered and without interference from anyone." To insure the judge's order was carried out Griffith had two deputy sheriffs accompany the men.

When Callan and Skipton arrived back at the Jungle Inn later that morning they found the casino open. As the state inspectors entered with their entourage, the two deputies questioned the presence of the newspaper people. Callan replied that he had been authorized to bring anyone he chose into the place.

When Skipton's work was complete, he rushed back to Columbus to meet with Woldman, who announced that the Jungle Inn would be padlocked. The state industrial relations director stated he would issue an order closing the club on two separate counts, 1) the inn buildings did not conform to the state building code; and 2) the inn was a public nuisance. Woldman explained, "They found virtually [the same] violations in the Mounds Club. We'll issue a forthwith order closing the building as a hazard to employees and frequenters. They will be ordered to stay closed until they comply with the code," said Woldman. He said the padlock citation would not be ready until the end of the week, at which time it would "probably" be served in person on the owners, operators and employees of the Jungle Inn. Since the structure was originally built without a permit, Woldman declared the Jungle Inn would have to be "rebuilt from the ground up to meet the state building code."

Mock declared he would fight Woldman's padlock order. Right after the casino was raided a rumor spread around Youngstown that the Jungle Inn would reopen as a "benefit-bingo" operation. After Woldman's exposure of the fire dangers, however, the "worthy cause" crusade to carry on the bingo tradition lost steam.

An order was issued and addressed to Mrs. Grace E. Farah, owner of the Jungle Inn property and John J. and Mazeed George, commander and adjutant, respectively, of the Army-Navy Union Garrison Post 504, notifying them to vacate the premises immediately. The order, issued by Harold Callan, directed Mrs. Farah to "tear down the buildings and to remove all materials to neat and orderly storage or otherwise dispose of the material."

In his order Callan outlines the violations that called for his decision to raze the buildings:

> "That it violated Ohio laws because of size, seating capacity and use; by its location to an adjacent restaurant; insufficient exits and exits improperly marked; electric wiring not in rigid conduit; heating equipment, fans and fuel not contained in separate, fireproof rooms; checkroom oil heater connected to steel pipe instead of chimney.
> "That oil tanks in the basement are not properly vented, opening in fan room wall would allow rapid fire spread and plywood interior wall coverings would burn with great rapidity if ignited.
> "The marshal found these alleged violations of state fire laws in inspection of the smaller, restaurant building.
> "Building heater not installed in fireproof room; electric wiring not in rigid conduit; stairs too narrow and only one exit provided from the second floor; fuel oil tanks outside the buildings not vented.
> "That the floor joints over the basement have been badly weakened and are at present held up by 11 steel screw jacks and by reason thereof, the life of building occupants is periled by the danger of building collapse."

In commenting on the building that housed the restaurant, attorney Mock claimed it had recently passed a state fire marshal's inspection. "I can't see how so many wrong things have cropped up in such a short time," Mock questioned. Nevertheless, he quickly filed a written notice of appeal contesting the order to raze the buildings. An appeal hearing was scheduled for August 26.

The August 26 appeal to raze the Jungle Inn was held during a five-hour hearing in Callan's sweltering Columbus office. Of the three people identified as principals in the matter – Grace Farah, John George and his brother Mazeed – only the latter appeared. He claimed the 95-member Army-Navy Union Garrison Post 504, of which the three George brothers were officials, operated the restaurant located in the smaller of the two buildings. The larger one, he referred to as the assembly hall.

Attorney Mock said the garrison had hired an architect to plan a remodeling of the building, which housed the restaurant, in an effort to conform to the building code. The changes that needed to be made were estimated at $9,000. As far as the "assembly hall" was concerned, Mock told the gathering, "The hall has been abandoned, its equipment moved and the owner has no intention of permitting its public use again." Then, in an impassioned plea, Mock declared, "It is unconstitutional and unreasonable to order these buildings torn down."

Others testifying at the hearing included James Santagada, the Jungle Inn's maintenance man; an architect; construction company representative; Anthony George, Mazeed and John's brother; and J. R. Shenk a professor of structural engineering at Ohio State University. The professor testified that birch plywood, used in construction of the interior of the "assembly hall" was inflammable. At the completion of the hearing Callan said he would take counsel's plea under advisement before deciding whether or not to "modify his order to raze the Jungle Inn."

On September 13 Callan stated in his decision:

> "On consideration of the evidence submitted by the appellants and the division of the state fire marshal, I find that the conditions violations of laws and circumstances as set forth in order No. 80506 to be true in their entirety.
>
> "Therefore, by reason of the premises and pursuant to the authority vested in me order No. 80506 is hereby affirmed and shall remain in full force and effect."

In addition to the rescue of the slot machines, attorneys Mock, Del-Bene and Buchwalter were busy trying to save the Jungle Inn itself from demolition in the wake of Callan's September 13 ruling. On September 26 in Columbus a Franklin County Common Pleas judge suspended the raze order indefinitely. The suspension of the order did not lift the ban on public use of the building. Grace Farah, along with John and Mazeed George filed the appeal. The next day the attorneys filed the same appeal in Trumbull County court, claiming Franklin County lacked jurisdiction over the property.

On January 4, 1950 the same court reversed Callan's order to have the Jungle Inn demolished, calling the order "unreasonable and invalid." The ruling claimed that the order did not give the owners enough time to make alterations that would comply with state fire regulations. Upset with the legal decision, Governor Lausche declared "the Jungle Inn will not reopen for any unlawful purpose if I can stop it."

On October 11, 1951 the *Vindicator* reported, "Jungle Inn – what's left of it – will stand unoccupied and shabby until it either falls down or the changing tides of politics allows a resumption of crap games, slot machine playing and other forms of gambling." That statement by the newspaper was the introductory paragraph to a story announcing that State Fire Marshal Callan would not appeal the ban to raze the once infamous casino to the Ohio State Supreme Court. Callan noted that the order to halt the building's demise was based on the fact that the owners had not been granted sufficient time in which to make appropriate alterations. Now, two years later, no attempt had been made to bring the building up to code.

Aftermath

In late January 1950 newly named Halls Corners' Mayor Elton Barber and members of the village council sought permission for a special election to un-incorporate the village. In early March a formal request was made to the Board of Elections.

On the most appropriate of days, April Fool's Day 1950, Halls Corners ceased to exist. An election was held to un-incorporate the village and 86 citizens (75 percent of the eligible voters) voted 55 to 31 to return the area to Liberty Township. The voters, who never had a municipal building in the village, cast their ballots at "Shorty" Lesnak's filling station as election officials from both parties looked on.

An April 2000 *Vindicator* article claimed, "In subsequent years, the inn briefly tried offbeat entertainment. Then it became a warehouse for a window-manufacturing business in which the Farahs were involved." In January 1957 the property was purchased by Bertram Zusman, who owned Bertram Builders. During the negotiations one of the Farahs told Zusman he was getting out because "this legitimate business is too crooked..."

In early 1979, almost 30 years after the highly publicized raid, the main building that once housed the casino was occupied by Bertram Builders & Supply Company, Leisure Homes, Inc., and Gateway Trucking Company. Around 3:00 on the morning of February 10 owner Bert Zusman was notified that a burglar alarm had been set off at the building. False alarms had occurred there before, so Zusman contacted his security provider, State Alarm and asked then to investigate and report back to him.

About an hour later a young couple, who lived on at Logangate Apartments, spotted flames and called the Liberty Township Fire Department. The couple then got into their automobile and attempted to drive down Logangate Road (Applegate Road had been renamed) in order to notify others who lived on the other side of the structure. Two stories resulted from this effort. The first reported one was that they became disoriented in the heavy smoke blowing across the road and crashed their car into the burning building. The other story claimed an explosion at the building caused their car to become "engulfed in smoke," and the vehicle went off the road and got stuck in the snow a few feet from the building. Unable to move the car, the couple fled on foot.

When Liberty Township firefighters arrived the road was impassible from the west, due to the flames shooting from the building. Firefighters from Hubbard Township and McKinley Heights were called upon to assist in fighting the blaze from the east. Helping to fuel the fire was a large inventory of lumber and prefabricated products used in the building industry. The frigid February temperatures hampered the efforts of the firemen. Papers had to be lit and held to the nozzles of some of the hoses to thaw them. The lack of hydrants in the area meant water had to be transported in to fight the blaze. Nine pumper-trucks and fifty firemen fought until 7:00 a.m. to bring the fire under control.

Liberty Township Fire Chief Arthur Carnahan suspected immediately that arson was the cause of the blaze, which was estimated at a $250,000 loss. Arson specialists from Youngstown and Boardman were called to the scene. A few days later, after state investigators viewed the remains, they determined that arson was the cause of the fire.

After the fire all that is left of the infamous gambling palace are pieces of the cement foundation scattered among brush, weed and scattered debris.[8] From the road it is hard to imagine that any structure was ever there, let alone the Mafia's most infamous gambling den.

4

The War Lords of Trumbull County: John & Mike Farah

Cleveland Beginnings

John and Michael George Farah were twin brothers, born in Syria on Christmas Day 1905. The boys grew up in Cleveland where the family attended St. George's Syrian Orthodox Church on West 14th Street and Starkweather Avenue.

John was described as the more aggressive brother. His first brush with the law was writing a fraudulent check in Cleveland on May 3, 1927; he was sentenced to a six-month jail term and fined $25. Around this time John and his wife Shamis were living with his parents, George and Freida on Walden Avenue down the street from Mike and his wife Grace Emily, in area known at the time as Miles Heights, a small village southeast of Cleveland which the city annexed in 1932. During the latter part of the 1920s the brothers ran a profitable retail trade in beer and whiskey. In December 1930 police raided a speakeasy in Miles Heights. Although they believed the Farahs were involved with the operation, a bartender took the fall and neither brother was arrested.

While still in Cleveland during the early 1930s the Farahs befriended Mickey Cohen. Brooklyn born, Cohen moved around a lot on his own as a teenager, earning a living as a prizefighter in Los Angeles, Cleveland and New York. While in Chicago he was close with Matthew Capone, a younger brother of "Big Al" Capone. Cohen's friendship with the Farahs would come to light in February 1950 after it was reported that Los Angeles police had a transcript of an alleged telephone call between Cohen and

Jungle Inn Nightclub
(Courtesy of Bruce Birrell)

Bingo players at a local nightclub, circa 1946
(Cleveland Press Collection, Cleveland State University)

Perry Como
(Cleveland Press Collection, Cleveland State University)

Flats area of Warren
(Courtesy of Bruce Birrell)

John Dillinger
(Cleveland Press Collection, Cleveland State University)

Alvin "Creepy" Karpis
(Courtesy Cleveland State University Library)

Scene of Karpis mail robbery in Warren
(Cleveland Press Collection, Cleveland State University)

Clarence S. Darrow
(Cleveland Press Collection, Cleveland State University)

George H. Birrell - Campaign poster for Prosecutor
(Courtesy of Bruce Birrell)

Hollyhock Gardens Nightclub
(Courtesy of Bruce Birrell)

Bar area of Hollyhock Gardens Nightclub - before Birrell raid
(Courtesy of Bruce Birrell)

Bar area of Hollyhock Gardens Nightclub - after Birrell raid
(Courtesy of Bruce Birrell)

Jimmy Munsene - playfully slugging heavy weight boxing champ Max Baer
(Courtesy of Bruce Birrell)

Horse racing results board at Jungle Inn Nightclub
(Courtesy of Bruce Birrell)

Bar area of Prime Steak House
(Courtesy of Bruce Birrell)

Felix Monfrino
(Courtesy of Bruce Birrell)

Mancini family burial plot in Oakwood Cemetery
(Author's Collection)

Tommy Viola - Detroit Police Mug Shot
(Courtesy of Paul Kavieff)

YOUR INFLUENCE AND SUPPORT WILL BE APPRECIATED

G. H. BIRRELL

Republican Nominee for

Common Pleas Judge

(Unexpired Term)

NON-PARTISAN BALLOT

General Election Tuesday, Nov. 3, 1936

George H. Birrell - Campaign poster for Judge
(Courtesy of Bruce Birrell)

Tommy Viola in court
(Courtesy of Bruce Birrell)

Jungle Inn Nightclub
(Courtesy of Bruce Birrell)

Bingo area of Jungle Inn Nightclub
(Courtesy of Bruce Birrell)

Dining area of Jungle Inn Nightclub
(Courtesy of Bruce Birrell)

Arrow Club
(Cleveland Press Collection, Cleveland State University)

Mounds Club
(Cleveland Press Collection, Cleveland State University)

Jasper J. "Fats" Aiello
(Courtesy of Youngstown Police Department)

Bingo area of Jungle Inn Nightclub
(Courtesy of Bruce Birrell)

Edward J. "Eddie" Allen - Youngstown Police Chief
(Courtesy Cleveland State University Library)

Ohio Governor Frank J. Lausche
(Cleveland Press Collection, Cleveland State University)

Mounds Club
(Cleveland Press Collection, Cleveland State University)

Anthony A. Rutkowski
(Cleveland Press Collection, Cleveland State University)

Oscar L. Fleckner
(Courtesy Cleveland State University Library)

Gun turret room of Jungle Inn - Note blackjacks hanging from chair
(Courtesy of Bruce Birrell)

John Farrah, Ralph Coletto and Edward Tobin
(Courtesy Cleveland Public Library)

State Fire Inspectors conducting investigation at Jungle Inn - Note turret at top of picture
(Courtesy of Bruce Birrell)

Remains of the Jungle Inn (Author's Collection)

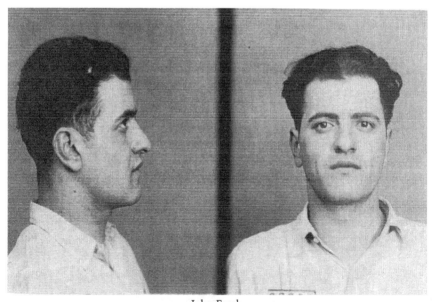

John Farah
(Courtesy of Cleveland Public Library)

Mike Farah
(Courtesy of Cleveland Public Library)

Dominick J. "Duke" LaPolla and James "Blackie" Licavoli
(Courtesy of Cleveland Public Library)

Arlene Steuer
(Cleveland Press Collection, Cleveland State University)

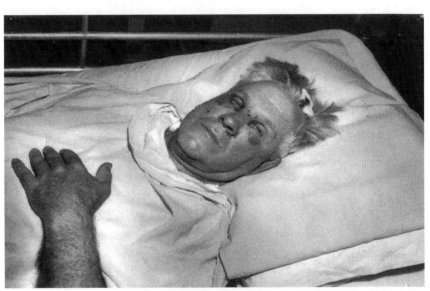

Jean Blair in hospital
(Courtesy of Bruce Birrell)

Mike Farah's grave in Lake View Cemetery
(Author's Collection)

John Farah's grave in Lake View Cemetery
(Author's Collection)

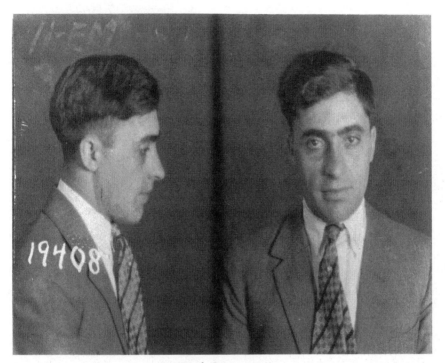

Frank Cammarata
(Courtesy of Paul Kavieff)

Joe "the Wolf" DiCarlo
(Author's Collection)

Licavoli Gang police photo
(Courtesy of Detroit Police Department)

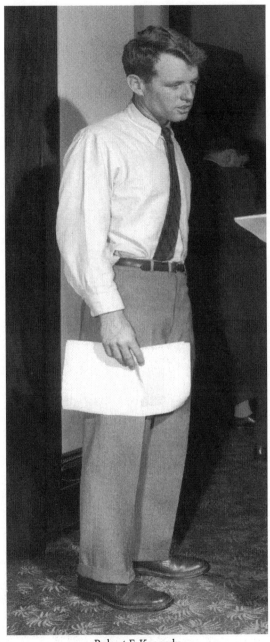
Robert F. Kennedy
(Cleveland Press Collection, Cleveland State University)

Leo "Lips" Moceri
(Courtesy of Youngstown Police Department)

Anthony "Tony Dope" Delsanter
(Courtesy of Youngstown Police Department)

Mike Farah made in August 1947. Police also found Farah's number in a telephone directory that was stolen from the pint-sized mobster's home during a break-in.

The brothers bootleg business had them purchasing a portion of their beer from Lawrence "Akron Larry" Rubin. The East Side Jewish mobster made a name for himself when he was acquitted of the murder of Sam Weiss in April 1928. Since then he had been arrested three times for suspicion, including another shooting in October 1928, and was on the rise in a gang led by Al Jaffe. During the mid-1920s Rubin lived on the fringes of the gangs that dominated the East Side Cleveland neighborhoods of Woodland Avenue/East 55th Street and the East 105th Street area. In the Weiss killing, Rubin proved to be a "stand up" guy by "taking the rap" for Jaffe and Hymie Martin,[1] both of whom were prime suspects in the murder. As Rubin moved up in the underworld he was said to have become a bootleg "big shot" having close ties to local politicians who aligned themselves with the gangster element.

Rubin's new "importance" may have gone to his head. Cuyahoga County Prosecutor Ray T. Miller revealed that "Akron Larry" had once threatened "to get" Emerich B. Freed, an assistant county prosecutor, who had successfully prosecuted two of Rubin's friends. The two men were convicted of illegal possession of explosives and sentenced from 10 to 15 in the Ohio Penitentiary. Rubin, who was in attendance throughout the trial, made his cavalier comments after the sentencing to a Cleveland detective assigned to the prosecutor's office.

By mid-1931 Rubin, who at the age of 29 was still living at home with his mother and three sisters, had developed a "lucrative whiskey business" with two downtown hotels. The *Cleveland Press* reported, "He was known as a source of 'good' whiskey and had what bootleggers term 'society folks' as his customers." Rubin was also known to be in the wholesaling end of illegal alcohol; once being referred to as a "collector for Cleveland's second largest syndicate."

That all ended on July 6, 1931 in Geauga County on a stretch of well-traveled highway called the Parkman – Middlefield Road, a mile outside the rural community of Parkman. Around 7:30 p.m. Mrs. Phyllis Pratt and her husband were on the highway when they spotted Rubin's automobile parked on the side of the road. The couple heard four gunshots and saw puffs of smoke rise from the front of the vehicle. A man in white flannel trousers, which were spattered with bloodstains, was waving automobiles past the scene. As the Pratt's moved slowly by they saw a man's legs protruding from under the car. When the couple stopped to see what happened the man in the white trousers took off on foot through the fields. In addition to the Pratts, three youths from Chardon, who had also stopped after being waved past, and two young farmers, one armed with a shotgun, watched the man flee. Phyllis Pratt summoned all the men together and the search was on. Soon two Geauga County deputy sheriffs, who happened by, joined the makeshift posse. Directed by Mrs. Pratt the group quickly tracked down John Farah, who was found cowering in the middle of a field of clover hay. With several guns trained on him Farah surrendered.

Returning to the car the posse viewed the reason for Farah's flight. "Akron Larry" Rubin's body, half-hidden under the front right fender, had four bullet holes in it – one below the right ear, another in the back of the neck and two in the chest. In addition, his skull had been fractured in two places by blows from a .38 murder weapon found nearby with its butt splintered.

Taken to the Geauga County jail in Chardon, Farah told Sheriff Ben Hotchkiss that he had been hitchhiking to Warren. "I heard some shots fired and ran, that's all I know," Farah declared. He offered no explanation for the bloodstains found on his white pants. Harold Bostwick, the Geauga County prosecutor claimed he had an "iron-clad case," against Farah and was prepared to seek a grand jury indictment immediately.

Through Rubin's "underworld acquaintances" it was ascertained that the "society" bootlegger was owed $900 by the Farahs. One newspaper acknowledged, "Following a custom of liquor wholesalers in trading with small dealers, Rubin, it was believed, accompanied the load of ale last night on its way to Warren driving his own sedan, that he might collect from the driver upon delivery." During the return trip an argument ensued resulting in the death of Rubin.

Police were waiting for Mike Farah when he returned home driving an empty truck during the early morning hours of July 7. He readily offered, "I just came back from delivering a load of beer to Warren. I passed right along the Parkman-Middlefield Road where the murder was committed. I don't know anything about my brother." When Detective Lieutenant Charles Cavolo notified Sheriff Hotchkiss of the arrest he was informed, "The murder is cleaned up. You can let him go." Cavolo released Mike Farah.

Later that morning attorney Edward Stanton, a former Cuyahoga County prosecutor, was hired to represent John Farah. He went to the jail with Mike Farah to confer with prosecutor Bostwick. While the two attorneysdiscussed legal matters a reporter approached Mike Farah.

"What was your brother's business?" the reporter inquired.

"Dry goods," Farah responded.

"Bootleg?" asked the reporter.

"I don't know," said Farah. "I don't know anything. I don't know anything but my wife and kids."

On July 8, during a preliminary hearing, Stanton argued that the charge against Farah should be reduced to manslaughter. "The state's evidence clearly shows that Rubin was killed in a fight and that is manslaughter," Stanton declared. A justice of the peace hearing the case did not agree and Farah was bound over to the grand jury on a charge of first-degree murder. The grand jury decided that a charge of second-degree murder was more appropriate, since no eye witness had actually seen the shooting, and John Farah was released on a $10,000 bond. On September 8 his trial began in Common Pleas Court in Chardon. The trial was to feature a rarity in this area – witnesses. One newspaper boasted, "The inside workings of the bootleg business are expected to be revealed in the trial." Stanton was prepared to produce evidence that the two men were "close friends" prior to the incident, thus setting the groundwork to prove the killing was not premeditated. Stanton also claimed his client was unarmed and that Rubin had been killed with his own weapon.

A panel of 40 prospective jurors was on hand as the jury selection process began. Several jurors had been impaneled before a 10-minute break was given. When the parties returned to continue the process, Stanton and Farah rose to address Judge Harlan Sperry. "At this time, I'd like to ask if I may be permitted to plead my client guilty to a charge of manslaughter," the attorney requested. Stanton maintained that the killing was a result of an argument over a bad check Farah had given to Rubin. While the plea was short of the second-degree murder conviction that was being sought, the newspapers noted that, "It was the first time in the history of Cleveland gang warfare that an admission was made to a killing."

Prosecutor Bostwick, who had balked at the request at the time of the arraignment convinced that he had the evidence to send Farah to the "hot seat," now consented to the plea. Sperry immediately sentenced Farah to one to twenty years in the Ohio Penitentiary. At the request of Stanton, bond was continued for six days to allow Farah to "straighten up" his business affairs in Cleveland. Meanwhile, the *Cleveland Press*, disappointed with the results, responded with the following editorial:

This Rural Justice

"John Farah is a bootlegger, whiskey dealer and hijacker.

"When he was captured running away from the murder of Akron Larry Rubin, another gangster, in a Geauga county wheat-field a lot of people said to themselves:

"'Ah, ha! Now we shall see how this stern and rigorous rural justice deals with these gangsters. There will be none of the monkey-business that goes on in the cities. Now we shall see something really hard-boiled!'

"Well, they let John plead guilty to manslaughter yesterday over at Chardon. One to 20 years."

John Farah's "One to 20 years" prison term lasted less than 14 months as he was pardoned by the charitable Governor George White on November 18, 1932.

On March 8, 1934, Farah was arrested on a suspicious persons' charge; the case was later dismissed. On May 20, 1935 John Farah was at the wheel of his automobile when he was fired upon. One bullet hit the top of the front windshield pane while the other went through the windshield and struck Farah in the left shoulder, near his neck. Around 3:00 that afternoon Farah was driven by friends to St. Luke's Hospital where attendants called the Shaker Heights Police while the patient was being treated. Farah's wound was dressed and he was told to return the next day to have the bullet removed.

Farah was uncooperative when police arrived. Asked several times where the shooting occurred, Farah gave four different locations. Police questioned residents in all four areas, failing to find anyone who heard or saw anything.

"Who shot you?" asked Shaker Heights Police Chief Bert Tilson

"I don't know." Farah answered.

"Don't you know what happened and didn't you see anybody?" the chief challenged.

"I don't know what happened and I didn't see anybody," Farah snapped.

"Did the killing of Larry Rubin have anything to do with you being shot today?" Tilson asked.

Farah responded by slowly shaking his head in the negative.

On June 26, less than six weeks after he was wounded, John Farah was arrested by an Ohio State Patrolman while in possession of 150 gallons of illegal alcohol. The patrolman came upon Farah around 4:00 in the afternoon near Auburn Corners. The officer became suspicious "because the back springs of his automobile sagged suspiciously." When the alcohol was discovered, Farah readily admitted who he was, but refused to say where he had obtained the alcohol or where he was headed with it. Farah was turned over to federal authorities for violating the revenue act. He was fined and sent to the federal penitentiary in Lewisburg, Pennsylvania, where he served a sentence of 15 months, one month longer than he did for the murder of "Akron Larry" Rubin. He was released in early 1937.

Mike Farah's rap sheet was less spectacular. He was arrested in Cleveland in September 1932 for carrying a concealed weapon. Farah went to a store on Buckeye Road and told the owner he wanted 15 pounds of yeast. When informed by the proprietor he didn't have that much Farah allegedly pulled a gun and declared, "You'll never sell anymore yeast or corn sugar in this store." Frightened, the owner fled the store and contacted police. The case was later dismissed. In May 1936 Mike Farah was arrested for a violation of the revenue act after the discovery of a whiskey still by government agents. He was sent to the federal prison in Milan, Michigan, serving a term from December 3, 1937 to October 2, 1938.

The Farahs moved into gambling and sometime before the end of the 1930s Mike Farah moved his family to Trumbull County. It's not sure if John and his wife Shamis made the move. Although John's residence was several times listed as the Warner Hotel in Warren, records showed he always kept a Cleveland address at 16404 Walden Avenue just a few doors from where Cleveland Mafia heavyweight Angelo "Big Ange" Lonardo lived. A report on the Farahs in 1952 claimed, "The Farah brothers were imported from Cleveland 20 years ago to coordinate bootleg activities in Warren."

Mike and his wife Grace, along with their five children, moved into a home at 243 Kenilworth Avenue in Warren. On Sunday, June 30, 1946 tragedy struck the Farah family. Robert, the oldest son, was spending the day with four friends at Geneva-on-the-Lake along the Lake Erie shore. The 17 year-old had just completed his junior year at Culver Military Academy in Indiana and was home for the summer break. After a hearty breakfast the youths swam out to a log about 200 yards from shore. After several minutes of playing on the log all of the boys, except Robert returned to shore. Some time passed and when Robert didn't show up one of the boys swam back out to the log. Unable to locate him there or on the shore, the youths were told to contact the Geneva police. Speedboats were quickly on their way to the scene and an hour after his disappearance Robert Farah was found in seven feet of water and pronounced dead at the scene. Officials speculated that the young man was overcome by cramps or the hot sun. The body was taken to Cleveland for the funeral and burial at Lake View Cemetery.

Less than two years after the tragic drowning, George Farah, the 86 year-old father of John and Mike passed away in Cleveland.

(The story of the Farah brothers picks up from this point after their Jungle Inn involvement.)

A Decade of Tax Woes

Although they would be known as the "rackets bosses" of Trumbull County throughout the 1940s and 1950s, the Farahs led a somewhat quiet existence after the highly publicized raid in August 1949 that closed the Jungle Inn. Several incidents, including the Kefauver Hearings in 1951, returned their names to the headlines.

The gambling activities of the Farahs seemed few and far between. One of the few occurred in early 1951. Around 4:00 on Friday afternoon, January 5, Niles police raided a bookie joint at 50 East State Street. News of the raid had been leaked to the right people because the operator, most of the patrons and key equipment, like the race wire ticker, had been removed. Arrested was Thomas Vecchione, an employee, while the owner watched outside from a safe distance. The *Vindicator* pointed out the significance of the raid when it reported:

> "The Friday raid was another chapter in the turbulent affairs of Niles bookies which has seen local men all but eliminated from the picture as outside mobsters moved into Niles to control the lucrative racket.
> "The syndicate's entrance into rackets which once were controlled completely by local people has been gradual but thorough."

It was clear though, at least to Niles Police Chief Charles S. Berline, who was behind the "outside mobsters." He warned "this joint is closed and it's going to stay closed. The Farahs are not going to operate in Niles." The newspaper chimed in, "It is hinted in racket circles that the latest moves by law enforcement officials indicate a determined effort to erase the Farah and syndicate influence in incorporated areas of Trumbull County."

While the Farahs may have gotten the message, local gambling interests didn't. The bookie joint re-opened for "brisk" business that Saturday. Berline, who was determined to make a point, posted an officer at the East State Street address and declared, "There is going to be no more bookie joint in Niles. Even if they move someplace else they're going to be closed if we have to have patrolmen stationed at a location at all times."

After the closing of the Jungle Inn, the Farah brother's cash cow, they sought to gain respectability by entering legitimate operations in Trumbull County. In March 1952 incorporation papers were drawn for Audrey's

Inc. and Farah's Inc., both in downtown Warren. Audrey's, an appliance store, was located at 152 Pine Street, while Farah's, which sold rugs and floor coverings, was at 138 Franklin. John Farah was listed as the agent of both corporations. Also listed as an incorporator was attorney Dominick J. "Duke" LaPolla.[2] The brothers were also reported to have invested in bars, restaurants and country clubs to supplement their income. In addition, the Farahs became active in Trumbull County politics.

After the Cleveland edition of the Kefauver Hearings the government went after Joe DiCarlo and James Licavoli for income tax evasion. John Farah also became a target. On May 12, 1951 it was announced that a tax lien had been filed in Cuyahoga County, where Farah still kept an address, for $5,101 in back taxes from 1949. Shamis Farah, John's wife, was also listed on the lien in case any of his property was listed in her name. The lien would prevent the Farahs from disposing of any of their assets. It also was a notice to creditors that if Farah had to liquefy, the government got the first shot at the proceeds.

This was just the beginning of the tax woes the Farah brothers would face during the 1950s. Before the year was out John found himself the defendant in another lawsuit in which he was being sued for $11,118 for appliances purchased through the Farah's Appliance Store at 903 North State Street in Girard. The suit to collect the money was filed by the Arnold Wholesale Corporation of Cleveland for television sets, irons and a chair, all delivered to relatives of the Farah family.

On February 12, 1952 the Warren *Tribune Chronicle* reported that Farah was purchasing the Elm Street Shopping Center with William Cafaro. According to the newspaper, Stephen Baytos, president of the Baytos Construction Company of Youngstown, "intimated that pressure was brought to bear upon him to give up his interest in the proposed center." The next day the newspaper reported that Cafaro was to be the sole purchaser of the Baytos interest. Cafaro claimed that the purchase was "arranged on mutually, friendly and satisfactory terms." An attorney for the construction company confirmed Cafaro's statement. Farah's name did not appear in the second article.

In June 1952 John and Shamis Farah sold the Farah Rug Company to a Euclid, Ohio man. The *Vindicator* reported, "It is rumored that Farah, short of cash following heavy primary election expenditures and without appreciable gambling returns, is liquidating some of his local holdings to meet heavy investment demands." Farah would later repurchase the store. Many sensed the Farahs were manipulative in their financial affairs. On August 14, 1952 a former employee of the Farah family's appliance store filed suit to collect $382 that he claimed was due him in unpaid commissions. When the Mahoning County Club in Girard was sold at a sheriff's auction in September 1952 John Farah held a $4,200 lien against it. The club was purchased by an unnamed group of investors represented by former Jungle Inn attorney Donald J. DelBene.

The big blow to Mike Farah came on August 29, 1952 when IRS agents filed a $302,356 tax lien, the largest ever filed in Trumbull County, against him and Grace for non-payment of income taxes for the years 1948 through 1950. The liens were effective against any and all possessions of the couple, and seals were placed on the ignitions of their automobiles rendering them inoperable. In addition to Mike and Grace Farah, a tax lien of $86,138 was filed against John Petercupo, described as "a silent and seldom-publicized but reputed associate in the Farah organization."

On March 11, 1954, in Federal Tax Court in Cleveland, Mike and Grace Farah agreed to a settlement of $74,000, which included interest and penalty against the lien of $302,356. At the same hearing, John Petercupo and James Licavoli also agreed to settlements. John Farah's problems were yet to come.

On July 1, 1954 John was back in the news after a deposition hearing involving the promotion of Warren Police Sergeant Victor Johns to a captaincy. Warren Safety Director Hyman Bruss helped block the appointment when it was believed that Johns, who was the top scorer in a recent promotional exam, was accused of receiving a stolen copy of the test. During the hearing Johns was questioned by Assistant City Solicitor Sam Petkovich, who asked the officer about recent discount purchases he had made at the Farah Rug Company, now a combination carpet and appliance store.

On May 11, 1955 the federal government filed tax liens against the former operators of the Jungle Inn. After determining that the gambling club grossed more than $1.3 million over a twenty month period during 1948 and 1949 the government's tax claim against the defendants was $343,000, of which 40% was assessed to Farah.

The case began in the United States Tax Court in the Federal Courthouse in Cleveland on May 24. The defendant's position was that the gross income figure estimated by the government was too high and they had all paid the taxes they owed.

In his opening statement James F. Kennedy, representing the government, told the court, "We have the right to recompute income where books and records are not properly kept. It was no easy job. They [the defendants] used no books. Property was in the name of strawmen." Kennedy claimed the club kept a general ledger showing daily profits, but gave no breakdown of income from its various games – bingo, dice, roulette, slot machines, etc. Agents were required to devise their own method of determining the club's profits, which, according to Kennedy, was developed from "lists of information" provided by former employees of the club.

Farah and his fellow defendants were represented by Arlene Steuer,[3] who told Federal Judge J. Gregory Bruce in her opening statement, "We don't have any more idea than the man in the moon how they arrived at such a huge figure."

Judge Bruce made it clear early on that the burden of proof would be on the defense to disprove the government's contention. "You know the club's sources of income," declared the judge.

It was quite a sight when the petite, five-foot, 100-pound attorney called her first witness. IRS Agent John A. Varley squeezed his six-foot, six-inch, 240-pound frame into the witness box, "then looked down at Miss Steuer as a St. Bernard dog might glance down at a Pekinese barking at his feet." Kennedy objected to the calling of Varley as a defense witness, claiming the agent was bound not to divulge confidential information. Varley himself was confused, asking the judge, "I want to know where I stand." During brief questioning on this first day of the trial, Steuer extracted from the agent that they had disregarded the figures provided to them by the defendants and came about their own conclusions by applying "tests."

Varley proved to be a difficult witness for Steuer. She clashed with Judge Bruce several times during her examination over her line of questioning. Steuer hammered away at the agent trying to obtain his formula for estimating the Jungle Inn's profit. At one point Bruce half rose from the bench and shouted at the feisty lawyer, "I said to go on to something else!" She was told on numerous occasions, "Don't argue with the court!"

One exchange began:

Steuer: Have you ever investigated a gambling casino before?
Varley: No.
Steuer: Do you know the odds of roulette?
Bruce: You can't examine the witness as to that. Go on to something else.

On the second day of the trial all four defendants took the stand to tell the court how the Jungle Inn operated. Farah stated that the partners kept a bankroll of $25,000, and that receipts and the accounting books were handled by attorney Dominick J. LaPolla. Farah claimed there were no records kept of the "periodic division of profits," which were handed out every four to six weeks. Farah denied that any of the profits made their way to public officials.

Both Farah and Tobin testified that the records kept by the operators were missing after a visit by the state fire marshal days after the August 1949 raid. During Tobin's testimony he was questioned by Russell Mock:

Mock: You couldn't lose on the slots, could you?
Tobin: That's right.
Mock: And the house couldn't lose on poker?
Tobin: No, it's standard to take a cut of the pot [5 percent].
Mock: And you could lose on dice?
Tobin: Definitely so. If you had a hot player. That's when you lose your money.

A reporter for the *Plain Dealer* summarized, "Slot machines were the big money makers, bingo only a come-on and chuck-a-luck was strictly a ladies game at the notorious Jungle Inn. Dice and poker tables were sure to turn profits for the house, too..."

Tobin had been a professional gambler for twenty years; a 20 percent holder of the club in 1948 and 25 percent holder the next year, he told the court. Farah, the 40 percent holder, was the only partner with the combination to the safe, Tobin stated.

Ralph Coletto testified he had a 25 percent stake in the operation and described himself as an overseer, watching the roulette wheel and the dice tables. He explained that the dice tables began each evening with $1,250 apiece and were run by a five-man crew.

Dominick LaPolla took the stand to discuss his roll in the accounting function. LaPolla was once an employee of the IRS, working out of the Youngstown office from 1940 to 1945. In 1947 he became the book-keeper for the Jungle Inn. When asked how he recorded the profits LaPolla answered, "I just took the figures they gave me."

Despite a staff of 65 catering to between 500 and 800 patrons a night, who entertained themselves at 80 slot machines, a roulette wheel, three dice tables, two poker tables, a chuck-a-luck game and horse bet bookies, the partners claimed they were hard pressed to make $250,000 a year.

At one point during the proceedings Kennedy asked, "Did Frank Brancato ever have an interest or get any profit from the Jungle Inn." The question apparently hit a nerve as all the attorneys jumped at the same time to object. Judge Bruce sustained the objection.

Brancato allegedly wielded a lot of influence over Trumbull County operations for the Cleveland Mafia, not that he ever admitted to it. Six days after this trial began Brancato was in Chicago for a hearing on a suspension of deportation. Credit records subpoenaed for the hearing showed Brancato listed himself as "manager for six years of Jungle Novelty Club in Youngstown and had no superiors." During the hearing Brancato gave the following testimony:

"I couldn't make any money in the fruit and vegetable business.

"That was in 1937 and I went looking for a job – any job. There weren't any jobs. So I ended up at the Jungle Club – the Jungle Inn, that is, in Youngstown.

"That was a gambling club – dice, cards, roulette, horses, a big bingo game. I dealt cards – blackjack – strictly a salaried man. Work all day, draw your pay.

"Then the war broke out and Jungle Inn closed for the duration. Well, instead of looking for another job I started selling sweaters."

The government re-called Varley to the stand, who revealed publicly that the slot machine revenues, judged the largest money yielders at he Jungle Inn, were calculated based on 79% profit of all the money poured into them. The *Plain Dealer* reported, "The agent casually admitted the figure of 79% was an arbitrary one taken from another agent who got it from a Columbiana [County] slot operator." The other formulas the agents used were based on investigations of other gambling joints nationwide. Two formulas revealed by Varley were:

HORSEBOOKS: Agents applied a 12% figure as representing profits, based on the clubs "action," or table bets. He said another method was to determine if a bookie's total bets equaled 10 times the cost of the horse-race wire service. He implied something was wrong with the bookie's figures if the test did not hold true.

DICE TABLES: The "standard" here is to figure that a stickman or croupier at the table is worth 10 times his pay in profits for the house.

The agents obtained the numbers to calculate the Jungle Inn's horse bet totals of $3,000 per day from Albert Antonelli,[4] a former horse-bet writer at the club. Based on these formulas Varley's investigation concluded that the Jungle Inn partners fell short in their income reporting some $500,000.

◆　◆　◆

By late July 1956 more than two years had passed and there had not been a single payment made on the $74,000 balance owed by Grace and Mike Farah. IRS agents, unhappy with the lack of effort on the part of the Farahs, entered their Kenilworth Avenue home and inventoried the furniture with plans to seize it for public sale. Farah quickly came up with $1,995 the appraised value of the furniture, to forestall the sale.

Farah agreed to meet with IRS agents on July 31 to decide upon a payment plan on the balance due. Farah, however, was a no-show at the meeting and nothing was accomplished other than the threat that further action "would undoubtedly be taken." The government made good on its threat. One week later IRS agents began confiscating pinball machines owned by Mike Farah throughout Trumbull County. After the first 15 were grabbed, Farah's men quickly rounded up 24 others and surrendered them voluntarily. This was not an act of goodwill on the part of the Trumbull mobster, but was done to empty all of the coin boxes before the government seized them. The 69 machines owned by Farah – placed at bars, restaurants and diners throughout Trumbull County – were valued at $30,000 and would be held until sold at public auction. Machines from competitors were quickly brought in as replacements.

Before the government could sell the pinball machines, Jess Soda of the Soda Construction Company filed an injunction in U.S. District Court in Cleveland to prevent the sale claiming he was a 50% owner. On October 20 the government called off the sale and allowed Soda to buy back the machines at the appraised value.

◆   ◆   ◆

On July 18, 1957, more than two years after the U.S tax trial of the Jungle Inn operators ended, a three judge panel ruled that the Jungle Inn partners were liable for the bulk of the money the government said it was due. The ruling stated that the partners had substantially underestimated the gambling profits for 1948 and 1949. The main points from their ruling were:

> The partners failed to prove that the government's formula in determining the gambling profits was arbitrary
> The burden of proof the partners tried to establish could not be met due to the destruction of financial records by their own hands
> The partners contention that they should be allowed a deduction due to the destruction of slot machines was denied
> A similar contention to allow depreciation on the slot machines was also denied

On July 25 a *Vindicator* article revealed the court's puzzlement with Anthony Delsanter's role:

"In the Tax Court's majority opinion, Judge Arnold Raum described Farah as the 'dominant figure.' In the Jungle Inn setup. Concerning Delsanter, the judge described his position as 'highly mysterious.'

"'The evidence does not show that he contributed any capital to the partnership or what if any services he rendered to it,' Judge Raum said. 'His 10 per cent interest in the venture could give rise to teasing speculation...'

"Observers take this to mean that Delsanter may have been the representative of a crime 'syndicate' with an interest in the gambling joint.

"Delsanter has played an obscure role in Youngstown rackets and at one time operated the National Cigarette Service Co. This is the enterprise in which Vincent J. DeNiro and Joseph (Fats) Aiello also have had an interest."

Except for their tax troubles, little was heard about the Farahs until January 8, 1958. A front-page *Vindicator* article stated, "gambling, dormant here [Warren] for many years except on a petty scale, reportedly burst wide open in the city over the weekend." The article reported that a "new gaming spot" in downtown Warren, above a South Main Street store, was in operation. The newspaper seemed to be very knowledgeable about what was going on, stating that:

> The opening came as a surprise because four-term Mayor William C. Burbank had kept a tight lid on the rackets during his administration
>
> Gambling equipment was brought into Warren, part of which was placed in the South Main Street location, the remainder stored in nearby locations
>
> The action was conducted behind locked doors and players were carefully screened. Admission was by recognition only
>
> The only games being offered were barbut and poker
>
> John Farah, "absent from the local gambling scene for several months" was a frequent visitor

The operation was chartered as the North End Athletic Club, with a certificate hanging on the wall. Running the reputed $100,000 game was Mike Farah, whom, the newspaper claimed, had just won $10,000 in one of his own games. Mike's alleged winnings couldn't have made the government happy, since they were still fighting him for back taxes he owed. The next chapter in Mike's drama came on February 8, 1958 when Peter F. Sindelar, Mike's father-in-law, filed a $34,500 suit in Trumbull County Common Pleas Court. The suit claimed Sindelar made loans totaling $35,000 in 1942 and 1952 and that for security Farah put up four pieces of property, including two tracts of land on which the former Jungle Inn was located.

Sindelar listed the First National Bank of Mercer, Pennsylvania as a co-plaintiff in the suit, claiming he borrowed the $30,000 from the institution to give to Farah, of which only $500 had been repaid. Bank officials claimed to have no knowledge of the suit. Defendants in the action also included Grace Farah, Sindelar's daughter, the United States government, the director of the Internal Revenue in Cleveland and Bertram Zusman, proprietor of a garage operating out of the old Jungle Inn building.

Sumner Canary, US District Attorney for Northern Ohio, stated that if Sindelar could prove the land was rightfully his at the time the federal liens were placed against it, the IRS would have to void its claim on the property. An investigation of the records proved that Sindelar had filed mortgages on the Farah properties previous to the tax liens.

Four months later, while the Sindelar lawsuit was still being considered, the IRS slapped a tax lien on Albert M. and John P. Farah, the sons of Mike and Grace, claiming that the parents had illegally transferred property to them for no consideration. The Farah brothers attempted a number of transactions during these years in an effort to beat the IRS. Each time the government taxing agency saw these transactions for what they were and challenged them. In one instance the IRS ordered son John Farah to pay $5,627 in taxes and interest on a 1951 Cadillac given to him by Grace Farah, who at the time couldn't pay her taxes. Albert Farah was billed for $3,253 for a Ford Victoria given to him by his father, Mike. Both men claimed they had been given the automobiles before the government filed the tax assessments. The cases were eventually settled out of court.

◆　◆　◆

The scene switches back to John Farah as the IRS filed a delinquent tax claim of $126, 958 against him and his wife Shamis on September 24, 1958. Liens were filed against John in Cuyahoga, Mahoning and Trumbull Counties. Farah reputedly kept a mailing address in Girard, but was said to spend nearly all his time in Cleveland at his Walden Avenue home.

◆　◆　◆

On December 16, 1958 the Jungle Inn property and Mike Farah's Kenilworth Avenue home were auctioned at a Trumbull County sheriff's sale. The Jungle Inn building, appraised at $30,000 was sold for $20,000, while the Farah home sold for $18,000. At the auction, in which there were few bidders, the purchases were made by attorney Arlene Steuer, who represented Peter Sindelar.

On April 20, 1959 the 6th Circuit Court of Appeals, after reviewing the tax figures, questioned double penalties that were being charged for failure to file both as underestimating the tax and as failure to file. The case was sent back to the Tax Court for clarification. In November 16, 1959 the United States Supreme Court, after a 6 to 3 decision finalized the amounts due for the Jungle Inn operators, reducing the total by nearly $14,000:

John & Shamis Farah	$80,024
Ralph & Tessie Coletto	$47,052
Estate of Mary Catherine & Edward Tobin	$38,586
Anthony Delsanter	$30,254

With the announcement of this ruling in the *Vindicator* it marked the last time the Jungle Inn tax case was publicly reported. There's no record of whether the individuals paid the amounts as shown.

Politics and the Jean Blair Incident

During the late 1940s and throughout the 1950s Mike Farah gained a reputation as being "the top boss of all commercial gambling throughout the county…and taking complete control of the Democratic Party." Many believed he was attempting to run the entire county government. James Maxwell became his first political enemy.

On December 14, 1950 Farah's political moves were challenged in court by Maxwell, the author of "The Lowdown on Warren." The publication, which was released before the 1947 mayoral campaign, attacked Mayor Henry C. Wagner. Describing himself as a "press agent and public relations man for steel companies," and claiming that his "means of livelihood" were being interfered with, Maxwell declared in his petition, which sought $50,000 in damages, that "Farah has taken control of the Democratic party and that he used undue influence in advising Maxwell's present and potential clients to refuse his services."

On February 16, 1951, just hours before the deadline for filing a response, George Buchwalter, counsel for Farah, filed a motion asking that Maxwell's petition be "stricken from the county files," because it was "redundant, irrelevant, scurrilous and mere sham pleading." A week later Maxwell withdrew the action in preparation of filing an amended petition. On April 27 he dropped the lawsuit.

The withdrawal of the lawsuit followed on the heels of yet another controversy started by Maxwell when he demanded that John and Mike Farah be subpoenaed before the Kefauver Committee and that he be allowed to testify. Maxwell was now attacking Chief Allen claiming that he had misled Senator Kefauver by naming only Frank Cammarata (see Chapter 5) from Trumbull County as someone the committee should investigate. In a letter to the committee Maxwell claimed Mike Farah was the "head of rackets in Trumbull County" and should be made to testify.

Chief Allen replied to the allegations stating, "The Licavoli or Purple Gang interests, which are headed by Cammarata in the Trumbull County area are striving with the Farah gang for monopoly of the rackets in that district. Any fair-minded citizen should do his utmost to get rid of them both immediately." Allen defended himself against Maxwell's accusations of dropping his campaign against Mike Farah by stating he had thoroughly discussed the Jungle Inn situation with investigators. "In fact," he claimed, "I left my whole file on the Jungle Inn case with them."

In the late spring of 1959 members of the Trumbull County Board of Elections met to vote on the removal of Laura DeJacimo, a member of the staff, for reasons of "inefficiency." The board consisted of – Frank Cickelli, Trumbull County Democratic Chairman; George Howe, a Democrat; Jean P. Blair, Trumbull County Republican Chairman; Peter Snyder, a Republican; and a fifth member. The vote was three to one for DeJacimo's dismissal, with Blair choosing to sit it out.

The dismissal ruffled the feathers of Mike Farah, but the reason for this or his connection to DeJacimo was never made clear, nor was it discussed in the newspapers. Farah, however, was determined to get the decision reversed and on Sunday morning, June 7 he telephoned Jean Blair, with whom he was acquainted. Just how well the two were acquainted would become part of a future court case. When Blair arrived at Farah's Kenilworth Avenue home he parked alongside the lawn on South Avenue and Mike climbed into the automobile.

Farah got right to the point. He wanted Blair to intercede on behalf of DeJacimo and get Snyder, the other Republican on the board, to change his vote. Farah told Blair he had "sufficient power and strength" to reverse the vote if he wanted. When Blair replied that he couldn't, Farah responded to the effect, "Why not? You control the board." The *Tribune Chronicle* reported that Democrats Cickelli and Howe had tried to remove DeJacimo, who was their own appointee, several months earlier, but were stonewalled when none of the Republicans supported them

Blair did not like the pressure Farah was imposing on him and moments later an angry exchange occurred after which, the party chairman claimed, the two men traded blows in the car. Blair's side of the story had Farah knocking his glasses off, which he later recovered on the floor of the back seat, pulling the keys from the automobile's ignition and throwing them out the window onto the lawn. As Blair attempted to recover them, Farah continued the assault. At one point the 61 year-old Blair took a wild swing, hitting Farah and knocking him to the ground. While Blair searched for his keys, Farah shouted "four or five times" for someone in the house to "bring him something." Blair later said he couldn't understand what Farah was calling for because he was not speaking English. Farah then scrambled to his feet, ran into the house and returned with a gun.

Blair recalled, "Suddenly, I saw Farah come out of the house with a gun in his hand. Farah rammed the gun into my stomach a couple of times and at one time as he rammed the gun, it clicked. 'I'll shoot your guts out.'" At this point Farah began pistol-whipping Blair about the face and head. "The blood streamed down my face after the blow with the gun and I was partially blinded," he remembered. Despite the beating, Blair continued to look for the car keys. It was Farah who found them. Throwing them at the bloodied politician Farah shouted, "Get the hell out of here."

At that moment John Farah arrived. Thinking that it was someone coming to his aid, Blair rushed over only to be disappointed when John ordered him off the property. Dazed and bleeding he got into the automobile and drove himself to Trumbull Memorial Hospital, just a few blocks away. Blair was treated for a fractured nose and stitches were required to close a head wound. Blair left the hospital and returned home, where he collapsed on the kitchen floor and was found unconscious by his wife.

Blair returned to the hospital where x-rays for a fractured skull proved negative. At the hospital Blair initially refused to identify his assailant. He told officers he wanted to confer with his wife and attorney first. The officers stated that Blair claimed he had been in an altercation with "either a friend or a good friend" over a political matter. The Republican County leader hadn't mentioned being beaten with a gun, referring only that he had been hit with a blunt object, even though earlier he told hospital personnel that he was hit over the head with a revolver. On Monday Blair claimed he was still "hazy" when questioned the previous day by police, but had now collected his thoughts.

Warren Police Chief Manley English spoke to Farah by telephone the day after the incident. His entire recollection of the conversation, which took place around midnight, was reported during a hearing held later that month. Here is the account as it appeared in the *Tribune Chronicle* on June 25, 1959:

"The chief said he had tried all day Monday to get in touch with Farah by phone, but got no answer at the home until shortly after midnight.

"'Mrs. Farah answered and when I asked to speak to her husband, she said 'he isn't talking to anyone.'

"I told her, 'Look, lady, I don't know if you realize your husband is in trouble and I want to get your husband's side of the story. It's important.'

"She said 'just a minute' and in a few seconds Mr. Farah came on the line. I told him I'd like to talk to him about the Sunday incident and asked him to meet me at the office to give his side of the story.

"He replied 'it's late and besides what good would it do?' I told him I couldn't say as to what good it would do, but it is part of formality to get statements from both parties. I have Blair's and I'd like to have yours.

"Farah replied to me 'I guess it can't hurt anything. Can I tell it to you now?'"

The chief said this wasn't regular, "but I decided that it would be my only chance to get his version of the story.

"So he told me how he called Blair and asked him to stop by the house for a few minutes on an important matter. After talking awhile Blair finally agreed to stop."

The chief said "Farah told me that not long afterwards he went outside to wait and it wasn't long until Blair drove up and parked on South St. alongside the house.

"I walked to the car and asked him to come in but Blair said he couldn't stay long, let's talk in the car," the chief quoted Farah as saying. Farah said he got in the car and they sat there and talked, the chief declared. The chief said he asked Farah what they talked about and "he told me, 'I said I wanted to talk about the DeJacimo firing and we talked about it for a while and Blair said he didn't have anything to do with it. He didn't even vote on it and couldn't do anything about it.' "So I commented," the chief quoted Farah as saying, "you are as bad as Cickelli and that gang." The chief said Farah told him: 'When I said that, [Blair] got mad." English said Farah told him that Blair swore and said "I've taken care of a lot of men up in the mill, some union fellows bigger than you are, and I can take care of you." English said Farah then told Blair "If you're going to talk to me like that you should take your glasses off and you shouldn't call me a name like that so Blair took off his glasses and laid them on the back seat. Then both of us got out of the car and we met on the lawn and he swung once and hit me. We traded blows, but didn't do much damage, but then he swung once and I ducked and as he swung he was wide open and I hit him on the nose. I hit him hard, and he fell and he fell hard and he stiffened right out. When he went down, he hit his head on some part of the front of the car." The chief quoted Farah as saying that during the fight they had apparently worked their way from the lawn to the parked car.

"I saw he was bleeding and I told him he better go and get fixed up. Just then my brother drove up, he looked out and said 'What ... is going on?' Blair walked up to the car and said 'Johnny, I want to talk to you.' He said that a couple of times, but John said 'no, you better go' so Blair got in his car and drove away." English said Farah told him.

English said that at this point he asked and Farah denied that he went back into the house for anything, that he had a gun in his pocket when he went out for the first time, and that he had taken the keys from Blair's car and thrown them on the lawn.

The chief said "I asked Farah 'are you sure you didn't go get a gun?'"

"Farah said, 'Look, I wouldn't lie, I swear on the graves of my mother and father and son that that's the truth.'

"Then Farah said "I stood and talked to my brother awhile and then we went inside.'"

On Tuesday, June 9 Farah was charged with assault with intent to kill after Blair signed an affidavit in his hospital bed. A warrant was issued for Farah's arrest and Detectives Walter Mackey and Joseph Mijic were dispatched to pick him up. Although the detectives failed to identify her in their report, a woman, obviously Grace Farah, informed the two that Mike Farah was not home. Detectives told her to have Farah call police headquarters as soon as he returned. Area newspapers assigned reporters and photographers to cover the booking and they headed to the police station at noon to await Farah, who was allegedly spending the afternoon in Cleveland at Thistledown Race Track. At 10:15 p.m. the news people were notified that Farah had called from his lawyer's office in Cleveland and said he would come in the next morning.

The news people concluded that they had been deceived and got together to discuss a strategy. They walked away, seemingly abandoning their vigil. They drove off, but returned shortly before 11:00 p.m., parking in a lot across from the police station from where they could see both entrances. As midnight approached an automobile pulled to the curb outside the station. Nothing happened for a few minutes and then the entrance to the police station opened up and a man signaled to someone in the vehicle. Mike Farah jumped out of the car and quickly disappeared into the police station. The newspapermen, who were parked about 100 yards away, got out of their vehicle and chased after him. Once inside the station they did not see Farah anywhere and were told by officers inside that he was not there. Some of the newsmen returned to their vigil outside and moments later they saw Farah dash out and jump into a taxicab. The *Tribune Chronicle* reported that the police blotter showed that "Farah was booked on the charge and released on bond, all in less than 60 seconds.

It appeared to the news media that Farah's crafty counsel – consisting of Cleveland attorney Michael Cozza, the law partner of Arlene Steuer, and from Hubbard former county judge and state senator J. Eugene Roberts – had worked out the logistics with the Warren Police Department to avoid publicity for their client. The booking took place in a second floor court office where detective William Poulos wrote out the arrest ticket and Court Clerk George Tablac handled the bond release paper. Earlier in the day a power of attorney had been given and bonding papers arranged by the Clerk of Municipal Court with bond set at $2,500. This had been arranged through Michael DeVincenzo, a bail bondsman and Democratic nominee for city councilman, who drove Farah to the police station that night. Members of the media immediately lodged a complaint about Farah's "special treatment" with Safety-Service Director Joseph Wyndham, who asked Chief English for an investigation and report on the matter.

The next morning Farah arrived at police headquarters with counsel to be photographed and fingerprinted; he then proceeded to the courthouse to await a 10:00 a.m. arraignment at which he pleaded not guilty. Afterwards Farah was in a congenial mood and allowed photographers to take his picture in the courthouse corridor. As he walked down the stairs Farah told photographers, "If the pictures don't develop, just call me up." Farah's friendly mood began to dissipate as the photographers followed him down the street. At one point Farah stopped and asked why they were still snapping pictures. Didn't they have enough?

On June 11 the *Tribune Chronicle* published an editorial entitled "Mike Farah's Power?" The editorial read in part:

> "Mike Farah has not been inactive. He has been prominently, if not openly, identified with political campaigns and has strongly backed candidates for public office. He has maintained interest in political activities, and the purpose of this interest has not always been visible.
>
> "The underworld cannot operate anywhere without connivance with public officials. That's a fact that cannot be refuted.
>
> "In the incident which culminated in the beating of Mr. Blair, the question arises why this public official, at the beck and call of Mike Farah, called at the latter's home.
>
> "How much power do Mike Farah or other racketeers hold in this city and county? The public has a right to know. A thorough investigation certainly would be in order."

Meanwhile, Warren Mayor William Burbank suspended Chief English "for negligence in not conducting a proper investigation by not arresting and grilling suspects in the vicious attempt on Jean Blair's life." The mayor said his actions had nothing to do with the "speedy booking" incident, although that matter was still under investigation. Burbank named veteran Detective Captain Verne Teeple acting police chief.

After his suspension order, Chief English said he would appeal the action with the Civil Service Commission. In an interview, he claimed the reason for the suspension was that he was being "sacrificed as a political pawn." The whole incident, he declared, "emanates from a difference within the Democratic Party." There was no mishandling of the case he claimed, the department followed every legal requirement according to the Ohio General Code. English insisted his men could not arrest Farah any earlier because Blair had not filed a formal complaint. The chief filed his appeal and a hearing was set for June 22.

On June 15, after a three day "intensive" investigation by Wyndham and City Solicitor Bruce Birrell, the director found no reason for disciplinary action against eight officers named by news reporters as being involved in the now notorious "speedy booking" escapade. The only disputed fact in the whole investigation seemed to hinge on which door Farah actually exited from. News people were adamant that Farah could not have come out the door police "swore" that he did. Instead, reporters claimed he was allowed to use a rear fire exit. It should be noted that in Wyndham's investigation the only interviewees were the police officers. Not a single newsperson from the group who maintained a 13-hour vigil outside the station was questioned.

The odious affair left a bad taste in the mouths of the citizenry of Warren. The incident remained a hot topic of discussion. The Crime & Public Relations Committee of the Warren Ministerial Association called a meeting to discuss the case while the Commission on Christian Relations of the First Methodist Church approved a resolution "expressing distaste of the preferential treatment" shown to Farah.

After his investigation, Wyndham issued a directive to Acting Police Chief Teeple stating that in all felony arrests the booking must take place in the downstairs area of the police station and that felony suspects be held a reasonable time until "trained" men are notified to fingerprint and photograph them. On the matter of Chief English, he made it clear that no orders were to be issued by him while he was on suspension and that he was not to be granted access to any department records.

On June 17 a preliminary hearing was held for Farah in Warren Municipal Court before Judge James A. Ravella. The preliminary hearing would produce one of three results. First, the judge could bind the defendant over to the grand jury on the assault to kill charge; second, the charge could be dismissed; or third, the charge could be reduced to a lesser degree under which the municipal court would have jurisdiction.

Outside the courthouse a crowd gathered to watch Blair and Farah enter. The 80-seat courtroom was filled to capacity with more than a dozen spectators standing. John Spain, the police prosecutor, handled the case for the city, while Farah was represented by Michael Cozza and Arlene Steuer.

The first witness was Jean Blair, who told the court how Farah had shoved a snub-nosed revolver into his stomach and threatened, "I'll shoot your guts out." He then testified that Farah pistol-whipped him and tried to kick him in the groin three times. Farah appeared calm sitting at the defense table, dressed in a blue suit and his signature black and white shoes. As Blair delivered his account of the fight, the defendant shook his head in disagreement and whispered to his counsel.

On cross-examination Steuer attacked like a pit bull causing Prosecutor Spain to object on a number of occasions. She focused on three areas. The first was Blair's actions at the time of the fight:

Steuer: Why didn't you leave instead of taking a beating?
Blair: I was looking for my keys so I could start my car.
Steuer: Did you consider finding you keys more important than
   your life!
Blair: I wanted to find them and get away.

The former deputy sheriff denied he had whipped off his glasses and told Farah, "I've licked better men than you."

Steuer next attacked the witnesses' statements to police. Blair said he had revealed very little to officers at the hospital because, "I was confused and battered from the beating I had received." Blair testified he felt he shouldn't tell the complete story because he was not represented by counsel and that they should be present in case "litigation ever came up on the fight." Blair admitted he didn't tell police at first he had been struck with a revolver, instead referring to the weapon as a blunt instrument. Police, he said, did not question him further about it.

The third item Steuer grilled Blair on was his relationship with Farah. Blair denied vehemently that the two were "close" friends. He declared he had never been inside Farah's home, that Farah had ever been in his home, or that the two had ever been out together in public. Although he had known Farah for ten years he considered the relationship as "neither friendly nor unfriendly."

The prosecution called two more witnesses that first day, an assistant medical records librarian at the Trumbull Memorial Hospital, and Dr. Charles A. Anderson. The latter testified that a "Y-shaped" laceration on Blair's head had been left by a "blunt instrument," never referring to it as a revolver. On cross-examination, he stated that the injury could not have been caused by a fall, as Farah had told Chief English, unless Blair "had been hanging upside down by his heels and then fallen." When Steuer questioned Blair's claim that he was dazed and confused, Dr. Anderson said, "He answered my questions in a rational manner every time I spoke to him." After Dr. Anderson's testimony the prosecution rested its case.

Steuer, who conducted the defense assisted by Cozza, called five witnesses, Grace Farah, criminologist David Cowles and the three police officers – Patrolmen Albert Timko and Ralph Marchio, and Detective Walter Mackey – who questioned Blair at the hospital after the attack. Grace Farah was called to the stand in an effort to poke holes in the politician's story. She testified that when Blair drove up she told her husband of his arrival and Farah went outside to greet him. This was contrary to Blair's claim that Farah was standing in the yard when he arrived. Grace claimed that her husband never came into the house in search of a weapon and that the only gun in the home was one hidden under an upstairs bed. In another contradictory statement, Grace Farah claimed Blair had been in the house on many occasions; Blair said he was never inside the Farah home.

Steuer called David Cowles, the legendary criminologist with 30 years experience with the Cleveland Police Department, to testify about the weapon. Blair stated the gun misfired when it was jammed into his stomach. Prosecutor Spain objected vehemently to the weapon being allowed into evidence, claiming there was no proof this gun was the one used in the assault. After Ravella overruled Spain's first objection, the prosecutor offered a general objection to all of Cowles' statements. Steuer claimed Spain should not be allowed a blanket exception and should have to object to each question. During Cowles' testimony each question by Steuer was met with an objection by Spain, an overruling by the judge, and then Spain asking that an exception be noted. For the next half-hour each question to Cowles was followed by:

"Objection!"

"Overruled!"

"Exception!"

As Ravella overruled the objections, Cowles told the court that the revolver, covered in dust when presented to him, was in perfect working condition even though the trigger had not been pulled in some time and that his investigation showed no traces of blood, hair or tissue from the attack.

After a day and a half of testimony both sides rested without Farah taking the stand. During closing arguments, Spain declared that evidence presented met the requirements to have the case bound over to the grand jury and that it met all the elements of the crime. He "dwelled" on the fact that the defendant did not take the stand in his own defense. "Since there were only two participants in the fight and since one of them has not testified, the court must accept the other's testimony as fact," Spain told the judge.

In her closing statement Steuer told the judge, "Are we to believe that a man frightened for his life would remain in the yard of his attacker looking for car keys? This was simply the case of a man who got licked in a fight and fabricated a charge. There was no proof offered of malice. His story is so improbable as to be beyond belief."

On the morning of June 18 Judge Ravella rendered a lengthy decision. In part the ruling stated:

> "The court is reluctant to believe that a man threatened with a gun does nothing but continue to look for his keys after being struck over the head with some instrument as he claims. He doesn't leave the scene but according to his testimony continues to look for his car keys.
>
> "This coupled with the fact that two or three strong blows with a gun would inflict more injury than that suffered by the complaining witness then would probably leave him in a condition where he could not leave the scene had he so desired.
>
> "The testimony of the complaining witness was that the defendant found his car keys and threw the same in the direction thus permitting him to start his car and drive away from the scene without any further difficulty.
>
> "It is difficult for the court to see any intent to kill when according to the testimony of the State a man has a gun, is beating another man over the head with it, and instead of continuing to beat him, stops the beating and produces his car keys for him so that he can leave the scene.
>
> "This being the situation and there being no question here but there was a fight between two men who were friendly prior to the fight, and the defendant having failed to tell his version of what happened at this hearing, the Court can do nothing other than find the defendant guilty of assault and battery.
>
> "Therefor the charge is reduced from one of assault with intent to kill to the offense of assault and battery, and the penalty will be imposed on that basis."

With that the judge fined Farah $200 and costs. The original charge, a felony, called for a prison sentence. The assault and battery charge was a misdemeanor and involved no prison time. Despite the favorable ruling to Farah, his lawyers announced they were appealing the decision and the fine. One point of the appeal was that there could be no assault and battery since no assault charge could exist "when two parties engage in a fight under mutual agreement." Farah was released and the current $2,500 bond was continued.

John Spain and Bruce Birrell, claiming Ravella's ruling was "contrary to the evidence," questioned the judge's power to reduce a felony charge down to a misdemeanor without dismissing the felony charge. Also disagreeing with Ravella's decision was Trumbull County Prosecutor Charles H. Anderson.[5] Despite there being no bind-over from the lower court, Anderson declared, "The prosecutor's office will be ready to take the case before the grand jury next September. We will ask the grand jury at that time if it wants to consider this case and I am sure it will."

The judge's decision elicited more public outcry and a demand for an independent outside investigation. In addition, Safety-Service Director Wyndham's earlier investigation into Farah's booking was called a "whitewash" by outraged citizens, who flooded the local newspapers with letters to the editor. Warren City Council rejected one councilman's proposal that Ohio Governor Michael DiSalle conduct a state investigation.

Newspapers around the state took shots at the Farah / Blair incident. The *Akron Beacon-Journal,* in an editorial wrote, "When it comes to showing consideration for the tender feelings of alleged criminals, the Warren police department has a record unmatched anywhere in the state." As far as the "lightning-quick" booking of Farah, the editorial added, "Warren should be mighty proud of a police department as efficient as that."

A *Vindicator* editorial on June 19 began:

> "Law abiding citizens of Warren who have no use for such men as Mike Farah and the bad name which his presence gives the city and Trumbull County were both disappointed and angry because of the lenient treatment accorded the racketeer in Warren's municipal court yesterday."

Next it was Chief English's turn on the hot seat. On late Friday afternoon, June 19, Mayor Burbank filed the following statement with the Warren Civil Service Commission detailing eight points for his suspension of the chief:

> "Further investigation discloses:
> ›   That Chief Manley English claims he was absent from the city on Sunday, June 7, when the assault occurred; that the police department made a routine check and that the victim at the end of the check failed to identify the assailant.

> That on Monday, June 8, Chief English had reason to suspect the identity of the assailant and was in fact informed the attempt on Blair's life was made by Mike Farah.

> That Chief English failed to take Mike Farah into custody for questioning on Monday, June 8, when Mike Farah was known to be in the city.

> That Chief English did not attempt to take Mike Farah into custody until Tuesday, June 9, by which time Mike Farah was supposed to have been gone from the city.

> That Chief English failed to make any attempt to locate Farah, contenting himself with the statement that Farah would give himself up when he was ready to do so.

> That Chief English did permit Mike Farah to set the time, place and manner of his apprehension.

> That Chief English permitted Farah to arrive at the police station with his bondsman and permitted him to ascend the stairway to Municipal Court and was permitted to leave the building within four minutes after arrival there.

> That Chief English permitted Farah's release without fingerprinting or photographs as required by law in cases involving a felony.

Therefore, on the foregoing, I charge Manley English with incompetence and gross neglect of duty and herewith order he be suspended from duty indefinitely."

On June 22 the appeal hearing on Chief English's suspension was held in Warren City Council Chambers. Deciding the issue would be three Civil Service Commission panel members. Chief English was represented by George Buchwalter, a seemingly strange choice for a law enforcement official as he had also represented the Farah brothers, James Munsene and Frank Cammarata. He was assisted by David F. McLain. The city was represented by Bruce Birrell and John Spain. Among the 50 spectators present were Mayor Burbank, Director Wyndham and representatives of the Ohio Police Chief's Association.

To be decided by the commission was whether they would uphold the mayor's indefinite suspension order, disaffirm it, or modify it. Before the hearing could get started the commissioners had to rule on three motions made by Buchwalter. One was for the dismissal of the suspension order due to the fact the order was signed by Wyndham and not Mayor Burbank as required by law; and two requesting that Burbank's detailed charges against English be stricken from the record, due to the fact it contained facts not included in the original suspension order. After nearly thirty minutes of hearing arguments the commission denied all three motions.

After opening statements, the first witness called was Warren Police Sergeant Harry Rhoda, who was working second shift the day of the incident. He testified that he received a telephone call from Trumbull Memorial Hospital from Dr. Anderson, who had treated Blair. He related that the doctor berated him for not knowing about the incident. Rhoda said he pulled the report, which had been filed by the sergeant on the previous shift. Sergeant Robert Darr went to the hospital to question Blair but, according to Rhoda, the report was "vague except to state that a man had been injured." When English arrived Rhoda discussed the casualty report with him, which did not identify the assailant. Rhoda said that at that time on Sunday afternoon, no detectives were available to investigate. Rhoda claimed that based on the information he had at hand, he couldn't ascertain if Blair's injuries were serious, his reports only indicated a misdemeanor had occurred. Rhoda said his conversation with the doctor ended with him telling Anderson "to call him again if Blair's condition worsened."

Rhoda was followed to the stand by six other officers – Detectives Joseph Mijic, Harold Lapp and Walter Mackey, Identification Bureau Clerk Robert Messett and Captains Harry Thomas and James A. Sullivan. Each testified that all phases of the investigation and booking followed procedure, and that at no time were they given any orders from the chief to give Farah special treatment.

When questioned about the trip he made to the Kenilworth Avenue home that Tuesday to arrest Farah, Detective Lapp was asked if he entered the Farah home to look for him. "It's not the policy on the first contact with a warrant to search a house unless we have good reason to believe the party is in there though someone says he isn't. We try to use a little public relations when serving any warrant and do not try to force the power of the warrant and the police badge unless we have to." Lapp pointed out that half of all suspects, once they are notified there is a warrant for their arrest, turn themselves in at the station. "We had reason to believe that this would happen in this case," Lapp told the commission.

Detective Mijic confirmed a *Vindicator* newspaper statement, which claimed one of their reporters tipped them off to Farah's whereabouts hours before he turned himself in. Mijic stated that *Vindicator* reporter David Durbin, of the newspaper's Warren Bureau, had mentioned this to him while he was standing in front of headquarters. Durbin stated that he had a reliable tip that Farah was in a house on the east side.

"I asked him where, but he either didn't hear me or he ignored me and went inside the police station, Mijic stated. Asked why he didn't seek out Durbin for more information Mijic's replied, "I had been ignored once and wasn't going to be ignored again." Mijic said he didn't think the tip was anymore significant than some of the rumors they had been hearing all day.

The next witness was Captain Thomas, who had command of the second shift at the station the night Farah surrendered himself. He told commission members about the call from the mobster. "Farah said he was in Cleveland and would not be in that night but would come in that morning to be booked. I called the chief immediately but was unable to contact him until about 10 p.m. when I gave him the message. At this time the chief suggested I tell the reporters who were at the station about Farah's call for their own information." Thomas said that English suggested he not tell the reporters to leave, just give them the information and let them decide for themselves if they wanted to wait.

On Tuesday morning Safety-Service Director Wyndham told the commission that "there was a complete lack of authority and direction" in the handling of Farah's arrest and booking. He said he suggested to English on more than one occasion that Farah be picked up, once it was learned he was the assailant. Wyndham stated that the chief's position was that since Blair had not yet filed charges he would not act. Wyndham responded, "I told the chief it's our right to do so." He related to the commission that suspects were frequently arrested on open charges and it would have been reasonable to make an arrest in Farah's case due to the serious nature of the crime. He stated, "If police waited to follow normal procedures in obtaining warrants before making arrests, the city would be in chaos."

Wyndham was followed to the stand by Municipal Court Clerk George Tablac, who handled the booking procedure for the city. He was incensed at the newspapers for reporting that Farah had been booked in less than 40 seconds. Tablac gave a detailed description of the events of that day and night. Tablac went to see Blair in the hospital that Tuesday morning to have him sign the affidavit. After the warrant was prepared it was given to the chief. That afternoon Tablac obtained from Judge Ravella the amount of the bond, $2,500. At 4:00 p.m. he was contacted by bondsman Michael DiVincenzo who arrived a half-hour later to make bond arrangements.

At 11:30 that night DiVincenzo contacted Tablac at his home and said Farah would be at the station in fifteen minutes to be bonded out. Tablac agreed to meet him, declaring to the commissioners this was not out of the ordinary. The clerk said he then called the station and informed Captain Sullivan that Farah was on his way. Tablac arrived at the station, mailed a letter at the corner and then told officers to send Farah up to his office once he arrived. Tablac stated that Officer William Poulos brought Farah upstairs for the procedure minutes later.

Tablac said he assumed the man Poulos brought in was Farah, as he had never seen him before. Once the booking procedure was over, Farah asked if he could leave using the fire escape. He was told to use the front door, which Tablac testified that Farah did.

During cross-examination, the clerk repeated that it was not at all unusual for him to come to the station to handle a booking at "off hours," that he had once come down at 3:30 in the morning. Tablac told commission members, "I want to get some stuff straightened out, especially what reporters wrote about us." He then called the stories of the 40-second booking "silly nonsense," stating that it took a minute and a half to two minutes just for the arrest record to be made out, let alone securing the suspects signature on release copies.

Officer William Poulos was the next witness. He testified he was given the warrant for Farah's arrest when he arrived at the station at 11:30 p.m. to begin his shift, but was given no information on where to serve the warrant, just told to try to serve it. Poulos was about to get in a squad car when he noticed Tablac's arrival, followed seconds later by Farah and his bondsman DeVincenzo. Poulos told Farah he had a warrant for his arrest and escorted him into the police station. At the booking room he was told to escort the prisoner upstairs. "At no time was Farah handcuffed because he had made no effort to resist arrest and because it was not customary to do so when they surrendered on their own. We attempt to use as much diplomacy as possible when handling suspects inside or outside the jail," Poulos explained.

Poulos testified, as Tablac had, that Farah asked if he could leave using the fire escape. Poulos stated, "I shook my head no to Tablac and Tablac told Farah he wold have to leave the way he came [through the prisoner entrance] or out the front door." Farah went down the front stairs before both men. "Farah opened the door, stuck his head out and was gone," Poulos declared.

Under cross-examination Poulos stated he had been given no special instructions from the chief as to how to handle the warrant or booking procedure. He also denied being contacted by Farah or an agent of Farah's to arrange a booking that would avoid publicity and photographers for the mobster.

After Poulos's testimony the city called Chief English to the stand for cross-examination, knowing that he was within his right not to testify. But, English agreed and began answering questions. He stated that as head of the department it was his responsibility to delegate orders and not be responsible for the actions of each and every officer. That being said, he stated that on the Monday morning after the incident he instructed Captain Verne Teeple to send officers to question Blair if he were up to it. Upon finding out that Farah was the assailant English began telephoning the Farah home, finally getting hold of Grace Farah sometime after midnight.

After a brief argument English got her to put her husband on the phone. It was at this time he got Farah's side of the incident.

The next day, after Blair signed the affidavit, English turned the warrant over the Teeple to execute. Asked by Birrell, "Did you issue any further orders?" The chief replied, "No. I had placed the matter in the hands of the detective captain and I felt he was well able to handle it."

The chief said he recalled mentioning to Wyndham that they place Farah's home under surveillance, but decided not to due to the cost of calling in additional officers.

Asked why he released Farah's comments about the fight to the newspapers, English answered, "That is a perfectly normal procedure. We don't withhold information from the press unless we feel to do so would be detrimental to the investigation of a case. In this instance, I failed to see any reason to withhold the information."

English's defense counsel postponed their questioning of the chief. Birrell, for his last witness, wanted to call *Vindicator* reporter David Durbin. Defense objected, correctly stating that Durbin had been present throughout the hearing. The commissioners upheld their objection and the city announced it was resting their case.

Buchwalter immediately asked that the case be dismissed claiming the city had failed to produce any evidence that was grounds for punishment. The commissioners overruled the request stating they were going to conduct a complete hearing before rendering their decision.

The defense began their case with the calling of Dayton Police Chief Paul J. Price. Over the objections of Birrell, the defense was granted permission to present hypothetical situations to the chief and then ask what he would do under the circumstances. These situations were similar, but not identical to the case at hand. In each instance Price's handling of the situation was the same as how it was handled by English. On cross-examination Birrell could not shake Price and his testimony proved to be very significant.

On Wednesday morning Sergeant Robert Darr appeared as the first witness that day. Darr had been in charge of the shift prior to Sergeant Rhoda. He testified that upon receiving word of an assault from the hospital he dispatched Patrolmen Ralph Marchio and Albert Timko to investigate. He stated that at the end of his shift he did not mention the Blair assault to Rhoda.

Patrolman Marchio then testified that at the hospital Blair told them that he "felt good," and didn't want to discuss the matter until he talked to his lawyer. According to Marchio, he was told by Blair that the fight followed a heated exchange after some political talk with a "friend." When one of the commissioners asked for confirmation of Blair's "friend" characterization, Marchio backtracked and replied, "I believe he said another person." Marchio repeated the story about referring Blair to his hospital report where he claimed to have been hit with a gun. Blair now stated that he was not sure it was a gun, but it was a "blunt instrument."

Next, Officer Jack Lubert testified that he and his partner Detective Gordon Herbert had been sent by Captain Teeple to canvas the neighborhood to see if any witnesses could be found. After a check of nine nearby homes, the officers came up empty.

Captain Verne Teeple, the acting police chief, was the next witness and he quickly confirmed many of the comments made by English. Teeple said he was not aware of the incident until arriving at work Monday morning. He said the matter quickly became "more than routine." Teeple admitted that he did not make the casualty report on Blair public because of the "prominence of the party" involved. "I felt that anything of this nature was the chief's responsibility," Teeple testified.

Chief English was the last defense witness to take the stand that Wednesday morning as commission members had "personal business matters" to attend to that afternoon. The chief's testimony was "in narrative form describing his actions from the time he first learned of the attack on Jean Blair Sunday evening until Mike Farah's arrest at midnight Tuesday."

During cross-examination by Birrell the day before, English admitted he had been to Farah's home. He was not asked how frequently or what the visits were for. On Thursday, June 24, the last day of the hearing, he was pressed to give more details of those visits. English claimed he had gone there to discuss the proposed padlocking of the Farah's new gambling club on South Main Street. Farah had called the chief at his home after the story appeared in the newspaper. Farah wanted to know if the story was true and what he could do to prevent it.

Instead of going to the station to discuss it in the chief's office, Farah instead asked English to come to his home. The chief told the commission, "Farah told me he didn't want to come to the station because 'if I go there and anyone sees me they will start gossip that we are connected which you and I both know is not true.'" The chief related that Farah had told him that "some young fellows had come to him and asked to use [the South Main St. facility] as a club." He guessed that some gambling had been going on, but asked English to hold off on the padlocking. Just why the hoodlum thought there would be less "gossip" if the chief's car was spotted at the Farah home wasn't asked, and that's exactly what happened. English said the next day Wyndham came to his office and said he had information that the chief had been seen at the Farah home.

English was next asked by counsel to discuss Jean Blair. "I have been a close friend of Blair's for the past 12 years," he said. "I gave Blair all the consideration I did because of this friendship and because I did not want to see him get hurt. I know he had already been hurt.

"There would have been completely different action if on Sunday he [Blair] had told the officers that Farah was his assailant. I feel that this business is a complete stall. If there was any evidence on the part of Blair to cooperate we would have had someone there [Sunday] to get the affidavit.

"It seems to me that Blair wasn't very anxious to take any action. The general idea seemed to be that everyone wanted us – the police department – to take action. If we had the evidence for support, we would have taken action. I have devoted more time to this case than any other similar case in my eight years as chief."

English told the commission his version of a conversation he had with John Spain. According to the chief the police prosecutor told him, "I have orders to prepare an affidavit charging assault with intent to kill." English said he responded with, "You're the police prosecutor, and it's none of my business, but in the past haven't you insisted on certain types of evidence before filing charges? Do you think you have that kind of evidence in this case?" The chief claimed Spain replied, "No, I don't see where we have evidence to that effect, but I've been ordered to do it."

Spain took exception to the chief's testimony and later explained to reporters, "Naturally as one of the lawyers involved in the hearing I could hardly appear on the witness stand. I cannot, however, allow the chief's statements to stand unchallenged. Chief English's version of our conversation is not consistent with the facts. Actually, I had determined as early as 5:30 p.m. Monday, June 8, after talking with Jean Blair in the hospital, that charges of assault with intent to kill should be filed."

Chief English's testimony lasted until almost 1:30 p.m. He admitted that he refused to file charges initially against Farah because he didn't have Blair's affidavit. He discussed his phone conversation with Farah the night after the incident, and went into the problems of running and trying to train a department with the budget he had to work with.

When his testimony was completed the hearing came to an end. Buchwalter asked for a third time that the charges be dropped. Again he was rebuffed. Attorneys on both sides were not permitted to make final arguments. They were told by commission members that a decision would be handed down sometime after July 1 and if they wanted to file closing briefs they had until that time to do so.

On July 8 the members of the Civil Service Commission delivered a 14-page opinion (See Appendix 3) which cleared Chief English of negligence charges and reinstated him as police chief retroactive to June 11, the day he was suspended. At a meeting announcing the decision English told the commissioners he was "grateful for their consideration." He told reporters the he "didn't see how the decision could have been anything else." He and his defense counsel refused to make further comment until they could read the full text of the opinion. Safety-Service Director Wyndham also declined comment pending his review of the document.

On the charge by Mayor Burbank that English had allowed Farah to "set the time, place and manner" of his arrest, the commissioners declared there was no evidence introduced during the four-day hearing that, "Chief English knew or in any way arranged the special handling of Farah at the time of his arrest, booking, bonding and subsequent release." The commissioners' opinion did not absolve English of "errors in judgment," but decided the errors were not greater than "those committed by other members of the department upon whom [English] had some right to rely."

With that, the opinion seemingly blasted everyone else involved. They "ripped" the department for "the slovenly and almost negligent manner in which our local police officers apparently operate the department." On the "speedy booking," the opinion stated that the circumstances were "too pat and showed excellent planning" despite the fact that "witnesses would have us believe the 'fast booking' was a series of coincidences." The commission concluded that steps were initiated beforehand to "make the apprehension, booking, and release of the wanted suspect as painless and easy as possible. We can assume the chief had no knowledge that Farah would be treated with 'kid gloves' by men in his department and-or employees of the Municipal Court of Warren." This was followed by "and most of the citizens of Warren are sickened by the fact that one Mike Farah…with no visible means of support and known to almost everyone as an overlord of the underworld in this area, should be given preferential treatment… than that which would be expected of any ordinary and respectable citizen of this city." Commission members declared, "The members of the police department should be summarily dismissed," if any of the offenses were committed again.

The city's top brass were not exempt from the commissions' wrath, who stated they were "amazed" that Wyndham's own investigation exonerated the officers involved in the "speedy booking" episode. It was apparent that the commission members seethed over the fact that "the arresting officers, and perhaps others, showed ignorance, indifference or pre-determined plan to aid and abet the quick arrival and departure of Farah." They noted on several occasions in their opinion that there was never any effort to bring Farah in for questioning.

Despite the apparent exoneration of the chief, in December 1959 Warren City Council defeated an ordinance proposal that would have reimbursed English for his legal expenses.

◆   ◆   ◆

On Tuesday, September 15, 1959, Mike Farah went before the Trumbull County Grand Jury. His appearance was brief and he slipped out the back door, accompanied by attorney Buchwalter, refusing to stop at the clerk of court's office to collect his $3 entitlement as a subpoenaed witness. On Thursday, after hearing testimony from Jean Blair that the fight was a result of the Republican County Chairman's failure to intercede after the firing of Laura DeJacimo, the grand jury returned "a lone secret indictment" of Farah charging him with assault with intent to kill.

The indictment was kept secret by County Prosecutor Anderson because they hoped to arrest Farah on Friday after 4:30 p.m. That way, with the courthouse closed for the weekend, Farah would have to remain behind bars until Monday morning's arraignment. A warrant was issued for his arrest at 4:00 p.m. Friday, but Farah was too crafty to fall into the trap. Anticipating the appearance of deputies at his door that afternoon, Farah left his house before noon. Attorney Buchwalter telephoned Chief Sheriff's Deputy Edward James and informed him that his client was on a "brief vacation," and would surrender himself to the Trumbull County Jail "sometime" on Monday.

On Monday morning Buchwalter appeared at the county jail at 10:00, apparently preparing the way for his client, who arrived 20 minutes later. Booked, photographed and fingerprinted during a procedure that lasted 15 minutes, Farah was then escorted across the street to the courthouse for his arraignment. He pleaded not guilty to the charge of assault with intent to kill before Common Pleas Judge George Birrell and was released after posting a $7,500 bond. Farah and counsel then left the courthouse, amid the cracking flashbulbs of newspaper cameras, to prepare for a November trial date.

On November 7 an incident was reported to the newspapers by Laura DeJacimo, the elections board member whose firing precipitated the Blair / Farah ordeal. On Tuesday morning Mrs. DeJacimo was at the East Market Street School serving as an election worker. During the day a smoke bomb was wired to the spark plugs under the hood of her car. The bomb was wired incorrectly and, instead of exploding, caused the vehicle not to operate properly. The next morning DeJacimo took the automobile to a service station where attendants discovered the device.

DeJacimo took the bomb to the police department and personally handed it to Chief English. By Thursday afternoon, after receiving no word back from the department, DeJacimo telephoned the newspapers. Reporters contacted Chief English the next day. He told them he felt the device was harmless and he "didn't want to take detectives off more important work." English stated he had the bomb dusted for fingerprints, but none were found. He said no attempt was made to retrieve prints from DeJacimo's automobile and no written report of the incident had been prepared for news people to view.

By mid-November both sides in the Blair / Farah incident were waiting for the Seventh District Court of Appeals to hand down a ruling on Municipal Judge Ravella's decision before proceeding with the new charges. On November 16 the appeals court met to hear arguments from both sides. Arlene Steuer, instead of arguing her client's case, asked to withdraw her appeal, claiming the defense was satisfied with the Municipal Court's finding of guilty of assault and battery. John Spain stood by his previous claim that Judge Ravella had no authority to find Farah guilty of a lesser charge when he was charged with a felony – assault with intent to kill. After waiting five months for the Appeals Court to hear the case, the hearing lasting a mere twenty minutes.

On November 20 the Seventh District Court of Appeals unanimously reversed Municipal Judge Ravella's ruling with the following decision:

> "A Municipal Court, had, in cases of felony, only power to discharge or recognize the defendant to appear before the proper court. It had no final jurisdiction in such cases or any power to impose any sentence."

The next day, at the request of County Prosecutor Charles Anderson, Judge Ravella dismissed the charge against Mike Farah and a trial date was set for Common Pleas Court. Before the trial began, both sides announced the witnesses they were subpoenaing. Police officers, former and present council members, and a surprise witness for the defense – Mrs. Jean Blair – were all served.

On Monday, December 14 the long awaited trial of Mike Farah for assault with intent to kill Jean Blair began. George Buchwalter and Arlene Steuer represented the defendant; Judge Birrell presided; and prosecutors Charles Anderson and J. Don Campbell represented the state. Courthouse officials were prepared to hang "standing room only" signs, anticipating that the spectators would be as plentiful as they were during the June hearing. There were few people in the courtroom that morning. It could have been that they expected a lengthy jury selection. But the selection of fourteen members to the panel went rather quickly, with most jurors readily admitting they had read articles about the Farah / Blair incident. Farah dressed in a brown suit and maroon tie sat patiently at the defense table as prospective jurors were questioned. By 1:30 twelve jurors and two alternatives were sworn in and then transported to the scene of the crime – Farah's Kenilworth Avenue home.

Upon the jury's return both sides presented their opening statements. "Farah intended to kill Blair," Assistant Prosecutor Campbell told the jury. The unprovoked attack and the injuries suffered by Blair indicate intent on Farah's part to kill Blair and the state feels that the evidence will prove all of the allegations in the indictment."

Audrey Steuer served up the opening statement for the defense declaring, "Farah has never given his version of the fight. It was not as dramatic as the state pictures it. It was merely a fight between two men who had been friends for years.

"The argument was not about the dismissal of Laura DeJacimo from the election board. We will give you the reason later on.

"Had the two men been less well known the incident would have ended right there. When confronted by his wife and police for an explanation of the injuries, Blair, trying to recover his dignity, blamed Farah.

"There was no gun involved and this was nothing more than a backyard brawl. Put the argument where it belongs by bringing in a not guilt verdict."

The rest of the afternoon was taken up with the testimony of Jean Blair, who returned to the stand the next morning. Blair basically repeated the same story he had told in Judge Ravella's courtroom the previous June with one exception. Blair now contended that Farah's threat was, "I'll shoot your guts out with a shot gun." It was a slip defense attorneys would not miss on cross.

Buchwalter questioned Blair during cross-examination. It was a brutal encounter for the politician. Tempers flared as Prosecutor Anderson strenuously objected to questions and aside remarks made by legal counsel. Judge Birrell told jurors to forget the heated exchange and to disregard remarks made by Buchwalter.

It became apparent quickly where the defense was going with the case in this second trial. Farah and his defense team were now contending that the fight was an argument over money loaned by the defendant to Blair.

"Not so," Blair angrily declared. "I never got any money from Farah under any circumstances. I don't remember getting a personal loan for $500 from Farah, or that he ever loaned me any."

Buchwalter then attempted to paint Blair and Farah as close personal friends. He questioned Blair about being at the Farah home and with him at several social functions. He dug into Blair's "frequent" visits to the Jungle Inn and meetings the two men had in Blair's home and at the Buchwalter house.

The questioning got around to the day of the altercation. Blair admitted that during the fracas he never attempted to flee or call out for help because, although in fear for his life, he didn't want to be a coward.

"I stood there and took a beating," Blair said. "It was hard to take."

Blair admitted he had no marks or bruises on his stomach or abdomen, where he said Farah shoved the revolver. There were also no marks on his groin where he claimed Farah had kicked him. It was then that Buchwalter brought up the shotgun statement. Blair explained that he didn't think the statements were contradictory since he only testified that Farah threatened to shoot him with a shotgun, not that he went and retrieved one.

Mariam Blair was the state's next witness. Examined by Campbell, she related how her husband had dropped her off at Trumbull Memorial Hospital about 12:15 that Sunday, where she worked as a "Gray Lady."[6] By 4:00 p.m., when she had not heard from her husband and could not contact him at home, she had a friend drive her home. The *Tribune Chronicle* picks up the story:

> "'I walked in the kitchen and saw my husband lying on the floor in a pool of blood, his face swollen and distorted....'
>
> "At this point Miss Steuer objected to 'characterizations' by Mrs. Blair and Judge Birrell instructed Mrs. Blair to refrain from such and just tell what she did.
>
> "'I knelt down and spoke to him,' she continued, 'and when he didn't answer I found he was unconscious and administered first aid to bring him to consciousness.'
>
> "'When my attempts failed, I went to the cellar and got some spirits of ammonia which I used with cold water, and brought him around.'
>
> "'I left him where he was, cleaned blood from his face and the floor, then attempted to summon a doctor.'
>
> "'I called eight or 10 doctors, but couldn't find one so I contacted my daughter (Mrs. Cole) and then Dr. Charles Anderson was called.'
>
> "'I helped my husband to the living room, then later took him to the hospital where he was admitted.'
>
> "Miss Steuer took up the cross-examination and asked Mrs. Blair if she felt that, because she was upset and because it was her husband involved, her concern was exaggerated.
>
> "'No,' Mrs. Blair replied."

The last witness called for the state was Dr. Charles Anderson (no relation to the prosecutor). He was asked to describe Blair's wounds for the jury. "I found he had a laceration of the scalp and adjoining bruises," the doctor began, "both eyes were black, the nose was fractured and there had been bleeding from the nostrils and the back of the throat."

At 10:45 a.m., on the second day of the trail, the prosecution rested its case.

Late Tuesday, Mike Farah took the stand. He claimed that the dispute was over money owed him by Blair. A fact that never came up in the recounting of the conversation Chief Manley claimed he had with Farah the night after the incident. When questioned about that conversation, Farah said he recalled that English had urged him to give his side of the story to the newspapers, but he said he never made a statement to the chief, such as English described.

Farah stated that he had known Blair for about 25 years and that over time the two had become better acquainted. He told the court that they would talk politics and go out and dine together, "we were good friends." Farah related that he had been to the Blair home on several occasions and that Blair was a frequent visitor to the Jungle Inn. The two would sit and chat for hours at a time.

Next Farah told a story about how the two went out for a drive one night. During the course of their conversation, Farah said Blair asked him for a $500 loan. When the two returned to the Farah home, Mike gave him the money. When Blair tried to explain what the money was for, Farah said he replied, "You don't have to explain, you can have it."

Farah said they discussed the firing of Laura DeJacimo, but he accepted Blair's explanation that there was nothing he could do. It was then that Farah claimed he asked Blair about repayment of the $500 loan. At this point he said Blair got angry and belligerent. According to Farah, this was not the first time he had inquired about repayment of the loan, but he had always been put off by the politician. This time however, Farah threatened to tell Blair's wife about the financial transaction.

The witness said he had once been warned by Blair not to say anything to Mariam Blair. Now, according to Farah, Blair responded, "You open your mouth, I'm not afraid of you."

With this, both men got out of the car and after Blair removed his glasses the former deputy took a swing at Farah. After ducking the punch Farah hit Blair on the nose, knocking him to the ground. Farah told the jury, "As he was trying to get up, I saw he was bleeding and told him to go to the hospital. I told him I was as sorry as he was about the fight and added, 'you started it.'"

"I never went into the house while Blair was on the lawn, I never got a gun and never used it. Farah concluded his direct examination with, "I never had a fight with Blair before. I never threatened to shoot his guts out. He was as close as my family to me."

During Farah's entire testimony he added asides to his answers directing them to the jury. This was especially so during cross-examination. In addition, he repeated continuously, "I'm telling the truth." He was cautioned on numerous occasions to "confine his answers to the questions."

In addition, Birrell had to caution the gallery twice, which had swelled to 200 spectators, against any outbursts or demonstrations, threatening to clear the courtroom if they didn't stop. "This is a public trial and you have a right to view it but you have no right to demonstrate or show any emotion to anything which occurs in the courtroom. If it occurs again, I will clear the courtroom. The state and defendant are both entitled to a fair trial and I expect to see to it that they receive it," Birrell declared.

During cross-examination by Prosecutor Anderson the exchanges got ugly. He began by reviewing Farah's criminal past – gambling arrests, liquor violations and his prison sentence in Milan, Michigan. Then questions got around to his activities in local politics. Farah told Anderson that he didn't want to answer any questions about politics as they might embarrass the prosecutor. Pressed, Farah related his interest in politics and elections and that he helped his friends regardless of which party they supported. He then stated he had once worked for the prosecutor's son.

Anderson's son John H. Anderson[7] was known as "an enemy of the racketeer" and participated in a number of vice raids. He died while in office in August 1951 at the age of 34.

Farah's cavalier comment incensed the prosecutor who barked, "You know why my son got elected prosecutor?"

Steuer immediately objected, but Anderson responded, "He [Farah] raised it. I don't have to take it from him and you know it. I'm not going to take it from this guy." Birrell ordered Anderson to continue with the examination. A few moments later Anderson apologized to the jury for his outburst.

Additional defense witnesses were called. Grace Farah testified that Blair had been a frequent guest at the Farah home and had often gone for rides with her husband. She testified that her husband did not come back into the house until after Blair had driven away. She said when Mike entered the house his hair and his T-shirt were "mussed," but she did not hear any commotion outside, despite the doors and windows being open. When questioned about the gun, she said it was kept loaded and under the bed upstairs. She stated there was no shotgun in the house.

Farah's son Albert said he and two children arrived at the home just prior to Blair pulling up. He said his father didn't come into the house until Blair drove away and he never heard any noises while in the house.

James R. Craig, a former safety-service director who was a neighbor of the Farah's was called. He testified that on the afternoon of the fight he heard "no screams, no shouting, and no loud noises" while he was outside. Another witness, John Conroy, said he was a horse-race bookie at the Jungle Inn and had been introduced to Blair and his wife by Farah. He claimed Blair was a frequent visitor to the gambling den.

Cleveland ballistics expert David Cowles was the final witness in the trial when testimony ended Wednesday morning. He was again called to state that the gun the defense claimed came from the Farah house was in working order.

During closing arguments Anderson and Campbell told the jury that they believed the state had proved its case for assault with intent to kill. Buchwalter and Steuer called for an acquittal, claiming the fight was a back-yard brawl between two old friends and never should have been brought to trial. In his instructions to the jury, Judge Birrell gave them the option of 1) finding Farah guilty of assault with intent to kill; 2) guilty of assault and battery; and 3) not guilty.

The jury of eight men and four women began deliberations at 1:12 p.m. Wednesday afternoon. There was quite a stir when the buzzer sounded at 2:45 p.m., but jury members simply wanted a pitcher of water. At 4:37 the jury submitted a question to the judge about the definition of assault and battery. After consulting with both sides the judge responded that a more specific question needed to be asked. The buzzer went off again at 5:43 and the judge and attorneys expected to get the question. Instead, they got a verdict – guilty of assault and battery. The jury had taken just three ballots. The first was an 11 to 1 vote of not guilty of assault with intent to kill. The second ballot was unanimous. After more deliberations they voted 12 to 0 in favor of conviction on the lesser charge.

During deliberations, Farah, who had switched to a blue suit and light-blue tie after two days of testimony, remained in the courtroom for the four hours and 35 minutes it took the jury to find him guilty of a reduced count of assault and battery, basically the same conclusion that Judge Ravella[8] had arrived at, but with a stiffer penalty.

When defense counsel announced they would seek a new trial Judge Birrell delayed sentencing until Friday. The *Vindicator* reported, "In its request for a new trial the defense cited seven reasons if felt the defendant had not received a fair hearing, including, 'Misconduct of the prosecuting attorney, errors in the charge to the jury, errors of law prejudicial to the defendant, evidence excluded which was offered by the defendant, evidence prejudicial to the defendant admitted over his objection, error by the court in refusing to give special instructions to the jury as requested and other errors apparent on the record.'"

On Friday, December 18, Birrell overruled defense counsel's motion for a new trial. He then asked Farah if he had anything to say before sentence was imposed. Buchwalter replied, "We have nothing to say, your honor."

Before passing formal sentence Birrell declared:

"The court has given the extent of your sentence very careful study. Your attorneys presented your case skillfully. They characterized the case as a back-yard brawl.

"Unfortunately, the court does not agree with the implications of this characterization. You requested a county official to stop at your home. He agreed to accommodate you. You were apparently dissatisfied by an action of the Board of Elections and asked him to change the action.

"You apparently became incensed when he didn't comply, started a fight and gave him a beating.

"You had a right to criticize actions by the board or an official, but no right to attack. We expect officers to respect all people and classes, but we can't expect them to do or not to do because one constituent stands in the background with a club, ready to give a beating if the action is not agreeable to him.

"Fear of physical violence must not be permitted to influence public officials' decisions. This was no mere back-yard brawl, but a serious public matter. Disapproval of such conduct must be registered in the sentence because of its widespread affect.

"Public officials must be protected from irate citizens who believe questions can be settled by physical violence."

During the sentencing statement Buchwalter interrupted by objecting to the judge's comments. He requested the objection become part of the record stating, "This is the first time I have ever objected during a sentencing by a judge."

Birrell noted the objection and then concluded, "Your sentence is four months in the county jail and a $200 fine and the court feels it is a fair and just sentence."

After the sentencing, defense counsel filed a notice of appeal and posted a $7,500 bond to continue Farah's freedom while the appeal was pending. Birrell had denied a request for probation for Farah due to his previous conviction in 1930 and because of his "connections." In the clerk's office while posting bond Farah sneered at reporters and barked, "If you don't belong to a certain clan, a private citizen doesn't have a chance to live around here. This was nothing but a fight and look what the clan did with it."

Taking exception to Farah's "clan" comments, the *Vindicator* shot back with an editorial on December 21 entitled "About This 'Clan,' Mr. Farah." In part the editorial stated:

"It seems to be very hard for some people to understand that there is a right way and a wrong way of living.

"The "clan" is made up of honest, decent, law-abiding people. Most of them have jobs, some of the white-collar variety, some in the mills and factories. They have varied interests and personal objectives. Some have families and some do not.

"However, the "clan" has a few characteristics which are common to nearly all its members. They work for the money they get and with it they pay their bills. They believe that the law, whether they like it or not, applies to everyone."

In April 1960, Lynn B. Griffith, the presiding officer of the 7th District Court of Appeals, revealed that an outside appeals court was being asked to hear Farah's appeal. No explanation for requesting this outside help was given. Defense counsel claimed that Farah had not received a fair and impartial trial and that the judge's charge to the jury regarding self-defense was in error. Within days it was announced that the 9th District Court of Appeals would hear the case.

On May 12 a three judge panel from the 9th District Court of Appeals[9] heard arguments. Arlene Steuer spoke for the defendant; Assistant Prosecutor Campbell represented the state. The feisty attorney stated that Farah was denied a fair trial because Judge Birrell refused to allow witnesses to testify as to the relationship between Farah and Blair. She said defense counsel was prepared to present several witnesses who would testify that the relationship between the two men went back to the 1940s. An objection was made by the state early on to this type of testimony, which Birrell sustained.

Don Campbell called the testimony "immaterial," and argued, "The testimony objected to by the prosecutor covered the years 1948 and 1949 and had no bearing on the relationship of Farah and Blair in 1959. We never had a chance to object to testimony which might have been offered by other witnesses in a similar vein because the witnesses were never on the stand."

In Steuer's rebuttal she claimed that after the first objection was sustained a lengthy conference took place in Birrell's chambers, after which she believed any testimony on the relationship would be disallowed.

The second point regarded the charge to the jury regarding self-defense. Steuer claimed that Birrell had failed to follow written instructions from defense counsel, in which he was to instruct jurors that "it was not necessary to wait until being struck to land a blow in self-defense." The attorney declared, "It was obvious the jury was confused as to the definition of assault and battery when it asked for further instructions during deliberations."

In response to this second point, Campbell simply allowed that it was not mandatory for a judge to give instructions offered from defense counsel.

On June 8 the 9th District Court of Appeals rendered its decision upholding Farah's conviction stating, "The court finds no prejudicial error." The judges ruled in part:

> "The jury believed the story told by Blair. The evidence fully supports the verdict returned by the jury.
>
> "The jury chose to believe, and we think properly so, that such a cut on the top of the head, requiring several sutures, was caused by some instrument wielded with great force.
>
> "The visual and silent evidence was such as to cause this court to conclude that the force used by Farah to repel the claimed first assault by Blair was so disproportionate to the need of self-defense that it (if it were believed Blair struck the first blow) lost its character of a defense and became aggression."

◆　　◆　　◆

Farah's $7,500 bond was continued after the Appellate Court ordered his sentence delayed 45 days pending an anticipated appeal to the Ohio Supreme Court. Farah fought the conviction throughout all of 1960 exhausting virtually every appeal. With his last chance with the United States Supreme Court at hand Farah changed his mind and accepted the sentence. On January 11, 1961 he began his sentence at the Trumbull County jail. Farah had served just 60 days when Judge Birrell granted him a "Good Friday" release on March 11.

Murder of Mike Farah

The early years of the 1960s in the Mahoning Valley were marked by a number of high profile murders – including Sandy and Billy Naples, Vince DeNiro, John Schuller and Charles Cavallaro. The murders spread into Trumbull County on June 10, 1961.

As with the murders of Sandy Naples and John Schuller, rumors surfaced that an attempt would be made on Farah's life in early 1961. One *Vindicator* article reported, "The same rumors said Cleveland gambling interests were unhappy with Farah and insisted the Cleveland group hoped to control gambling in the area with Farah out of the picture."

On the warm, sunny Saturday morning of June 10, Farah was out in his yard hitting golf balls and waiting for a golfing partner to arrive. Shortly after 9:15 a 1959 Chevrolet sedan arrived at the home on the corner of Kenilworth and South Avenues. Farah had no time to notice the strange set-up of one man driving and a second man in the backseat before the first shot was fired. The blast, from a .12 gauge shotgun loaded with nine pellets of "double-O-buck" shot, tore open the ground near Farah's feet. A second shot ripped into the basement window casing on Farah's home behind him. Perhaps frozen in terror, Farah didn't move and the last blast caught him in the abdomen, hip and thigh.

Mortally wounded, Farah was helped from the yard into the kitchen by his wife, Grace, and his 16 year-old daughter, also named Grace. Both women witnessed the shooting from the kitchen window, which looked out onto the lawn where Farah was standing when he was shot. Police arrived quickly after being summoned by the daughter. Warren Police Sergeant Herbert Rising was the first to speak to Farah. The dying man gave Rising a description of the automobile, but said he didn't recognize the occupants.

Farah, in a semi-conscious state, was rushed to Trumbull Memorial Hospital bleeding profusely from the damage caused by the nine shotgun pellets. Gathered at the hospital were his wife and daughter, son Albert and Farah's brother John. They were waiting near the entrance of the emergency room when the bad news came. Another son John, who arrived late, was informed by his brother that their father had passed away.

An emergency room physician informed the press that Farah had died at 10:25, but was revived and lived for another 40 minutes. At 11:15 a.m. he succumbed to internal bleeding and shock on an emergency room table.

Farah's oldest son, John, barked out, "They ought to pick up Tony and the whole fucking bunch." Although he would later refuse to elaborate, the "Tony" he was referring to was Anthony "Tony Dope" Delsanter, the onetime partner of the Farah brothers in the Jungle Inn. Another family member would deny John ever made the outburst.

Albert Farah told police he couldn't understand "why anyone would want to harm his father since he retired from active business about ten years ago." Trumbull County Sheriff Robert Barnett was also perplexed. "We have some hit and run numbers business and some sporadic floating gambling, but I have been making my own checks for some time and I know the county is quiet," he explained.

Just hours after the shooting Warren detectives found the automobile used in the killing a half mile from the murder scene abandoned in the parking lot of the Heltzel Steel Form Company on Niles Road. The vehicle had been stolen on March 15 in Canton. This was the third shooting in just over a year with a Canton connection. The shotgun found at the Sandy Naples murder scene was stolen from a Canton police cruiser and the automobile that was used in the shooting of Joseph Romano was stolen in Canton. Searching the area around the car detectives discovered the murder weapon – a .12 gauge Remington shotgun – in some bushes behind the automobile. The weapon was equipped with a device called a "choke." The device helps to keep the shotgun pellets from spreading as they leave the barrel.

Farah's body "lay in state" in an auditorium-type room in the basement of St. George Syrian Orthodox Church on West 14th Street in Cleveland. The room had been constructed with a $20,000 donation Farah gave to the church after the death of his son Robert in 1946. Farah's bronze casket was draped with a blanket of red and white carnations and chrysanthemums. The words "In Loving Memory" adorned a silk ribbon.

Funeral services were held on June 13 for the 56 year-old Farah. Warren detectives were dispatched to look for "anyone of importance from the rackets world." Among the 70 mourners, mostly family and friends from Cleveland's Syrian community, were two "minor" police characters. The *Vindicator* reported Reverend Philip Saliba "chastised a society which encourages crime and violence and said that society should be put on trial since it condones crime." Saliba declared Farah had made mistakes, "Who has not? He did a lot of good things, too." After the church service Farah was buried in Cleveland's historic Lake View Cemetery, the final resting-place of President James A. Garfield, multi-millionaire industrialist John D. Rockefeller, and fabled crime-fighter Eliot Ness.

After the murder, Chief English denied published reports that Tony Delsanter was the "prime suspect" in the investigation. English said police were looking to question Farah's ex-partner Delsanter, along with "many other characters." Still, Warren police issued a "pick up" order for Delsanter. The day after the funeral Delsanter was picked up in a Mahoning Avenue restaurant while he "nonchalantly munched" a sandwich. The 50 year-old Delsanter was questioned and released after his alibi of playing golf in Akron was confirmed by detectives from that city. A second suspect, Nicholas "Nick Brown" Papalas, was also picked up. Papalas, a former employee of Farah had recently been found working with Delsanter, claimed he was at home asleep at the time of the murder.

Other men questioned in the killing included Phil Mainer and Joseph Drago. On the day of the funeral the *Warren Tribune Chronicle* reported:

> "Various reports circulating in the area have said that Farah's slaying was ordered because periodic payments to his overseers in Cleveland

rackets had started to dwindle. Rumors of a possible attempt on Farah's life began circulating about six weeks ago, it was learned. Informants said the Cleveland racketeers were concerned by only a trickle in Trumbull gambling take and had decided to give another Warren man control of the county's gambling."

On June 18 the *Vindicator* revealed the results of the Warren Police Department's investigation. Farah had allegedly made two trips to Niles during the twelve hours prior to his death. The first was Friday evening to "confer with other racketeers." The second was reported to have taken place at 3:00 a.m., during which time Farah got into a heated argument on State Street. This was followed by a brawl and an attempt by several men to force Farah into an automobile and "take him on a death ride." Captain Verne Teeple, spearheading the investigation, said police were unable to substantiate the story.

The *Vindicator* concluded:

> "Long the front man for the Cleveland rackets syndicate…Farah in recent months saw his underworld prestige wane. Newcomers were muscling in on what he considered his exclusive domain, and he did not gracefully fade into oblivion as he allegedly was warned to do.
> "When Sandy Naples was murdered…it had been rumored that Farah was high on the priority list for a gangland slaying if he did not bow out of the picture."

The flaw with the newspaper's conclusion was that it was not "newcomers" who took over in the wake of Farah's murder. It was Anthony Delsanter. In a 1981 book about Mafia turncoat Aladena "Jimmy the Weasel" Fratianno titled *The Last Mafiosi*, author Ovid Demaris in discussing Fratianno's lifelong friendship with Delsanter writes, "[Delsanter] had recently done some work [Mafia terminology for taking a life], clipping Mike Farah, who had fronted the Jungle Inn for Blackie Licavoli." There seems little doubt that Delsanter was behind the murder of Mike Farah, if not indeed the triggerman himself.

Despite the apparent mob war raging in the Valley the FBI office in Youngstown indicated it would not pursue the matter because no federal statutes had been violated.

The murder of Mike Farah marked the end of the Farah brothers influence in Trumbull County.[10] John and his wife Shamis, after the closing of the Jungle Inn, had spent most of their time at their Cleveland home. At some point the couple returned to the Mahoning Valley and took up residence in Girard. It was there that John suffered a fatal heart attack on April 6, 1980.

By the time his obituary appeared in the *Vindicator* the funeral services had already been held. The brief notice mentioned Mike Farah as John's brother, but stated "the family would give no information other than the time of the services," which had already been conducted.

Mike's son John moved to Costa Mesa, California shortly after his father's murder. He died there after a short illness two days after his 30th birthday on March 9, 1962. Mike's other son Albert died in May 1980. Grace Farah passed away on July 28, 1989 at the age of 80 and Shamis Farah died January 5, 1997, four days after her 91st birthday.

"Here is a thug who has violated nearly every law and rule of decent citizenship in the book. Yet he manages to defy the Government for years and years – escaping deportation and prosecution for deliberately avoiding the taxes most other people are forced to pay. Who is running this country, the hoodlums or the honorable citizens?" – Republican Senator John J. Williams Delaware, *Washington D.C. Daily News,* December 8, 1958.

5

The Saga of Frank Cammarata

Transplanted Detroit mobster Frank Cammarata committed such crimes as armed robbery and carrying a concealed weapon, both of which he was convicted and served time for. His biggest mistake, however, was falling into the cross-hairs of Youngstown Police Chief Eddie Allen.

Detroit Beginnings

Francesca Cammarata[1] was born in S. Cataldo, Sicily on March 16, 1898. At the age of 15, after the death of both parents, he set sail for the United States. On April 15, 1913 Cammarata arrived at Ellis Island after crossing the Atlantic aboard the *SS Napoli.* Cammarata took out citizenship papers in 1920, but did not follow through with the complete naturalization process and never became an American citizen.

He first settled in Rochester, New York at the home of a married sister. Sometime during the latter half of the 1910s Cammarata relocated to St. Louis where he became associated with members of the Licavoli clan in a gang known as the Hammerheads, a juvenile gang with a penchant for violence. The principals of the Licavoli gang were two sets of brothers – Peter and Thomas, known as "Yonnie," and their cousins, brothers James, who because of his dark complexion was known as "Jack White" or "Blackie" and Pete, called "Horseface"[2] to distinguish him from his more infamous cousin of the same name. While in St. Louis, Cammarata was arrested for a robbery and released after bail was provided. With this began a practice that he would follow many times throughout his life – bond jumping.

In the early 1920s the Licavolis moved from St. Louis to Detroit, where the bloody Giannola / Vitale Gang War had depleted the city's supply of hoodlums. In the book *The Violent Years* author Paul R. Kavieff states, "Over a period of approximately 10 years, more than 100 men were killed as a result of the strife." The Licavolis and Cammarata arrived in the city as "new recruits." Yonnie Licavoli soon helped organize the Moceri / Licavoli River Gang, which took its name from an area along the upper Detroit River.

A historical note to the reader, many organized crime enthusiasts have always assumed that the Detroit underworld of the 1920s and 1930s was the Purple Gang, regardless of the ethnic background of the gangster. While the origin of the gang's name has been disputed over the years, it has been established by Paul Kavieff of Wayne State University, an organized crime historian who authored *The Purple Gang*, that the gang was made up of the Jewish underworld element of Detroit and did not include members of the Italian Mafia. For years Licavoli clan members, including Frank Cammarata, have erroneously been identified and referred to as the Purple Gang. Kavieff has not been able to pinpoint just when this association began, but he declares it is nothing more than another fable in a long line of Mafia folklore.

In the mid-1920s Cammarata married Grace Licavoli, the sister of "Yonnie" and Peter. The couple had their first child, a daughter, in 1927. A second daughter followed in 1931. The year 1925 was a benchmark year in the criminal career of Cammarata. On June 12 he was indicted with Yonnie Licavoli and Pete Carrado in Federal Court for violation of the Dyer Act, the law which tripped up notorious bank robber John Dillinger – transporting a stolen vehicle across state lines. The men were believed to be operating a stolen automobile ring, taking the cars to Buffalo, obtaining New York State plates and returning the vehicles to Detroit for resale. The case was never prosecuted.

On July 1 Cammarata was one of four gunmen involved in the armed robbery of the People's State Bank of Wayne County at Brooklyn and Grand River Avenues in Detroit. The robbers were waiting when the bookkeeper arrived that morning at 8:15. As the young man unlocked the door one ofthe robbers thrust a gun into his side. Once inside the bookkeeper and a janitor were forced to lie on the floor. The robbers huddled, and then had the bookkeeper unlock a small vault where several bags of silver were kept.

The robbers removed the bags, which contained about $2,100. While this was going on the janitor managed to set off two alarms, one a gong at the front of the bank. The robbers fled instantly never getting a chance to loot the main vault, which was on a timelock due to open at 9:00. Unfortunately for Cammarata, he stood guard at the bank door drawing the attention of passersby before and after the gong sounded, and was the only robber witnesses got a good look at. Arrested on September 22 and charged with armed robbery, he was released on a $10,000 bond.

On November 7, Cammarata again was identified as a participant in a holdup and shootout involving the payroll of the Kleiner Cigar Manufacturing Company in Detroit. A Detroit police officer assigned to guard the company payroll was wounded during the robbery, which netted the bandits between $8,700 and $10,000. Four days later, Cammarata was arrested and charged with the Kleiner robbery. He provided a $20,000 bond, which he forfeited on November 18 when he failed to make a scheduled court appearance. Cammarata fled the Motor City and returned to St. Louis where he was arrested on January 2, 1926 and returned to Detroit.

During the first Kleiner robbery trial a woman spectator found her way into the presence of jury members during a lunch break and told them that Cammarata was innocent. After learning of the encounter, the judge promptly declared a mistrial and sent the woman to the Detroit House of Corrections for 30 days.

Before the second trial the wounded police officer, now fully recovered, was shot again while on duty. The officer believed that Cammarata was behind the attack, hoping to silence him. During the trial Cammarata took the stand in his own defense and claimed he was sleeping in his apartment at the time of the robbery. During cross-examination, however, he could not remember the address of where he lived. The jury deliberated more than 24 hours without reaching a verdict before the judge declared mistrial. A subsequent trial was ordered but never held.

In addition to the Licavolis and Cammarata, high ranking members of the River Gang included Joseph Moceri, brother of Leo "Lips" Moceri a hoodlum who would figure in the Mahoning Valley underworld activities in the 1960s and in Cleveland's Mafia leadership in the 1970s; Joseph Massei, a highly respected member of the Detroit Mafia; and Angelo Meli, with whom Cammarata would be associated in the juke box rackets in the late 1940s.

On September 7 Cammarata and Yonnie Licavoli were prime suspects in the attempted killing of a Detroit policeman after the officer was found severely beaten. The two escaped to Windsor, Ontario located just across the Detroit River. The next day, after the Windsor Police Department received an anonymous tip, officers raided a hotel room and arrested Cammarata and Licavoli. A .45 automatic was found under Yonnie's pillow, while a .38 was uncovered in Cammarata's vehicle. The two were charged with possession of "offensive weapons" and held on $15,000 bonds, which neither could produce, while they awaited trial. To raise the bond it was rumored that from their cells they engineered the kidnapping of a rival bootlegger and ordered several liquor shipments of the rival hijacked. The target of their efforts was a competitor the two felt had "dropped a dime" on them to the Windsor police. The rival was shot to death one year later.

On October 24 Cammarata and Yonnie Licavoli were found guilty and subsequently sentenced to three years in the Kingston Penitentiary. Held in the county jail until all appeals were exhausted, the two entered the prison on November 28. They served two-years and seven-months. On May 15, 1930, after Cammarata's release he re-entered the United States at Cape Vincent, New York, directly across the border from Kingston. A Department of Justice report stated that Cammarata was re-admitted "under a reciprocal agreement with Canada covering such matters." Despite the fact that Cammarata had yet to be tried for the People's State Bank robbery in July 1925, there was no attempt to arrest him upon his release. By now the bond for the crimes he had been arrested for totaled $50,000.

Cammarata and Yonnie Licavoli returned to a Detroit that resembled a Wild West town. In January 1930 gunmen in a speeding automobile attempted to murder Police Inspector Henry J. Garvin. The attackers wounded Garvin and left an eleven year-old girl in critical condition. Members of the River Gang were suspects in the attempted murder and a citywide crackdown by police was underway. Just two weeks after Cammarata was released from prison a murder spree began in the Motor City. Between May 31 and July 23 fourteen people were murdered at the hands of gangsters. The most sensational of these killings was the murder of popular radio crime crusader Gerald F. "Jerry" Buckley, who was shot eleven times while sitting in the lobby of the LaSalle Hotel after the recall of Detroit Mayor Charles Bowles.

Buckley himself had been a witness to a double murder during the spree, which occurred near a side entrance to the LaSalle Hotel. After the successful recall election, in which he played a major role, Buckley had dinner with his personal secretary before returning to the hotel lobby. Buckley had been lured back to the lobby by a young lady who had called him earlier in the day with the promise of a story. As he sat waiting, gunmen entered the lobby shortly after 1:30 and killed him. River Gang gunmen Angelo Livecchi, Joseph "Scarface" Bommarito and Ted Pizzino were later arrested. Warrants were also issued for Frank Cammarata, Peter Licavoli and Joseph Massei. It was believed that a lady friend of Pete Licavoli actually placed the telephone call that lured Buckley to his death. No convictions were ever obtained. The three arrested men were tried and acquitted.

The public outrage from the radio commentator's vicious murder resulted in what came to be known as the Buckley Grand Jury, which was formed to investigate his death and the brazen crime wave. The heat put on the underworld, especially the River Gang, forced the Licavolis and a number of their close associates to move to Toledo, located southeast of Detroit in neighboring Ohio, during the spring of 1931. The Licavoli Gang quickly took over the bootlegging rackets there. The last obstacle to their power grab, however, would cost the gang the services of Yonnie Licavoli. A gang war that ended in the murder of popular Toledo bootlegger Jackie Kennedy on July 7, 1933 resulted in Yonnie being convicted of complicity and conspiracy in four murders. He was sentenced to life imprisonment in the Ohio penitentiary in October 1934.[3]

Cammarata missed most of the action. Even before his return to Detroit from the Kingston prison, Michigan officials had begun an effort to deport him. On April 29, 1930 a court date was set for Cammarata's trial for the 1925 bank robbery. Even though Cammarata was still running free on a $50,000 bail, prosecutors were confident his bondsman would have him in court on time. In mid-February 1931 Cammarata finally went on trial for the bank robbery. Several witnesses took the stand and identified him as the man standing guard at the front door as his companions robbed the People's State Bank. After deliberations that lasted less than three hours the jury returned a guilty verdict. On February 26 Cammarata was sentenced to 15 to 30 years in the State Prison of Southern Michigan, referred to as Jackson Prison. In the courtroom at the time of sentencing were immigration officials who asked the judge to enter into the court record that Cammarata be turned over to federal authorities when he was through serving his sentence. A month earlier an arrest warrant was issued for Cammarata as an undesirable alien and on June 4, 1932 he would be ordered deported upon his release.

Deportation and Return

While Cammarata was serving his sentence efforts were underway by his friends and family to have him deported. The effort was focused on Parole Commissioner Joseph C. Armstrong. In 1935 the official told those making the advances, "Why should Cammarata, a convicted bank robber, be allowed to go back to Italy and enjoy freedom, while other prisoners convicted at the same time for the same sort of offense have to remain in prison here merely because they happen to be American citizens? I am opposed to issuing too many deportation paroles. A man should be required to pay the same penalty whether he is born in this county or any other country."

The next year Armstrong changed his tune. He made a recommendation to Michigan Governor Frank D. Fitzgerald that Cammarata's sentence be reduced, then parole him so he could be deported. Armstrong now claimed, "Except for the fact that he will be deported, I would not have recommended the commutation of sentence. This will make it possible to deport Cammarata to Italy with the next group of deportees."

Fitzgerald went along with the recommendation, which drew a lot of criticism. One of the most vocal critics was Federal Judge Arthur F. Lederle, who prophetically declared, "Deported aliens often return to the United States illegally." Later, Fitzgerald apologized for his decision stating he wouldn't do it over again, if he had the chance.

On December 20, 1936, having served less than six years of his minimum fifteen-year sentence, Cammarata was released. As he left the prison Cammarata stated, "I will never see this country again. I will live in my home country with a house and great big garden."

The language in the parole papers signed by Governor Fitzgerald on December 16 was very specific:

> "Where as it is desired to parole Frank Cammarata No. 29806 in custody of warden for delivery to Immigration Officials if and when called for, for deportation to Sicily. In the event subject is not deportable this action is void. Immigration authorities to hold this inmate against bail should he attempt to stay deportation. MUST NEVER RETURN TO THE UNITED STATES."

Allowed to spend the holidays with his family, Cammarata was deported to Italy on January 9, 1937. In an interview with Youngstown Police in 1952, Cammarata re-capped his brief time in Italy:

> "I stayed there for about 3 years. My family came over to Italy about two weeks after I was deported and stayed with me for about 6 months. My wife was in a family way so I sent her back to the States. In 1939 the war was about to start in Italy and I knew that if I didn't get back to the States then I would have to fight with the Italian Army and if I was going to fight I would fight for the country where my family was, so I got on the last boat that left Italy before the war started."

Reports locally stated Cammarata was conscripted into the fascist army of Italian dictator Benito Mussolini and ordered to serve in Ethiopia. In 1939 he went AWOL and was believed to have re-entered the United States through New York City sometime between September and December of that year.[4] Once back, he was reported to have settled in East Liberty, Pennsylvania, located in suburban Pittsburgh, before moving to Solon, Ohio. Grace was reported back in the Detroit area by 1938, where she gave birth to the couple's third child, a son.

By the time Cammarata reconnected with the Licavolis, around 1940, the gang had spread its influence from Detroit across Northern Ohio, including Cleveland and the Akron / Canton area, to the Mahoning Valley. The Prohibition Era money train rolled out of existence and the policy racket, gambling and labor racketeering became the main staple for the mob. It was during this time that the war over the control of slot machines was taking place, in which Nate Weisenberg and Jerry Pascarella became casualties. James Licavoli, Cammarata's cousin by marriage, was the prime suspect in both incidents.

Cammarata moved around wholly unnoticed for nearly seven years. It was difficult to track his movements once he re-entered the country or to determine what his new role was in the gang during these years. On July 19, 1946 U.S. Immigration inspectors and local police, acting on an informant's tip, arrested Cammarata at the home of his daughter and son-in-law, Emanuel Amato, in Solon, Ohio, a suburb located southeast of Cleveland in Cuyahoga County. The information provided to authorities was that Cammarata had been living at the home for four years. A report in the *Cleveland Press* claimed Cammarata "was linked with rackets in Cleveland recently, including a gambling joint and an after-hours liquor spot." Other reports described Cammarata as a liquor salesman; his son-in-law was listed as the president of Bessie's Tavern.

According to a later statement by Cammarata, he came back to America as a stowaway on a boat from Italy. After landing in New York City he traveled to Pittsburgh by train. While there he sold cheese door to door for Charlie Gallo. In 1940 he moved to Solon, Ohio where he got another job selling cheese for Gallo.

Cammarata was held on a $50,000 bond, reportedly the highest bond ever set on an immigration violation in Cleveland. On August 1 the Central Office of the Immigration & Naturalization Service in Philadelphia reduced it to $10,000. The next day Cammarata was a free man and, as was his habit, he soon jumped bail. While seemingly hiding in plain sight, Cammarata hired lawyers to clear up his parole / pardon problems with the state of Michigan. On the following dates – October 1, 1946, February 27,

1948 and January 4, 1950 – Cammarata filed applications for a pardon with the state of Michigan. All the requests were denied, yet there was never any attempt to apprehend the fugitive.

Like the trail leading up to his arrest in Solon, the next two years were hard to follow. It's not for certain just when or why he ended up in the Mahoning Valley. After jumping bond in Cleveland, Cammarata claimed he looked for a place to live in Warren, but was unsuccessful. By his own admission he went to Youngstown and lived at the home of Sam Belinky on Rush Blvd. After eight months in the Belinky household he relocated to Warren. What can be pieced together is that Cammarata was asked to intercede in a juke box dispute in Detroit during the mid-1940s. The dispute involved the placing of a new style of juke box, distributed by the Seeburg Company, into bars and restaurants in a city that was monopolized by machines provided from Wurlitzer Company and overseen by Vincent Meli. Due to Cammarata's association with Angelo Meli in his River Gang days, he was able to convince the respected Mafioso's nephew, Vincent, not to take such a hard-line stand with the Seeburg distributor. Many believed it was Cammarata's success in this endeavor that resulted in his relocating to the Mahoning Valley to serve as an intermediary in the same type of dispute that was occurring in Youngstown, but of a more destructive nature. Whatever the case, Cammarata moved into a modest home at 161 Avondale Avenue, on the city's south side with Grace and their three children.

After the January 1948 inauguration of Republican Charles Henderson as mayor, a number of Youngstown hoodlums vacated the city. One of them was Frank Vitale, who had a record in both Cleveland and Youngstown. On the night of March 8, 1948 Vitale was arrested in Detroit by detectives, members of the Holdup Squad, at Kercheval and Beaconsfield Avenue. His apprehension came during a citywide cleanup campaign under the direction of Police Commissioner Harry S. Toy, in which nearly 100 hoodlums were picked up. Police questioned Vitale for nearly two hours, during which time he said he had come to the city with Cammarata to distribute wedding invitations for his April 19 marriage to a member of the Licavoli family. While one of the local newspapers reported a check of marriage license records in the Mahoning County Courthouse failed to confirm Vitale's statement, another claimed he had several wedding invitations in his pocket.

Shortly after the interrogation, which ended near midnight, the police officers were joined by FBI agents and went to the home of Peter Licavoli in the upscale Detroit suburb of Grosse Pointe. The FBI was interested in the whereabouts of Mike Rubino, a Detroit Mafia figure and Federal fugitive, who was wanted in the wake of an $800,000 gasoline coupon scandal back

in 1945. Arrested inside the home were Cammarata, Joseph "Scarface" Bommarito; Joseph "Long Joe" Bommarito, a parolee from Southern Michigan
Prison, David Feldman, an ex-con who served time on a narcotics charge;
and Dominic and John Licavoli, said to be cousins of Peter. The men claimed
they were staying at the house while Peter Licavoli was in Tucson. The six
men were lined up at the police station for the infamous photo that in later
years incorrectly identified them as members of the Purple Gang.[5]

The next day a Detroit judge declared, "These arrests were basically illegal arrests by the FBI and Detroit police."[6] All of the prisoners except Cammarata and "Long Joe" Bommarito, who was wanted for a parole violation,
were released after a habeas corpus hearing. There was no apparenteffort on
the part of Michigan lawmen to return Cammarata to prison to serve out
the remainder of the 1925 bank robbery sentence; the focus of authorities
seemed strictly on the re-deportation.

The *Detroit News* reported, Cammarata "had been scheduled to
surrender next week in Cleveland on a warrant ordering his deportation,
but immigration officers said they would not wait for the surrender date."
On March 11, 1948, Cammarata was taken from his Detroit jail cell in
shackles and, surrounded by police, FBI and U.S. Immigration officers,
placed aboard the Pennsylvania Red Arrow train for a trip to Ellis Island
in New York Harbor. During the half-hour wait for the train to leave, five
Border Patrol officers stood guard.

Cammarata was handcuffed to his seat the entire trip. Once in New
York, an attorney hired by Cammarata filed a petition in federal court
asking for a stay of the deportation order. The 1925 bank robbery conviction had been commuted after another person confessed. Attorneys were
seeking a review of the deportation order in lieu of this, asking that the
order be stayed until motion for a retrial in the bank robbery could be
heard. On the petition Cammarata listed his home address as Avondale
Avenue, and his profession as cheese salesman.

While a judge reviewed the request, friends and relatives sought the
help of Michael J. Kirwan[7] the Mahoning Valley's powerful Congressman.
Kirwan served in the United States House of Representatives from the 19th
Congressional District of Ohio from 1937 until his death in 1970. His most
important move in the House of Representatives came when he replaced J.
Buell Snyder of Pennsylvania, who died in February 1946, on the powerful
appropriations subcommittee that handled funds for all rivers, harbors and
flood control projects in the United States. The Appropriations Committee Group was recognized as one of the most powerful and influential in
Congress.

On April 20, 1948 Kirwan placed a bill in Congress to hold back the deportation until the Department of Justice could do a "thorough investigation." House Bill H.R. 6286, "A Bill For the relief of Francesca Cammarata," stated:

> Be it enacted by the Senate and House of Representatives of the United States of America in Congress assembled, That the Attorney General is authorized and directed to cancel the deportation proceedings presently pending against Francesca Cammarata, and that the facts upon which such proceedings are based shall not hereafter be made the basis for deportation proceedings.

A simple reading of the bill indicates the Congressman was asking that the deportation order be cancelled and the charges that formed the basis of the order be prevented from being used again.

The next day the *Vindicator* reported, without mention of Kirwan's house bill, that Federal Judge Sylvester Ryan of New York held up the deportation order after hearing arguments. An assistant U.S. attorney explained that after another man confessed to the bank robbery the governor of Michigan commuted Cammarata's sentence, but the deportation order remained valid due to the failure of the governor to grant the prisoner an outright pardon. It is imperative that one remembers while reading through the narrative of this long legal battle that the arrest order requesting Cammarata's deportation in January 1931 was for crimes other than the bank robbery, which at the time of the order he had yet to be convicted for. Cammarata and his lawyers waged their entire fight on the fact that another convict, on his deathbed, had confessed to the crime. Judge Ryan ordered that Cammarata be released by immigration officials for 30 days "so he could seek exoneration." A bond of $10,000 was set and Cammarata was once again set free.

House Bill 6286 endured the 80th Congress, 2nd Session, without being voted upon. On March 29, 1949 Kirwan introduced H.R. 3890, a second bill with precisely the same language. The Congressman stated, "Mr. Cammarata has a fine wife and children. They have suffered a great deal and, since Mr. Cammarata is now devoting his life and efforts to their personal welfare, I beg your indulgence in their behalf." At the same time Kirwan introduced the second bill, he sent a letter to the Commissioner of United States Immigration & Naturalization Service asking for the board of appeals to review Cammarata's case. The letter stated that, "Since 1939 when he re-entered the United States Mr. Cammarata has been of good moral character and has conducted himself in a gentlemanly manner. He has a fine home, a good wife, and children and his present status is a tremendous economic hardship to them."

Kirwan wasn't the only political figure the Licavoli family sought help from. Republican U.S. Senator Homer Capehart of Indiana was also approached. Capehart had been the president of the Wurlitzer Company, a major player in the juke box trade, until 1939. He was acquainted with Peter Licavoli, who most likely made the request for political help. Before Capehart had time to act, Federal Judge Ryan ordered a stay and the senator was off the hook. The information, in the form of a telegram dated June 25, 1948, was brought to the attention of the Kefauver Committee in February 1951 in Detroit and Peter Licavoli was subpoenaed and questioned. Although he admitted he knew Senator Capehart he offered no other useful information, denying he had ever asked the politician to intervene on his brother-in-law's behalf. When Capehart was appointed to the Senate Rackets Committee in February 1959 by the GOP Policy Committee he immediately came under fire for his prior connections to Cammarata and Licavoli.

At Odds with Eddie Allen

During this time Cammarata remained free on bond moving between Detroit, Cleveland and the Mahoning Valley plying his criminal trade unmolested. After his successful intervention in the Detroit jukebox "war," the Detroit mob used Cammarata in Youngstown, where a similar situation existed, to achieve the same results. It depends on which narrative you read, and believe, to determine if he was successful. In *Merchants of Menace: The Mafia*, Chief Allen wrote:

> "Cammarata was not as successful in his juke box negotiations in Youngstown as he was in Detroit, and coupled with his own court battles to stay out of jail and in the United States, he finally abandoned the juke box venture."

Compare Allen's assessment to that of Assistant Committee Counsel Arthur Kaplan reporting to the Senate Racket's Committee in December 1958:

> "Due to Cammarata's success in Detroit, 'They had no difficulty at all in placing these machines [juke boxes] in [Youngstown] establishments they previously couldn't get into,' Kaplan stated. He indicated that it was a fear of Cammarata that made this possible."

On April 10, 1959 during another session of the Senate Rackets Committee, Joseph Nemesh, president of Music Systems Inc., a distributor of the Seeburg jukeboxes, testified about his problems in placing the machines in Youngstown during the late 1940s. The *Vindicator* reported:

> "Nemesh testified that he had success in Ohio selling a new model juke box produced by Seeburg in the late 1940s but could not crack a boycott in Youngstown.
>
> "As fast as he could line up someone to handle a Youngstown juke box route for him, he said, the man would be driven out. He said one man was beaten and his bar stench-bombed. The home of another...was stench-bombed and he too 'immediately lost interest,' Nemesh testified.
>
> "Nemesh said he then invited Edward Amato, whom he identified as a son-in-law of Detroit gangster Frank Cammarata, to take the route. He said Cammarata himself advised them to give up in Youngstown after trying to help."

Whatever the case, during Chief Allen's investigation of violence in the local juke box industry during June 1950 the deportation delay resulting from Congressman Kirwan's bill came to his attention. It's not for certain if Kirwan's efforts were made public before this, but at this juncture they exploded in the headlines right as the Kefauver Crime Hearings were beginning their 14-city tour of America.

Allen admits it was Youngstown's "juke box war" that initially brought Cammarata to his attention. He wrote: "The monopolistic practices of owners and union leaders in and around the juke box business were the cause of this war, which had begun to erupt in the hurling of stink bombs, acid bombs and dynamite bombs by those who wished to retain control and those who were trying to muscle in." Cammarata was allegedly overseeing this muscling-in and in June 1950 Allen had Cammarata brought in for questioning. The mobster informed the chief that he was president of the American Records Company, which had a branch office in Cleveland. He claimed at the moment the company was "not very active" locally, but if it did get active he was entitled to receive 45 percent of the profits. Despite repeated questioning from the chief, Cammarata never explained his duties or responsibilities with the record company. Cammarata did reveal he was compensated to the tune of $100 each week from the Berger Music Machine Company of Lorain, Ohio (located west of Cleveland), but again refused to explain his responsibilities.

During their conversation Allen said he was told by Cammarata the first congressional bill was introduced by Kirwan at the insistence of his wife, Grace. On the second one, he "personally went to see Congressman Kirwan in Washington D.C. and requested Mr. Kirwan to introduce another such bill." He said the Congressman assured him that he would continue to do whatever he could for him. (Kirwan claimed that the introduction for the second bill came at the request of others.)

After questioning Cammarata, Allen called in James Licavoli. The suspected killer of Jerry Pascarella and Cleveland's Nate Weisenberg had recently been named by Virgil Peterson, director of the Chicago Crime Commission, as one of the "most powerful racketeers in Youngstown and Trumbull County," during his July 7 testimony before the Kefauver Committee.

On Sunday, July 9 the *Vindicator* reported that Allen had sent a registered letter to Kefauver in Washington D.C. accusing a politician, "with good White House connections," of blocking federal prosecution of a local racketeer. Allen wrote, "The official's intercession is so powerful that he has been able up to now, to stop the wheels of justice of the investigating agencies which are pushing the case against this criminal." When asked why the letter was sent to the crime-crusading Senator, Allen replied that it was "prompted by a request from Kefauver for information on enforcement officers or politicians," who were protecting criminals.

The chief then revealed details of his meeting with James Licavoli. According to Allen, "This criminal only last week told me that he had enough influence in Washington to force his racketeering operations into Youngstown. So far, we've heard endless testimony in Washington charging that powerful connections were safeguarding criminals. As yet, I haven't heard anyone mention the name of a powerful politician. Now one name is in the hands of the Senate committee. I named this politician in my letter, together with a request that the Senate committee aid me in keeping this racketeer [Licavoli] out of Youngstown."

Allen claimed Licavoli would extend his gambling operations into Youngstown, "as long as this national political figure stands in front of him and protects him." The chief promised that if the Senate committee didn't release the name of the politician, he would…and soon. "If the Senate doesn't help us in exposing this Washington politician, then [Licavoli] is right," Allen declared. "Neither federal agencies nor local police can curb the criminals if this type of high influence continues in the nation's capital."

The next day a front-page *Vindicator* story revealed the politician to be Congressman Michael Kirwan. Upon receipt of the letter Senator Kefauver spoke directly with Kirwan about the accusations. Kefauver told reporters that Kirwan had relayed to him that he had received "an adverse report" from immigration officials on Cammarata and was dropping the case. (On June 28, 1950 Democratic Representative Francis E. Walter of Pennsylvania, Chairman of the House Immigration Sub-Committee notified Kirwan in writing that, "in view of an unfavorable report from the Department of Justice on Cammarata's present activities, the bill was being tabled[8] by the House Judiciary Committee.)

Kefauver sought to appease both parties. He stated, "Chief Allen is a good man trying to do a diligent job, and his assistance has been invaluable." The Senator in support of Kirwan, a fellow Congressman, said he believed the representative "acted out of good motives."

Allen's comments proved to be the first time Kirwan had been attacked publicly for introducing the bills. He responded with a formal statement in which he declared, "I have no apology for introducing a bill in behalf of the Cammarata family." Then, in a stinging rebuke to Chief Allen, he ended the statement with "the faster the citizens of Youngstown deport you back to Erie, it will be a much better city." Incensed by Kirwan's comments, Chief Allen challenged the Congressman to appear before the Kefauver Committee and "tell his story" publicly.

On July 28, 1950 the final step to table the Kirwan deportation bill was scheduled to take place during a hearing of the House Judicial Sub-Committee on Immigration. Due to an emergency meeting to discuss the escalating crisis in Korea, however, the hearing was cancelled. The newspaper reported, "The bill is now in the subcommittee archives and will die when Congress adjourns unless a motion to table it is passed." Cammarata remained at liberty while the legal wrangling continued.

In November 1950 the Michigan parole board finally charged Cammarata with parole violation and sought his arrest. Michigan authorities had been giving consideration to a full pardon for Cammarata until Chief Allen's investigation resulted in a label of "influential racketeer" being place on him. The *Vindicator* explained, "The parole violation thus is actually a violation of commutation of sentence and Cammarata would be liable toserve out the remainder of his sentence." This followed the three applications over the years for a complete pardon from the governor of Michigan, all of which were denied.

On December 14 Cammarata was arrested by Warren Police Chief Manley English and three officials from the Ohio Parole Board. The arrest was made in the back room of the Pine Street Cigar Store, a Warren gambling joint that was raided a number of times. Cammarata was booked in Warren, but transferred to the Youngstown jail where he was held without charge while extradition details were worked out. The prisoner would be handed over to Michigan authorities unless he decided to fight extradition. On December 16 Cammarata's attorneys, Russell Mock and Patrick J. Melillo, filed a writ of habeas corpus demanding the release of their still uncharged client. Judge Erskine Maiden, Jr. set a hearing date for Monday, but refused to free the prisoner. Mock met with Chief Allen and offered to provide a bond of $15,000 to insure Cammarata's appearance in court. Allen refused, after conferring with Michigan officials, citing Cammarata's "record as a bail jumper."

Before the habeas corpus hearing could be held that Monday morning, December 18, a fugitive-from-justice warrant was officially served on Cammarata making the point of the hearing moot. The legal scene then switched from Maiden's courtroom to Judge Robert Nevin's. That afternoon a motion for dismissal of fugitive and parole violation charges against Cammarata was in the hands of Nevin. Attorney Joseph W. Louisell of Detroit, the newest addition to Cammarata's high-priced legal team, argued before Nevin stating four reasons why the charges should be dismissed. Louisell charged, "That the warrant was defective, that the court is without jurisdiction, that the prosecution had failed to produce any element of crime and that the arrest …was wholly illegal and improper." In addition, if the charges were not dropped, the attorneys wanted bond for their client.

On Tuesday afternoon Chief Allen was called to testify as to why Cammarata was a bad risk for being granted bond. Questioned by Assistant Law Director P. Richard Schumann, Allen stated that Cammarata "probably will not be here when extradition papers arrive from the governor of Michigan to return him as a parole violator." Allen backed up his statements with newspaper clippings from the *Detroit Free Press*, which reported how Cammarata had jumped bond after his 1925 arrest in Detroit for the bank robbery. A *Vindicator* article reported:

> "Allen said that the Black Hand Society known as the Mafia, is greatly interested in Cammarata's hearing and that the chief indicated that Cammarata's son-in-law Emmanuel Amato of Cleveland, a front man for juke boxes in Youngstown, appeared in court Tuesday along with a local cafe owner. The latter, Allen said, had attempted to take over the entire vending machine business in the Youngstown district.
>
> "The Chief said he began his investigation when he learned that Cammarata was 'trying to muscle in on the juke box business here." He named the café owner as Charles Vizzini of 848 Fifth Ave., and said he was the head of the Mafia in the Youngstown area. Vizzini has denied any connections with the Mafia."

Mock responded that Cammarata had "lived an exemplary life," claiming that his arrest record held only two convictions – the concealed weapons charge in 1927 and one for armed robbery, for which he had served his jail sentence. As for "bail jumping," Mock pointed out that Cammarata was still under bond to immigration officials for $10,000 since 1948.

After Allen shared his comments with the court, which were reported by national syndicated columnist Drew Pearson[9] regarding Cammarata's connections with the Mafia and the Detroit Mob, an angry exchange took place between the chief and defense counsel. Attorney Melillo insisted that the court stenographer record Allen's words. Nevin didn't agree. Words between the judge and lawyer then became heated and when Melillo refused to sit down Nevin ordered him jailed for contempt of court. The attorney was taken to a cell at 3:10 p.m., but was released a half-hour later on Nevin's order, just before court recessed for the day. Nevin overruled the defense motion for dismissal of the charges. On Wednesday afternoon Judge Nevin denied Cammarata's petition for bond and committed him to the county jail, setting a 30-day limit for the extradition process to take place.

Cammarata's attorneys immediately filed another habeas corpus petition with Judge Maiden. On Thursday morning, after an hour-long hearing, Maiden denied the petition for bail citing that the law provides for bail only before a man is tried for a crime. In Cammarata's situation, he had already been tried and convicted, but was now in violation of his parole agreement. Mock and Melillo announced that they would file a motion with the court of appeals.

Their attempt to rush an Appellate Court hearing turned into a fiasco. Only two of the three judges on the panel were present and one had not "expected a formal hearing" to be presented. Assistant County Prosecutor Harold Hull was in common pleas court on another matter when notified of the hearing and was "wholly unprepared" to proceed with the case. The time spent in the courtroom allowed defense counsel to do some Chief Allen bashing.

Melillo, still irate over his contempt of court jailing, called the Municipal Court a "glorified justice of the peace court." He then "waxed hot" stating that a grand jury should investigate "those people in Youngstown who are engaged in this giant persecution" of Cammarata. While Melillo did not articulate who "those people" were, Russell Mock was more specific in his criticism. He claimed Cammarata was a victim of a "letter writing" campaign between Chief Allen and a Michigan state parole officer. The crux of the defense's argument was that Michigan didn't want Cammarata. He had appeared before the Michigan Parole Board several times since his re-entry into the country and that after an arrest in March 1948 he was photographed and fingerprinted by Detroit police and then released to immigration officials.

Despite his request for a delay until Tuesday, the day after Christmas, Hull was forced to present legal opinions and previous opinions by 2:00 that afternoon. In spite of the fact that only two judges heard the appeal, they were determined to study the case and reach a decision before Christmas Day.

Just minutes after 6:00 p.m. on Saturday, December 23, Cammarata posted a $15,000 bond and walked out of the Mahoning County jail. The Christmas present was a gift from the 7th District Court of Appeals, whose distorted ruling stated, "The evidence is clear that there has been no trial, no judgment of conviction or bail. Therefore, it is our opinion that until such time as trial is had, the accused is entitled to reasonable bail as guaranteed by the federal and state constitutions."

Mock and Melillo then stated that if Michigan authorities didn't extradite Cammarata by January 19 he would be free. To help insure this, attorneys scheduled a meeting with Michigan Governor G. Mennen "Soapy" Williams on December 28. On the day of the meeting a three-week delay was granted to attorneys representing the State of Michigan Corrections Department by an aide of Governor Williams. The delay was allowed to give the department additional time to prepare legal briefs. A legal advisor to the governor would then make his recommendation. If the state wanted Cammarata back, the governor would then issue a request to Ohio Governor Frank Lausche, who would then issue a "governor's warrant" for Cammarata to be returned. Upon his return to Michigan Cammarata would have to serve out the remaining time on his old sentence.

On December 29 subpoenas were issued for Cammarata, Joseph DiCarlo and several other Mahoning Valley figures to appear before the Kefauver Committee during its upcoming hearings in Cleveland in mid-January. Despite Chief Allen claims that Cammarata was "the most powerful racket figure in Trumbull County," the Warren hood was one of several men that were not called to testify.

Meanwhile, the deportation proceedings continued and on February 28, 1951 a Federal Court in Cleveland ruled that Cammarata must leave the country by March 23. The *Vindicator* reported, "He may choose any country he wishes, but if the country of his choice refuses to accept him, he will be deported to Italy, his birthplace." Cammarata was allowed to remain free on the $10,000 federal bond from 1948, but had to report in person to authorities in Cleveland (later Youngstown) every two weeks and was not free to leave the Northern Ohio judicial district.

Two days after this ruling the state of Michigan decided it wanted Cammarata back. In asking Ohio Governor Lausche to return Cammarata, Michigan Governor Williams stated, "I can see no basic difference between this case and any other parole-violation case. This man is a powerful and important underworld figure. He was sentenced to a term of 15 to 30 years in prison for armed robbery. He was paroled on condition that he be deported to Italy, but instead of remaining in his native land he returned here in violation of his parole and in violation of American immigration laws. Cammarata should not be permitted to escape his prison sentence by making a visit to a foreign country. Deportation cannot be a substitute of Michigan law."

On March 5, Lausche issued an executive warrant for the arrest and extradition of Cammarata. In the affidavit for his arrest, in addition to outlining the history of the case, it claimed that Cammarata had "no visible means of support, yet appeared to be living in comfortable circumstances." Attorney Melillo immediately announced he would battle the extradition attempt in order for his client to remain free. Although Cammarata still had a pending deportation date of March 23, an immigration official confirmed that the action would be postponed if he were returned to Michigan to complete the prison sentence.

Cammarata was arrested at his new home at 241 Overlook Drive in Warren on March 7 and taken to the city jail, where some confusion existed over where he would be held.[10] Cammarata spent one night in the Trumbull County Jail and the next day a hearing was held before Judge William K. Thomas in Warren. The judge continued Cammarata's $15,000 bond and set a hearing date of March 26 for arguments on whether the hoodlum would be returned to Michigan to complete his sentence.

Perhaps in anticipation of Cammarata going away for a long time – if not forever – the day after the hearing the Austin-Burke Company of Youngstown, an interior decorating firm, filed suit to collect $1,200 for draperies, curtains and furnishings purchased from their firm since April 1949 by the Cammarata family. The lawsuit was dropped the next year.

Cammarata's extradition trial in Trumbull County Common Pleas Court got underway on Monday, March 26. The defense chose not to have the case heard before a jury; instead Judge William Thomas would listen to testimony and decide the case. The former Detroit Mob member found himself between a rock and a hard place. If his attorneys – Melillo and Mock – were successful in defeating the legal team from Michigan, who wanted Cammarata to complete a 15 to 30 year prison sentence, then he would be deported. That same day in Washington D.C., Senator Kefauver inquired on the status of Cammarata. He was assured by an official of the immigration service that 1) if Cammarata was successful in his extradition fight, he would be deported immediately and 2) if he were returned to Michigan to complete the sentence, he would be deported upon release.

Members of the Michigan legal team finally made public their side of the issue in their opening statement. The *Vindicator* reported:

"Prosecutor John H. Anderson of Trumbull and Asst. Atty. Gen. Perry A. Maynard of Michigan said that Cammarata's sentence was commuted on the ground that he leave this country. They said that when he returned late in 1939, they claim illegally, he violated his parole. Maynard said that the terms 'commutation' and 'parole' must be considered the same in the case.

"Maynard declared that under the indeterminate sentence law in Michigan a full pardon can be gained only by discharge of the balance of a maximum sentence, by the discharge at the expiration of parole time, or by the granting of an unconditional pardon."

Defense counsel tried unsuccessfully to place the correspondence of Chief Allen into record. The attorneys claimed the letters created a "change in attitude" on the part of Michigan parole board officials, and proved Allen's influence brought about the extradition hearings. To which the judge claimed, "So what!"

On Tuesday, the second and last day of the hearing, the judge refused to allow, as an exhibit, the confession of James Shoules, the dying prisoner who claimed he carried out the 1925 armed robbery of which Cammarata was convicted. The newspaper reported:

"Judge Thomas decided that his court is not concerned with the guilt or innocence of Cammarata in the robbery case, but only with the possibility that he has violated parole, is a fugitive from justice or is under the jurisdiction of Michigan authorities."

At the end of the hearing, during which Cammarata did not testify, Thomas gave both sides 15 days to file their closing briefs. The judge's decision on Cammarata was long in coming. More than three months passed and on July 11 it was reported that Cammarata sold his Overlook Drive home in Warren to the sales manager of a local steel company. Whether the home was sold because Cammarata anticipated a return to Michigan or some foreign land, or if he needed the money from the sale of the house (reportedly $41,000) for legal fees, the newspaper didn't specify.

On August 24, the *Vindicator* reported that in a 16-page ruling Judge Thomas "found that the Michigan parole order, to which Cammarata agreed, only sanctioned his release from prison for the purpose of deportation and 'ceased to validate his further release…at the moment he unlawfully returned to this country. The deportee is not only required to leave this country. He is also obliged not to return.'"

The judge then denied Cammarata's petition for a writ of habeas corpus and revoked his $15,000 bond. Just in case Thomas's ruling had gone the other way, two U.S. Immigration officials were on hand to arrest Cammarata on an illegal entry charge.

After the decision, Cammarata, "friendly and jovial," spoke with reporters at the courthouse while his attorneys conferred with Judge Thomas. Cammarata used this opportunity to deny any role in the Michigan bank robbery, claiming he was 42 miles away at the time. According to Cammarata, Michigan Governor Frank D. Fitzgerald commuted his sentence when Shoules confessed to the crime. The governor then promised a full pardon within a year of his deportation. Cammarata claimed, "The governor died in the meanwhile so I returned and sought aid from various officials."

There was no immediate action against Cammarata. Mock and Melillo were seeking to arrange a continuation of the bond while they appealed the decision before the 7th District Court of Appeals. Thomas consented and allowed Cammarata to remain free while the appeals process dragged on. The newspaper reported that Judge Thomas would first have to post a formal journal entry of his decision. "Until the court's ruling that Cammarata must go back to Michigan is on the clerk of courts' books he is at liberty under $15,000 bond," the newspaper reported. "The entry is expected to be filed Wednesday, August 29."

During the mayoral race in the fall of 1951, Mayor Charles Henderson and Michael J. Kirwan traded heated barbs, triggered by the congressman's bill to keep Cammarata from being deported. Kirwan came out in support of John A. Bannon, the Democratic candidate for mayor. Henderson claimed Kirwan "injected" himself into the campaign because of his personal resentment over Police Chief Edward J. Allen's exposure of Kirwan's sordid role in keeping the convict Frank Cammarata from being deported."

Kirwan countered with a formal statement defending his decision. He claimed he was approached by a Washington D.C. attorney by the name of Roy St. Louis who asked him to introduce the bill. St. Louis told the lawmaker that Cammarata's wife and three children "are your constituents," and if he didn't introduce the bill, who would?

In defense of his bill the Congressman said, "There were 2,700 special bills introduced in that 81st Congress. Some were to stay deportation of men who had sold dope to children, some on men who had committed murders and other crimes and some for re-admittance of men deported." Kirwan then explained that Cammarata had served a sentence for a crime he didn't commit and was then deported. "His wife and three children, American-born and good people, also went to Italy with him," Kirwan declared. "They did not like Italy and they came back to their native country, America. He came back into this country illegally – following his own wife and three children and not somebody else's wife, showing the good that was in this man.

"I'm tossing this challenge out now to any man or woman in this town, to the states of Ohio and Michigan and to the U.S. government and its Department of Justice – show me the time when this man was taken into court for some offense he committed or any law he has broken – after coming back to this country.

"If they can and have proof, I'll immediately go to Washington and ask them to take the $10,000 bond he is under and deport him."

In response to the congressman's assertions, Henderson pointed out that this was the third version Kirwan had given for introducing the bill. In the November election Henderson was elected to a third term when he beat Bannon by 7,500 votes.

Cammarata's appeal, scheduled to be heard in mid-September 1951, would take another five months to make its way into the courtroom. In Warren, on February 27, 1952, Cammarata was again represented by Russell Mock as both sides made lengthy arguments before the appeals court. One month to-the-day later, the 7th District Court of Appeals ruled unanimously that Cammarata must be returned to Michigan authorities. In announcing the court's decision, Judge John C. Nichols said that federal immigration officials advised that Cammarata be returned to Michigan, as opposed to being deported, due to Kirwan's pending bill before Congress. Mock announced he would appeal to the Ohio Supreme Court and take the case all the way to the U.S. Supreme Court if necessary.

On June 2 the appeal was filed with the Ohio Supreme Court. The court did not hear the appeal until October 17. Three days later vice squad officers in Youngstown picked up Cammarata in the Post Office Building. Cammarata told Lieutenant Dan Maggianetti that he was self-employed in Warren as a house builder. (Another report had the 54 year-old mobster working as a bouncer in a McKinley Heights nightclub.) Cammarata said he made a trip to Youngstown every two weeks to report to immigration officials or to consult with legal counsel. Police released him later that day.

On October 29, the Ohio Supreme Court ruled that Cammarata could be returned to Michigan. To no one's surprise, the next day attorney Melillo announced they would appeal the case to the U.S. Supreme Court. On November 3 Cammarata was granted a 90-day stay of execution by the Ohio Supreme Court so Melillo could prepare his case for the higher court. The attorney was preparing a writ of certiorari[11] an appeal to review the lower court's decision. During the whole appeals process Cammarata remained free on a $15,000 bond.

The year 1953 was a new year with new problems for Cammarata. On January 14 the Internal Revenue Service filed tax liens against Cammarata and his wife Grace to the tune of $12,584. The liens represented unpaid taxes for the years 1949 and 1950. This legal struggle would continue into the 1960s.

The next month it was Cammarata's service in the Italian army that was drawing news. Despite the fact newspapers had reported for several years Cammarata was a deserter from the Italian army, it wasn't until February 1953 that the mobster disclaimed the stories. The *Vindicator* stated that the original report of Cammarata's desertion came from U.S. Department of Justice officials. An examination of their files revealed there was no support to the claim. On February 4 Cammarata suddenly produced discharge papers showing he had served from May 13, 1937 to September 6, 1937. According to the documents he was discharged on March 13, 1952, some 15 years later. Many questioned the authenticity of the documents.

Cammarata's 90-day stay expired in early February 1953, but the U.S. Supreme Court granted him an extension on the filing of his appeal until late March. Still the process dragged on…

Finally…Back to Jail

On Monday night, June 15, 1953 nearly seven years since Cammarata was arrested outside of Cleveland, the U.S. Supreme Court denied a hearing to contest the State of Ohio's extradition decision to send the former Detroit mobster back to Michigan. Springing into action were U.S. Immigration officials, who raced to the new Bonnie Brae Avenue home of Cammarata in Warren and took him into custody. What happened next had all the precision of a Chinese fire drill. Prison officials in Michigan weren't even clear on what was to happen with Cammarata. When questioned by reporters, State Corrections Commissioner Ernest C. Brooks stated, "There's nothing we can do about Cammarata. It's been held that we waived our rights to him as a parole violator. Federal officials should send him back to Italy."

Immigration officials, on orders from Washington D.C., drove Cammarata to Cleveland and placed him in the Cuyahoga County jail. While Cammarata was technically being held in Cleveland for deportation, this action was seen as a move to get Cammarata to a neutral site while Michigan officials filed the necessary documents to return him to the state penitentiary to complete his sentence; as well as due to the hood's propensity to jump bail. Michigan Assistant Attorney General Perry Maynard immediately requested a "hold" order be placed on Cammarata. On June 17, after affirming that the prisoner would be returned to Michigan to serve out his sentence, Michigan Attorney General Frank G. Millard outlined the legal plan to bring the prisoner back:

"We have to send the Ohio State Supreme Court a copy of the U.S. Supreme Court order refusing to review Cammarata's case. Then the Ohio court must notify the Trumbull County Common Pleas Court. After that Cammarata's bail can be canceled and the Trumbull County sheriff can serve Ohio Governor Frank J. Lausche's warrant to extradite Cammarata to Michigan."

A simplistic plan? Not at all.

On June 20 a wrench was thrown into the works by Cleveland attorney Paul W. Walter[12] who appeared before Cuyahoga County Common Pleas Judge Joseph H. Silbert. Representing Cammarata, Walter told the court that a motion was being prepared seeking a re-hearing for Cammarata with the U.S. Supreme Court on the fight to block the Michigan extradition. While Silbert claimed he was confident that Cammarata would be extradited to Michigan, he said a "legal point" needed to be decided. The "legal point" was defined as "whether the county sheriff from Warren (Trumbull County) can take him back there from Cleveland (Cuyahoga County) for release to Michigan authorities."

Judge Silbert told both sides that a decision on the matter would be made on July 10. Both sides questioned the significance of the July 10 date, but were told the matter would be settled at that time. It was later revealed that Silbert was leaving for vacation and would not return to the bench until then. In the meantime, Silbert ordered Cammarata held in the Cuyahoga County jail without bond.

All along Cammarata felt the worst that could happen would be deportation, and on several occasions he made it known he preferred Mexico to his native land. With a return to the Michigan prison staring him in the face, he now announced he would rather go back to sunny Italy instead of the steel bars of a cold prison. While Cammarata was locked up in the Cuyahoga County jail he claimed he was destitute. Deputies believed the mobster until they saw him shelling out money to purchase special meals for himself and fellow prisoners, sometimes to the tune of $70 per meal. When deputies finally decided to search the prisoner they found five $100 bills hidden in his shoes.

On July 1 Perry Maynard and Ohio Governor Frank Lausche "ran an end around" on the legal system and Frank Cammarata was finally on his way back to Michigan. Maynard was informed that Cammarata could not be removed from the Cuyahoga County jail – even though they had signed extradition papers from Lausche – until given an order from the common pleas court. With Silbert on vacation no order would be forthcoming. Lausche then sent extradition orders to Trumbull County and authorities there drove to Cleveland and reclaimed their prisoner. Attorney Walter screamed "foul," calling the action a "low-handed trick." He immediately contacted the vacationing Silbert, who told him to request that Trumbull County officials hold off releasing Cammarata until the judge returned and "dealt with the Cleveland end of the case."

By the time Silbert's request was relayed to Trumbull County, Cammarata was long gone. Perry Maynard and two Michigan State Patrolmen, armed with a new extradition order from Lausche, removed Cammarata from the Trumbull County jail at 3:30 in the morning. The prisoner was refused permission to go to his home and tell his wife goodbye. Even then it seemed as if luck were running against the Wolverine State. On the way to the prison in Jackson, Michigan the automobile the men were traveling in broke down and the rest of the trip had to be completed in a borrowed vehicle. At 11:00 a.m. on July 2 Cammarata was back behind the bars of a Michigan prison after a reprieve of sixteen and a half years.

The re-incarceration of Cammarata was a true victory for Perry Maynard. The Michigan Assistant Attorney General put up a relentless fight to bring Cammarata back to Michigan, after every hearing and dogging prosecutors and government officials every step of the way along the five-year legal process. A *Vindicator* article stated, Cammarata's lawyers have used every possible section in the law books to avoid extradition, and, despite a five-year fight all the way to the U. S. Supreme Court and many exasperating delays, Maynard followed up on every angle of the case and was ready to seize Cammarata once the high court refused to prevent his return to Michigan."

Back in Cleveland, attorney Walter was still raging over the incident. In court before Judge Silbert, he blamed Cuyahoga County Sheriff Joseph M. Sweeney for allowing his client to be returned to Michigan. Cuyahoga County Prosecutor Frank T. Cullitan responded, "This Cammarata has no right to be walking the streets. The sheriff had nothing on which to hold him." After hearing both sides, Silbert upheld Sweeney's actions stating that Cammarata should never have been brought to Cleveland and that Cuyahoga County had absolutely no jurisdiction in the matter.

Walter, a prominent Republican politician, lost after delivering an impassioned speech. As the parties were leaving the courthouse, Frank Cullitan told a reporter, "Paul Walter is a man who is being mentioned for United States district attorney. Isn't it interesting how vitally he is concerned with what happens to a man who was adjudged an undesirable alien, a man who sneaked illegally back into this country after he was once deported and who is wanted for a prison term for bank robbery?" Overhearing the comment, Walter hurried to another reporter and loudly stated, "Cullitan better sweep his own doorway before making such a statement."

Judge Silbert was correct when he had declared the matter would be resolved on July 10. On that date the Cammarata case was officially closed in Cleveland when the judge placed a journal entry on record simply stating that the extradition warrant, sent to the Cuyahoga County Court of Common Pleas, had been withdrawn.

Once back in the Jackson prison, Cammarata wasted no time making his next move. Although facing a maximum 23 and a half-year sentence, the prisoner was allowed a parole hearing within sixty days. Lawyers went to work immediately. Cammarata's trail of lawyers stretched from Detroit, to New York to Cleveland, to Warren and back to Detroit. The costs, which had to be enormous, were said to have come from the cash laden pockets of brother-in-law Peter Licavoli.

As Cammarata whiled away his time in prison he seemed unable to stay out of the public eye as the government continued to pursue him. In January 1954 it was Cammarata's tax returns – or lack thereof – that made headlines. Republican U.S. Senator John J. Williams of Delaware ripped his Democratic counterparts calling the work of federal tax officials under the previous administration a "disgusting example of gangster coddling." Using Cammarata as an example, he stated that in place of bringing an indictment against the criminal, "the Treasury Department allowed this gangster to file belated tax returns for each of the years involved and dropped all efforts for prosecution. Just who in the Treasury Department is responsible for this extreme leniency to another racketeer is a question which thus far I have been unable to obtain."

Senator Williams then attacked Kirwan for introducing his "stinker" bills to Congress to protect Cammarata with a stay of deportation. Kirwan, Chairman of the Democratic Congressional Campaign Committee, was quick to respond, "Certainly I gave Cammarata protection, the protection that every human being is entitled to – his day in court." When asked if he thought politics were involved, he answered, "It couldn't be anything else. There were 2,700 private relief bills introduced that year, [some] involving white slavers, dope peddlers and everything else, and they pick on me."

In the years following Kirwan's misguided efforts, the House Judiciary Committee adopted new procedures for deportation bills. In the past the mere introduction of a bill was enough to stay a deportation order. New rules stated the bill's sponsor must convince committee members of the merits of the bill and provide evidence to support the claim.

On January 13, 1954, the same day Senator Williams was berating Cammarata in the Senate, the prisoner filed an appeal for release. The basis was a recent Supreme Court ruling which, "held that Michigan cannot return a parole violator to prison if it has previously refused an opportunity to regain custody of him." Cammarata's attorneys presented the claim that the state turned down three opportunities to regain him after his 1946 arrest in Ohio. On April 16 the Michigan Supreme Court agreed to reviewthe re-arrest of Cammarata. Eight months passed before the court rendered a decision. On December 30 the court rejected Cammarata's argument that the arrest was improper.

In May 1955 the government began going after underworld tax evaders in the Mahoning Valley. Included in a wave of trials were principals from the Jungle Inn – John Farah and his wife, Ralph Coletti and his wife, Anthony Delsanter and Edward Tobin. A separate trial was being prepared against Cammarata. His attorneys filed a motion to have the case heard in Michigan so Cammarata could appear as a witness. The judge and the IRS attorneys approved the request.

Fourteen months passed and still no progress was made on the case. Then on July 25, 1956 IRS agents seized the newest home of Grace Cammarata at 634 Belvedere Avenue in Warren to help satisfy a government lien of $12,586. A review of the amount by the U.S. District Tax Court reduced the amount to less than half. On August 14 Grace paid $1,138 leaving a balance of $5,500. Despite the payment, an IRS supervisor set a sale date of September 10. After an additional $3,334 was paid IRS agents abandoned their plans to sell the house at auction.

On May 29, 1958 Michigan authorities determined that Cammarata had served enough time and were ready to release him for immediate deportation to Italy. The next day, after Cammarata was released from the Jackson prison, he was picked up by U.S. Immigration agents, who were ready to fly him immediately out of the country. Cammarata's attorneys argued in Federal Court that the deportation would cause hardship to his family. Another long legal affray was about to begin. Federal Judge Thomas P. Thornton granted a stay while both sides "gathered evidence." Cammarata was ordered held with out bond in the Wayne County Jail.

On June 12 an additional week's postponement was granted at the request of the government who asked for additional time "to obtain more information and evidence from Washington to present at the hearing." When the week was up Judge Thornton dismissed Cammarata's plea for a temporary injunction to block his deportation. The judge gave Cammarata ten days in which to decide whether to appeal the ruling to the U.S. Court of Appeals in Cincinnati.

On June 25 attorneys for the 60 year-old Cammarata, who was now being referred to in the newspapers as a "Prohibition Era figure," filed notice they would appeal the decision. The court allowed Cammarata to be released after posting a $10,000 bond.

Less than a week after being released on bond, and allowed to return to his Warren home, Cammarata successfully eluded government agents who attempted to serve him with a subpoena to appear before the Senate Rackets Committee, which were being conducted in Washington D.C. Underworld figures with Youngstown connections called to testify included members of the Licavoli clan, and Joe and Sam DiCarlo of Buffalo.

In mid-August Cammarata's name came up during testimony at the hearings. Robert Scott, a former Detroit teamster's official, testified that he had been directed by Teamster's President James R. "Jimmy" Hoffa to approach Michigan Governor G. Mennen Williams in regards to a pardon for Cammarata. Scott went on to make a number of allegations against Hoffa. The Cammarata accusation, however, was the only one the powerful labor leader would confirm. Hoffa claimed he made the request on behalf of an attorney whose name he couldn't recall.

On December 1 it was announced that Cammarata would be called to testify before the committee in Washington D.C., along with Youngstown Teamster's business agent Joseph Blumetti. Cammarata's appearance was amusing.

The hearings were under the leadership of Arkansas Democratic Senator John L. McClellan. The body of senators conducting the investigation, which included John F. Kennedy of Massachusetts, was known as the McClellan Committee. Lead counsel for the committee was Robert F. "Bobby" Kennedy.

This segment of the hearings was to expose how underworld figures were in collusion with union officials and businessmen to control the coin-operated machine industry. Described as a multibillion-dollar business, it included vending machines and jukeboxes. Since the Teamster's Union would figure prominently in the juke box trade, members of the committee, particularly Bobby Kennedy, were anxious to question Cammarata about Hoffa's efforts to get a pardon for him. In addition, the committee attempted to tie him to Detroit Local 985, known as the "juke box local," of the teamster's Union, which was about to come under investigation.

On Wednesday, December 4 Cammarata arrived at the committee offices early. He told Bobby Kennedy he had decided to give up his deportation fight because he was "sick of the people." Since his return to Warren from Michigan he had been working as a bricklayer's assistant. His 21 year-old son was forced to leave school in order to help support his mother. Cammarata said his Warren home was for sale and that Grace would follow him on his return trek. The plan was to leave from Miami on December 8, then on to Cuba two days later. From there he would board a ship for Sicily.

When Cammarata was called to testify he entered and took the witness seat. Bobby Kennedy announced that Cammarata was being called at this time because it would be the committee's last chance to question him before he left on his self-imposed exile. The committee would soon be taking a Christmas break and would not return until January 7, 1959. Cammarata appeared without legal counsel. When asked why by Kennedy, Cammarata explained, "I don't need a lawyer. I don't know anything about the vending machine business and I have only visited Youngstown a couple of times in the past few years." Later he told the committee he couldn't afford one, to which Bobby Kennedy reminded him that he had an expensive house built and purchased a new automobile while serving time in prison in Jackson, Michigan.

When asked to give his name Cammarata refused until Senator McClellan ordered him to do so. He would not even acknowledge that his wife's maiden name was Licavoli. McClellan then asked Assistant Committee Counsel Arthur Kaplan to present information on Cammarata's criminal career and ties to the jukebox industry. According to the *Vindicator*:

> "Kaplan linked Cammarata to a secret meeting of juke-box distributors and Teamster officials in 1950 which broke a stranglehold on juke-box distribution activities in Detroit.
>
> "Kaplan said that the Music Systems Inc. of Detroit had its machines boycotted in 1950 because of Teamster opposition. After failing to break the boycott by forming another union, Kaplan said, the company called in Cammarata.
>
> "After a meeting attended by Teamster official "big Vince" Meli and Music System officials, the stranglehold was broken because, Kaplan said, Cammarata told Big Vince to 'be nice to Music Systems."
>
> "Kaplan told the committee Cammarata next appeared to break up a juke box monopoly then held by the International Brotherhood of Electrical Workers.
>
> "Cammarata, with his uncle, Emmaneul deAmato [sic], took over the Youngstown area distribution of MSI juke boxes after a previous distributor had failed to break the IBEW blockade against the Seeburg machines, Kaplan said.
>
> "'The individual who was supposed to distribute the machines quit trying because he was harassed by the competing group,' Kaplan said.
>
> "'He was told by the Detroit distributor to hang on a while longer because Cammarata was on the way and his troubles would be over.'
>
> "According to Kaplan, the previous distributor, whom he declined to name, quit anyway, leaving the way clear for Cammarata and deAmato to take over in Youngstown.
>
> "'They had no difficulty at all in placing these machines in establishments they previously couldn't get into.' Kaplan stated. He indicted that it was fear of Cammarata that made this possible.
>
> "Kaplan listed briefly some of Cammarata's underworld associates which included the Farahs of Girard, operators of the defunct Jungle Inn.

"'Cammarata was connected with the more ranking echelon of Detroit hoodlums and his job was to look out for the interests of the Warren-Youngstown boys, Kaplan said."

When the overview by Kaplan was completed Bobby Kennedy again began to question the aging mobster. Cammarata's first response was to take the Fifth Amendment. In executing this task he spoke in "guttural broken English." Clearly annoyed, Kennedy asked, "Why are you putting on this act? You talked to me just a few minutes ago in perfect English."

When Robert Kennedy asked if he received a percentage of the juke box take in Youngstown, Cammarata mumbled his refusal to answer. He then asked if he also got a percentage of the gambling take from the same area. Again, same answer. When the questioning got around to Cammarata failing to file income tax statements, Senator John Kennedy stated that the Treasury Department should be forced to produce all the documents they had so government investigators could determine who interceded on Cammarata's behalf. The committee members were clearly incensed that the gangster had not filed returns from 1939 to 1946 and during the other years had filed false returns.

When Cammarata's testimony was completed Senator McClellan said that it was a blessing for Americans that he was leaving the country. He was reminded that if he were still around when the committee reconvened on January 7, that he was still under subpoena and would be expected to testify. For the first time during the hearing the mobster's answer changed. He clearly stated, "Yes, sir, I will do this."

Of his appearance the *Detroit Free Press* wrote:

> "Old-time Michigan hoodlum Frank Cammarata – on his way to catch a boat to his native Sicily, or somewhere – wouldn't give the Senate Rackets Committee the time of day Thursday.
> "Asked in a dozen or more skillfully varied ways whether he knew anything about underworld infiltration of the Detroit jukebox business, Cammarata did his best to sound like Tony the peanut vender as he pleaded the Fifth Amendment in broken English.
> "'I might incriminal myself,' he said at one point."

Cammarata then returned to the committee's offices where he again spoke freely. The *Vindicator* printed the following exchange between Cammarata and Kennedy:

> Kennedy: "How'd you sneak back into this country in 1939 after you were deported?"

Cammarata: "I came in through New York."
Kennedy: "How did you do that? How did you get through immigration authorities?"
Cammarata: "I just walk in. Nobody was there."
Kennedy: What are you going to do when you get to Sicily?"
Cammarata: "Maybe go into business."
Kennedy: "What business, bank robbing?"
Cammarata (laughing): "Nah, I never rob a bank."
Kennedy: "You're trying to tell us you're broke. What about that nice house you built in Warren?"
Cammarata (waving): "That's my wife's house."
Kennedy (feeling Cammarata's shirt collar): Don't try to tell me that's a $2.98 shirt; that cost at least $15."
Cammarata (also feeling the collar with reminiscing air): "Yeah, but that was when things were better."

At this point, Cammarata showed the palms of his callused hands to the chief counsel.

Cammarata: "See, that's where I make my money. I'm a bricklayer's helper. I do honest work."
Kennedy: "You never had anything to do with these juke boxes did you."
Cammarata: "Nah, I never even seen one except when I take my wife out to dinner."

When discussing Cammarata's pending departure Kennedy stated, "I understand he is going to Cuba to set up a gambling establishment." Cammarata claimed that he was only going to take a two-week vacation in Cuba before returning to Italy.

On Saturday, December 7 the government announced a judgment of $4,197 was filed against Cammarata in Cleveland Federal Court. IRS agents moved quickly filing a lien on December 12 against the Cammarata's Belvedere Avenue home so Grace could not sell the property without paying her husband's tax debt. In addition, the city's banking institutions were notified and liens were to be placed against any of the couple's accounts. When questioned as to where her husband was, Grace claimed she didn't know. In March 1959 the IRS billed Grace Cammarata $5,150 for back income taxes and penalties. Grace appealed to the US Tax Court in Washington D.C. claiming she owed nothing, that her husband had never transferred any assets to her.

Cuban Demise

Apparently Cammarata executed his self-imposed deportation as promised, arriving in Cuba that Thursday, December 12. Reports from the island nation said Cammarata was arrested by officials of the Fulgencio Batista government the night he arrived while he was speaking with Santo Trafficante, Jr., who operated a gambling casino in Havana. Trafficante was the most powerful Mafia boss in the southeastern United States.

Bobby Kennedy was informed by federal immigration officials of Cammarata's arrest, and that the Cuban government was planning to deport him to Italy. Kennedy said if the deportation were carried out it would mark the end of the committee's interest in the hood. Kennedy, however, was determined to find out from IRS officials why Cammarata had never been prosecuted for tax evasion. Records that had been requested from the agency had yet to be delivered to the committee.

On December 14 Cuban authorities officially announced they had arrested Cammarata as a "very dangerous person," and were holding him in the Tiscornia Immigration Camp, across the bay from Havana. Cuban immigration officials said they had decided to deport Cammarata, but wanted to find out if the United States wanted him on any charges. If not, he would be placed on a ship for Italy. Before any official action could be taken by Cuban officials the Batista government was overthrown by Fidel Castro.

On January 2, 1959 the *Vindicator* reported in a front page headline: "Cammarata's Trail Lost in Fury of Revolution" While the general attitude of the government was, "We don't care where he is as long as he's not here," the whereabouts of Cammarata was a mystery to immigration authorities. In April 1960, more than 15 months after he was last heard of, Osorio Davilla, Director of Cuban Immigration, reported Cammarata had been released from the Tiscornia Immigration Camp in January 1959, along with all the other detainees there, on orders from Fidel Castro. Davilla reported they were still holding Cammarata's Italian passport. An official from the Italian Embassy in Havana reported they had no information on the hood's whereabouts. United States immigration authorities claimed they would have been informed if Cammarata had reached Italy. On June 15 Davilla stated, "We have checked his record and we know where he is in Cuba." The immigration director declared as long as Cammarata obeyed Cuban laws he was free to remain in the country. Meanwhile the U.S. Immigration agency was keeping a close watch to make sure Cammarata and other gangsters didn't slip back into the country since the Castro takeover. Cammarata's tenure as a law-abiding citizen of Castro's Communist Cuba was short-lived. On July 30, 1960 the *Vindicator* headlines screamed:

Cuban Police Jail Cammarata
As Leader of Narcotics Ring

After his release from the immigrant camp, Cammarata decided to stay in Cuba. During the early months of the new Castro regime Cammarata openly met with known gamblers and underworld figures. As the new government began a crackdown on organized crime, Cammarata's meetings with these people became more discreet. He purchased a small bar (some reports referred to it as a nightclub) called the Mermaid Club in a poor section of Havana. He soon began using the place as a front for selling drugs. It wasn't clear how he had entered the trade, but the Cuban police claimed he was associated with "Lucky" Luciano.[13]

On July 29 a Cuban undercover agent, posing as a drug buyer, made plans to purchase cocaine from Cammarata at his Havana apartment. After the drugs arrived the police closed in and arrested Cammarata, Harold Fieldman and three Cubans. Police seized $14,000 worth of cocaine and a quantity of cash. The newspaper claimed Cuban officials were "extremely tough" on dope dealers and that conviction could bring up to ten years in prison. Police immediately closed Cammarata's Mermaid Club, concluding that the bar was being used as a front for his drug operations.

The American arrested with Cammarata, Harold Fieldman, operated Exchange Auto Sales and Fieldman Marine Sales with his wife back in Girard, Ohio in Trumbull County. Fieldman had a police record in Trumbull County, which included white slavery. A *Vindicator* reporter questioned Mrs. Fieldman, who claimed to be "shocked" at the arrest, not even knowing her estranged husband was in Cuba. She was reportedly running the Girard business and considered herself "separated" from her husband. Cuban authorities described Fieldman as Cammarata's "secretary and assistant." Answering questions about the arrest, a Cuban immigration official was asked if the two would be deported. He replied that "is still a long way off – they must face Cuba courts and a probable prison sentence first."

More than six months passed before any more information was released about the arrest. On St. Valentine's Day 1961 the Associated Press reported that Cammarata was in Principe Prison in Cuba awaiting trial, unable to post a $20,000 bond. After taking care of all his legal finances in the past, it seems as though the Licavolis had finally given up on bailing out their troubled brother-in-law. As for his "secretary and assistant," Fieldman pulled a Cammarata. On August 29, 1960, after posting a $5,000 bond, he fled the country. Callers to his Girard businesses were told that he was "out of the state."

The February 1961 dispatch was the last time Cammarata's whereabouts would be known. Three months after the resolution of the Cuban Missile Crisis, Castro began clearing Cuban prisons, mostly those who had been taken prisoner during the failed Bay of Pigs invasion in April 1961.[14] On January 14, 1963 a boat arrived in Miami with 89 persons aboard. Cammarata was not among them. On April 23 another 21 arrived; again no Cammarata. An attorney, who negotiated the release of this latest batch, reported that three other prisoners elected to be flown to South America and that nine others were still listed as being in Cuba, but Cammarata's name was not on either list. One prisoner, incarcerated in Cleveland, told reporters he did not know Cammarata, but had heard a rumor he was in a new "concentration camp" in southeast Cuba.

More than two years passed before Cammarata was reported on again. On May 14, 1965 the *Vindicator* reported that Frank Cammarata had died eleven days earlier in a Havana hospital. According to the death certificate, the 66 year-old died of acute edema of the lung and hypertension of the heart. There was no mention of what he had been doing during the last few years of his life; one can only assume they were spent in prison. At the time of his death Grace was still living in Warren and their children were in the Cleveland / Youngstown area.

Frank Cammarata was not the typical gangster. He married into the Licavoli clan and was considered an elite mobster as a member of the Detroit Mafia. But from 1925 until the day he died, some 40 years later, Cammarata was either in jail or on the run from law enforcement and immigration officials. Cammarata seemingly did nothing to help his situation. A notorious bail jumper, he managed to get arrested time and again while on the lam. In the end, the toll of his enormous legal fees was exceeded only by the toll his criminal exploits placed on the lives of his wife and children.

6

The Story of "Tony Dope""

Known to his underworld associates as "Tony Dope," Anthony Delsanter was born on March 11, 1911, one of four boys in a six-sibling family. He grew up on East 126th Street in Cleveland's "Little Italy" section. One of Delsanter's earliest arrests was for truancy in 1928, when he was 17 years old. His first jail term came the next year when he was arrested for reckless driving and spent 60 days in the county workhouse. In 1931 a conviction for violation of a traffic ordinance would cost him another 20 days.

By the end of Prohibition two things were clear, Delsanter was on the road to being a habitual criminal and he was expanding his base of operations in Northeastern Ohio. A burglary and larceny conviction in the spring of 1934 resulted in a term at the Ohio Penitentiary. In November he was held as a suspicious person in three different cities – Akron, Canton and Mansfield.

At a young age Delsanter formed a friendship with a neighborhood boy, two years his junior – Aladena "Jimmy" Fratianno. The two ingratiated themselves with the local gangsters in "Little Italy," members of the infamous Mayfield Road Mob. Both were tough youngsters and as they moved into their late teens and early twenties they began to make a name for themselves initially, as strike breakers.

On February 9, 1935 Delsanter was convicted on another burglary and larceny charge and sentenced to a 1 to 15 year term. He was paroled on September 1, 1936. Returning to Cleveland he hooked up with Fratianno and decided to make some quick money by holding up a few gambling joints. In their first effort they collected $5,800 after ordering nine men to strip to their underwear at gunpoint.

The next score, set up by Pittsburgh Mafia member and future Rochester boss Frank Valenti earned them a whopping $70,000. In July 1937 Fratianno decided to rob a layoff bookie who was slow in paying him. At one of downtown Cleveland's busiest street corners they waylaid the man in his car and drove off. After administering a savage beating they collected $1,600, far short of the $10,000 Fratianno was due. Unfortunately for him and Delsanter, the police swooped down on them while they were changing automobiles. On October 9 the two men and an accomplice were given 10 to 25 year sentences.

Delsanter spent over eight years in the Ohio Penitentiary before he was paroled on January 24, 1946. Shortly after his release Delsanter relocated to the Warren area. In *The Last Mafiosi*, the biography of Jimmy Fratianno, author Ovid Demaris writes, "His old friend Tony Dope Delsanter was now a made guy and running things in Warren for Johnny Scalish [Cleveland Mafia boss]." There is no information giving insight as to how or why Delsanter was initiated into the Cleveland Mafia or why he was sent to the Warren area. He was considered, however, the Cleveland Mafia's man at the Jungle Inn to oversee the operation and earned ten percent of the profits according to the IRS suit filed against the owners of record in the mid-1950s (see chapter 4).

Delsanter remained free of legal problems for about two years. Then on February 21, 1948 he was arrested at Detroit's Willow Run Airport with Joseph "Red' Giordano from New Kensington, Pennsylvania and Max Stern, described as a lieutenant of Peter Licavoli in Detroit. In their possession were two expensive furs – a silver blue mink and a gray stone marten – along with a loaded .38 revolver. Rumors swirled as to why the men were in Detroit. One alleged the pair was there to kill two Detroit men who were believed to be behind the September 1947 robbery of the Mounds Club outside Cleveland.

In April 1949, more than a year after the arrest, the three went to trial. Delsanter was acquitted on a directed verdict. Giordano and Stern were convicted and sentenced to four years, though a long, drawn-out appeals process ensued.

Around this time Delsanter came into possession of the National Cigarette Service, a vending machine concern at which he employed notorious Valley mobster "Fats" Aiello, who had been ordered to get a job by Chief Allen or face constant police harassment. Delsanter held onto the company for a few years before selling his interest to Vince DeNiro in September 1952.

In March 1951 Delsanter was arrested for a double slaying that took place in Pittsburgh. On May 17, 1946 the bodies of two men were found in the rear of an automobile riddled with bullets near the Pittsburgh City Tuberculosis Hospital. Now, nearly five years later, a Pittsburgh newspaper published an expose on the murders naming Delsanter as the triggerman and Frank Valenti as the alleged mastermind. Delsanter was arrested at the offices of the National Cigarette Service and through his attorney, Russell Mock, announced he was anxious to go to Pittsburgh to clear his name before the Allegheny County Grand Jury.

On April 2 Delsanter was released on a $1,000 bond by Judge David Jenkins. Before he left he was grilled by officials from several Pennsylvania law enforcement agencies. After some delay Delsanter finally went before the grand jury on the morning of May 8. After his testimony an assistant district attorney told reporters that Delsanter was a cooperative witness and that "the grand jury was satisfied with his testimony and attitude." They wouldn't feel the same towards Valenti, who refused to testify. A judge ruled that since Valenti may become a defendant in the case that he had the right to refuse to answer questions that could incriminate him. Valenti had once been charged as an accessory in the murders, but the charges were dropped for lack of evidence. On May 17, exactly five years after the killings, the grand jury completed their re-investigation of the dual murders (due to the newspaper expose) and concluded there was not enough evidence on which to indict either Delsanter or Valenti.

Aside from his tax woes in 1955, when he was charged with owing more than $30,000 in back taxes from his days at the Jungle Inn, Delsanter spent the 1950s avoiding problems with the law.

That changed on November 19, 1960. Delsanter had been running a bookie operation out of a "cozy country tavern" called the Log Cabin. The bar, located on Palmyra Road southwest of Warren, handled sports betting, horse race wagers and lottery bets. The raid on a pleasant autumn afternoon followed raids nationwide in 56 cities by agents of the Internal Revenue Service cracking down on football betting. There were about 25 patrons in the bar that afternoon, but only five were placed under arrest – Delsanter, the proprietor of the Log Cabin; Carmen Perfette and his nephew Joseph described as pickup men; and the manager and a bartender. All five were charged with violating the federal gambling tax law. In addition to recovering hundreds of football, horse bet and "bug" slips, the agents confiscated nearly $3,000 in cash and two revolvers.

On Monday morning Trumbull County prosecutor Charles Anderson filed padlock proceedings against the Log Cabin and four other alleged bookie and lottery joints. After several postponements the five men were finally arraigned in Federal Court in Cleveland before Judge James C. Connell on February 10, 1961.

While Delsanter was waiting for the case to come to trial he was arrested for reckless driving in Warren on March 13. Delsanter hit a tractor-trailer rig at West Market Street and Highland Avenue. Arrested by Patrolmen

Albert Timko and Ronald McCracken, Delsanter resisted arrest, used profane language and threatened both officers while being examined at St. Joseph Hospital.

The *Vindicator* article that reported the arrest stated that Delsanter was "in competition with racket lord Mike Farah." That "competition," if indeed it did exist, came to an end less than three months later when Farah was cut down by an assassin while practicing golf shots on his lawn on a Saturday morning. Delsanter, the prime suspect in the murder, produced an airtight alibi.

On July 20, four of the five defendants in the Log Cabin raid case were found guilty in U.S. District Court and fined $1,050. Joseph Perfette was acquitted due to lack of evidence. Attorneys for the men announced they would file a motion for a retrial, which was denied.

Nearly two months after the death of Billy Naples in July 1961, police arrested Delsanter and charged him with being a suspicious person. During questioning he was asked about rumors that were circulating about his connection with a barbut game in Campbell. He denied the claims. When asked about his work, Delsanter claimed he had been out of work for the last eight months and living off money he had made up until that time. When the suspicious person's case came to trial City Prosecutor William Green argued that Delsanter failed to give satisfactory answers to questions about his job and residence. Police found $686 on his person, despite the fact Delsanter said he hadn't worked in eight months. He explained the money came from winnings on the golf course and racetrack bets. When his attorney Eugene Fox asked for a dismissal of the charges, Municipal Court Judge John Leskovyansky agreed.

It would be nearly ten years before Delsanter's name appeared again in local newspapers. In the years after the tragic November 1962 bombing death of Charles "Cadillac Charlie" Cavallaro, which also killed one young son and maimed another, the presence of the FBI and the Justice Department became more pronounced in the Mahoning Valley. In December 1970 the Justice Department's Organized Crime Strike Force raided the business office of Cleveland Mafia associate John P. Calandra. The raid was one of several taking place in Ohio, Pennsylvania, New York and New Orleans. In Cleveland agents uncovered evidence of a loan-sharking operation that included Delsanter, Leo "Lips" Moceri and John Licavoli. On December 15 Delsanter's home was one of several targets in the Mahoning Valley that was searched by FBI agents. One of the other Trumbull County places hit was Cherry's Top of the Mall Restaurant at Eastwood Mall, which was described as "one of the area's plush eating and drinking spots." One of the stock holders of Cherry's Inc., which owned the establishment, was Anthony Cafaro. The information gathered for the warrants to raid these locations came from court-authorized telephone bugs. Affidavits provided to the court by the FBI claimed Delsanter "runs gambling in Warren."

In May 1971 a Federal grand jury in Cleveland began reviewing the seized evidence. The affidavits stated Delsanter was linked to Joseph Lanese of Euclid, a large suburb along Cleveland's eastern border. Lanese was accused of obtaining the betting lines on college and pro football games from the Cihal Brothers in Pittsburgh and providing them to Delsanter. On July 20 Delsanter was one of several men arrested after indictments were issued by the grand jury. He was charged with conspiracy in interstate transportation of wagering information. At Delsanter's home agents seized several customer lists. One of the interesting items found was four copies of a paper that set forth the provisions of the Federal Organized Crime Act. Despite the charges later being dropped, for the remainder of his life Delsanter would be referred to as the gambling boss of Trumbull County and Warren.

On August 21, 1974 Delsanter was indicted by another Federal grand jury in Cleveland. He and old sidekick Carmen Perfette were charged in an 11-count indictment with a scheme to defraud Teamster Local 377's health and welfare fund of $34,000 between January 1967 and December 1972. Two un-indicted conspirators in the case were Joseph Perfette and Joseph Giordano; the latter had passed away the previous April.

The indictment charged the men with plotting to make illegal claims on the fund even though none of them were members of the union. They set up a dummy corporation called P & R Construction Company that used Carmen Perfette's home as its business address. Delsanter and Carmen Perfette were accused of collecting $25,750 in direct benefits and $8,560 in benefits paid directly to doctors and hospitals for treatments. In addition, the two were charged with "causing false entries to be made in documents required by labor laws to be kept in the fund." On September 24, 1975 Delsanter pled guilty in Federal Court in Cleveland to a reduced charge of "willfully causing inaccurate information to be published" in the Health & Welfare Fund Teamster Local 377's annual report during 1971 – 1972. Delsanter was fined $2,000, ordered to make restitution and placed on a year's probation. Carmen Perfette received the same sentence for pleading guilty to the charge of "concealing information" in the same report. In January 1977 the Teamsters' Local 377 had to file suit in Trumbull County common pleas court to recover the money due them.

Just days after his indictment for the health and welfare fund charge, Delsanter was one of four men charged with tampering with a pay telephone. Delsanter was caught in the act while under surveillance. He was seen using a "wire device" to make $300 worth of calls from an East Market

Street service station that was owned by one of the other men. All four pled not guilty during arraignment in Warren Municipal Court and demanded jury trials. In December a jury acquitted the four men.

◆   ◆   ◆

After the death of long-time Cleveland Mafia boss John Scalish in 1976 the Cleveland Family found itself at war. James Licavoli became the reluctant boss of the Cleveland Family in a surprise move that overlooked Angelo "Big Ange" Lonardo, who was the reported underboss to Scalish. Licavoli named Leo "Lips" Moceri, his cousin, as his underboss. After the disappearance of Moceri in August 1976, some sources claim Delsanter was named the new underboss. In two books about "Jimmy the Weasel" Fratianno, Delsanter is described at various times as the underboss and the *consigliere* of the family. Whatever Delsanter's position was it was short-lived.

Delsanter and his wife Martha resided at 373 Central Parkway in Warren. Martha passed away on September 1, 1972. In the years after her death Delsanter enjoyed vacationing at the home of his son, Larry in Hollywood, Florida. On July 31, 1977 he told friends at the Mosquito Yacht Club that he was leaving for Florida for the last in a series of treatments for a medical condition. Delsanter had recently had an operation for hemorrhoids. Around 2:30 a.m. on August 2 Delsanter suffered a massive heart attack at his son's home and died. The 66 year-old Delsanter was buried in All Souls Cemetery.[1]

7

A Few Selected Biographies

George H. Birrell

One of the most respected and longest serving jurists in the history of Trumbull County was George H. Birrell. Born in Kinsman, Ohio on January 6, 1890, Birrell graduated from Oberlin College in 1911. After a short career as a teacher and a stint in the Army Air Corps during World War I, he attended law school at Western Reserve College in Cleveland. Birrell received his law degree, passed the bar and began his law practice all in the same year – 1919.

Making Warren his home, Birrell ran for public office in 1926 being elected city solicitor (law director). He served two terms and was then elected Trumbull County prosecutor in 1929, serving in that position until 1932. During this time he handled the last two bribery trials of James Munsene, reaching a plea bargain in the annual court case.

As prosecutor during the Prohibition Era, Birrell was known as the "Ax-buster" for his assaults on speakeasies. In the company of city police or county deputies, Birrell would wait as he sent his "stool pigeons" into the establishment to purchase liquor. Then the prosecutor would come in swinging and destroy bars, mirrors, tables, chairs and merchandise – keeping just enough evidence to make a successful prosecution.

According to a *Vindicator* article, Birrell "was one of Trumbull County's biggest vote-getters and one of the most successful candidates in the history of the Republican Party here. He served as GOP chairman for a period of time and was one of the party leaders for years."

In 1944 Birrell was elected judge of the Common Pleas Court. He was re-elected to three more six-year terms serving on the bench for 24 years, the longest period ever served by a Trumbull County judge. In 1968 he declined to seek re-election to a fifth term.

During his years as judge, Birrell presided over the case of Thomas Viola, on trial for the murder of Munsene, and the assault trial of Mike Farah for the beating of Jean Blair. During the 1950s Birrell's son Bruce served as Warren city law director. In this capacity he handled the city's case against Police Chief Manley English during his civil service trial in 1959.

A member of the Trumbull County Bar Association, Birrell served as its president in 1945. In 1969 that body honored him for 50 years of dedicated service. He received a similar honor, the "golden gavel" award, from the Ohio Judges Association.

Birrell died in Trumbull Memorial Hospital on December 4, 1971. He was 81 years old. Two of his son followed in his footsteps as lawyers. A third son was a casualty of World War II.

George Buchwalter

Attorney George Buchwalter seemingly had his hand in every major trial in Warren and Trumbull County involving underworld leaders here. Among his top clients were James Munsene, the owners of the Jungle Inn and Mike Farah.

The son of Jay Buchwalter, an attorney and key witness in the bribery trials of James Munsene in the 1920s, George Buchwalter attended Adelbert College of Western Reserve University in Cleveland. He graduated from Western Reserve Law School before becoming an attorney. Early in his career he served as city solicitor (law director) of Warren. In this capacity he once filed a padlock order against Munsene's Prime Steak House restaurant.

In the 1960s the Trumbull County Republican Party recommended Buchwalter as a replacement for outgoing Common Pleas Judge William McCain. Buchwalter had been on opposite sides of the courtroom from McLain many times when the latter served as Trumbull County prosecutor. The recommendation was accepted by Governor James A. Rhodes and Buchwalter was appointed to the bench in 1965.

The next year Buchwalter was elected to a six-year term as common pleas judge. Ironically, the man he beat was attorney David F. McLain his old adversary's son.

In 1972 Buchwalter was elected to a second six-year term on the bench. Poor health, however, forced him to retire on February 15, 1976. Buchwalter lived another ten years before passing away at the age of 81 on February 10, 1986 at St. Joseph Riverside Hospital.

Last Days of the Hollyhock

After the 1936 arson blaze the Hollyhock Gardens Night Club never regained its popularity. The next year, during the famous "Little Steel" strike, the CIO used the remnants of the building as a base of operations and a "soup" center.

In May 1938 John Venetta filed a lawsuit against James Munsene, Alfonso Fiore and four others to dissolve a partnership that owned both the Hollyhock Gardens and the Prime Steak House. The lawsuit called for Venetta to recover $33,356, which he declared, was his share of the partnership as of April 1, 1935 when he retired from the business. Venetta claimed he entered into a partnership involving both establishments with Munsene and Fiore on January 1, 1934 and served as a fiscal agent until a disagreement with Munsene ended the partnership in April 1935. At that time he claimed he and Fiore each had a 30 percent share, while Munsene owned 40 percent.

Sometime after the March 1941 murder of James Munsene the Hollyhock reopened with a restaurant on the first floor and gambling den on the second. A horse betting room was later added adjacent to the dining room. From Munsene's death until the Hollyhock closed for good, George Mustakes was reportedly in charge of the operation.

On March 11, 1944 a *Vindicator* reporter, exposing the easy availability of slot machines in Trumbull County, wrote about the current state of the new Hollyhock Club. He pointed out that the restaurant still occupied the first floor of the club, but the gambling room on the second floor was accessible only by an outside stairway. Upstairs a 60 by 175-foot room was dedicated to bingo, while the more serious gamblers could entertain themselves with one of 50 slot machines, black jack, craps and a chuck-a-luck game. All of this took place while the Jungle Inn was on a hiatus during World War II. Four years after Jimmy Munsene's murder, the reporter noted, some employees were recognized as being former associates of his.

The Hollyhock Club tried to promote itself as a bingo parlor, but there were always slot machines and other gambling devices nearby, which were the real moneymakers for the proprietors. In October 1946 a gambling raid again closed the club. It re-opened two months later again featuring bingo. On December 7 Trumbull County sheriff's deputies raided the Hollyhock Club, breaking up a bingo game and arresting Sam Sanfillipo and Harry Furst. The large crowd of players left in "orderly fashion." Three nights later another squad of deputies, including Henry Rose and Earl Bash, raided the club again. This time the crowd of nearly 300 bingo players, mostly women, roundly booed the deputies. Sanfillipo was arrested for a second time. A hearing for the pair was set for December 12. Neither Furst nor Sanfillipo appeared, but attorney George Buchwalter was there to plead both men guilty. A Cortland justice of the peace fined both men $50 and court costs. George Mustakes, who reputedly owned the Hollyhock at this time, accompanied Buchwalter and paid the total of $116.

On the eve of Election Day, November 3, 1947 police were surprised to find the Hollyhock Club closed. They discovered this after being called to the restaurant after two men created a disturbance because they arrived there to find they couldn't gamble. Both men were arrested.

In late December 1947 a letter from a member of the Central Committee of the Republican Party, referring to a resolution calling upon the Trumbull County sheriff, prosecutor and mayor of Warren to cleanup the county and city, specifically naming the Jungle Inn and the Hollyhock Club, was revealed. On December 30, just days before a new administration was to be sworn in, the Hollyhock Club was reported closed. The horse betting rooms were dark and the slot machines and all other gambling equipment had been removed. On March 4, 1948, after police discovered bookies had moved in, they raided the club and arrested two men. Warren Police Chief William E. Johnson promised, "That is one bookie joint that is down and is going to stay down."

On July 21, 1951 it was announced that the building that formerly housed the Hollyhock Gardens Night Club and the Hollyhock Club was being sold to the Warren Rescue Mission for $21,000. Attorney Dominick J. LaPolla represented the current owner of the building, John Petercupo, an alleged "associate" of the Farah brothers. Plans for the former nightclub and gambling parlor included a chapel, storeroom and ladies auxiliary on the first floor and a dormitory and sleeping quarters on the second floor.

The Warren Rescue Mission occupied the building until the late 1960s. In 1973 the building was razed under Warren's Phase Two Urban Renewal program. Today there is nothing left to indicate where the old nightclub stood. That section of the Warren "flats" is occupied by a few small business concerns and empty lots.

Jennings Family

The DiGenero / Jennings family and their activities in Niles, Ohio is worthy of a book on its own. In 1952 early organized crime investigative journalist Ed Reid wrote the book *Mafia*, one of the first comprehensive books about this nefarious organization and its countrywide influence. In one chapter he listed the top 83 mob figures in the United States, ranking them in order of importance. Ranked number 8 and number 16 were Anthony De Janero (Barney Jennings) and James De Janero (James Jennings) of Warren, Ohio. The early nature of the book is one reason Reid made a number of mistakes. No one can blame him, it's simply the nature of the subject that prevents the writer from getting a clear understanding and accurate information. Despite the misspelling of the last name and the mystery of who Anthony a.k.a. Barney Jennings actually was, it was clear that the Jennings' family had made enough of a splash locally that they were considered influential Mafia members on a national level.

Marco and Rosa DiGenero were typical of the tens of thousands of Italians who immigrated to the United States in the late 19th Century. The couple arrived at Ellis Island from Naples in the mid-1880s. The DiGeneros settled in Niles, Ohio where they decided to raise their four children – sons James "Sunny Jim," Joseph and Leo "Shine" and daughter Theresa. Somewhere between Ellis Island and Niles the family surname changed from DiGenero to Jennings, something not all that unusual for Italian immigrants.

During the next two decades the Jennings family became prominent in the Niles area. A grocery concern run by Marco became a speakeasy once Prohibition began. In addition, it housed a gambling den and a popular athletic club, which sponsored local boxers and a semi-professional football team. The brothers built a political base in the East End and their power was apparent when their candidate Vincent LaPolla became the only Italian on Niles City Council. Throughout their lives the Jennings brothers would be active in many facets of the Niles community – both legitimate and illegitimate.

James Jennings was a popular political leader and a wealthy construction contractor. During the Depression years he helped take care of nearly 300 Niles families. During the holidays his building concern, McDermott & Jennings Construction Company, distributed food to those in need.

Associated with the Jennings brothers were Martin "Marty" Flask, a cousin, and Thomas "Chippy" Mango. Flask and Mango lived near the Jennings on Mason Street and were involved in many of their activities. After an October 1930 raid, in which Marty Flask was arrested and charged with possession of alcohol and slot machines, James exploded. Charged with interfering with police, he filed affidavits the next day charging the Niles police with taking bribes to protect rival speakeasies and gambling dens. In a courtroom filled with family and friends James declared, "I am going through with this." Prosecutor George Birrell took the threat seriously and began questioning the men suspected of paying off the police. It was later reported that Jennings charges "implicated practically every man on the night force." Ten Niles bootleggers, including Flask, filed charges that bribes had been paid to seven members of the police force.

The incident became known as the "Nile police scandal," but Jennings' outburst backfired. Mango turned state's witness and testified that he acted as the payoff man for the group. Then Flask unexpectedly pleaded guilty to paying a bribe and was sentenced by Judge William M. Carter to one to ten years in the Ohio Penitentiary. James ended up being charged with offering a bribe to Niles Police Lieutenant Edward Kennedy for protection of his slot machine racket. Convicted, Jennings fought it all the way to the U.S. Supreme Court. He called it quits in May 1932 and turned himself over to authorities in Columbus. After serving six months of a one to ten year term, he had his sentence commuted by Governor George White on November 10. The paperwork was rushed to the London Prison Farm and Jennings was home by nightfall where he was greeted by dozens of the poor he helped support.

Around 2:00 in the morning on June 6, 1933 a bomb exploded under the front porch of the Jennings' Mason Road home. The Jennings' son, Marty, had returned home from an outing at Lake Milton just 40 minutes before the blast. He was eating a sandwich and reading the newspaper in the sunroom. During this time he heard an automobile pull to a stop and watched as a man walked up Mason Street. Moments later the car drove away. Marty soon went to his room to prepare for bed. It was then that the bomb went off.

Throughout the 1930s the Jennings Night Club remained the popular gambling joint in Niles, but trouble was never far away. James Infante, a next door neighbor of the Jennings, used part of his home as headquarters for the Niles "bug" racket. On September 15, 1936 a bomb went off under the front porch of the building. Authorities said the bomb was to serve as a warning to Infante.

In early January 1941 a Niles newsstand operated by a Jennings' associate was the target of another bombing, this time a stench bomb. This was followed a short time later by a bomb thrown at the nightclub from an automobile. The gambling room at the nightclub had recently opened under new management – Frank Budak, who had previously run the Poland Country Club casino. The club was closed on January 15 when the bomb was tossed. The bomb blew out the windows in the Infante home leaving the parents and their four children covered with glass.

The gambling room was located on the second floor of the nightclub building. Joseph Jennings, who owned the place, claimed his operation was not the target of the bomber. "It was for the 'Bug' Headquarters next door [the Infantes], and I have absolutely nothing to do with that. All I'm interested in is the nightclub. I don't even have anything to do with affairs on the second floor of my building." Two days after the bombing, Joseph Jennings claimed Budak was talked out of operating the gambling room.

Fourteen months after the sensational closing of the Jungle Inn, the Jennings Night Club was the target of State Liquor Enforcement Chief Anthony Rutkowski. In mid-December 1950, a *Vindicator* reporter entered the gambling den to find 25 slot machines, three horse racing boards, two chuck-a-luck games, a dice table and a bingo game in operation. Rutkowski's men had visited the place and saw the same gambling equipment, but no liquor. Twice Rutkowski sent registered letters to Trumbull County Sheriff Ralph Millikin. Except for the signed receipts there was no further acknowledgment.

While the newspaper report did nothing to arouse Millikin, it did draw the attention of Trumbull County prosecutor John H. Anderson, who pressured the Jennings into removing the equipment. Shortly after that a new operation opened on Mason Street – the Pastime Club, operating as a bingo parlor under the auspices of a woman's service league.

Shortly before 3:00 a.m. on June 19, 1951 an anonymous woman caller phoned the Niles Police station and said, "There is a lot of noise and commotion over at the Jennings." The "Jennings" she was referring to was the notorious Jennings Club, which at the time was "only" being used for bingo. As a police cruiser sped to the scene it narrowly missed hitting a man running from the club on Mason Street. Police took off after him and the chase ended when the suspect hit a fence and fell to the ground. He was soon identified as Youngstown underworld figure John "Pinky" Walsh.

Less than two hours later, based on a description given of another man seen fleeing the club along Mason Street, Niles police arrested Sandy Naples near a Crandon Avenue Street corner. At the crime scene, the second floor apartment of Joseph "Pobo" Jennings, Jr., who was vacationing in Canada, police found four smashed doors and the combinations knocked off two strong boxes. Police could not tell how much money, if any, had been stolen. When the two men were searched at the station they had $28 between them.

Both men were indignant while police questioned them. Walsh stated, "I've been coming to Niles for 30 years and nothing like this ever happened before. I was just up here doing a little drinking. Asked why he ran from police Walsh replied, "There was lights and yelling and who wouldn't run!" Naples insisted that, "I came up to shoot some craps, that's all. I got in a fight, that's all." Sandy stated that he had come to the city alone. When told that Walsh had already admitted that the two came together Naples became abusive and began swearing at his interrogators.

The next day Naples and Walsh pled guilty to suspicious person's charges and were fined $50 and costs before being released from the Niles jail. Police lacked evidence and witnesses to tie them to the break-in at the Jennings Club.

On June 18, 1952 Niles police arrested Joseph "Pobo" Jennings, Jr. for possession of gambling equipment. Jennings was apprehended in a Wood Street dwelling he had hoped to open as a gambling joint. A chuck-a-luck game was confiscated. Released on a $100 bond, he forfeited it by not appearing at his hearing.

After the Kefauver Hearings and the introduction of the new Federal Gambling Stamp law, James Jennings was one of several Niles gamblers to obtain one. Niles was reported to be the only city in Trumbull County where the stamps were issued. The address Jennings used was 8 State Street, the same one used by Mike Naples to obtain his stamp. This address was reputed to be the "bug" headquarters for Niles, which was believed to be operated by Jennings and Naples. Two other "bug" operators used the same address on their applications for the stamp. The newspaper reported, "All recipients are engaged in writing, selling or banking numbers, or in displaying punchboards."

In the movie *The Godfather*, Michael Corleone promised that one day his family would be completely legitimate. James Jennings may have been looking to do the same when he purchased the area franchise of the Canada Dry Bottling Company at 1141 State Street in December 1952. The purchase group included his sons, James, Jr. and Martin. The family had been operating Purity Bottling Company at the time the Youngstown operators of the Canada Dry distributorship became defunct. The Jennings operation would be responsible for the distribution of Canada Dry products in Warren, Youngstown and Sharon, Pennsylvania. A *Vindicator* article announcing the change referred to James Jennings as "one of Trumbull

County's most notorious racket and gambling figures." The company was a target of bombers on May 25, 1954 when a dynamite bomb was thrown on the roof of the building causing about $55 in damage.

During the fall of 1953 "Pobo" Jennings' gambling den at 137 Wood Street, dubbed the "Little Jungle Inn," was visited by state liquor agents. They reported to Trumbull County Prosecutor John Anderson that there were gambling devices on the premises. A padlock was ordered put on the club by Judge George Birrell.

James Jennings died on February 27, 1964. He was stricken enroute to his winter home in Fort Pierce, Florida and flown home. He died at North Side Hospital at the age of 77.

Murder of Marty Flask

On March 16, 1939 Flask was working as a bartender for Joe Jennings in the nightclub. He was serving drinks behind the bar. In the club that night was "Chippy" Mango. A little guy at 5-feet, 3-inches tall and 140 pounds, Mango had a reputation for having quick temper. In April 1934 he found his path interrupted by a freight train on his way to South Pine Avenue. He took a shot at the train's engineer, who in turn filed an affidavit charging Mango with shooting to kill. Mango served jail time for the incident. In May 1936 he was arrested for possession of a still and transporting liquor; a federal crime, he served 17 months in Lewisburg, Pennsylvania.

Around 3:00 a.m. Mango was sitting at a table in the nightclub with Mike "Bree" Naples and James "Bananas" Matash, both numbers runners, all three were drinking. Naples and Matash had "a difference of opinion" regarding each man's share in some recent "numbers business." Matash began shoving Naples. Flask, who was known to have a violent reputation, attempted to reason with the two men, suggesting to them, "Why don't you fellows settle this in a different way." When this didn't solve the problem Flask told them to take the fight outside. At this point Mango insisted, "I'll stop it. Let me stop it."

Flask, angered because of the drunken man's interrupting, slugged Mango in the face with a pair of brass knuckles knocking him senseless before he crashed to the floor. In a daze, Mango got to his feet and staggered out of the club. Flask then "ejected" the fighting patrons, who resumed their fisticuffs on the sidewalk in front of the club. Flask took his place in the crowd to watch the outcome.

Mango climbed the stairs to the gambling den on the second floor of the club, where he grabbed a loaded double-barreled, sawed-off shotgun. He went down to where the fight between Matash and Naples was just ending. As he came around the corner someone shouted, "Lookout, Mango's got a gun."

Flask was standing about ten feet away when Mango leveled the shotgun and pulled both triggers. Witnesses heard Mango cry out, "Where's the other SOB?" He then turned and fled leaving his hat and coat where he had placed them in the club. Flask had put up his arm instinctively to ward off the blast. The charge struck his arm and the left side of his chest, near the heart.

Standing in the crowd watching the fracas that night was Joseph Jennings' 19 year-old son, known as "Pobo." The young man was struck in the leg by one of the pellets. He related what happened next. "I was standing a few feet from Marty when the shot was fired," he stated. "Marty staggered across Mason Street to a telephone pole where he slumped to the ground. I ran to him, shouting to Mango, 'Don't shoot any more.'" When "Pobo" Jennings reached his relative, Flask was bleeding heavily from his wounds and having a hard time breathing. He told Jennings, "I believe I'm a goner, Pobo."

He was driven to Warren City Hospital by Mike Naples, but died in "Pobo's" arms before they arrived. The official cause of death was a lung hemorrhage and heart puncture. At the time of his death the 34 year-old Flask had been a newlywed for five weeks. He and his wife lived in an apartment about the nightclub. Flask was buried in St. Stephen's Cemetery.

The *Vindicator* reported, "Witnesses said Mango had had only a few drinks but his friends said that as a result of an operation at the federal penitentiary at Lewisburg, Pa., a few years ago, he became intoxicated easily." No one offered any details on this mysterious medical procedure. Police couldn't question Mango – he was long gone.

The next day an inquest was held. One of the witnesses was Jess Soda, who would become a partner of Mike Farah in the Trumbull County pinball machine trade. After the hearing an affidavit was filed charging Mango with first-degree murder on the recommendation of Trumbull County Prosecutor Paul Reagen. While Reagen announced there was no evidence to show any "ill-feelings" existed between the two men, the *Vindicator* reported that during the ensuing investigation it was revealed that the shooting may have been linked to a "long-brewing feud" between the two men over the organizing of slot machines and the "bug" racket, which was said to be attempting to squeeze Mango out.

Mango would remain a fugitive for 14 years. During the mid-1940s

Mango's wife, Nellie tried to have her husband declared legally dead in Probate Court. At the time he fled town Mango operated a taxicab business in Niles, which was taken over by his sons Frank and Joseph.

Mango fled to Boston where he changed his name and opened a gasoline station and a tire store. In May 1953 Mango was arrested by Boston police officers after stolen tires were found at his station. Although Mango was cleared of any wrongdoing in the theft, as a matter of routine police work his fingerprints were taken and a set forwarded to the FBI in Washington D.C. When the prints were matched to a set the FBI had on file from the Flask murder, Mango was arrested. When questioned by Boston police Mango admitted that he had shot Flask to death. He agreed to waive his right to an extradition hearing and be returned to Niles.

The trial of Thomas "Chippy" Mango began on November 30, 1953 with jury selection in the courtroom of Judge George H. Birrell. Attorney George Buchwalter represented the defendant; the prosecution was handled by Charles H. Anderson. By noon the next day a panel of six men and six women had been chosen, many of whom were in their teens when the crime took place. Before opening statements were made the panel was taken to the scene of the killing at the Jennings Night Club.

In his opening statement, in which he told the jury that he would be seeking the death penalty, Prosecutor Anderson stated, "The shooting was done with premeditation and deliberate malice and you should find Mango guilty as charged. He went upstairs in the nightclub, got a sawed-off shotgun, came down and then shot Flask as he was about to go back inside the club."

Buchwalter then took his turn, trying to paint a broader picture than just the shooting of a man. "The Jennings crowd was connected in different ways with the 'Business' and Mango was its 'whipping boy' and used for all sorts of purposes," the attorney claimed.

"Flask, an unsavory character, used 'brass knuckles' on Mango, cutting his cheek bone. Mango was crazy with pain and fear and he went out of his mind and his actions were beyond control. He went upstairs, got the gun and shot Flask whom he had heard threaten his own life.

"Mango did not leave Niles after the shooting because he was afraid of police. He was afraid of what the 'gang' might do if he stayed."

One of the first witnesses called was a stenographer from the Boston Police Department, who stated that during interrogation Mango said, "I knocked off Marty Flask. I pulled the trigger of the shotgun. I killed him in Niles." Mango told his interrogators he discarded the shotgun in the Union Cemetery in Niles.

Defense counsel fought hard to keep the notes from Mango's Boston confession from being read to the jury, but to no avail; Birrell ruled they were admissible. On cross-examination – in these years before the Miranda Rights were enacted – Mango was not advised his statements could be used against him, asked if he wanted an attorney, or asked to sign the notes.

Another witness called by the state was Joseph Jennings, Sr. who testified that he was the sole owner of the club in 1939 and still was today in 1953. He claimed he was not aware that gambling was going on in the upstairs in 1939. On cross-examination, he recanted, now simply denying that he had any interest in the venture.

Jess Soda testified that he was playing poker upstairs when he heard the commotion downstairs. When he went to investigate Soda saw Mango holding his face and Flask "swearing and cursing," and threatening to "kill that little SOB."

By 11:00 a.m. on the second day of trial the state had concluded its case. The defense placed a number of witnesses on the stand that testified to the character of Marty Flask. The consensus, in the words of one witness was that Flask "was known as a man of violent temper and was given to violence."

The highlight of the trial took place when Chippy Mango took the stand. "I'll never know why I got a gun. I am really ashamed of my conduct and for the humiliation I am now bringing to my family. I had no intention of killing any one when I got that gun, but I feel I was justified in doing what I did on account of the abuse I stood from Marty. I shot only after Flask came toward me."

During his testimony tears welled up in Mango's eyes and several times he had to pause in order to regain his composure. Family members in the gallery, including his wife and two sons, were seen wiping tears from their eyes.

He told the court of several incidents involving Flask. He claimed he had been shoved around during crap games, that Flask had once spit in his face, and that on one occasion he had picked his son Joseph up by his ears. After the assault by Flask, Mango said he had difficulty with his hearing, he suffered from headaches and bleeding. He was unable to eat for several weeks after he was hit.

The Warren *Tribune Chronicle* reported that Mango revealed after the shooting he went "to Cleveland where an X-ray taken by a doctor showed his jaw had been fractured. After five weeks in Cleveland he went to Boston where he wound up owning a gas station after working for an undertaker and as an attendant at a service station."

During cross-examination Mango admitted that he had a one-third interest in slot machines in the area and a fifteen percent interest in the gambling operation at the Jennings Night Club. He said that after he obtained the slot machine interest that Flask "seemed to have a grudge" against him. He claimed, "My mind couldn't have been working when I took the gun from the cupboard." Still, he stated he acted in self-defense repeating that he shot only after Flask had come toward him.

The defense ended its case on December 3 after putting a doctor on the stand, who testified that Mango did not have "full powers of reasoning" due to the blow he suffered at the hand of Flask. In his opinion Mango had suffered a concussion from the hit and a recent examination showed that he had deafness in his right ear.

The state followed with a rebuttal witness, the superintendent of the Lima State Hospital for the Criminally Insane. Mango had been sent to the facility for 30 days after his return to Trumbull County from Boston. During this observation period it was reported, "Mango was very agreeable, frank, co-operative and talked quite intelligently throughout his stay at the institution and showed no brain disturbance."

The closing statements were colorful. Anderson declared there was no dispute that Mango had killed Flask. He said it was foolish for the defense to claim that Mango was insane, but shot in self-defense, because the two conditions were incompatible.

"Why didn't you go home instead of going for a gun?" Anderson asked. "Why did you pursue the course you did? It was the greatest mistake you ever made.

"Mango's acts in this instance speak louder than his words. It was a brutal killing, intentional, malicious, deliberate and premeditated. Mango was boiling mad. His pride had been hurt and he had been pushed around. Mango's mind was working all the time. There can be no excuse for this crime."

It should be noted that, unlike his opening statement, Prosecutor Anderson did not ask the jury to send Mango to the electric chair. Instead, he pointed out it could make a recommendation for mercy. Mango's testimony and the defense's case in general showed Mango to be a sympathetic character. Perhaps Anderson bought into the fact that Mango may have some claim for self-defense.

Buchwalter's closing came off as tantamount to letting a little boy come out of the corner after being punished for some misdeed. "I am asking the jury in all good faith to turn Chippy free, to let him go home and sit down with is wife, two sons and grandchildren this Christmas for the first time in 15 years," the lawyer pleaded.

"You will feel better in your own mind and your conscience won't be any happier this holiday season than if you bring in a verdict of acquittal, and there isn't a single reason why you shouldn't.

"It's been a long and weary road for Chippy."

It was a masterful performance. The whole time Buchwalter walked around clutching the brass knuckles that were used to hit Mango. At one point he struck the defense table with the knuckles causing nearly everyone in the jammed courtroom to jump. "Just imagine what damage could be done by a blow with this set of knuckles," he said.

After closing statements Judge Birrell gave his charge to the jury. He told them they could arrive at one of six verdicts:

> Guilty of first-degree murder, with a death sentence in the electric chair
> Guilty of first-degree murder with a recommendation of mercy, life in the Ohio Penitentiary with a possibility of parole after 20 years
> Guilty of second degree murder, life in the Ohio Penitentiary with a possibility of parole after 10 years
> Guilty of first degree manslaughter, one to 20 years in the Ohio Penitentiary
> Not guilty, freedom for Mango
> Not guilty by reason of insanity at the moment of the crime, further commitment and observation at the Lima State Hospital

The jury began deliberations at 11:07 a.m., they finish at 4:03; a little under five hours, which included lunch. The courtroom exploded in applause and whistling as the words "not guilty" were read. As the verdict was read several jury members wiped tears from their eyes. It was later learned that on the first ballot the panel voted nine to three for acquittal and then spent the rest of the time deliberating between manslaughter and acquittal before reaching a unanimous decision.

Mango cried out, "I thank this jury from the bottom of my heart. I want to thank you for your confidence in me." Mango even thanked Prosecutor Anderson, who wished the newly freed man "good luck."

John L. Kocevar

One of the controversial figures to emerge for the Jungle Inn raid was agent John L. Kocevar of the Ohio Liquor Enforcement Department. Kocevar was born and raised in Cleveland, where he graduated from East Tech High School. During World War II he served in Europe with the 392nd Bomb Group. Returning to Cleveland after the war, Kocevar began work with the Ohio Department of Liquor Control in 1947, transferring to the department's enforcement arm shortly thereafter.

On September 3, 1949, just weeks after the Jungle Inn raid, Kocevar led a raid on the Flamingo Club in Cleveland. Despite there only being 20 customers in the saloon, Kocevar faced the same dangerous situation he had encountered at the Halls Corner's casino. While the raid was in progress the owner of the club and another man arrived. Running in the owner shouted, "Get a gun and give these guys the business!"

One man closed the door and locked it, while another shoved a gun in Kocevar's back. The agent was forced to a back door and outside, while four men with him were terrorized inside. Kocevar was able to flee to a neighboring home and call Cleveland police. When they arrived the occupants of the Flamingo Club scattered through windows and the back door to escape.

Kocevar was transferred to the Toledo district. In March 1952 he took sick leave. Shortly afterward a rumor surfaced that Kocevar was seen in the company of two Toledo underworld figures – Roy Kerr, a pinball machine operator and beer distributor and James Duggan, a bootlegger and gambler. The three flew from Miami to San Juan, Puerto Rico to Antigua, returning a week later. When this activity was exposed two years later, Kocevar simply stated that their presence on the same flights was coincidental, and the fact that they stayed at the same beach club was "completely accidental."

In the meantime, Kocevar was appointed supervisor of liquor enforcement for the Canton and Portsmouth districts. During July 1954 Kocevar disappeared in the middle of a departmental investigation directed by former Youngstown Police Chief Edward J. Allen, now the Ohio Liquor Enforcement Chief. Allen accused Kocevar of shaking down tavern owners and of being behind the disappearance of a truckload of whiskey from a Belmont County bootlegger. His disappearance was widely reported and after a ten-day period his position in the state liquor agency was terminated due to an "automatic resignation" clause in the Civil Service rules.

The next month Kocevar returned to appeal the "resignation" saying he had requested sick leave and had "assumed" it was granted. At a Civil Service Commission hearing in October, Allen told board members he had enough evidence to dismiss Kocevar earlier, but Ohio Liquor Director Anthony Rutkowski "failed to act." Rutkowski, when called to testify, said Kocevar was a good officer and recalled how he had saved his life during the Jungle Inn raid. Despite the commission's ruling to support the resignation, a Franklin County (Columbus) Common Pleas Court restored Kocevar to his former position in September 1955. The case was appealed all the way to the Ohio Supreme Court and when Kocevar was finally able to return to duty, in July 1956, it was with full back pay.

In 1959 Kocevar led the state in liquor arrests. Called "one of Ohio's most able liquor enforcement agents," he was promoted to the top liquor department post in Cleveland, his hometown. It didn't take long for Kocevar to begin receiving death threats for his efforts against cheat spots and underage drinking. The liquor agent's activities drew the wrath of police and politicians as well as liquor cheats. Kocevar had a positive image during his years as the District Enforcement Chief in Cleveland, which he resigned in March 1963.

In July 1963, impressed by his reputation, Cuyahoga County Sheriff James McGettrick hired Kocevar as his chief aide. The sheriff said he was looking for "a hard, street-wise operator to help him in his pledge to keep the county free of racket operations." On his first day on the job Cleveland underworld figure Alex "Shondor" Birns called Kocevar to make surrender arrangements for his latest arrest.

In October 1965 it was reported that Kocevar was arrested for drunk driving in Valley View, a suburb just south of Cleveland. The arrest, a month earlier, followed a raid by the sheriff's department during a picnic held by volunteer firefighters for Valley View. During a Cleveland *Plain Dealer* investigation in November 1965 it was revealed that Kocevar and his wife were officers of Kitchen Reddy Foods, Inc. which held the contract to supply food to prisoners in the Cuyahoga County Jail. Due to the negative publicity, Kocevar asked for a leave of absence on November 26 citing "malicious attacks by a local newspaper." When McGettrick denied the request a loud argument ensued in the sheriff's office and Kocevar resigned.

In December Kocevar went to trial on the drunken driving charge. He declared from the witness stand that he had been framed. The jury agreed and acquitted him. Kocevar was not as fortunate, however, when he went on trial for conflict of interest charges involving the county jail food scandal. After an eight-day trial in March 1967, the jury took just two and a half-hours, taking only one ballot, before convicting Kocevar. The judge gave Kocevar a suspended sentence and ordered him to pay court costs.

Kocevar went into private business and later retired only to be called back to public life as Service Director of Seven Hills. In 1992 he was named Public Works Coordinator of Parma. A Eucharistic Minister, he remained active in Democratic politics for years serving in various executive capacities. On September 28, 1998 Kocevar died at Parma Community General Hospital of a heart attack at the age of 75.

Charles J. Margiotti

Although he was described as "one of the greatest of trial lawyers," Margiotti may best be remembered for his work as a prosecutor.

Charles Joseph Margiotti was born on April 4, 1981 in Punxsutawney, Pennsylvania. After college, law school and passing the state bar exam he tried his first cases in his home town.

In 1930 Margiotti, said to be "one of the legal profession's rising stars," was selected to handle the prosecution in the Brady C. Paul murder case. Paul was a corporal in the Pennsylvania State Highway Patrol, who was senselessly murdered in December 1929 by two Bonnie and Clyde type "thrill killers," W. Glen Dague and Irene Crawford Shrader (also spelled Shroeder), who had committed several robberies and stolen a few automobiles. Paul's partner was wounded in the exchange. At the time of the shooting Shrader had her young son with her. The boy was dropped of at his grandfathers and later, when questioned by police about the incident, stated, "I saw Mommy shoot two cops."

The two were captured in Arizona 19 days later, after a number of robberies and shootouts, and brought back for trial. During her time on the run Shrader was dubbed the "blonde tiger" by the media and was identified as the actual shooter of Paul.

The case reportedly received the type of media blitz that the Dr. Sam Shepard trial would receive fourteen years later. Attorney Kedgwin Powell, a former Youngstown police chief, served as co-defense counsel opposing Margiotti. After a colorful trial Dague and Shrader were found guilty. Both were executed in the electric chair during the summer of 1930. Shrader, at the age of 22, was the first woman to die in the Pennsylvania death chair.

An article in the *Vindicator* describing Margiotti's career stated, "Irene [Shrader] was the ninth killer to be sent to the electric chair by Charles J. Margiotti. Irene was his 100th murder case. Ninety-one killers he has defended escaped the death penalty. One of those 91 was Thomas Viola, convicted of the murder of Jimmy Munsene."

In discussing Margiotti's abilities as a lawyer, Kedgwin Powell stated, "He could read over a whole trial transcript, then close it up and tell you what was said in it. His cross-examination was good because he knew all the facts." The former chief claimed Margiotti's preparation and fine keen sense of public relations was his formula for success.

In 1934 Margiotti campaigned for the Republic nomination for governor of Pennsylvania and lost. He then jumped ship and campaigned heavily for the man nominated by the Democrats. From 1935 to 1938 he held the position of Pennsylvania State Attorney General under both Democratic and Republican administrations. In 1936 he was a delegate to the Democratic National Convention.

In 1956 the book *Tiger at the Bar: The Life Story of Charles J. Margiotti* was published. The book devoted only a sentence or two to the Thomas Viola case, which the attorney had lost. On August 25, 1956 Margiotti died at the age of 65 in Pittsburgh. He was buried at Calvary Cemetery in Punxsutawney.

James Maxwell / George Mustakes Incident

Little is known of the criminal career of George Mustakes, but that didn't keep James Maxwell from proclaiming him Warren's number one mobster. Maxwell was a former newspaper reporter from Chicago. He became a radio broadcaster in Warren, where his weekly news program gave the "low-down" on city crime and politics.

In late October 1947, just prior to the November mayoral election, Maxwell published a pamphlet entitled "The Lowdown on Warren." In the pamphlet Maxwell stated "Warren's Capone is Big George [Mustakes], owner of the Hollyhock." The eight-page pamphlet referred to Warren as "a little Chicago," and declared Mayor Henry C. Wagner was "tied up with Attorney [George] Buchwalter in exploiting the city." Maxwell said he invited the filing of any libel suits in connection with statements made by him in the publication. Maxwell claimed the pamphlet was paid for by "Republican citizens who are interested in good government." He failed to identify any of those "citizens."

One of the charges against Wagner in the pamphlet was that the mayor had failed in his pledge to keep Warren clean. Proof of this was "George the Turk" Mustakes, whom Maxwell called the mob boss of the city. At the time the city directory listed Mustakes as the operator of the Hollyhock Restaurant, from which, according to Maxwell, he "bossed" Warren.

Mustakes arrived in Warren during the early 1920s and built his reputation as a chef (as opposed to a mob boss) by working at several restaurants before opening his own eatery on Pine Street late in the decade. In the 1930s he worked for Jimmy Munsene as manager of the Hollyhock Gardens. Mustakes also worked for Munsene at the Prime Steak House.

Maxwell stated on page one, "My investigation shows nothing against any elected official except the mayor. All others seeking re-election, both Republican and Democrat, are in my opinion honest and capable men." He printed Wagner's campaign pledge to the citizens of Warren. Maxwell charged Buchwalter with being the brains of the operation; the police department with failing to enforce; and that Floyd Pardee, the safety-service director, was just "an errand boy." Maxwell also made statements about alleged payoffs to racketeers and where and when they were made. He finished with, "the charges made in this booklet are very serious charges. If they are not true I should be sent to jail for criminal libel."

While many scoffed at the allegations, one man who was taking them seriously was Judge George Birrell. He recommended that the Trumbull County grand jury investigate Maxwell's accusations. Another who took them seriously was the mayor. The November elections were just days away when the pamphlet was released. On November 1 Wagner filed a $100,000 libel suit in Common Pleas Court charging Maxwell with "false, deliberate, and malicious intent to injure the reputation of the plaintiff now seeking a second term as Republican mayor of Warren." Wagner added in his suit that "the defendant has a criminal record in Trumbull and in Cook County, Illinois."

Maxwell called Wagner's suit "a last minute political effort…attacking the character of the defendant." Maxwell claimed there had been threats made upon his life, and although he claimed not to be in fear, he began carrying a weapon. Whatever the basis for the charge and countercharge one thing was for certain, the voters put Wagner out of office on Election Day.

In May 1948 Maxwell was summoned to appear before attorney Harvey A. Burgess to testify at a deposition hearing. During the course of the hearing Maxwell refused to answer a question put to him about his source of information in the pamphlet. He was immediately jailed for contempt of court. On May 28, after a petition was filed for a writ of habeas corpus, Maxwell was ordered released by a Portage County common pleas judge who ruled that the defendant could not be compelled to reveal his source at a deposition hearing.

Maxwell then filed his own lawsuit against Burgess, seeking $75,000 in damages. He claimed Burgess was not acting as a notary public when he had Maxwell jailed for refusing to answer a question during the deposition for the upcoming libel case filed by Wagner. Burgess then filed a motion to have the suit thrown out. At the hearing, Maxwell told Judge Birrell, who was hearing the motion, that he would "make his dissatisfaction known" if the ruling didn't go his way. On October 28, 1948, Birrell chastised Maxwell in his courtroom before dismissing his lawsuit against Burgess.

If "Big George the Turk" Mustakes was the Al Capone of Warren, it was a well-kept secret. Mustakes' nickname came from the fact that he was born in Turkey. As for Maxwell, he disappeared from public view except for a short while in 1950 and 1951 when he worked in a public relations capacity for the steel industry and filed an ill-fated lawsuit against Mike Farah. On January 7, 1948 Mustakes and four others – his son, George, Jr., Charles Murgie, Sam "Mollie" Sanfillipo[1] and Dominic Bastardi – were arrested while loitering in the lobby of the Hollenden Hotel in downtown Cleveland. The men said they were in town to do some shopping. A search of their automobile uncovered ammunition for a rifle, a baseball bat and a police nightstick. Also in the car police found a copy of the *Vindicator* from October 28, 1947 in which an article on Maxwell's pamphlet appeared. The men were kept overnight and released the next morning.

During the mid-to-late 1940s Mustakes owned the Hollyhock Restaurant. Before the decade came to an end Mustakes moved his family to Arizona. He took up residence in Tucson, where he operated Red Wagon Marine Products, a fish market.

In 1952 he became involved in a perjury case, which attracted statewide attention. The charge evolved from a preliminary hearing in October 1952 in which Arizona State Attorney General Fred O. Wilson was charged with bribery and conspiracy. The official was accused by a political opponent of attempting to pave the way for an illegal gambling operation in Pima County, Arizona. During the hearing, which was to determine if there was sufficient evidence to indict Wilson, Mustakes was called to the stand, where he denied knowing the official or ever meeting him. After Wilson admitted he had met Mustakes and had spoken to him by phone, the former Warren resident was charged with perjury.

Mustakes' trial, held in late December, featured Wilson as the state's key witness. According to Arizona law corroborating testimony is required in a perjury case. In addition to Wilson's testimony, the corroboration was to come from telephone records. Wilson claimed he had met Mustakes in a Tucson hotel and had spoken to him on three occasions by phone. All the state could produce was documentation that calls had been placed between Wilson's hotel room and the Mustakes home. There was no proof that the two men actually spoke.

On New Years' Eve 1952 Mustakes' counsel requested and received a directed verdict of acquittal form the judge before a single defense witness was called. The judge declared, "I am unable to find any evidence of corroboration whatsoever, except the barest of inference."

In 1954 Mustakes was investigated by a Pima County grand jury regarding the "secret" ownership of the Rillito Race Track. By this time

Mustakes was diagnosed with cancer. The disease claimed his life on February 10, 1958. The 58 year-old was buried in Grantwood Memorial Park in Tucson.

Wick W. Pierson

Wick Woodford Pierson was a respected trial lawyer and a one-time Trumbull County prosecutor. In 1926 he prosecuted the first bribery trail against James Munsene. Twenty years later he would serve as co-defense counsel for Munsene's slayer.

Pierson was born in Vienna Township on February 2, 1880. After high school he married and for a while resided with his wife's family in Richmond, Virginia. Pierson returned to Trumbull County around 1902 and tried farming for a few years.

Pierson decided to return to school and earn a law degree. In 1907 he graduated from Ohio Northern University in Ada. During the bar exam that same year he received the highest grade in the group. After practicing law for a time in Youngstown, Pierson decided to hang his shingle in Girard, where he made his home for the next three decades. During that time he served as city solicitor.

In November 1924 he ran for the office of Trumbull County prosecutor. He served one term, which ended in December 1926. During this time he prosecuted the first of Munsene's five bribery trials, winning the case only to have the verdict overturned.

After two years of elected office Pierson returned to private practice. His most famous case was serving as co-counsel during the murder trial of Thomas Viola, who was being tried for the murder of Munsene and his nephew.

In 1941 Pierson moved to Warren and formed a law practice with his son. He remained active in the firm until his death. On May 12, 1955 Pierson died at Trumbull Memorial Hospital after a long illness. He was 75 years old.

Paul J. Reagen

Attorney and prosecutor Paul J. Reagen was born on September 13, 1895 in Port Jervis, New York. His family moved to the Trumbull County area when Reagen was a young man. After college Reagen attended Youngstown Lay School, where he received his law degree. He moved to Girard, where he would reside for the remainder of his life.

Reagen won election as Trumbull County prosecutor in 1936 and was re-elected to four-year terms in 1940 and 1944. During May 1948 he was again the Republican Party nominee for prosecutor.

Reagen's busy schedule may have led to health problems. He suffered from asthma and had a heart condition. On Saturday, August 7, 1948, seven months after a Trumbull County grand jury had exonerated him after an investigation of the Jungle Inn, Reagen spent a busy morning in his office. During the afternoon while was watching an Indians-Yankees baseball game on television with his assistant William McLain, he began to complain of not feeling well. Reagen asked McLain to drive him home.

During the drive home Reagen began to experience chest pains. At the Reagen home an ambulance was called, but the popular prosecutor slumped over and died before it arrived. He was 52 years old.

A well liked and respected figure in the community, Reagen was involved with numerous civic organization and clubs. On the day of his funeral, the county court house, municipal court and other public offices were closed in his honor.

Chapter End Notes

Chapter 2 – James "Jimmy" Munsene

1.   In Clarence Darrow's autobiography, *Farmington*, he claims to have been born in Farmington as opposed to Farmdale where he was actually born. Darrow later admitted he had made a mistake.

2.   Jay Buchwalter was born on January 18, 1874 in Dalton, Ohio. He moved to Trumbull County when he was ten. Buchwalter attended Canfield Academy and then went to Mount Union College where he graduated in 1900. He passed the Ohio Bar the next year. He was a respected attorney for more than 40 years in Trumbull County and was a noted public speaker. Buchwalter was an avid student of the Bible and taught classes at the First Methodist Church. He died on October 5, 1944.

3.   During the first two decades of the 20th Century Evelyn Nesbit was one of America's most provocative female personalities. As a 16 year-old chorus girl in New York she caught the attention of 47 year-old Stanford White, a wealthy and successful architect. Though married, White had a sexual appetite for young beautiful girls. In his lavish tower apartment in Manhattan, his bedroom was adorned with mirrors and a red velvet swing from which he gained sexual pleasure by watching his young dates frolic upon. After they stopped seeing each other Nesbit married Harry Kendall Thaw the wealthy son of a Pittsburgh coal and railroad baron in 1905. Thaw was described as a "neurotic, jealous millionaire" and a "sexual sadist" who was addicted to cocaine.

In June 1906 Nesbit and Thaw attended a roof top theatre performance at Madison Square Garden, at which White was in attendance. During one number Thaw approached White and shot him three times in the face, killing him instantly. The ensuing trial was the first of many that the media would dub the "Trial of the Century." After a hung jury in the first trial, Thaw was found insane at the second one and incarcerated in an asylum for the criminally insane in Matawan, New Jersey.

In the years after the trial Nesbit became a vaudeville personality, acted in silent movies, performed in the Follies Bergere in Atlantic City and managed cafes. Between 1914 and 1922 she was in 11 Hollywood films, including 4 in 1919. It was at Jimmy Munsene's cabaret "Follies Bergere" that Nesbit worked briefly as a hostess in the mid-1920s.

Nesbit's life spiraled downward and was highlighted by a number of suicide attempts brought on by her addiction to alcohol and morphine. She survived, however, and in 1955 served as technical adviser for the film *The Girl in the Red Velvet Swing*, in which Nesbit was played by actress Joan Collins; in Sanford White's role was Ray Milland. In a later movie, *Ragtime* (1981), Elizabeth McGovern portrayed her.

Nesbit died on January 17, 1967 at the age of 82 at a nursing home in Santa Monica, California.

4.   Darrow's desire to finish his career with a win near his hometown failed to materialize. He continued with his legal career until his death on March 13, 1938.

5.   Sophie Tucker was known as the "Jazz Age Hot Mamma." The Russian born entertainer was a comic, singer and vaudeville and movie star.

"Pinky" Hunter was a local singer, who became a radio personality as a broadcast announcer for the Cleveland Indians.

Estelle Taylor, a beautiful model, Broadway and Hollywood actress, is best remembered for being the wife of heavyweight boxing champion Jack Dempsey.

Irene Bordini, born in France, was a popular Broadway star of the 1920s.

Fifi D'Orsay was known as "The French Bombshell," even though she never stepped foot out of North America. The Canadian born actress starred in films and appeared on television from 1929 to 1968.

- Information obtained from the Internet Move Data base (IMBd.com) website.

6.   The Ted Weems Orchestra had their first big hit in 1929 with the novelty song "Piccolo Pete." His band was nationally known in the 1930s, making regular radio broadcasts, including a national program with Jack Benny. The Ted Weems Orchestra was the first band Perry Como recorded with, beginning his long and illustrious career.

Perry Como was born Pierino Ronald Como in Canonsburg, Pennsylvania in 1912. A high school singer, he opened his own barbershop after graduation. Como honed his singing skills by performing at wedding receptions and other social functions. While vacationing in Cleveland in 1933, Como auditioned for Freddie Carlone's band and was hired at twenty-five dollars a week. Sometime during the mid-1930s he was heard at the Hollyhock Gardens Night Club by popular orchestra conductor Ted Weems. Como's popularity skyrocketed in the late 1930s after he became the featured vocalist with the Ted Weems orchestra. When the Weems band broke up in the early 1940s, NBC offered him a contract to share star billing with singer Jo Stafford on the Chesterfield Supper Club, a radio show broadcast Monday through Friday. His exclusive recording contract with RCA Victor in 1943 began an association that would last for almost fifty years. He sold sixty million records during his career. Como remained a popular singer until his death on May 12, 2001. – various Internet web sites

7.   The Prime Steak House was leveled during urban renewal around 1970. Nothing remains of the restaurant where Jimmy Munsene and Felix Monfrino were murdered. The exact location of the place cannot be found today. Nearly all of the buildings which once occupied the "flats" area of Warren from the 1920s through the 1950s are gone.

8.   The Warren *Tribune Chronicle* printed the following details from the Munsene autopsy:

"Dr. Henshaw and Dr. E.M. Chalker, who performed the autopsy, declared that Munsene may have been struck by as many as six or eight bullets, some of them going clear thru his body. A thoro [sic] examination of the body shows 12 punctures in the skin."

No. 1 is near the anterior surface of the right shoulder and the shot apparently took a medial course the chest cavity.

No. 2 is in the back of the right shoulder and the probe shows the slug passed to the soft issues of the back under the right shoulder blade.

No. 3 is on the right side about in line with the 11th rib and into the chest cavity.

No. 4 is in the back on a level with the fifth lumbar one inch to the right of the spine.

No. 5 is in the back on the level with the fourth lumbar, one inch to the left of the spine. Probes showed that both holes lead to the abdominal cavity.

No. 6 is on the left side, four inches to the left of the left nipple. The hole leads into the chest cavity.

No. 7 is on the same level as No. 6 but eight inches to the left of the left nipple and leading to the chest cavity.

No. 8 is two inches below No. 7 and leads to the abdominal cavity.
No. 9 is in the stomach, two inches to the left of the midline.
No. 10 is on the same level only three inches below No. 9.
No. 11 is thru the flesh in the lower left abdomen but the course was not determined.
No. 12 is a superficial wound. The bullet passed thru the skin above the left elbow.

One of the slugs taken from Munsene's body was fired from a .38 revolver, indicating that both gunmen took shots at the man. (The guns were identified as a .45 automatic and a .38 revolver).

9. Police Chief Barney J. Gillen began his career on March 24, 1906. He moved up the ranks, serving as a detective and captain, until May 21, 1919 when he was appointed chief of police by Mayor Ed Parks. Gillen served as Warren Police Chief for 27 years, retiring on June 1, 1946. He remained in his hometown of Warren until his death on September 19, 1960 at the age of 89.

10. The prison, said to be the largest walled prison in the world, opened in Jackson, Michigan, located 60 miles west of Detroit and 40 miles north of the Ohio border, in 1839. It was Michigan's first state prison. The prison was rebuilt north of the city of Jackson in the mid-1940s and was operational until January 4, 2002.

11. Charles J. Monazym was released from Leavenworth by 1961. In December of that year he was charged with running a dice game in north Detroit, but acquitted at trial. In 1963 his name came up during a Senate Committee hearing as "being connected" to the Detroit Mafia. Monazym steered clear of publicity until March 1977 when he was indicted in a Detroit-Miami bookmaking operation; he was acquitted in April 1978. In April 1977 Monazym, along with his old friend James Tamer and Detroit Mafia figure Vito "Billy Jack" Giacalone were investigated by a federal grand jury as to their role in a secret ownership of the Aladdin Hotel and Casino in Las Vegas. The allegations were that the men secretly owned the casino, in violation of federal and Nevada gaming laws, but reported to Anthony "Tony Jack" Giacalone, a Detroit Mafia heavyweight. Monazym died on May 20, 1997.

12. William E. Johnson replaced Barney J. Gillen as Warren Police Chief upon the latter's retirement on June 1, 1946. Johnson joined the police force in May 1929. In 1937 he was named head of the Bureau of Identification for the department.

13. Once the Wright Family's homestead, Wrightstown became part of Tucson city proper as the city expanded. It is now a neighborhood of Tucson.

14. Samuel "Gameboy" Miller was the brother-in-law of another Cleveland Syndicate member, Morris "Mushy" Wexler, who ran the Theatrical Grill in Cleveland, located next door to the Hollenden Hotel. The two established the Empire News service, the Ohio chapter of Arthur "Mickey" McBride's Cleveland based Continental Press the country's premier wire service. Miller became a "casino troubleshooter" for the Cleveland Syndicate. His new responsibilities took him to Covington, Kentucky; Miami, Florida; and Tucson Arizona.

15. Members of the Tucson Police Department assisting in the arrest were Joseph Herron, Ellmont Saylor, Herman King, Kenneth Yeazell and Thomas Burke according to an August 9, 1945 article in the *Arizona Daily Star.*

16. It is interesting to note that the out-of-town newspapers always referred to the murder victim as James Mancini, not Munsene. The family marker in Oakwood Cemetery bears the name "Mancini."

17. Russell Syracuse was a high-ranking member of the Licavoli gang. Along with John Mirabella and Joe "the Wop" English the three were prime suspects in the murder of Detroit radio crusader Gerald "Jerry" Buckley on July 23, 1930, though none was ever indicted. The ensuing "Buckley Grand Jury" pushed the Licavoli gang out of Detroit and into Toledo, Ohio. In taking over the bootlegging business there the Licavoli gang murdered popular local gangster Jack Kennedy on July 7, 1933. Among those indicted for the murder were English and Mirabella, who were the alleged triggermen; Syracuse, the suspected driver; and Thomas "Yonnie" Licavoli, the mastermind who ordered the killing. English and Licavoli were found guilty and sent to the Ohio Penitentiary. According to organized crime investigative journalist Hank Messick:

> "The FBI discovered that Syracuse and Mirabella came to Youngstown in 1934. Whether English was also there, they were unable to determine. But Syracuse lived with Mirabella until, in 1945, as Paul Mangine, Mirabella married a local woman. Two years later Syracuse vanished, at least as far as the FBI could ascertain."

Messick's work is somewhat questionable, since English was arrested in Akron, Ohio on August 29, 1933. Syracuse, however, was never heard from again.

18. Davis-Monthan Air Force Base became a military base and was dedicated on November 1, 1925. When the airfield was first established in July 1919 it was the first municipal aviation field in the United States. Named for two local World War I pilots – Samuel Davis and Oscar Monthan – who died in separate military aircraft accidents. During World War II the airfield served as a training base for B-18, B-24 and B-29 aircraft. At war's end the base found itself a storage ground for decommissioned airplanes. In 1946 the Strategic Air Command took over the base and ran it for 30 years. In 1976 the base was transferred to Tactical Air Command. The base, a key Air Combat Command facility, is still in full operation today employing approximately 6,000 military and 1,700 civilian personnel.

19. I was unable to uncover any information to explain why the transfer of Thomas Viola from Arizona to Ohio took so long. A December 13, 1945 Warren *Tribune Chronicle* article reported that Viola had been lodged in the Cuyahoga County Jail in Cleveland and that he was being held incommunicado, having arrived the previous evening. The article also stated that Bernard Monfrino had identified Viola at a "recent hearing in Tucson." Neither the date nor purpose of that "recent" hearing was reported in the local newspapers.

20. A septic arthritis caused by gonorrheal infection.

21. The 13-day trial tied the record of the murder trial of Louis Vitullo of Youngstown, for the murder of Elizabeth "Betty" Palko conducted in 1931. During that trial George Birrell was still Trumbull County Prosecutor. The jury deadlocked 6 to 6 on the verdict. Vitullo later pled guilty to manslaughter and received a 1 to 20 year prison sentence.

22. Writ of Certiorari, informally called a "Cert Petition," is a document which a losing party files with the Supreme Court asking the Supreme Court to review the decision of a lower court. It includes a list of the parties, a statement of the facts of the case, the legal questions presented for review, and arguments as to why the Court should grant the writ. "Review on writ of certiorari is not a matter of right, but a judicial discretion. A petition for writ of certiorari will be granted only for compelling reasons." Rule 10,

Rules of the U.S. Supreme Court. – *www.techlawjournal*

23. Manley English was born October 4, 1904 in North Carolina. English joined the Warren Police Department in 1930 and rose through the ranks. He made sergeant in 1946, captain in 1948, and was sworn in as chief of police on December 2, 1950 by Mayor Harold C. Smith. English retired in 1971 and moved to Lehigh Acres, Florida where he died of a heart attack on December 26, 1979 at the age of 75.

24. The article was entitled "The FBI's greatest chase – 20,000 miles to Leavenworth." J. Edgar Hoover wrote about the Bureau's success with its "Ten Most Wanted Fugitive" list, detailing their latest arrest of fugitive Joseph Franklin Bent, Jr. In the article were photographs of "Today's Ten Most Wanted Men," with Viola in the number 10 position.

Chapter 3 – The Jungle Inn

1. The 1950 census showed that Halls Corners had grown to a population of 254, many described as "trailer camp dwellers." According to the Trumbull County Board of Elections the following persons made up the village government as of November 1947: Charles E. Sedore, Jr., mayor; Genevieve Barber, clerk; Clara Dehn, treasurer; and council members Roy Barber, Leo Dehn, Howard Halliday, Wilson Kohn, Charles E. Sedore, Sr., and Agnes Sedore (the mayor's wife) and Agnes Stiteler. Within days of the August 1949 raid. Leo Dehn and Howard Halliday resigned their positions, with one claiming, "I didn't like the way they were running the village." Agnes Stiteler claimed she had not been a member of council since 1946.

2. In April 1942, after the bombing of Youngstown Police Sergeant William Davis' home, a runaway grand jury recommended that a special grand jury be called under the guidance of a special outside prosecutor. Ohio Governor John W. Bricker agreed and a secret investigation was begun. The resulting action ended the rule of the lottery houses in Youngstown the next year with arrests and convictions of all the major operators.

3. The number of slot machines reported by the various newspapers, books and magazines fluctuated between 80 and 100. In Anthony Rutkowski's official accounting of the machines after the raid he listed the total as 83.

4. After Governor Frank Lausche's order to close the Mounds Club and the Jungle Inn, his next two targets were the Colony Club located in Chesapeake, Ohio in Lawrence County in December 1949 and the Pettibone Club in Geauga County which was closed in June 1950.

5. Over the years this story was embellished. A later version had John Farah running to the turret in an attempt to get the shotgun and shoot Rutkowski.

6. During the Kefauver Committee hearings held in Cleveland in January 1951 Sheriff Ralph Millikin was subpoenaed to answer the questions of the senators regarding his actions during the August 1949 raid. The committee received a letter from Dr. John R. McKay of Warren, Ohio, stating that Millikin, who "suffers from severe angina," has been admitted to the Trumbull Memorial Hospital where he is receiving "large doses of morphine to quiet him." The committee had sent Dr. Razinsky of Warren out to see Sheriff Millikin in response to the letter received from Dr. McKay. Razinsky confirmed the condition of Millikin and agreed he should have a few days of rest.

7. On November 11, 1954 Governor Lausche promoted Rutkowski to a judgeship on the Cleveland municipal bench. It was the second time Lausche had promoted him. In 1946 Rutkowski was handed a vacated seat only to be defeated for election the next year. Rutkowski assumed the seat held by Charles A. Vanik who was running for Congress. There was much speculation at the time that Lausche would move Edward Allen, now the former police chief of Youngstown, into the position.

Rutkowski was not without problems on the bench. In the late 1960s the judge's son, Raymond served as his bailiff. In October 1969 Raymond was indicted after he allegedly took money to fix cases. He was convicted of "larceny by trick" in June 1970 and resigned. Raymond was replaced as his father's bailiff by his 32 year-old wife, Joan. In March 1971 Joan Rutkowski resigned after a Cleveland Bar Association inquiry into judicial ethics. These problems helped lead to Rukowski's unseating in November 1973 by Ann A. Manamon. Rutkowski passed away on July 10, 1982 at the age of 78.

8. As the years have passed since the August 1949 closing of the Jungle Inn tales of the raid have become embellished. In 1951 Senator Estes Kefauver wrote a series of articles for the *Saturday Evening Post* about the crime hearings he was conducting. In an article titled, "What I Found Out

About The Ohio Hoodlums," the senator writes that Anthony Rutkowski told his committee members that the goon that had been ordered to shoot him, "had been slow in obeying his master's orders. When there was no gunfire, Farah himself ran to the turret, but one of Rutkowski's agents beat him there. The agent grappled with the gunman, took away his shotgun, and thus was able to prevent Farah from shooting the chief raider."

In a November 1990 article by a reporter from the *Tribune Chronicle*, he states authorities entered the club "with guns drawn." In the same article he talks about one-time Cleveland Mayor Carl B. Stokes being a member of the raiding party.

"I started my career as a public servant with the liquor department when I was fresh out of school," said Stokes, who wound up being in on the raid.

"We got in through the front door OK," Stokes recalled. "Then there was a second door and one of the agents manhandled the doorman. We all stepped inside and were greeted by a man with a machine gun up in the cat-walk. He told us to freeze and that's just what I did."

Stokes' memory must have faded some 40 years after the raid. Not only were there no reports of a man with a machinegun ordering the raiders to "freeze," but in Stokes' own autobiography, *Promises of Power* published in 1973, he claims he didn't join the Ohio Department of Liquor Control until late December 1949, some four months after the raid.

Another rumor had it that singer Dean Martin, a native of Steubenville, Ohio, worked the dice tables before making it big as an entertainer.

One of the more popular stories was about a "cigar-chewing" dice player who was laying down as much as $300 a roll on a summer night during August 1947. The dice roller, a big man said to be about 60, was a stranger who no one ever saw before that night. By the end of the evening he was reported to have been $7,000 ahead of the house.

Chapter 4 The War Lords of Trumbull County: John & Mike Farah

1. Hymie Martin was convicted of the murder of former Cleveland Councilman William F. "Rarin' Bill" Potter. The victim's body was found on February 8, 1931 in an East Side Cleveland apartment several days after he was shot through the head. Martin, known as "Pittsburgh Hymie," was convicted at trial less than two months later and sentenced to life in prison. During a retrial in June 1932 he was acquitted when a key witness disap-

peared, but not before supplying defense counsel with an affidavit repudiating her previous testimony. The sensational killing was the most highly publicized murder case in Cleveland until 1954 when Dr. Sam Shepard was arrested for the murder of his wife Marilyn. In later years Martin was associated with the Jewish Cleveland Syndicate.

2.   Dominick J. "Duke" LaPolla was long active in legal matters in the Mahoning Valley. A relative of Judge James A. Ravella, LaPolla, like the judge, was born in Niles (June 7, 1903) and earned his law degree from Ohio Northern University (1927). Although he later served as a municipal judge in Niles, LaPolla was noted for representing a long list of underworld clients in the Valley, including the notorious Farah brothers. During the January 1951 Kefauver Committee hearings in Cleveland, LaPolla was counsel of record for James Licavoli. LaPolla was an attorney for more than 70 years. He died on March 20, 2000 at Auburn Hills Care Center in Niles. He was 96 years old.

3.   Arlene Barbara Charlotte Steuer was described as a modern day Portia when she graduated with top honors from Cleveland Marshall Law School in June 1952. The slight built, 5-foot tall brunet spent seven years attending night school after turning down offers at Fenn College (now Cleveland State University) and Cleveland College, in order to work and provide support to her widowed mother. When she graduated she had recorded the highest grades in the school's history. After law school she joined classmate Michael E. Cozza in the firm of Cozza & Steuer with offices in the Leader Building in downtown Cleveland. Once, during an interview, Steuer recalled her first trial, a case over a $67 grocery bill. She stated, "I was glad I wore a long skirt because my knees were knocking." During the 1950s Steuer represented the Farahs in other matters possibly making her the first woman attorney who could be called a "mob lawyer."

4.   Albert Antonelli was a watchmaker and jeweler who operated Foster Jewelers in Youngstown for 60 years, from 1930 to 1990. In 1930 he was questioned in the double murder of Cleveland bootlegger Joe Porrello and his bodyguard Salvatore Tilocco. Revolvers recovered from both of the dead men were traced to Antonelli in Youngstown.

5.   Charles H. Anderson, Sr. was a longtime attorney and Republic political leader in Trumbull County, at one time serving as county chairman. Born in Mercer County, Pennsylvania, on August 30, 1883, Anderson's family moved to Trumbull County when he was six. Anderson

earned a bachelor's degree from Muskingum College and then attended Youngstown University, where he earned his law degree. Living in Hubbard Anderson became involved in politics, becoming Hubbard solicitor (law director) and serving two terms as mayor, 1920 to 1923. In 1940 he won the Republican nomination to run for Congress against Democrat incumbent Michael Kirwan.

In November 1950 Anderson's son was elected Trumbull County prosecutor. The young prosecutor quickly named his father as his chief assistant. When the younger Anderson died in August 1951, his father was named as his replacement and continued the fight his son started against vice and brothels in the county. Anderson was re-elected in 1952 and in 1956, when he defeated Donald J. DelBene. He had served nine years by the time he left the prosecutor's office. In November 1960 Anderson was elected Probate Court judge. He served in that capacity until his death on March 10, 1966. Anderson was buried in Hubbard Union Cemetery.

6.　A Gray Lady was a woman who provided non-medical, personal services with the American Red Cross Gray Lady Service.

7.　John H. Anderson, Jr. was born in 1916 in Ashtabula, Ohio and moved to Hubbard in Trumbull County as a child. His father served two terms as mayor of Hubbard and was long involved in Trumbull County Republican politics, serving at one time as county chairman. Not long after earning his law degree from Ohio State University, Anderson joined the FBI, serving in New Orleans, Miami and Pittsburgh. When World War II began he resigned from the bureau. He served in the Army's Criminal Investigation Division as a special agent in the Southwest Pacific. While in the service he contracted a disease he battled for the rest of his life. When he returned to Ohio he joined his father's law office in Warren.

Anderson was elected Trumbull County Prosecutor in November 1950, the first Republic elected to that position in 14 years. As a prosecutor Anderson battled vice conditions in the county. He closed bookie joints and padlocked houses of prostitution.

When Anderson took office he appointed his father chief assistant prosecutor. The last year of his life was spent fighting the disease he became afflicted with overseas. He died in Trumbull Memorial Hospital on August 10, 1951 at the age of 34. Common Pleas Judges George Birrell and William McLain appointed his father to replace him.

8.　James A. Ravella was born on April 16, 1906 in Niles. He was a

1928 graduate of Ohio Northern University where he earned his law degree. After practicing law in Youngstown he served in World War II as a Navy lieutenant. In 1948 he became an assistant prosecutor in Warren. The next year he was appointed special counsel to the Ohio State attorney general. In 1950 Governor Frank Lausche appointed Ravella Municipal Judge of Warren, a position he would hold until his retirement from the bench in 1981.

On March 15, 1961 a bomb was detonated at the home of Municipal Judge James A. Ravella at 3076 Overlook Drive in Warren, at the opposite end of the street from where Frank Cammarata once lived. While police could not determine a motive for the bombing, they theorized it was a scare tactic and that the culprits knew the judge and his wife were vacationing in Florida at the time. The blast, estimated to be caused by three or four sticks of dynamite, ripped through an outside wall and caused damage to the living room and basement of the home located in an upper class neighborhood of Warren.

Ravella died on August 18, 1990 from congestive heart failure at Trumbull Memorial Hospital. He was 84 years old.

9. The 9th District Court of Appeals had jurisdiction for Lorain, Medina, Summit and Wayne Counties. Originally scheduled to hear the case were Judges Oscar Hunsicker, Arthur Doyle and Perry Stevens. By the time the hearing began Judge Stevens had taken ill and was replaced by Judge Lee Skeel, a Cleveland judge from the 8th District. Judge Hunsicker wrote the opinion.

10. In late September 1961 the *Akron Beacon Journal* reported that Mike Farah had been involved in a bid-rigging scheme earlier that year involving a Warren sewage contract. The bids came in some $750,000 over the engineering estimate for the project. The newspaper claimed, "There was talk downtown that at least $500,000 of the amount bid had been demanded by mobsters supposedly then under the control of the handsome, raspy-voiced Mike Farah. There was also talk that Farah, failing to get the full amount asked, 'came down' in his 'price' to the $200,000-$250,000 level and said the rest could be made up in contract extras."

Chapter 5 – The Saga of Frank Cammarata

1. According to Ellis Island records Cammarata's first name was listed as Francisco. The name used later in the congressional petition to keep him from being deported was Francesca.

2.   On August 21, 1930 Pete "Horseface" Licavoli was convicted of the murder of Henry Trupancy, a Detroit bootlegger. Licavoli pumped nine bullets into Trupancy on July 14 as the victim sat in an automobile with another man. The killing was part of an on-going mob war in which Trupancy was the ninth victim in ten days. Licavoli was sentenced to life in prison and died in the Marquette Branch Prison in 1951 after serving 21 years.

3.   In October 1934 Thomas "Yonnie" Licavoli was convicted of the murders of Jackie Kennedy, Louise Bell, Abe Lubitsky and Norman Blatt. Originally slated for the electric chair his sentence was commuted to life in prison. Author Paul Kavieff believes this may have been the first capital murder case in which a mob leader, who did not actually pull the trigger but ordered the murder, was convicted.

4.   Some reports claim Cammarata returned through Mexico with the help of Frank Milano, who maintained a home there. Between the time of his arrest in Solon in 1946 and his arrest in Grosse Pointe in 1948, several dates were used in speculating his actual return to the United States. Cammarata told Robert F. Kennedy, after his testimony before the Senate Rackets Committee in 1958, that he came in "walking freely" past immigration authorities in New York City.

5.   It should be noted that the *Detroit Free Press*, which first printed the photograph, showed only Cammarata, "Long Joe" Bommarito, "Scarface" Bommarito and David Feldman. They labeled the picture, "The Cream of the Crop," never falsely mentioning that the mobsters were part of the Purple Gang. It is possible that the photograph, with all seven men, used by Edward Allen in his *Merchants of Menace* book, could have been the first instance that the men were incorrectly identified as members of the Purple Gang.

6.   It was alleged the men were gathered at the Grosse Pointe home to select a successor to James Tamer, reputed to be the head of a "nationwide gambling syndicate," and the man who handled the "Sicilian mob's" gambling interests in the Motor City. Tamer had recently been returned to the Jackson Prison for a parole violation. In a Michigan Corrections Department report, Tamer was said to be "the only hoodlum who can tell Licavoli where to get off, and get away with it."
     Earlier that day Holdup Squad detectives Ralph Mahanna and Wesley Nosworthy were suspended after charges of aiding Tamer had been lodged against them. The officers were charged with "conduct unbecoming a police

officer, neglect of duty, falsification of reports, violation of police regulations, and release of a prisoner without proper authority." The prisoner was Mike Thomas, whose brother Marty was one of Tamer's chief lieutenants.

7. In one of the versions Congressman Michael Kirwan gave he stated that one of the people who urged the introduction of the bill for Frank Cammarata was former Mahoning County Democratic Chairman John Vitullo.

8. Politically speaking, "tabled" means to lay aside for future discussion with a view for postponement or shelving.

9. Drew Pearson was a popular and controversial journalist for the *Washington Post*, who wrote a syndicated newspaper column which appeared in newspapers across the country. Pearson reputedly was the first to make public General George S. Patton's infamous slapping incident in Sicily during World War II. In the early 1950 Pearson's staunch anti-McCarthyism stand resulted in him being labeled pro-Communist by the fiery senator's supporters.

10. The confusion began in Columbus when Governor Lausche directed the arrest warrant to Mahoning County Sheriff Paul Langley instead of Trumbull County Sheriff Ralph Millikin. Having already been aware of Millikin's track record from the Jungle Inn days, perhaps it might have been a deliberate oversight on the part of Lausche. After Langley delivered Cammarata from the Trumbull County jail to the courthouse in Warren, Judge William K. Thomas, who was sitting in for the ailing Judge George H. Birrell, discharged Sheriff Langley from any further duties and responsibilities in the case. Governor Lausche later claimed the confusion was caused by the fact Langley's name appeared on the paperwork received from Michigan.

11. Writ of Certiorari, See Note 22 in the Chapter End notes for Chapter 2.

12. Paul W. Walter was a leading figure in Republican politics in Cleveland and Cuyahoga County during the late 1940s and early 1950s. A prominent attorney in the city, he was referred to as "the political right hand" of U.S. Senator Robert A. Taft. Due to his close association with Taft, Walter was the leading candidate to be named United States Attorney when the Republican administration of President Dwight D. Eisenhower moved into the White House in January 1953, replacing John J. Kane, Jr. of Youngstown.

In April 1953 Walter chose not to be considered for the position.

13. In February 1946 Charles "Lucky Luciano" Lucania was released from a New York prison and deported back to his native Italy. Sometime in late 1946 he entered Havana, but after pressure from the U.S. Government, Cuban officials deported him in March 1947. Throughout the 1950s U.S. and Italian law enforcement officials believed Luciano was behind a major narcotics ring that was shipping drugs to America. But they were never able to pin anything on him. In March 1959 Francesco Scibilia, a 26 year-old recent deportee from the Unites States, who had falsely charged Luciano and four others with narcotics trafficking, was sentenced to 30 months in prison for making the malicious accusations. There is no information that links Luciano in anyway to Frank Cammarata or his arrest in Havana. Luciano died of a massive heart attack on January 26, 1962.

14. In January 1963, after the United States agreed to pay a ransom ($53 million in food and medicine) for the prisoners captured during the failed Bay of Pigs invasion, Castro allowed the return. The first 100 U.S. citizens returned on a Pan Am flight which had brought 15,000 pounds of medicine to the island. Some 300 Americans, most of Latin descent, registered at the Swiss Embassy in Havana for permission to leave. Persons leaving Cuba had to surrender all possessions, being allowed just three changes of clothing. In all more than 3,600 people eventually left the island, many were family members of the ill-fated Bay of Pigs' invaders.

Chapter 6 – The Story of "Tony Dope"

1. During the wake of Anthony Delsanter, Jimmy Fratianno was approached by Cleveland Mafia Family boss James Licavoli and told that they were able to bribe a clerk in the Cleveland FBI office and obtain a listing of the Bureaus' confidential informants. Although Fratianno was a paid informant, his name would not have appeared in the Cleveland records since he was working with the California office. Still, it was this incident that sent a scared Fratianno into the Witness Protection Program making him one of the most important mob turncoats of all time.

Chapter 7 – A Few Selected Biographies

1. Sam Sanfillipo was the cousin of Tom Sanfillipo of Cleveland who was charged with the murder of Robert L. Firestone in the mid-1940s. Tom hid at the home of Sam after the killing. At trial Tom was acquitted of the murder.

Appendix

Appendix 1:

The Ohio State Department of Liquor agents who participated in the Jungle Inn raid on August 12, 1949:

Anthony J. Rutkowski, State Liquor Enforcement Chief
Oscar L. Fleckner, State Liquor Director
Frank M. Acton, Inspector-in-charge – Cincinnati
Carson C. Davis, Inspector-in charge – Dayton District
Joseph F. Harrell, Supervising Inspector – Toledo-Sandusky District
Homer Hilliard, Assistant Chief Inspector – Cincinnati
John Joyce, Inspector – Cleveland
John J. Kocevar, Inspector – Cleveland
Attila G. Kopan, Inspector – Sandusky
Noble Rains, Inspector – Dayton
Charles D. Marts, Inspector-in-charge – Cleveland District
Corwin Matthews, Inspector – Cleveland
Charles C. McCue, Inspector – Cleveland
Raymond S. McDonough, Inspector – Cleveland
Steven Nemeth, Inspector – Cincinnati
Nicholas Ragus, Inspector – Cleveland
Henry Searon, Inspector – Cleveland
Malcolm H. Simpson, Cleveland – Inspector
James Stillwell, Special Investigator
John Weaver, Supervising Inspector – Cleveland-Akron-Canton District
Wade Webb, Inspector - Sandusky

Appendix 2:

The 20 men arrested at the Jungle Inn during the August 12, 1949 raid:

Christ Bourekas, 36, Warren – bartender
Harold Burman, 49, Youngstown - clerk
George S. Calboran, 34, Youngstown – bartender
Anthony Chance, 39, Youngstown - clerk
Ralph Coletto, 61, Cleveland Heights – clerk
Sam Cretella, 38, Girard – clerk
Myron Elias, 38, Niles
John Farah, 43, Cleveland – proprietor
Claude M. Hoagland, 57, Garfield Heights
Cecil Johnson, 41, Youngstown - clerk
Walter Lisko, 26, Warren – clerk
Charles Marino, 34, Girard – clerk
Jerry Mazzano, 28, Youngstown – clerk
James V. McGuire, 47, Youngstown - clerk
Steve E. Paparodis, 32, Youngstown
James Santagada 40, McDonald – maintenance man
Albert Sudetic, 24, Youngstown – clerk
Sam Teslar, 45, Warren – clerk
Edward F. Tobin, 42, Girard
Joseph Wright, 28, Youngstown – clerk

All of the men were charged with 1) keeping a gaming room, 2) keeping gambling devices. And 3) gambling, with the exception of Calboran and Paparodis, who were only charged in the first two counts.

Appendix 3:

Opinion of the Civil Service Commission in the Matter of Chief Manley English delivered on July 8, 1959:

This cause came on for hearing before the Civil Service Commission of the City of Warren on the appeal of the respondent, Chief Manley R. English, from an order of indefinite suspension by Mayor William C. Burbank. The order of suspension arose from the alleged neglect and incompetence of the respondent in respect to the investigation into and the handling of an altercation involving one Jean Blair and Mike Farah. Upon the evidence in the record before the commission, which included the testimony of some 16 witnesses, we have come to the following conclusions:

(1) First, we can conclude that the events and occurrences surrounding the Blair-Farah affair from Sunday, June 7, to Wednesday, June 10, showed an appalling lack of what we would consider even elementary police procedures. These deficiencies we would enumerate as follows:

(A)Officers Marchio and Timko failed to make a proper casualty report on Sunday, June 7. These officers negligently omitted any reference on their report concerning the possibility that a gun had been involved in the Blair-Farah fracas. It was admitted in the testimony that the hospital report contained such a statement, that one or both of the officers had inspected this report, yet no mention was made of the gun on the casualty report. This was a serious omission. Had the question of the gun been inserted at the outset of this affair, possibly more serious attention would have been given to it and an immediate investigation would have been made.

(B)Sergeant Rhoda was informed at 6:30 o'clock on June 7 that Blair had been re-admitted to the hospital with a possible skull fracture. While Rhoda did, by his testimony, instruct the doctor in attendance to call the department if the victim grew worse, we feel that, in view of the possibility of serious injury and-or death, Sergeant Rhoda could have and should have, taken immediate steps to obtain a statement or to otherwise begin an immediate investigation into the matter. This is especially true since it was admitted that the attending physician questioned the fact that no investigation or arrest had been made, and, according to Rhoda's testimony, "berated the department" for its inactivity. We believe these facts would have aroused a prudent officer that the incident might involve more than a "friendly fist fight." Instead only a simple notation was added to the casualty report and no further action taken.

(C)When Chief English visited police headquarters at 6:10 o'clock p.m. on June 7 he was informed of the incident and inspected the casualty report. Since that report contained no mention of the gun and-or the re-admittance of Blair to the hospital, there was possibly no reason at that time for Chief English to order an immediate and complete investigation of the Blair-Farah affair. The failure on the part of his subordinates to fully inform the Chief of the facts involved left him without important facts on which to make a decision.

(D)The testimony before the Commission indicated that on Monday, June 8, Chief English phoned Captain Teeple from his home concerning the Blair-Farah incident and shortly thereafter talked to Teeple regarding the matter. The testimony further indicated that at about 8:00 o'clock a.m. on Monday, Chief English directed Captain Teeple to "send a couple of men" to the hospital to get a statement from Blair "as soon as the hospital was cleared." Yet further testimony indicated that it was necessary for Chief English to personally direct Detectives Mijic and Mackey to go to the hospital and obtain a statement at 12:15 o'clock p.m. Apparently the directives of the chief were not carried out for over four hours. We can only conclude that Captain Teeple failed to carry out this assignment within a reasonable time. The testimony offered no explanation for this failure within the chain of command in the department. Further, the evidence indicates that it took another two hours more for Detectives Mijic and Mackey to obtain the first statement from Blair. It thus took approximately six and one-half hours to obtain a simple statement from Blair and carry out an assignment given to Captain Teeple at 8:00 o'clock that morning.

(E)While there was widespread rumor in the City of Warren known even to members of this commission as early as Sunday night, June 7th, that one Mike Farah was the assailant of Jean Blair and had assaulted him with a pistol, the evidence before the commission does not show that respondent English knew of this rumor or was advised of this rumor until such a time as he was in the office of Safety-Service Director Wyndham at approximately 10:30 o'clock a.m. on Monday, June 8. [It was not until] upon receipt of the typed statement signed by Jean Blair at approximately 3:30 o'clock p.m. on Monday, June 8, we find that Chief English knew at that time that the victim of the attack, Jean Blair, had stated Mike Farah had attacked him with a pistol, that Farah had shoved the gun into the stomach of Blair, that an attempt was made to discharge the pistol and that he (Blair) had been pistol-whipped. As the respondent himself stated during this hearing, signed statements are made and secured from participants in a felony to insure the fact that there will be no substantial change in the story of witnesses subsequent to the signing of the statement. Consequently, we feel that the chief could rely upon the statements made in the signed statement of Blair and that circumstances of the affair were as set forth in such statement. We further find that Chief English knew that a police officer can arrest a suspect when he has probable cause to believe that a felony has been committed, even though he did not witness the crime. Upon the statement given by Blair, we find that the chief should have concluded that a felony probably had been committed by Farah and further investigation of the crime should have proceeded along that assumption. While we do not find that it is necessary for the Chief of Police of Warren to personally conduct every investigation into every crime committed in the city, we do find that in this case the respondent, through conversation with the Safety-Service Director, had stated that he (English) would "take care of the matter." Consequently, he had at least in this instance, assumed personal direction of the investigation into the affair. However, between the period from 3:00 o'clock p.m. when the respondent first read the statement of Blair until approximately 6:00 o'clock p.m., respondent English was primarily concerned with conferences with Safety-Service Director Wyndham and a trip to Trumbull Memorial Hospital with Police Prosecutor Spain for a third interview with the victim of the assault. From and after 6:00 o'clock p.m. on Monday, however, it is our opinion, based upon the evidence presented to the commission, that Chief English should have taken immediate steps to apprehend the named assailant, Mike Farah and obtain from him, or at least attempt to obtain from him, a written, signed statement of his (Farah's) version of the altercation, if there were no detectives on duty, it would seem to us that the chief could well have ordered uniformed officers to arrest Farah for questioning. Also, since he had assumed direction of the investigation, he himself could have gone out to the Farah residence and either obtained a statement from Farah or arrested him for questioning on an open charge. Instead the chief contented himself with a series of telephone calls to the Farah residence, none of which were successful in locating Farah until shortly after midnight on Tuesday, June 9, and during that particular telephone conversation the respondent did obtain an oral statement from Farah as to his version of the fight between himself and Blair. From the testimony of the chief concerning this telephone conference and from the rapid booking that took place on the felony charge filed against Farah, we can conclude that Farah has a definite aversion to visiting police stations, but we do not conclude that based on the facts known to the chief that he should have tolerated Farah's aversion. He should have insisted upon Farah coming to the police station and giving a signed statement of his version of the fight. This insistence should have been backed up with the threat of arrest or actual arrest if Farah refused to come in. It is a well known fact that any suspected felon may be arrested on an open charge (regardless of the hour) if the arresting officer has reason to believe a felony has been committed. The only evidence then available to the respondent at that time was Blair's statement which clearly indicated that a felony had been committed.

Moving to the events of Tuesday, June 9, we find that the warrant for Farah's arrest was issued to Officer Lapp and he, accompanied by Officer Messett, went to the Farah home. They were advised by a woman that Farah was not at home, was not in the house and was out of town. When the woman was advised that the officers had a warrant for Farah's arrest, the woman told them that they were expecting such a warrant and that she would tell Farah of the warrant when he returned. He would either call the police or come down to the station. This apparently satisfied Officers Lapp and Messett, but again it seems to us that even elementary police procedure would have required these officers to have found out who the woman was and how much reliance they could place on her statement as to the whereabouts of a wanted felon would call the police or turn himself in. There is nothing in the record to indicate that they knew who the woman was or that they were justified in their blind acceptance of her statements concerning Farah. These officers made no further attempt to question others in or about the residence or to ascertain whether Farah was in the home or not. We feel that these failures on the part of Officers Lapp and Messett reflected either their ignorance of what they should do or a lackadaisical attitude in the performance of their duties as investigators.

Upon the changing of shifts at 3:00 o'clock p.m. on Tuesday, the warrant for the arrest of Farah was given to Detectives Mackey and Mijic. There was testimony to the effect that Mackey assumed, or was told, to stand by and be ready to serve the warrant. By Mackey's testimony, "the day was quiet" and he had little to do but wait. Yet no further effort was made to locate Farah. No one checked the residence again, no one checked the homes of relatives in the homes of relatives in the city, no one checked any of the places where Farah might possibly be within the city of Warren. In short, for eight hours the detectives charged with the responsibility of arresting a suspected felon thought it fit to do nothing in respect to that responsibility. Further, there was some testimony to the effect that these officers and perhaps Captain Thomas had either ignored or refused to accept or investigate information concerning the whereabouts of the wanted felon.

This would amount to a complete irresponsibility in the discharge of their duties. It appeared as though these officers either couldn't think of where they might look for Farah, were afraid to look for him or just didn't care whether he was apprehended or not. They had little else to do according to their testimony, yet they were not the least bit inclined to pursue this matter.

At about 7:30 o'clock p.m. on Tuesday, June 9, the testimony indicated that Captain Thomas received a telephone call from Farah. Once again, we are astounded that an experienced police officer did not make some attempt to find out where Farah was in Cleveland, did not order him to come to the station at once on a threat of pursuit or a request to the Cleveland police authorities to arrest him on sight. This was a wanted and suspected felon on the phone, but Captain Thomas, by his lack of questioning, by his failure to assert the authority of the police in this matter, treated the call as though it were some stranger inquiring about a lost dog. This was further evidence of a complete ignorance or disdain for the normal practices of an experienced police officer under the circumstances.

(1)At approximately 11:30 o'clock p.m. on Tuesday, June 9 Captain Sullivan received a telephone call from one George Tablac indicating that Farah was on his way to accept the warrant. This information was then relayed to the respondent, Chief English. However, after spending much of the previous night trying to reach Farah on the telephone, the respondent was not inclined to try to question the suspect if and when he did come in. The respondent need only to have told Captain Sullivan to hold the suspect after booking, to call him (English) so that he might come down and question him. In the alternative, the respondent could have directed Captain Sullivan to question the suspect and obtain, or attempt to obtain, a statement. Neither of these things were ordered by the respondent and Captain Sullivan did not take it upon himself to try to accomplish these things although it would be normal police procedure for him to do so. In fact, it appears to the commission that instead of effort being made to meet and question this wanted suspect, there was concerted effort on the part of the officers then within the police station to avoid seeing or meeting Farah. Captain Sullivan, though he knew that Farah was expected momentarily, left no instructions to the desk man to notify him when Farah presented himself. According to the testimony no one saw Farah in the police station except Officer Poulos, although Farah apparently walked THROUGH the station and WAS EXPECTED. The testimony offers no excuse for this failure to be on the alert by Captain Sullivan and the other members of the department then within the station. We think this tantamount to the indifference in the performance of their duties if not incompetence.

(J)Turning to the evidence surrounding the fast booking of Farah and his release from police custody, based upon the evidence presented to this Commission, we can state only that Chief English was informed by Captain Sullivan that Farah was on the way to the police station to give himself up. For this purpose we may assume that the Chief of Police upon receiving this information had the right to rely upon the detectives and-or the policemen who were on duty to see that proper procedures would be taken and that the chief had no knowledge that Farah would be treated with "kid gloves" by men under his department and-or by employees of the Municipal Court of Warren. Before leaving this point, however, we must state that we feel the evidence clearly shows that starting in the afternoon of June 8, steps were started to make the apprehension, booking and release of the wanted suspect as painless and easy as possible. We cannot come to any other conclusion but that Farah was given preferential treatment. The amount of bond set before the Municipal Court could have any idea of the seriousness of the attack or the nature of the evidence against Farah and long before the police or anyone else had any idea that Farah would be apprehended. The power of attorney of the bondsman was deposited with the clerk and the clerk apparently held himself ready upon a moment's notice to appear at the Municipal Court to sign the necessary release papers. The evidence leads us to the conclusion that Farah could have come to the station at almost any time during June 8, but that he absented himself from his usual haunts until such time as he was assured that he would not be hounded by newspaper reporters and when the time was right for his quick appearance and disappearance from the police station. We must conclude from the testimony of Officer Poulos and perhaps others, either in ignorance, indifference or pre-determined plan contravening normal police procedure, at least aided and abetted the quick arrival and departure of Farah. We deem it completely inconceivable that any police officer, upon arresting a person charged with as serious a felony as assault with intent to kill would not make an attempt while that person was in police custody to obtain a signed statement from the person charged with the crime and obtain from him all information that the arresting officer could about the crime. This is especially true when the arresting officer was one of the Warren city detectives whose main and almost sole function is the investigation of felonies and other serious crimes. Officer Poulos failed to perform, in our opinion, the following elementary duties in respect to this arrest:

(1)Failed to "book" the suspect at the police desk where it should have been accomplished.

(2)Failed to question the suspect or attempt to obtain a statement.

(3)Failed to retain the suspect for questioning by his superiors and for fingerprinting and photographing and failed to inquire of his superiors whether he should be retained until these procedures were carried out.

Having pointed out the many failures, omissions and deficiencies on the part of several members of the police department involved, we must point out that only the case of the respondent, Chief English is before us. Accordingly, we are limited to evidence presented to this commission concerning the respondent's status. While we are of the opinion that Chief English committed errors of judgment and omissions in the matter, these were no greater and often less important than those committed by other members of the department upon whom the respondent has some right to rely in the performance of their admittedly known duties. There is no testimony or evidence in the record before this commission in a very lengthy hearing that in any way shows that the respondent, Chief Manley R. English, knew or in any way arranged or attempted to arrange or permitted the special handling of Farah at the time of his arrest, booking, bonding and subsequent release.

What has been printed in the newspapers concerning the evidence and the statements of the various parties and witnesses that have found their way into the newspapers are not evidence before this commission and have not been taken into consideration. We may suspect many things, but suspicion and evidence are two different things and we are limited to the evidence. For instance, the witnesses would have us believe that the "fast booking" was a series of coincidences, but in our opinion they are too pat and showed excellent planning and execution. We believe that there was a definite plan to give Farah far more consideration than the ordinary citizen of this community would have received. But having reached that conclusion, we must point out that the plan could have originated in the Municipal Court, in the Chief's office, or in any level of the police department organization beneath the Chief's office, and could have been carried out without the slightest knowledge of the plan being revealed to Chief English, and the evidence presented does not show that Chief English planned or had anything to do with Farah's fast booking.

We will say further at this point that we are amazed that the investigation by the safety-service director of the members of the police department involved in this affair apparently indicated no responsibility on their part for this fiasco. We cannot understand that conclusion from the evidence before us, but again, those personnel are not before us here.

In conclusion we would like to say for the record that this commission and most of the citizens of Warren are sickened at the fact that one Mike Farah, a person with a known criminal record, reportedly associated with gambling and other illegal activities within our city in the past, having no visible means of support, and known to almost everyone as the overlord of the underworld in this area, and, in fact, deserving less respect than any ordinary citizen, should be given preferential treatment in the matter of his arrest, booking and subsequent release far beyond that which would be expected by any ordinary and respectable citizen of this city. For this reason, this commission has taken pains to point out the slovenly and almost negligent manner in which our local police officers apparently operate the police department. By this opinion we consider that they have been admonished and warned that similar omissions, indifference and elements of incompetence will not be tolerated by this commission or the people of Warren.

We therefore advise the safety-service director of this city and every member of the police department, from the Chief to the newest "rookie," that if any of the acts herein specified are committed or omitted by them in the future they should be summarily dismissed from the police department. We would further state that in the event the appointing authority or department heads fail to carry out their responsibilities in this regard, this commission, under the authority of State Law, shall make its own investigation into the possible abuse of this power by such appointing authority or department head. We further instruct the safety-service director of this city to have copies of this opinion prepared and presented to each member of the police department so that they may be aware of the deficiencies herein pointed out and so that they may have no excuses for their failures in these respects in any way in the future. They should be further directed to diligently study the Police Manual and be prepared to stand inquiry on its contents.

While the decision we have reached may not be a popular one because of the hue and cry raised for "someone's scalp" by the newspapers and citizenry of this community, we cannot come to any other conclusion under the evidence presented to us.

We therefore disaffirm the order of suspension of the Chief of Police by Mayor William C. Burbank and order the respondent reinstated to duty as of June 11, 1959.

Respectfully submitted,
CHARLES F. ATKINSON
President
JOHN F. DAVIS
Vice President
LESTER R. STAUFFER
Secretary

Bibliography

Newspapers:

Akron Beacon Journal
Arizona Daily Star
Ashtabula Star-Beacon
Cleveland News
Cleveland Plain Dealer
Cleveland Press
Jefferson Gazette
Newton Falls Herald
Niles Daily Times
Steel Valley News
Toledo Blade
Tucson Daily Citizen
Warren Tribune Chronicle
Youngstown Vindicator

Government Publications:

Third Interim Report of the Special Committee to Investigate Organized Crime in Interstate Commerce – May 1, 1951

Tax Court Of The United States – Anthony Delsanter, et al., Petitioners, v. Commissioner of Internal Revenue, Respondent – July 18, 1957.

Hearings before the Permanent Subcommittee on Investigations of the Committee on Government Operations United States Senate, Part 2, October 10, 11, 15 and 16, 1963
Hearings before the Permanent Subcommittee on the Investigations of the Committee on Governmental Affairs United States Senate One Hundredth Congress Second Session, October 11, 15, 21, 22, 29, 1988 (aka Organized Crime: 25 Years After Valachi)

Books:

Allen, Edward J. – Merchants of Menace – The Mafia: A Study of Organized Crime – 1962 – Charles C. Thomas – Publisher

Demaris, Ovid – *The Last Mafiosi* – 1981 – Times Books

Federal Writer's Project of Ohio Works Progress Administration (Complied by) – *Warren and Trumbull County* - 1938

Griffin, Joseph E. with Don DeNevi – *Mob Nemesis: How the FBI Crippled Organized Crime* – 2002 – Prometheus Books

Illman, Harry R. – *Unholy Toledo* – 1985 – Polemic Press Publications

Jenkins, William D. – *Steel Valley Klan: The Ku Klux Klan in Ohio's Mahoning Valley* – 1990 – The Kent State University Press

Kavieff, Paul R. – *The Violent Years: Prohibition and the Detroit Mobs* – 2001 – Barricade Books

Messick, Hank – *The Silent Syndicate* – 1967 – The MacMillan Company

Messick, Hank and Burt Goldblatt – *The Only Game In Town* – 1976 – Thomas Y. Crowell Company

Porrello, Rick – *The Rise and Fall of the Cleveland Mafia: Corn Sugar and Blood* – 1995 – Barricade Books, Inc.

Reid, Ed – *Mafia* – 1952 – Random House

Vinson, L.C. – *The Book of Warren* – 1920 – The Perkinswood Press Companies

Youngstown Vindicator – *These Hundred Years: A Chronicle of the Twentieth Century as Recorded in the Pages of The Youngstown Vindicator* – 2000 – The Vindicator Printing Company

Index

(Names from Chapter End Notes
and Appendix are not indexed, (p)
denotes photo)

Aaran, Jimmy 49, 50
Aiello, Jasper J. "Fats" 78, 107, 136(p),
     163, 232
Allen, Edward J. xi, xiii, xv, xvi, 137(p),
     166, 251
  efforts to close Jungle Inn, 63, 64,
     65, 84-89, 91, 94, 97, 102, 103
  pursuit of Cammarata, 198, 208-
     214, 216-17,232
Allen, Margaret 47
Alvin Karpis Story, The 15
Amato, Emanuel (Edward) 204, 209,
     212, 225
Anderson, Dr. Charles A. 173, 177,
     187
Anderson, Charles H. 233
  Jean Blair assault case, 175, 184-86,
     189, 190
  Marty Flask murder, 247, 249, 250
Anderson, John H. 104, 189, 215, 243,
     245
Antonelli, Albert 161
Applegate, Calvin 63
Armstrong, Joseph C. 202-3
Arrow Club xiii, 71-74, 92, 135(p)

Baer, Max 35, 37, 127(p)
Ballo, Sargon John 62
Bane, James 29
Bannon, John A. 217, 218
Barbarus, Cyril 56-57
Barbe, J.M. 102, 110-11, 112

Barber, Elton 116
Barker-Karpis Gang 14
Barker, "Doc" 15
Barker, Freddie 15
Barker, "Ma" 12, 15
Barnett, Robert 194
Barrasso, Buddy 49
Barrasso, Ralph 49
Bash, Earl J. 51, 60, 75, 85, 105, 240
Bastardi, Dominic 256
Batista, Fulgencio 228
Baytos, Stephen 157
Belinky, Sam 205
Belledaire, Viola 10
Benore Club 92
Berline, Charles S. 156
Birns, Alex "Shondor" 252
Birrell, Bruce 171, 175, 176, 180, 181
Birrell, George H. 80-81, 125(p),
     131(p), 242, 245, 255
  biographical info 237-38
  judge during Blair assault trial, 184,
     185-87, 189-93
  judge during Viola trial, 51-54, 57,
     59-60
  prosecutor during Munsene
     bribery trial, 32-33, 35
Blair, Jean P. xvi, 43, 145(p), 166-73,
     175-82, 184-90, 192-93, 238
Blair, Mariam 187, 188
Blumetti, Joseph 224
Bommarito, Joseph "Long Joe" 206
Bommarito, Joseph "Scarface" 201,
     206
Bonnie and Clyde 12, 253
Bordoni, Irene 35

Bostwick, Harold K. 72, 152-53
Bowles, Charles 201
Brancato, Frank 65, 160
Brandt, Joseph 2
Bremer, Edward G. 14
Bricker, John W. xiii, 72-74
Brooks, Ernest C. 219
Bruce, J. Gregory 159, 160
Bruss, Hyman 158
Bryan, William Jennings 25
Buchwalter, George 40, 42, 166, 240,
    254-55
  biographical info, 238
  representing Chief English, 176,
    180, 182
  representing Jungle Inn owners, 98,
    104, 105, 115
  representing Mango, 247, 249-50
  representing Mike Farah in Blair
    assault case, 184-87, 190-91
Buchwalter, Jay 18, 19, 21, 28, 31, 40,
    238
Buckley, Gerald F. "Jerry" 201-02
Buckley, John J. 85
Budak, Frank 101, 243
Burbank, William C. 163, 171, 175-
    76, 183
Burgess, Harvey A. 18, 21, 22, 26, 32,
    255
Burner, W.L. 45

Cafaro, Anthony 234
Cafaro, William 157
Cage, Thomas 55
Calandra, John P. 234
Callan, Harold 93, 103, 112-16
Cammarata, Frank xvi, 65, 147(p),
    166, 176
  Chief Allen's pursuit and legal
    proceedings, 208-19
  Cuban activities, 228-230
  early years, 198-202
  death of, 230
  deportation and return, 202-08
  efforts of Congressman Kirwan,

    206-08, 209-11, 217-18, 222
  jailed, 219-23
  juke box activities, 200, 205, 208-09,
    212, 224-27
  McClellan Committee and Robert
    Kennedy, 224-27
  release from Michigan prison,
    223-24
Cammarata, Grace 199, 204, 205, 209,
    218, 223, 224, 225, 227, 230
Campbell, Harry 15
Campbell, J. Don 185-87, 190, 192
Canary, Sumner 164
Capehart, Homer 208
Capone, Al xii, 118, 256
Capone, Matthew 118
Caputo, Dominic B. "Moosey" 67, 68,
    78
Caputo, Frank 67
Carnahan, Arthur 117
Carrado, Pete 199
Carter, William M. 22, 24, 33, 60, 242
Castro, Fidel 228-29, 230
Cavallaro, Charles "Cadillac Charlie"
    193, 234
Cavolo, Charles 152
Cickelli, Frank 166, 167, 168
Clampitt, C. Wayne 50
Cleaveland, Moses 2, 3
Clemens, Charles 17, 32
Cohen, Mickey 118
Coletto, Ralph 83, 105, 106, 140(p),
    160, 165
Coletto, Tessie 83, 165
Collins, James 92
Como, Perry xv, 35, 120(p)
Connell, James C. 233
Conroy, John 190
Continental Club 92
Costello, Frank 83
Cowles, David 173, 190
Cozza, Michael 170, 172, 173
Craig, James R. 189
Cullitan, Frank T. 221

D'Orsay, Fifi 35
Dague, W. Glen 253
Dalitz, Moe 72
Darr, Robert 177, 180
Darrow, Clarence Seward xv, 24-33,
    124(p)
Darrow, Mrs. 26, 32
Davilla, Osorio 228
Day, Luther S. 22-23, 24
Day, William L. 22
DeJacimo, Laura 166-68, 184-85, 186,
    188
DelBene, Donald J. 51, 104, 107, 111,
    158
Delsanter, Anthony "Tony Dope" xvi,
    65, 150(p)
    death of, 236
    early years, 231
    friendship with Jimmy Fratianno,
        231-32, 236
    Log Cabin operation, 233-34
    member of Cleveland Mafia, 232,
        234, 236
    murder of Mike Farah, 194, 195,
        196
    role in Jungle Inn and tax trial, 83,
        162-63, 165, 223, 233
    Teamster's fraud case, 235
Delsanter, Martha 236
Demaris, Ovid 196, 232
DeNiro, Vincent J. 163, 193, 232
DeVincenzo, Michael 170, 179
Diamond, Jack "Legs" 13-14
DiCarlo, Joe "the Wolf" 78, 84, 148(p),
    157, 214, 224
DiCarlo, Sam 224
DiCenso, Anthony 55
DiGenero, Marco 241
DiGenero, Rosa 241
DiGenero Family (See Jennings)
Dillas, William 49
Dillinger, John 12-14, 122(p), 199
DiPaola, Ambrose 41
DiSalle, Michael 175
Drago, James 195

Duncan, William C. 18, 19, 21-22
Dupuy, Emmanuel H. 68
Durandetti, Lucy 16
Duggan, James 251
Durbin, David 177, 180
Durkin, P.J. 20

English, Manley 61, 168-69, 170-71,
    173, 175-84, 185, 188, 195, 211,
    238

Fagadore, Thomas 20, 29
Farah brothers xv, xvi, 39, 51, 65, 76,
    82, 83, 99, 118, 155-58, 163, 164,
    194, 196, 225, 240
Farah, Albert M. 164, 194, 197
Farah, Freida 118
Farah, George 118, 155
Farah, Grace (daughter) 194
Farah, Grace E. (wife) 118, 155, 197
    Jean Blair assault incident, 169, 173,
        179, 189
    Jungle Inn ownership and tax trial,
        104, 114, 115, 158, 161, 164
    murder of Mike Farah, 194
Farah, John xv, xvi, 39, 51, 142(p),
    146(p)
    aftermath of raid, 99, 101-02
    assault trial, 107-110
    death, 196-97
    destruction of Jungle Inn equipment,
        112
    early years, 118, 154, 155
    gambling activities, 65, 155, 156, 163
    Jean Blair incident, 167
    Jungle Inn operation, 65, 76, 83, 84,
        87
    Jungle Inn raid, 94, 96-99
    legitimate businesses, 83, 116, 156-57
    murder of Larry Rubin, 152
    murder of Mike Farah, 194, 196
    raid court case, 104-06
    tax problems, 157-58, 163, 164
    tax trials, 159-60, 165, 223
    trial for Rubin murder, 153-54

Farah, John P. 164, 194, 197
Farah, Michael George (Mike) xv, xvi,
    39, 51, 143(p), 146(p), 156, 238,
    240, 246
  death of son Robert, 155
  dismissal of Laura DeJacimo, 166,
    185, 188
  early years, 118, 155
  friendship with Mickey Cohen,
    118, 151
  funeral of, 195
  gambling activities, 65, 155, 156,
    163, 181
  Jean Blair assault trial, 184-93, 238
  Jean Blair booking scandal and
    inquiry, 169-74, 177-83
  Jean Blair incident, 166-69
  Jungle Inn operation, 65, 68, 76, 83,
    84, 104
  Jungle Inn raid, 96, 99
  legitimate businesses, 83, 116, 156-57
  move to Trumbull County, 155
  murder of, 193-94, 195-96, 197, 234
  murder of Larry Rubin, 152-53
  suspension and hearing of Chief
    Manley English, 175-76
  tax cases, 157, 158, 161-62, 164-65
  Trumbull County politics, 157, 165-
    66, 256
Farah, Robert 155
Farah, Shamis 83, 118, 155, 157, 164,
    165, 196, 197
Fearon, Henry 96
Fedele, Pietro 10-12
Feldman, David 206
Fieldman, Harold 229-30
Fieldman, Mrs. 229
Fiore, Alfonso 239
Fitzgerald, Frank D. 203, 217
Flannigan, Edward A. "Sheriff" 64, 68
Flask, Martin "Marty" 242, 245-49
Fleckner, Oscar L. 93, 94-99, 101, 104,
    106, 107-08, 110, 139(p)
Floyd, Charles Arthur "Pretty Boy" 12
Follies Bergere 17, 32

Fox, Eugene 234
Franks, Robert 25
Fratianno, Aladena, Jimmy the Weasel"
    xvi, 196, 231-32, 236
Freed, Emerich B. 151
Furst, Harry 239-40

Gallo, Charlie 204
Garfield, James A. 195
Garmone, Fred 79
Garvin, Harry J. 201
George, Anthony 115
George, Captain 4
George, John J. 114-15
George, Mazeed 114-15
Giannola / Vitale Gang War 199
Gillen, Barney J. 39, 45, 46
Gillett, Michael 21
Gillmer, R.I. 18, 19, 21
Giordano, Joseph "Red" 232, 235
Green Acres casino 84
Green, William 234
Griffith, Lynn B. 40
  bribery trial of Munsene, prosecutor,
    22-24, 26-29, 31-32
  judge during Jungle Inn raid, 94,
    98-99, 102, 104-06, 107, 110-13
  judge of appeals court 192
Guarnieri, Louis L. 33
Gust, Thomas 10
Gutelius, Daniel 39

Halls, Calvin 63
Hamm, Jr., William A. 14
Hardman, Roy S. 66-67
Harlan, Stuart 72, 92
Harris, Jack 42, 53, 55, 56
Harvard Inn 14
Heinlein, John O. 38, 81
Helman, Clyde 107
Henderson, Charles P. 84, 205, 217,
    218
Henshaw, J.C. 10, 44
Herbert, Gordon 181
Herbert, Paul 40

Herbert, Thomas J. 76, 78, 91
Hickory Grill 76, 88, 103
Hildebrand, Robert 85
Hoagland, Claude 105
Hoffa, James R. "Jimmy" 224
Hollyhock Gardens Night Club xv, 16,
    35, 37-38, 39, 40, 64, 125(p),
    126(p), 239-40,   254, 256
Hooper, Warren G. 46
Hoover, J. Edgar 13, 15, 47, 60, 61, 84
Hotchkiss, Ben 152
Howe, George 166
Huffman, Earl B. 42-43, 57
Huffman, J.C. 12
Hull, Harold 213
Hunter, "Pinky" 35
Hurley, John 80

Infante, James 242-43
Ingle, Helene 67-68

Jaffe, Al 151
James, Edward 184
Jenkins, David G. 69, 233
Jennings Night Club 242, 247, 248
Jennings, Jr., James 244
Jennings, Sr., James "Sunny Jim" 241,
    242, 244, 245
Jennings, Jr., Joseph "Pobo" 243, 244,
    245, 246
Jennings, Sr., Joseph 241, 243, 245,
    248
Jennings, Leo "Shine" 241
Jennings, Marty 242, 244
Jennings, Theresa 241
John, Spotted 4
Johns, Victor 158
Johnson, William E. 44, 46, 47-48, 50,
    52, 54-57, 61, 240
Jones, Lloyd S. 101-02, 106, 108, 109-10

Kaplan, Arthur 208, 225-26
Karpis, Alvin "Creepy" 12, 14-15, 122(p)
Karpowicz, Albin (See Karpis, Alvin)
Kavieff, Paul R. 199

Kelly, George "Machine Gun" 12
Kennedy, Edward 242
Kennedy, Jackie (Toledo bootlegger)
    202
Kennedy, James F. 158-59, 160
Kennedy, John F. 224
Kennedy, Robert F. xvi, 149(p), 224-28,
Kerr, Roy 251
Kirwan, Michael J. xvi, 206-08, 209-
    11, 217-18, 222
Kistler, Charles D. 8
Kleinman, Morris 72
Kocevar, John L. 93, 96, 103, 105
    biographical info, 250-52
Kory, Joseph F. "Eddie" 62
Ku Klux Klan 22, 28

Lacey, Robert 83
Lanese, Joseph 235
Lansky, Meyer 83
LaPolla, Dominick J. "Duke" 144(p),
    157, 159, 160, 240
LaPolla, Vincent 241
Lapp, Harold 177
Latona, Sebastian F. 54-55, 58, 59, 60
Lausche, Frank J. xv, 138(p)
    efforts to close gambling dens,
        91-92, 97, 99, 102-04, 107-08, 115
    efforts to extradite Cammarata,
        214, 215, 220, 221
Lederle, Arthur F. 47, 203
Leisy, James 102, 106
Leopold-Loeb murder case 25, 28
Lerner, Jacob 49, 50
Leskovyansky, John 234
Lesnak, "Shorty" 116
Licavoli Clan, Family or Gang xvi, 39,
    74, 148(p), 166, 198, 199, 202,
    204, 208, 224, 229, 230
Licavoli, Dominic 206
Licavoli, Grace (See Cammarata)
Licavoli, James "Blackie" "Jack White"
    65, 74, 144(p), 157, 158, 196, 199-
    200, 204,   210, 236
Licavoli, John 206, 234

Licavoli, Pete "Horseface" 199
Licavoli, Peter 48, 198, 201-02, 205, 206, 208, 222, 232
Licavoli, Thomas "Yonnie" 198, 199, 200-01, 202
Little Canada 11
Little Man: Meyer Lansky and the Gangster Life 83
Livecchi, Angelo 201
Locke, G.C. 22
Log Cabin 233-34
Lombardi, Guy 41
Lonardo-Porrello Corn Sugar War 10, 11
Lonardo, Angelo "Big Ange" 155, 236
Louisell, Joseph W. 62, 212
Lubert, Jack 181
Luciano, Lucky 229
Luhman, Dr. Roland A. xiv, 88-89

Maccagnone, James "Biffo" 61-62
Mackey, Walter 169, 173, 177
Macklin, Elmer 46
Macris, Gus 12
Maggianetti, Dan 85, 218
Maiden, Jr., Erskine 212, 213
Mainer, Phil 195
Mallo, James 10
Mancini, James (see Munsene)
Mango, Frank 247
Mango, Joseph 247
Mango, Nellie 247
Mango, Thomas "Chippy" 242, 245-50
Mann Act 10
Mansell, Irving L. 97-98
Marchio, Ralph 173, 180-81
Margiotti, Charles 51-60
    biographical info 253-54
Marshall, John 3
Martin, Hymie 151
Marts, Charles 95, 103
Marts, Frances 95
Mashorda, Raymond S. "Legs" 85
Massei, Joseph 200, 202
Matash, James "Bananas" 245-46

Maxwell, James 80, 165-66, 254-56
Mayfield Road Mob 39, 231
Maynard, Perry A. 215-16, 219, 220-21
McClellan, John L. xvi, 61, 224, 225, 226
McCracken, Ronald 234
McGettrick, James 252
McGinty, Thomas J. "Tommy" 72, 78, 92
McLain, David F. 176, 238
McLain, Louis 87
McLain, William M. 64, 238, 258
    assistant prosecutor during Munsene bribery trial, 26, 29, 51, 55, 56, 58, 60
    prosecutor during Jungle Inn closing, 92, 98, 99, 103-04, 106, 107, 110
McMahon, James 4
Meli, Angelo 200, 205
Meli, Vincent 205, 225
Melillo, Patrick J. 211, 213-14, 215, 217, 218
Merchants of Menace 65, 208
Messett, Robert 177
Mijic, Joseph 169, 177
Millard, Frank G. 219
Miller, Don C. 50
Miller, Ray T. 151
Miller, Sam "Gameboy" 48-49
Millikin, Ralph R. 51, 59-60, 75-77, 80, 85-86, 92, 95, 96, 98-99, 102, 105, 107, 112, 243
Moceri, Joseph 200
Moceri, Leo "Lips" 150(p), 200, 234, 236
Mock, George 39
Mock, Russell,
    representing Cammarata, 211-12, 213, 214, 215, 217, 218
    representing Delsanter 233
    representing Jungle Inn owners, 101, 104-06, 107, 110, 113, 114-15
    representing Jungle Inn owners at tax trial, 159-60
    representing Sedore, 88

Monachino, Sam Jerry 85-86
Monazym, Charles "Black Charlie" 46-47, 48, 52-55, 58
Monfrino, Bernard 16-17, 40, 42, 50, 52-58
Monfrino, Felix 40, 42-44, 45-48, 55, 129(p)
Monfrino, Genevieve 44
Mounds Club 72, 78, 84, 92-93, 94, 104, 113, 135(p), 138(p), 232
Muche, James "Jimmy" 65-66
Muche, Louis 66
Muche, Margaret 66
Munsene, James "Jimmy" xv, 64, 65, 69, 127(p), 176, 237, 238, 239, 253, 254, 257
    Atlantic City operation, 17
    attempted bribe of Sheriff Smith, 18
    bribery trials, 19-33
    Darrow representation, 24-33
    dog racing, 40-41
    early years, 16-17
    fatal car accident, 41-42
    funeral of, 45-46
    Hollyhock Gardens nightclub, 34-39
    murder, 42-46
    murder investigation, 44-45, 46-48
    Prime Steak House, 39-40, 42
    Viola arrest of, 47-51
    Viola court trial of, 51-60
    Viola escape from prison and recapture, 61-62
Munsene, Marian 16
Munsene, Nofry 16, 42, 45, 51, 53, 56, 58
Munsene, Tony 42
Munsene, Tullio 16, 45
Munsene, Warren 16, 45, 51
Murgie, Charles 256
Murphy's restaurant 21, 23, 29
Mussolini, Benito 204
Mustakes, Jr., George 256
Mustakes, Sr., George 40, 239, 240, 254, 256-57

Naples, Billy 193, 234
Naples, Mike "Bree" 244, 245-46
Naples, Sandy 193, 195, 196, 243-44
Nelson, "Baby Face" 12
Nemesh, Joe 209
Nesbit, Evelyn 32
Ness, Eliot 14, 71, 195
Nevin, Robert 212, 213
Nichols, John C. 218

Oldacres, Edwin 39
Ormeroid, Dr. George 9
Ormeroid, Mrs. George 9
Osborne, Clyde W. 68
Owens, Jesse 41

Packard, J. Ward 6-7
Packard, William 6-7
Papalas, Nicholas "Nick Brown" 195
Paparodis, Steve 78-80, 82
Pardee, Floyd 255
Pascarella, Jerry 74, 204, 210
Paul, Brady C. 51
Paull, Walter 39
Pearson, Drew 213
Perfette, Carmen 233, 235
Perfette, Joseph 234, 235
Perillo, Joseph 9
Petercupo, John 158, 240
Peterson, K. Berry 50
Peterson, Virgil 210
Petkovich, Sam 158
Petro, Julius 84
Petrosky, Walter 78
Pettibone Club 72, 92
Pieri, Sam 47
Pierson, Wick W. 18, 19-20, 22, 51-52
    biographical info, 257
Pizzino, Ted 201
Porrello, James 10, 11
Porrello, Joe 10, 11
Poulos, William 170, 178, 179
Poulson, Francis 26
Powell, Kedgwin 253
Pratt, Phyllis 151-52

Price, Paul J. 180
Prime Steak House xv, 37, 38, 39, 40, 42, 52, 54, 55, 57, 58, 65, 128(p), 238, 239, 254
Pugalise, Bruno 9
Pugalise, Pasquale "Patsy" 9
Purple Gang 166, 199, 206
Purple Gang, The 199
Purvis, Melvin 15

Quinby, Ephraim 3-4

Randazzo, Salvatore 10
Raum, Arnold 163
Ravella, James A. 78, 171, 173-75, 178, 185, 186, 190
Reagen, Paul J.
  biographical info, 258
  during Jungle Inn years, 75, 76-77, 80-81
  Mango trial, 246
  Viola trial, 51, 53, 54-55, 57, 60
Redmond, H.J. 26-27, 33
Republic Steel 7, 16
Rhoda, Harry 177, 180
Rhodes, James A. 62, 238
Rich, Joe 15,
Risher, Jack 12
Rising, Herbert 194
Roberts, J. Eugene 170
Rock, Frank 41
Rockefeller, John D. 195
Romano, Joseph 195
Rose, Henry 51, 240
Rossi, Dominic "Muggsy" 41
Rothkopf, Louis "Lou Rhody" 72
Rubin, Lawrence "Akron Larry" 151-54
Rubino, Mike 46, 205
Rutkowski, Anthony A. 93, 94-96, 98-99, 101, 103, 104-112, 139(p), 243, 251
Ryan, Sylvester 207-08

Sacks, Beryle C. 61
St. Clair, Arthur 3-4

St. Louis, Roy 217
Salen, George 36, 39, 44
Saliba, Rev. Philip 195
Sanfillipo, Sam "Mollie" 68, 239-40, 256
Sansone, Augustino 37-38
Santagada, James 115
Sargent, Andrew 21
Sargent, Charles F. 27, 29, 31, 32, 33
Sarkesian, Eddie 46
Sarkis, Louis LaHood 61
Saylor, Ellmonte 55
Scalish, John 232, 236
Scallechia, Dominick 9
Scarpitti, Donato 38
Schnur, Charles G. 79
Schuller, John 193
Schumann, P. Richard 212
Scopes "Monkey Trial" 25
Scopes, John T. 25
Scott, Charles R. 112
Scott, Robert 224
Sedore, Charles E. 63-64, 69, 75-76, 77, 79, 80, 81, 86-88, 90, 102-03
Sferra, Angeline 40, 44
Shenk, J.R. 115
Shepard, Dr. Sam 253
Shero, Anthony "Tony the Hawk" 42, 44, 52-53, 56, 58
Shoules, James 216, 217
Shrader, Irene Crawford 253
Shuba, Edward 97-98
Silbert, Joseph H. 220-22
Silver, James 50
Sindelar, Peter F. 163-65
Skipton, Roy A. 112-13
Slifka, Adrian M. 97, 101-02, 106, 108-09
Sloan, Gertrude M. 61-62
Smith, John H. "Jack" 17-23, 28-29, 32
Smith, Mrs. John H. 17, 19-21, 23, 27-28, 30, 32
Snyder, J. Buell 206
Snyder, Peter 166
Soda, Jess 162, 246, 248

Spain, John 172-76, 182, 185
Sperry, Harlan 153
Stanton, Edward 152-53
Stein, Russell 69, 73-74
Stern, Max 232
Steuer, Arlene 145(p)
   Jean Blair assault trial, 170, 172-74,
      185-87, 189-90, 192
   Jungle Inn tax trial, 159, 165
Storer, Richard 3, 4
Sudetic, Albert 106, 107, 110
Sullivan, James A. 177, 178
Sweeney, Joseph M. 221
Syracuse, Russell 49
Syracuse, Samuel 49

Tablac, George 170, 178-79
Tamer, James 47
Taylor, Estelle 35
Teeple, Verne 171, 179-80, 181, 196
Thomas, Harry 177, 178
Thomas, Thomas 28-29, 30
Thomas, William K. 215, 216-17
Thornton, Thomas P. 223
Tiberio, Lee 56
Tiberio, Louis 56
Tickel, Herman E. 49, 53-54, 55, 57
Tilocco, Salvatore "Sam" 11
Tilson, Bert 154
Timko, Albert 173, 180, 234
Tobin, Mary Catherine 83, 165
Tobin, Edward F. 83, 105, 106, 140(p),
   159-60, 165, 223
Toy, Harry S. 205
Trafficante, Jr., Santo 228
Trigg, Howard 85
Trumbull Steel Company 6, 16
Trumbull, John 3
Tucker, Sammy 72
Tucker, Sophie 35

Valenti, Frank 232-33
Van Buskirk, John L. 50
Varley, John A. 159, 161
Vecchione, Thomas 156

Venetta, John 239
Viola, Thomas "Tommy" xv, 46, 48,
   130(p), 131(p)
   capture, 47-49, 50, 51
   death of, 62
   escape from prison, 61-62
   trial 51-60
Vitale, Frank 205
Vizzini, Charles 212

Wagner, Henry C. 80, 165, 254-55
Walker, Helen Wilkins (see Helen
   Wilkins)
Walsh, John "Pinky" 243-44
Walter, Francis E. 210
Walter, Paul W. 220-21
Warren, Moses 3
Washington, George 1
Wayne, "Mad Anthony" 2
Weems, Ted 35
Weisenberg, Nate 74, 204, 210
Weiss, Sam 151
White, George 154, 242
Wilkins, Helen 17, 20, 23, 28
Williams, G. Mennen "Soapy" 214,
   224
Williams, John J. 222
Wilson, Cliff 60
Wilson, Fred O. 256
Wilson, Lillian Jane 8
Woldman, Albert 104, 113
Women's Christian Temperance
   Union 26
Wyndham, Joseph 170, 171, 175, 176,
   178, 180, 181, 183

Yavorsky, John 78
Youngstown Sheet & Tube Company
   8, 14

Zusman, Bertram 116, 164

Made in the USA
Columbia, SC
02 August 2021